Dead in the Water

NEW PERSPECTIVES IN

SOUTHEAST ASIAN STUDIES

DEAD IN THE WATER

*Global Lessons
from the World Bank's
Model Hydropower Project
in Laos*

Edited by
BRUCE SHOEMAKER
and
WILLIAM ROBICHAUD

The University of Wisconsin Press

Publication of this book has been made possible, in part, through support from The McKnight Foundation, Oxfam Australia, and Global Wildlife Conservation.

The University of Wisconsin Press
728 State Street, Suite 443
Madison, Wisconsin 53706
uwpress.wisc.edu

Gray's Inn House, 127 Clerkenwell Road
London EC1R 5DB, United Kingdom
eurospanbookstore.com

Library of Congress Cataloging-in-Publication Data
Names: Shoemaker, Bruce, editor. | Robichaud, William, editor.
Title: Dead in the water: global lessons from the World Bank's
    model hydropower project in Laos / edited by Bruce Shoemaker
    and William Robichaud.
Other titles: New perspectives in Southeast Asian studies.
Description: Madison, Wisconsin: The University of Wisconsin Press, [2018]
    | Series: New perspectives in Southeast Asian studies | Includes
    bibliographical references and index.
Identifiers: LCCN 2017044548 | ISBN 9780299317904 (cloth: alk. paper)
Subjects: LCSH: Hydroelectric power plants—Economic aspects—Laos—Nam
    Theun River. | Hydroelectric power plants—Social aspects—Laos—Nam
    Theun River. | Hydroelectric power plants—Environmental aspects—Laos—
    Nam Theun River. | Dams—Laos—Nam Theun River. | Economic
    development projects—Laos. | Nam Theun 2 Hydroelectric Project.
Classification: LCC TK1513.L28 D43 2018 | DDC 333.91/409594—dc23
LC record available at https://lccn.loc.gov/2017044548

ISBN 9780299317942 (pbk.: alk. paper)

This book is dedicated to Sombath Somphone—Lao community development worker, civil society leader and founder of the Participatory Development Training Center in Laos. Sombath was born in 1952 and raised in a small village on the banks of the Mekong River in Nong Bok district of Khammouane province, not far from the confluence of the Mekong with the Xe Bang Fai, a river that features prominently in this book. Sombath's dedication to assisting rural people and communities in Laos and the natural world, along with his kindness and friendship, have been an inspiration to many people in Laos, including several contributors to this volume.

Contents

Contents

Contents

Foreword

Dams and Dreams in Lao PDR

YOS SANTASOMBAT

Lao PDR has few options for driving economic growth other than its potential to exploit timber and export hydropower.

World Bank Public Expenditure Review (1997)

In 1986, just eleven years after the end of the Lao civil war and the establishment of the Lao People's Democratic Republic (Lao PDR, also known as Laos), the country shifted its political economy paradigm from socialist to what was termed a "new imagination" policy—a less doctrinaire and more open form of centralized planning and control. The Lao People's Revolutionary Party introduced a new economic mechanism as a means of effecting comprehensive socioeconomic and political reforms that aimed to establish the foundation for a market economy. The reform was designed to promote growth in foreign direct investments, especially in the areas of infrastructural services, hydropower, mining, transportation and urban development. Since then Laos has embraced globalization and a neoliberal market economy. Free enterprise and private property have been recognized and promoted, and development projects have been designed and launched with the support of grants from donor countries and loans from international financial institutions, especially the World Bank. Laos was informed by Western advisors that it had no viable option but to develop its hydropower resources and sell electricity to its neighbors. In the 1990s, a number of hydroelectric projects were designed with promises and expectations that there would be a huge influx of foreign exchange and capital, which, in turn, would enable land-locked Laos to fulfill its dreams of modernity.

Nam Theun 2 (NT2) is the largest and most controversial of all the hydro-electric projects planned and implemented in Laos. This megaproject is the first industrial development project that has been jointly funded by private shareholders and the Lao government, with the support of the World Bank and the Asian Development Bank as key financial lenders. The Lao government supported the project on the grounds that such state-private sector partnerships are an important strategy by which the country can reduce its dependence on official development assistance. The design and implementation of NT2 thus paved the way for a new national strategy of turning resources into capital. Dam development and land concessions in Laos have proceeded rapidly, and the Lao government, along with private investors and some international donors, have invariably ignored calls from international nongovernmental organizations (INGOs) and local stakeholders for further assessments of environmental and social impact and costs.

Despite the rapid economic growth averaging 7–8 percent a year that decentralization and private enterprise have made possible, Laos remains one of the least developed and poorest countries in Southeast Asia. The disparity of income between urban and rural dwellers is widening. The majority of rural households remain under or close to the poverty line, and the natural resources vital to their livelihoods are being threatened by megaprojects designed to exploit natural wealth for corporate profit. A combination of state and private investments in hydropower dams, mining, tree and fruit plantations, casinos and entertainment complexes, and other infrastructural projects, implemented through concessions to foreign companies, are transforming land, forest, fish, and water—the essence of local livelihood security—into expendable resources for commercial investment. Despite promises that megaprojects such as NT2 would benefit local ethnic groups as well as wider populations in the country, it is highly questionable whether they have.

The expansion of the market economy has led to the "transnational enclosure" of the country's resources, which means that management systems are increasingly centralized.[1] Increased centralization and authoritarianism enable the government and commercial interests to gain control of and transform territories traditionally utilized by local peoples into marketable resources. Enclosure redefines how the resource is managed—by whom and for whose benefit. Enclosure tears local people and their rivers, land, forest, and knowledge out of the conceptual framework in which they are embedded and forces them into a new framework—which reflects the interests of the state and dominant groups. In this way, natural resources are excluded and disembedded from the local fabrics of livelihoods and redefined as state property. Rivers are transformed into exploitable economic resources and turned into a series of hydropower dams for national and transnational production and development.

In theory, the transition to a market-oriented economy is an important factor contributing to the "connectivity" and viability of economic cooperation among ASEAN (Association of Southeast Asian Nations) Economic Community member countries. Regional economic reforms and agendas have created an environment conducive to increased trade, investment, and other forms of economic cooperation. Economies of scale and specialization resulting from regional cooperation facilitate investment in member countries as a whole, exceeding individual countries' abilities to attract investors. By generating affordable energy, economic synergy, and dynamism, regional cooperation contributes to the goal of sustained economic growth and helps improve living conditions of poor and marginal communities in the new and emerging economies. In reality, however, the implications of large-scale development are diverse and complex. While potential economic returns from increased exploitation of natural resources are great, the socioeconomic and environmental risks are also very high. More importantly, the benefits of development are not shared evenly among all social strata and stakeholders, creating a fragmented and uneven distribution of resources. The factors behind this uneven development include inequalities within and between countries, social hierarchies leading to exclusion and skewed access to resources, globalization, and the character of neoliberal political economy, which tends to place economic growth before equity, social justice, and sustainability.

This volume, edited by Bruce Shoemaker and William Robichaud, is not just about a dam. By tracing the two-decade long history of NT2 it also provides us with an overall historical description and thought-provoking analysis of how national development has taken place in Laos, detailing the sociocultural and environmental outcomes of a megaproject, the process of resettlement of local ethnic communities and resultant impact on their livelihoods, and the unmet expectations of development—the vast gap between what was promised, dreamt of and anticipated, and the actual outcome. This volume offers a new understanding of Laos in a difficult period of nation building and development, providing a vital lesson to policy planners, scholars, and international nongovernmental organizations encountering the illusory success of a globalizing economy, and revealing the different dreams of modernity that are formed within the mainstream development discourse.

NOTES

1. See Keith Barney, "China and the Production of Forestlands in Lao PDR: A Political Ecology of Transnational Enclosure," in *Taking Southeast Asia to Market: Commodities, Nature and People in the Neoliberal Age*, ed. Joseph Nevins and Nancy Lee Peluso (Ithaca, NY: Cornell University Press, 2008), 91–92, and Yos Santasombat, *The River of Life: Changing Ecosystems of the Mekong River* (Chiang Mai: Mekong Press, 2011), 31–34.

Preface

In 1990, the *New Yorker* magazine published an article about Laos titled "Forgotten Country."[1] Within a few years, however, Laos would come under intense attention by the World Bank and various other institutions around the world, as it moved toward developing what soon became the most contentious hydropower dam in Southeast Asia, Nam Theun 2 (NT2). This book is about that controversial project. Both of our personal histories with NT2 extend back to the early years of the project, to a time when it was little more than a concept, seemingly too massive for Laos to undertake.

Vientiane, 1991

On a humid and sultry day toward the end of the annual rainy season in 1991, I filed, along with other invitees, into the drab and musty environs of the Lane Xang Hotel in central Vientiane, the capital of Laos. The country was just starting its gradual shift from a doctrinaire communist economy, and the Lane Xang, like most businesses in the country, was government owned and operated. The hotel was a bit rough around the edges from years of deferred maintenance. Noisy Russian air conditioners were the norm among those who could afford them in Vientiane, but in the Lane Xang's cavernous meeting room these had to be supplemented with creaky ceiling fans. As a representative of one of the only international nongovernmental organizations then permitted to operate in the country, the American Friends Service Committee, I had been invited to attend a joint meeting between the World Bank, United Nations Development Program and the government of the Lao PDR. The agenda was the presentation of a technical feasibility study on an ambitious and complex hydropower project that would be difficult to carry out, especially in a country still lacking paved roads between its major towns and cities. It was to be situated in central Laos—an area distant from my own work in the country. I felt obligated to attend, but it seemed like a dull way to spend a perfectly good afternoon.

As the meeting started, it looked like my suspicions were right. The main presentation, by a representative of the Australian Snowy Mountain Engineering Company, was dry and technical—all about how one river, the Nam Theun, could be dammed where it traversed a plateau and the water sent off the edge of an escarpment to drop more than 1000 feet at high speed to power turbines to generate electricity. The outflow would be directed to join a different river, the Xe Bang Fai. The engineers were convinced this was all very feasible and that, while some details needed to be worked out, the project would generate large amounts of electricity to help power Thailand's fast-growing economy and provide significant revenue for Laos, which might well soon need such funds, given that its traditional socialist allies and donors were foundering. The Berlin Wall was already down, and at the close of 1990 the rapidly collapsing Soviet Union, which had been Laos's most stalwart ally, had recalled most of its advisors. The cessation of much of the Eastern bloc aid on which Laos was heavily dependent would soon follow.

At the time I knew next to nothing about hydropower. I had come to Laos with an agency that had a mandate to seek reconciliation in the wake of the Second Indochina War by working to build ties with a place seen by many in my own country as an enemy. In whatever small ways we could, we were trying to address the enormous legacy of the American bombing of the country during the war, as well as supporting small-scale, community-level development projects.

The World Bank team, led by a senior staff member, Jamil Sopher, seemed enthusiastic about the project's potential. Bank staff also seemed pleased by the polite, nonconfrontational and, one might say, deferential atmosphere in the Lane Xang. The annual World Bank/International Monetary Fund (IMF) meetings recently held in neighboring Thailand had been contentious. Hundreds of activists had attended the parallel international People's Forum at which there had been nonstop criticism of the Bank, most notably over its support for hydropower projects in India, as well as its expected decision to support the controversial Pak Mun hydropower project in northeastern Thailand, just a short distance across the Mekong River from Laos. During a dialogue meeting set up by the Bank to hear the concerns of some of its most prominent critics, the situation had degenerated to the point where the critics had turned their backs and walked out of the meeting, which garnered considerable media attention and yet more negative publicity for the World Bank. In contrast, in Laos, run by a one-party government with no independent media or any recent history of independent local activism, perhaps Bank staff assumed they had found a "safe haven," a place where they might be spared the types of challenges, controversies, and conflicts they increasingly had to endure in Thailand and other more open societies.

But then into the harmonious atmosphere in the Lane Xang strolled an unexpected visitor, Bruce Rich, a well-known environmental and human rights lawyer, senior attorney at the Environmental Defense Fund, and author of numerous articles, reports and books, many scathingly critical of the World Bank. As the gregarious and animated Rich stood to introduce himself, Bank staff visibly tensed. His claim of being "on vacation" in Laos elicited nervous laughs and smiles of disbelief.[2] Rich had attended the People's Forum at the World Bank/IMF meetings in Bangkok, and now here he was in Vientiane. While Rich maintained a generally low profile at the meeting, his presence kept the World Bank staff on their toes and provided the rest of us with the confidence to ask a few questions about the project. It was clear that virtually no consideration had yet been given to any of the most basic social and environmental concerns of the type that were making Pak Mun so controversial in Thailand.

As was the case in most subsequent NT2 consultations in Laos, the initial presentation had taken up most of the allotted time for the meeting, and there was relatively little left for detailed discussion. But in more ways than one the stage was set. From the start, NT2 was to prove much more contentious than the Bank had anticipated or hoped.

BRUCE SHOEMAKER

Nakai Plateau, 1992–2008

On a quiet morning during the rainy season of 1992, I sat in a café in Vientiane reading the English-language *Bangkok Post* newspaper. Twice each week one shopkeeper in Vientiane brought some copies of the paper across the Mekong from Thailand. In those halcyon pre-internet days, it was one of the few sources in Laos of news from the outside world. I had come to Laos to conduct biological surveys at a time when the country was just emerging from a long period of self-imposed, post–Indochina War, and postcommunist revolution isolation. An ornithological survey I had done for a few days in a small patch of degraded but protected forest near the capital of Vientiane was only the second government-sanctioned wildlife field survey that had been conducted in the country since the Communist Party took control in 1975.

Turning the pages of the *Post*, I was met by a photo of biologist John MacKinnon holding a pair of long, spectacular animal horns. They looked like something from Africa. The photo accompanied a story, picked up from the Vietnamese press, about the startling discovery of a new and unusual species of large mammal in Vietnam. The species had not yet been officially described and named, but would become known to the world as the saola, *Pseudoryx nghetinhensis*.[3]

Like probably every other biologist in the world, I was stunned by the announcement. It was arguably the most surprising zoological find of the twentieth century. Few biologists, if any, would have guessed that an animal both this large (estimated to weigh up to 100 kilograms) and this distinctive (not only a new species but an entirely new genus of large mammal unlike anything known from Southeast Asia) could go undetected by the outside world until then, especially in a densely populated country like Vietnam. Not even Vietnamese biologists in Hanoi had known of the animal. It was like picking up the paper to read about the scientific discovery of a unicorn.

The article included a small map showing the site of discovery, Vu Quang Nature Reserve, a small protected area in the Annamite Mountains, on the border with central Laos. There seemed little doubt that the species also roamed the Lao side of the Annamites. Within days I left the capital by bus, then continued on foot to get as close as I could to the area of the animal's discovery. I found myself, for the first time, on the Nakai Plateau.

I spent about three days walking across the plateau, drinking from streams and stringing up a small hammock at night. I had not yet heard of Nam Theun 2 and had no idea what was coming. The town of Nakai (also known locally as Oudomsouk), which today is a bustling commercial center owing to prosperity from construction of the dam, didn't yet exist in any recognizable form. The plateau was dominated by an open, tropical pine forest. I was aware that this was almost certainly not saola habitat. They would be in the denser, broadleaf forest, visible in the Annamite foothills that rose on the other side of the Nam Theun River, from the edge of the plateau up toward the Vietnam border. Still, at that time the plateau was home to significant populations of wild elephants, wild cattle, and tigers, among other wildlife. Perhaps fortunately, I encountered some of their tracks, only. What I remember most was the plateau's extraordinarily beautiful pines, some of which measured more than 1.5 meters in diameter (a few years later, a forester would tell me that the Nakai Plateau held the most valuable remaining stand of wild, uncut pine in the world). It was like walking among the columns of a cathedral. Large, richly hued woodpeckers known as flamebacks called as they flew from tree to tree. Even absent saola, the plateau held wonders.

Figure P.1. Buddhist monks on the Nam Theun River, April 9, 2008, the evening before the gates of the NT2 dam were closed. Photo by William Robichaud.

Fast forward sixteen years from that first visit to the plateau to April 9, 2008. I am returning by boat to the now burgeoning town of Nakai from a field survey for saola in the montane forests that now comprise the Nakai-Nam Theun National Protected Area and the catchment of the Nam Theun River; the same dense forest I saw from the plateau in 1992. As our survey team's long-tailed boat descends one of the forested tributaries and enters the Nam Theun, the sun is finishing its descent toward the horizon. I jot an entry into my field notebook, look at the date, and realize we are on the Nam Theun on the last evening of the river's natural life, a life that has probably flowed for more than a million years. The gates of the new NT2 dam are to be closed the next morning, and the reservoir will begin to fill. The world will never be the same, in ways both certain yet incalculable. I take photos of the river in a vain attempt at preservation, like cutting a lock of hair from the dead.

Much had happened in the intervening sixteen years since my trek across the plateau. Most obvious, from my view in the boat, is the disappearance of nearly all of the magnificent pine forest, the trees having been cut and removed by Vietnamese loggers, with only a fraction of their value paid into a few pockets in Laos. Much of what remains is dusty, impoverished scrub, absent the call of flamebacks or the tracks of tigers, and waiting to be buried under millions of tons of water. One scar covered by another.

As our boat rounds a bend in the river, we meet a surreal scene: a dozen Buddhist monks, in orange robes and orange life jackets, stand on a sandbank in the middle of the river. A few staff of the NT2 Power Company are arranging them for a photo, and I realize what it is happening: to safeguard the project, the company has brought in monks, perhaps to give last rites to the river, or to ask its forgiveness.

We pause, in the quiet ending of the day, and I take my own photos of the curious assemblage. Then we push back into the current and continue to Nakai, as the sun sets on the Nam Theun River for the last time.

WILLIAM ROBICHAUD

Much has transpired in the more than two and a half decades since our first experiences with NT2. As plans for the project were developed, sides formed and a line was drawn, defined by opposing predictions of how the project would play out—would it be a positive transformation and model of global importance or a repeat of past failures? This volume is a record of NT2's development and a reflection on which prognosis was more accurate.

The book includes contributions from seventeen observers of the NT2 enterprise. Their experience and perspectives are diverse. Some of the chapter authors have worked as consultants or staff for the project and the World Bank, while others spent years campaigning against NT2. Several pursued and published research on various aspects of the project. In addition, many others involved in the project have contributed other information and perspectives to the book. Most of them are listed in the acknowledgements; some wish to remain anonymous.

Still others who could have provided important insights on NT2 declined to do so. Commonly cited reasons were either contractually mandated censorship or self-censorship; that is, they were barred from sharing what they know through contractual obligations to institutions involved in NT2, or they were concerned that contributing to the book would compromise their jobs at these institutions or their livelihoods in Laos generally. Most importantly, we regret that there is no direct inclusion of Lao voices in the book, voices which are often constrained by fear of speaking out (a theme touched on in chapter 10). Still, we have aimed for a diversity of analysis and insight about the planning for NT2, the true impact of the project, and the project's legacy—within Laos, the Mekong region, and beyond.

NOTES

1. Stan Sesser, "Forgotten Country," *New Yorker*, August 20, 1990.

2. Ironically, Rich really was on vacation and happened to be staying at the Lane Xang, one of the few hotel options for a foreign tourist at that time. He had run into a World Bank consultant he knew over breakfast in the hotel coffee shop, who told him about the meeting and suggested he attend.

3. Vu Van Dung, Pham Mong Giao, Nguyen Ngoc Chinh, Do Tuoc, Peter Arctander, and John MacKinnon, "A New Species of Living Bovid from Vietnam," *Nature* 363 (1993).

Acknowledgments

Foremost, the editors and authors are grateful to the many Lao villagers—in the Nam Theun catchment, on the Nakai Plateau, and in the Xe Bang Fai River basin—who in the course of our many visits to these areas, shared their views, answered our questions, and extended their warm hospitality. We also thank many other Lao people—academics, staff of government and nongovernmental organizations, consultants and others—who shared their insights and observations. For their confidentiality and safety, we have opted not to identify most of them by name.

We are deeply indebted to our insightful, patient and supportive editor at the University of Wisconsin Press, Gwen Walker (whose enthusiasm when we broached the idea of this book inspired us to actually follow through!), and her very capable staff and colleagues at the press, in particular Matthew Cosby, Terry Emmrich, Sarah Knapp, Anna Muenchrath, MJ Devaney, and Adam Mehring.

George Allez and Avery Shoemaker provided invaluable assistance in the editing of the manuscript and preparation of the bibliography. Camille Coudrat and Laura Poplett assisted with preparation of the maps.

During preparation of the book many colleagues generously contributed information and advice and/or read and commented on drafts of the text. Some requested anonymity; the others, in alphabetical order, are John Baker, Ramesh Boonratana, Natalie Bugalski, Mike Carroll, Jacqui Chagnon, Stuart Chape, Andrea Claassen, Cameron Cooper, Camille Coudrat, Premrudee Daoroung, Piaporn Deetes, Stephen Duthy, Mike Dwyer, Daryl Fields, Sean Foley, Richard Frankel, Stephanie Fried, Kate Geary, Kim Geheb, Anne-Sophie Gindroz, Chuenchom Sangarasri Greacen, Richard Hackman, Troy Hansel, Benjamin Hodgdon, Aviva Imhof, Arlyne Johnson, Julie Tallard Johnson, Melody Kemp, Josh Klemm, Shannon Lawrence, Robert Mather, Patrick McCully, David McDowell, Alex McWilliam, Shui Meng Ng, Francois Obein, John Parr, Alan Rabinowitz, Bruce Rich, John Robinson, Tanya Roberts-Davis, Anna Roggenbuck, Thayer Scudder, Stephan Sparks, Rob

Steinmetz, Lee Talbot, Shane Tarr, Rob Timmins, Michael Victor, Chanthavy Vongkhamheng, and Tony Zola. We would also like to thank two anonymous peer reviewers whose comments and suggestions made the book better.

The McKnight Foundation, through the assistance of its international programs director Jane Maland Cady and program assistant Karyn Sciortino Johnson, and Oxfam Australia, facilitated by Pauline Taylor McKeown, Socheata Sim, Gary Lee, and Michael Simon, provided funding and inspiration for the research and preparation of the book. Global Wildlife Conservation, with the assistance of its CEO Wes Sechrest and financial managers Samantha Reza and Alex Quintero provided fiscal management of this project. All of these organizations and individuals have been extremely supportive and helpful. A number of other funding organizations supported portions of earlier research that has been incorporated into this volume, including Blue Moon Fund and Open Society Foundations. The views expressed in this volume, however, are those of the authors only and not necessarily those of these supporting institutions.

Abbreviations

ADB	Asian Development Bank
ASEAN	Association of Southeast Asian Nations
BOOT	build-own-operate-transfer
CCGT	combined cycle gas turbine
CPAWM	Centre for Protected Areas and Watershed Management
DUDCP	District Upland Development and Conservation Project
EdF	Électricité de France
EdL	Électricité du Laos
EGAT	Electrical Generating Authority of Thailand
EGCO	Electricity Generating Public Company Limited
GEF	Global Environment Facility
GoL	government of the Lao People's Democratic Republic
ha	hectare
HSAP	Hydropower Sustainability Assessment Protocol
IAG	International Advisory Group
IDA	International Development Agency
IFC	International Finance Corporation
IFI	international financial institutions
IHA	International Hydropower Association
IMF	International Monetary Fund
INGO	international nongovernmental organization
IRN	International Rivers Network
IUCN	International Union for the Conservation of Nature
Lao PDR	Lao People's Democratic Republic
LTA	Lenders' Technical Advisory Group
MEENet	Mekong Energy and Ecology Network
MOU	memorandum of understanding
M-POWER	Mekong Program on Water Environment and Resilience
NBCA	National Biodiversity Conservation Area
NGO	nongovernmental organization

NNT	Nakai-Nam Theun
NNT BCC	Nakai-Nam Theun Biodiversity Conservation Consortium
NPA	National Protected Area
NT2	Nam Theun 2
NTEC	Nam Theun 2 Electricity Consortium
NTPC	Nam Theun 2 Power Company
PDG	Project Development Group
PoE	International Environmental and Social Panel of Experts
PRSP	poverty reduction strategy paper
REMP	Revenues and Expenditure Management Program
SMEC	Snowy Mountain Engineering Company
TERRA	Towards Ecological Recovery and Regional Alliances
UNDP	United Nations Development Program
VFA	village forestry association
WCD	World Commission on Dams
WCS	Wildlife Conservation Society
WMPA	Watershed Management Protection Authority
WWF	World Wide Fund for Nature
XBF	Xe Bang Fai

Dead in the Water

Introduction

Stepping into the Current

WILLIAM ROBICHAUD and

BRUCE SHOEMAKER

Laos is a country of extremes: it has the lowest population density and highest percentage of forest cover in Southeast Asia; it is the most bombed country per capita in history, yet home to Southeast Asia's best-preserved city (the former royal capital of Luang Prabang) and Indochina's largest protected area (Nakai-Nam Theun National Protected Area [NTT NPA]).[1] It has one of the world's most discouraging levels of press freedom (ranked 173rd out of 180 countries) and lowest measures of democracy (ranked 155th out of 167 countries assessed).[2] And although considered by the United Nations to be one of the world's "least developed countries," it recently became home to one of Southeast Asia's largest development projects, the Nam Theun 2 (NT2) hydropower dam.

NT2 was made possible by support from the World Bank, which once called the dam its "largest and most controversial project" of any kind.[3] The president of the World Bank and the prime ministers of Lao PDR and Thailand visited the project site during construction. Not just another large hydropower dam, NT2 was to be a new model of "dams as development"—an endeavor that would alleviate poverty and contribute to biodiversity conservation, while generating profit for a public/private commercial enterprise. Ultimately, NT2 became the highest profile, most studied, and most controversial hydropower dam in Southeast Asia. For more than two decades—from early planning in the 1990s through project approval by the World Bank in 2005, the dam's construction, the commencement of commercial operation in 2010, and ongoing attempts to mitigate its impacts—NT2 has been a contentious focal point of

3

the debate over natural resources, hydropower, and local livelihoods in Laos, the Mekong region, and beyond.

When the World Bank approved the project in 2005, the social and environmental problems of large hydropower around the world were increasingly well recognized, and many observers believed that the promises of the NT2 model were too good to be true.[4]

A Large Dam in a Small Country

NT2 is a massive project, constructed at a cost of $1.3 billion and generating 1070 megawatts of electricity. Yet it was built in a small country with almost no industrial base, and which had only recently emerged from decades of conflict, a communist doctrinaire economy, and self-imposed isolation from the West. What in the West is generally called the "Vietnam War" and thought of as occurring from the mid-1960s to early 1970s was in fact a much broader conflict, in time and space. It enmeshed Laos starting in the 1950s, after the country gained independence from more than six decades of colonial rule by France. The next two decades were consumed by a struggle for control between an American-backed royal government that held power in some areas of the country, including the capital city (Vientiane) and other urban centers, and a North Vietnamese–backed communist movement, known as the Pathet Lao (Lao Nation), which controlled parts of the countryside. For a short period, a third element, an armed Lao neutralist movement (aligned with neither North Vietnam nor the United States), jostled for control.

Attempts to resolve the impasse evolved through rounds of peace negotiations, armed ground conflict (including the development of a large, irregular fighting force of ethnic Hmong organized, supported, and advised by the CIA), years of intense US bombing of parts of the country, and an uneasy, short-lived power-sharing arrangement between the Pathet Lao and the royal government. Finally, in a last, bloodless step, the communist Pathet Lao seized full political control of Laos in December 1975 (seven months after the capture of Saigon, which had completed the ascension of communist power throughout Vietnam) and established the present Lao state, the Lao People's Democratic Republic (or Lao PDR).

This soon had two consequences. One was a loss from Lao society of substantial numbers of citizens with advanced education and technical expertise. Many Lao who were associated with the royal government, especially those in senior political and administrative positions, either fled to safety in neighboring Thailand (along with thousands of Hmong villagers from the mountains) or were interred by the new government in reeducation camps ("seminar camps"). Second, the government promptly turned toward the Eastern Bloc and drew the country into a prolonged period of communist consolidation as well as separation and isolation from the West (and also from neighboring Thailand—a cultural and linguistic kinsman to Laos, but also a US ally). Only limited information about life in the new Lao PDR reached the outside world during this time.

The eventual collapse of the Soviet Union and the ensuing loss of Soviet and Eastern Bloc technical and financial assistance necessitated a reorientation in Lao PDR's foreign policy and a cautious reopening to the West and to its wealthier neighbor and sometime adversary, Thailand. The fall of the Berlin Wall in 1989 was undoubtedly a significant catalyst for the revival of the Nam Theun 2 concept and the project's eventual implementation.

Yet despite the shifting political and economic winds, key elements of the project did not change: it would still alter the flow of two major Mekong tributaries, disrupt the lives of thousands of people, and bring substantial risk of harm to a globally significant natural area. Given NT2's size and the extent of its impacts, throughout the extended period of its planning and development it dominated discussions, consultations, campaigns, debates, and strategies for a broad swath of people and institutions—government officials, development practitioners, international banks, aid agencies, wildlife conservationists, and campaigners for human rights and the environment. It garnered considerable media attention, both positive and negative. The American magazine *Newsweek* once called it a "kinder, gentler megaproject" compared to dam projects in other countries.[5]

The dam was constructed on one of the largest tributaries of the Mekong, the Nam Theun (see figures I.1 and I.2). The river has its source in the Annamite Mountains, a densely forested global biodiversity hotspot. Most of the NT2 catchment is within Nakai-Nam Theun National Protected Area (NNT NPA) along Laos's eastern border with Vietnam. Several large streams flow down through the mountainous protected area to the Nakai Plateau, where they converge to form the Nam Theun River. Before the dam was built, the river meandered across the plateau and cascaded off its northern end. Below the plateau and the dam, the river (or what remains of it today) bisects another national protected area before reaching the Mekong (in its lower reaches, the name of the river changes to Nam Kading). NT2 is a trans-basin hydropower project. Water from the reservoir does not generate power by flowing through the dam but is dropped off a more precipitous point at the southern end of the plateau and upper reaches of the reservoir to a power station below. After

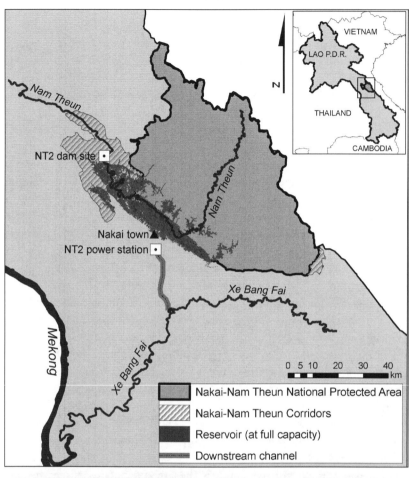

emerging from the turbines, the water passes through a long artificial channel to another river, the Xe Bang Fai (XBF), which enters the Mekong well downstream from the mouth of the Nam Theun/Nam Kading.

The area affected by NT2-induced changes in water flow is extensive. It includes flooding of about 40 percent of the Nakai Plateau, home to several thousand Indigenous Peoples. Their traditional livelihoods were based on the rich natural resources of the plateau and included raising livestock on its grasses, planting rain-fed rice, fishing, and collecting forest resources. The plateau and the Nam Theun River are—or were—also home to many threatened species of wild animals and plants. Other people live downstream in the Nam Theun/Nam Kading and XBF River basins. These communities, predominantly made up of lowland Lao but also of thousands of Indigenous Peoples, live largely from these rivers, being highly dependent on them as sources of food and cash income. By diverting flow from the Nam Theun to the XBF, NT2 greatly affected the livelihoods of people living along the banks of both rivers. Fish migrations were disrupted, and in many areas fishing is less productive. Finally, the protected area that comprises most of dam's catchment, Nakai-Nam Theun, is of high global significance. Increased ease of access to the area via the NT2 reservoir and other socioeconomic changes wrought by the project have significantly increased pressure on the protected area.

The NT2 project is owned by a public-private partnership of companies from France and Thailand together with the government of Lao PDR (GoL), known collectively as the Nam Theun 2 Power Company (NTPC). Following several years of construction, ultimately requiring a US$1.297 billion financing package, filling of the reservoir began in 2008, and commercial electricity generation commenced in 2010.[6] At full-supply level the reservoir inundates 430 square kilometers of the Nakai Plateau, which required the relocation of more than six thousand residents of the plateau.

Most of the dam's electricity is exported to neighboring Thailand—which has far higher electricity use than Laos but far less potential for hydropower projects (most of the main tributaries of the Mekong flow through Laos). For Laos, the core function of NT2 is to generate national revenue rather than electricity for domestic use. Through 2016 the project contributed around 1 percent of the country's annual budget, several times less proportionally than initial projections.[7]

Top left: figure I.1. Map of the NT2 project area.

Bottom left: figure I.2. The NT2 dam, looking downstream in February 2012. Photo by William Robichaud.

The World Bank has been heavily involved in NT2 almost from the time the project was conceived in the late 1980s. At the time, the Bank was smarting from extended bad publicity over a number of high-profile projects that had had severe social and environmental impacts and that were widely seen as public relations disasters. Many of these projects were large hydropower dams, in India, Africa, Thailand, and elsewhere. The World Bank increased its engagement with Laos at a time when the country was emerging from a period of doctrinaire socialism, while still retaining an authoritarian one-party government. In choosing Laos as the site for what it hoped would be a new model of hydropower, one in which the social and environmental benefits of the project would surpass the project's social and environmental costs, the Bank had to overcome a number of serious constraints. NT2 triggered all of the Bank's safeguard policies—guidelines and requirements designed to ensure that its projects are implemented with high standards and do not cause net social and environmental damage. At the time, it was widely debated whether fulfillment of the Bank's safeguards was realistic given the political economy that existed in Laos. The findings of this book suggest that it was not.

The Bank's role has been less as a direct financier than as a guarantor for the project's private investors against the risk of financial loss from potential political instability. This key role gave the Bank leverage to act as the project's chief architect in terms of fiscal, social, and environmental requirements. The Asian Development Bank and a number of other international finance agencies, mostly from European countries, also supported the project.

Doing a Dam Better?

Barely before the gates of the dam closed in 2008, Ian C. Porter and Jayasankar Shivakumar, two former senior staff of the World Bank turned consultants, set out to document the project's development in a book that would be published by the Bank in 2011 under the title *Doing a Dam Better: The Lao People's Democratic Republic and the Story of Nam Theun 2*. The work is a multiauthor volume, with chapters by various Bank staff and consultants, and covers the planning, development, and expected outcomes of NT2. As reflected in the title, the general tone and content of the book are positive and congratulatory. Although there is a certain amount of critical self-assessment, the book rarely questions the appropriateness or success of NT2, only how aspects of its implementation could have been better managed. The book's final chapter is titled "NT2: A Transformative Endeavor."[8]

8

We believe this positive conclusion was premature and that a more nuanced and diverse examination is now warranted. When *Doing a Dam Better* was published in 2011, many of NT2's promised social and environmental benefits were more conjecture than reality.[9] The book is also confined to just the World Bank's perspective and focuses mainly on internal World Bank processes, overlooking other important aspects of the project. Still, *Doing a Dam Better* has been presented by the World Bank as its summary of a promising new model, as the Bank attempts to justify its reengagement in large hydropower projects. This follows a period during which the Bank refrained from supporting such projects due to widespread criticism of the social and environmental impacts of hydro projects undertaken in the 1980s and 1990s. Then, in May 2013, the World Bank announced that it was ready to resume lending for large hydropower worldwide.[10] As Rachel Kyte, the Bank's vice president for sustainable development—and an influential advisor to the Bank's president, Jim Yong Kim—put it, "Large hydro is a very big part of the solution for Africa and South Asia and Southeast Asia. . . . I fundamentally believe we have to be involved." The earlier move away from hydro, she stated, "was the wrong message." She added, "That was then. This is now. We are back."[11]

The World Bank has continued to promote NT2's purported success as justification for its reentry into large hydropower. "[NT2] provides strong evidence of the World Bank's re-engagement in the hydropower sector."[12] "With [NT2's] large geographic footprint and multiple impacts, it constitutes a test case for project-specific environmental and social protection policies that have the potential to be broadly replicated."[13] Based on this purported success, the Bank has recently moved ahead with plans to support new large hydropower dams in various parts of the world, including the Congo, Zambia, and Nepal.[14] In 2015 it launched a major initiative to support development of hydropower in Myanmar through its International Finance Corporation arm, and staff have implied that it is the Bank's experience in Laos that justifies its move into Myanmar.[15] Even as NT2's social and environmental outcomes are increasingly questioned, the World Bank has organized study tours to Laos for decision makers and NGO representatives from countries such as Nepal and Vietnam, where NT2 has been put forward as a positive model of poverty alleviation and livelihood restoration.[16]

Among those who differ with this rosy assessment of NT2 is world-renowned scholar of hydropower resettlement Thayer Scudder of the California Institute of Technology. He was once a strong proponent of the NT2 project and served for twenty years as one of three members of the project's International Environmental and Social Panel of Experts (the PoE). More recently,

Scudder's view of NT2 has been characterized as his "final disappointment" in a long career of trying to ensure that hydropower projects improve the lives of the people they affect.[17] Later PoE reports indicate that, among the panel members, it is not only Scudder who has become increasingly critical of NT2's social and environmental outcomes and disillusioned with the project. This suggests significant and myopic gaps in the Bank's self-published history of the project.

Our book is a multiauthor volume that encompasses a diversity of viewpoints and voices. That said, a shared perspective of these voices is that *Doing a Dam Better*, and the World Bank more generally, have overstated the success of NT2 and the degree to which it should serve as a positive model worthy of replication. Because *Dead in the Water* has been written with a deeper passage time since the dam commenced operation, it has the benefit of more information on the challenges and the lessons of this controversial project. In particular, the book examines the consequences of disrupting two major river basins to create one of the largest reservoirs in Asia, while promising to secure the conservation of an adjacent area of globally significant biodiversity, to significantly improve the lives of several thousand resettled Indigenous People and many more people affected downstream, and to apply the dam's revenues to national poverty alleviation in a country with well-documented governance issues.[18]

Perhaps unsurprisingly, it is not clear that any of these promises have been met. The World Bank and its financial partners miscalculated the potential for the NT2 enterprise to overcome significant barriers and achieve its lofty goals. The chapters of this book examine what happened and why.

Over the years, NT2 has been the subject of intense examination from many quarters. Dozens of journal articles have been published about the project, and the project's own planning documents, studies, and reports would fill many filing cabinets. There is a rich store of information; the challenge lies in winnowing it down to a concise and coherent summary. This book focuses on the social and environmental outcomes of the project within Laos, since these were to make NT2 different from large hydropower projects of the past.

The book is organized in three parts. Part One, "The World Bank Promotes a New Model of Hydropower," sets the stage by reviewing the early history of the project and the institutional and political setting in which it was developed and describes how the World Bank sought to implement and portray NT2 as a new model, including through the use of independent monitors and nongovernmental organizations.

Part Two, "Social and Environmental Context and Outcomes," takes an in-depth look at what has happened on the ground since NT2 commenced commercial operation in 2010, in terms of the projected benefits for affected communities, biodiversity conservation, and national poverty reduction. Finally, Part Three, "Nam Theun 2's Wider Legacy," questions the validity of framing NT2 as a successful new model for hydropower, regionally and globally. Contrary to predictions, NT2 did not transform the socioeconomics of Laos, nor demonstrate how to do dams better. Instead, the project is better framed as a disappointment, which can and should stimulate the World Bank to change its approach to such projects.

The book concludes with reflections on why the dam was constructed given that so many of its goals were not reached, its relationship to the findings of the World Commission on Dams (WCD) and what can be learned from both the process of the decision to go ahead with NT2 and its consequences in light of current global trends for development finance and hydropower.

On balance, some readers may find this book overly critical of NT2. However, we believe that if more people with intimate knowledge of the project had felt free to share their experiences and perspectives, the collective conclusion would likely be more critical of the project, not less, than is reflected in these pages.

The final sentence of *Doing a Dam Better* reads, "The more complete body of experiences and lessons available down the road will enrich a deeper analysis and assessment, which should be documented and shared at an opportune point in the future."[19] We believe that time has arrived and offer this volume as a contribution to that assessment.

NOTES

1. Richard Waters, "Luang Prabang: Why You Should Visit South-east Asia's Best Preserved City Now," *Telegraph*, December 7, 2015, www.telegraph.co.uk/travel/destinations/asia/laos/articles/Luang-Prabang-Why-you-should-visit-South-east-Asias-best-preserved-city-now.

2. Reporters without Borders, 2016 World Press Freedom Index, https://rsf.org/en/ranking; Economist Intelligence Unit, Democracy Index, https://en.wikipedia.org/wiki/Democracy_Index#Democracy_index_by_country_.282015.29.

3. Peter Stephens, "The Communications Challenge," in *Doing a Dam Better: The Lao People's Democratic Republic and the Story of Nam Theun 2*, ed. Ian C. Porter and Jayasankar Shivakumar (Washington, DC: World Bank, 2011).

4. The recognition of these problems culminated in the WCD process, described in chapter 2, which cast doubt on the viability of large-scale hydropower dams due to their severe social and environmental impacts. NT2 was the first large hydropower dam to be supported by the World Bank following the WCD process. Prior to NT2 approval in 2005

a robust debate occurred between NT2 supporters and critics over whether or not NT2 was "WCD compliant."

5. Jonathan Kent, "Laos Dam Raises Ethical Bar," *Newsweek*, August 11, 2011, www .newsweek.com/laos-dam-raises-ethical-bar-99271.

6. Daryl Fields, NT2 project manager, World Bank, personal communication to Bruce Shoemaker, January 23, 2017.

7. World Bank, *Nam Theun 2 Hydropower Project Update: Revenue Management*, 2. See chapter 9 for a detailed discussion of project revenues and the GoL budget.

8. Patchamuthu Illangovan, "NT2: A Transformative Endeavor," in *Doing a Dam Better*, 157.

9. At the time Porter and Shivakumar were preparing their book in 2010, they told William Robichaud that the book's working title was "Doing a Dam Right." Robichaud (and maybe others) provided them with feedback along the lines of "Because the project is just now becoming operational and the hoped-for environmental and social outcomes are at this point more theory then reality, perhaps this title is a bit presumptuous?" They agreed and changed the title to the less conclusive but still optimistic "Doing a Dam Better."

10. Howard Schneider, "World Bank Turns to Hydropower to Square Development with Climate Change," *Washington Post*, May 8, 2013, www.washingtonpost.com/business /economy/world-bank-turns-to-hydropower-to-square-development-with-climate-change/2013/05/08/b9d60332-b1bd-11e2-9a98-4be1688d7d84_story.html?utm_term=.498f3ef8a497.

11. Quoted in Schneider, "World Bank Turns to Hydropower."

12. Ian C. Porter and Jayasankar Shivakumar, "Overview," in *Doing a Dam Better*, 2.

13. Porter and Shivakumar, "Overview," 8.

14. Schneider, "World Bank Turns to Hydropower."

15. Kate Lazarus. "Driving Change in the Hydro Sector," *International Water Power and Dam Construction*, Hydropower Developers Working Group, April 14, 2015, www .waterpowermagazine.com/opinion/opiniondriving-change-in-the-hydro-sector-4553422.

16. Shane Tarr, personal communication to Bruce Shoemaker, October, 2016. "The World Bank in Vietnam organized a 2013 study tour for government decision-makers and the World Bank–supported Trung Son Hydro Power Co Ltd to NT2 with a theme of demonstrating how effective NT2 had been at restoring the livelihoods of displaced people." Similar tours have been sponsored by the World Bank from Nepal to Laos.

17. Jacques Leslie, "Large Dams Just Aren't Worth the Cost," *New York Times*, August 22, 2014, www.nytimes.com/2014/08/24/opinion/sunday/large-dams-just-arent-worth-the-cost.html?mcubz=3.

18. Transparency International, Corruptions Perception Index 2015, www.transparency .org/cpi2015.

19. Illangovan, "NT2," 175.

Part One

The World Bank Promotes a New Model of Hydropower

1

Nam Theun 2's Winding History

Studies, Setbacks, and Rebrandings

BRUCE SHOEMAKER and

WILLIAM ROBICHAUD

Like the winding Nam Theun River, the development of the Nam Theun 2 hydropower project (NT2) saw many twists and turns, from the first conception of the dam up to the 2005 approval of the project by the World Bank, the Asian Development Bank (ADB), and their financial partners. The project was subjected to the vagaries of World Bank policy, as the Bank attempted to create a new model of development assistance, to issues that arose from unforeseen regional and international events, and to intense international opposition. But eventually it was the dam, and not the river, that survived.

The Early Years of Project Development

According to some reports, the idea of damming the Nam Theun River dates back to 1927, in French colonial times.[1] Subsequent decades of war and instability in the region made the construction of large infrastructure projects difficult, particularly in remote areas. One large hydropower project, Nam Ngum, was completed in Laos in the early 1970s, during the Second Indochina War, under the auspices of the Mekong Committee. The committee was formed in 1957 at the recommendation of the United Nations after Indochina's emergence from the French colonial era to coordinate use and development of water resources in the Mekong basin.[2] The Nam Ngum dam was located near the site of the country's highest electricity demand, the capital city of Vientiane (60 kilometers north of the city), which was a relatively stable area in the war years, compared to large swaths of other parts of the country. The first phase of the Nam Ngum dam was completed in 1971. At about the same time, the concept of the trans-basin project in the Nam Theun and Xe Bang Fai (XBF) River basins that would become NT2 was first explored. The Mekong Committee supported the idea, and in 1973 it was enthusiastically promoted as a project with great potential by Khamsing Ngonvorarath, then the director of Électricité du Laos.[3] The project's justification, which was to change repeatedly over the years, was that it would produce electricity in southern and central Laos, although the idea of exporting electricity to both Bangkok and Hanoi was also mentioned.[4] Following the 1975 communist revolution, Laos entered a period of self-imposed isolation from many Western and international institutions. Most of its aid came from Soviet-bloc countries, and the fledgling government was not equipped to implement major infrastructure projects. In the mid-1980s, a successor to the Mekong Committee, the Interim Mekong Committee (a realignment in response to the Khmer Rouge's takeover of Cambodia), scaled back the Mekong Committee's ambitious plans for large dams in the Mekong basin. After the formation of the new committee, nothing further happened for some time.

In 1986, the government of the Lao PDR (GoL) instituted a policy of a slow opening, known as *chinthanakan mai* (new imagination or direction) out of which emerged *konlakai sethakit mai* (new economic mechanism), a less doctrinaire form of communist economic planning. During this period, international aid agencies stepped up their assistance to Laos. One priority was to increase the country's electricity generating capacity. That same year, the United Nations Development Program (UNDP), with the World Bank as executing agency, agreed to fund an evaluation of potential sites for hydropower dams, which was to be conducted by an Australian consulting firm, Snowy Mountain Engineering Compomy (SMEC). This led to a prefeasibility assessment of NT2 in 1988, and then, in 1989, the same parties agreed to support a full feasibility study. These later two studies were also conducted by SMEC.

The findings were presented to the GoL and international organizations in September 1991. The study concluded that the concept of taking advantage of the unique physiography of the area through construction of a trans-basin diversion project had immense potential for economically generating large amounts of electricity. This was due to the close proximity of the Nam Theun

River, elevated on the Nakai Plateau, to the XBF River below. Water could be diverted from the Nam Theun and sent down the plateau's escarpment, generating enormous momentum; at the bottom of the escarpment, turbines could then convert the water's potential energy into large amounts of electricity. The realization of the project's large potential just as Lao PDR and Thailand were beginning to explore closer ties after a prolonged period of poor relations led to NT2's redefinition as a project primarily for revenue generation through the export of electricity to Thailand.

In October 1991, Philip Hirsch of the University of Sydney published a review of the environmental and social aspects of the SMEC study, which criticized the study's lack of participatory methods and its failure to identify or highlight many of the proposed project's key environmental and social issues.[5] This paper, the first independent published report on NT2, was prescient in that it identified many of the core issues that defined debate over the project in the coming years.

After the SMEC feasibility study, and at a time when the World Bank was increasingly supportive of public–private partnerships, Bank staff advised the GoL that NT2's projected cost meant that a partnership with the private sector would be required to finance, construct, and operate the ambitious dam. GoL leaders, perhaps still wary of opening up too quickly to Western investment and influence, responded by putting NT2 on the backburner and instead proceeded with another hydropower project downstream of NT2's proposed location known as Theun-Hinboun. With Theun-Hinboun the GoL could work with a donor, the ADB, with which it was more familiar, as well as with Scandinavian backers associated with governments that had long been sympathetic and supportive of the revolutionary Lao state. Due to its much smaller reservoir, which did not require substantial resettlement or the flooding of a large area of high conservation importance, Theun-Hinboun was first promoted as a more environmentally and socially friendly alternative to NT2. Unlike NT2, Theun-Hinboun was structured in a way that retained majority GoL ownership from the beginning.

But by early 1993 the pace of change in Laos had quickened. In June, the Thai and Lao governments signed a memorandum of understanding (MOU) under which Laos agreed to export 1500 megawatts of hydroelectric power to Thailand by the year 2000 (revised in 1996 to 2000 megawatts). While this agreement more immediately resulted in the initiation of Theun-Hinboun, the GoL also expressed interest in the development of the much larger NT2 project and indicated a willingness to move ahead with structuring NT2 as a private sector–led project. "The level of communism at the time when we started seemed impenetrable," NT2's first World Bank project director, Jamil Sopher, later noted, and getting the GoL to accept private sector involvement was one of the project's biggest obstacles.[6]

In March 1993, a preliminary MOU for the development of NT2 was signed between SMEC, the GoL, and the Thai government. SMEC then invited the Australian construction firm Transfield to join a consortium formed to build NT2, first known as the Project Development Group (PDG). In December 1993, the PDG was reconstituted with Transfield taking over the lead development role from SMEC. A "joint participation agreement" was signed that formally founded the Nam Theun 2 Electricity Consortium (NTEC).[7] This was quickly followed in January 1994 with the signing of a full MOU for NT2's development between NTEC, the Electricity Generating Authority of Thailand (EGAT), and the GoL, through its state enterprise Électricité du Laos (EdL).

In 1994, NTEC contracted with TEAM Consulting, based in Thailand, to conduct a social and environmental assessment of the project. The study, released in 1995, was considered inadequate by both World Bank environmental staff and observers from international nongovernment organizations (NGOs) and was quickly rejected by the Bank as an unsuitable basis for project decision making.[8]

In March 1995, a power purchase agreement was signed between EGAT, the GoL, and NTEC. The developers then began looking for funding for the project. Due to the perceived difficulty of attracting private financing to communist Laos (see text box on political risk guarantees), NTEC began exploring potential sources of foreign aid—especially for the GoL's equity share. Reportedly concerned about the World Bank's stringent guidelines, NTEC first approached ADB for financing. However, already committed to another hydro project in the same river system (Theun-Hinboun) and worried about overexposure, ADB declined. The government of Japan, which was at the time increasing its profile in Laos, was also approached but was reportedly worried about the considerable environmental and social risks of the project.[9] After eleven months, NTEC and the GoL turned to the World Bank, requesting US$300–400 million in loans. However, the Bank moved cautiously, saying that NT2 would be a "complicated financing package," and that there were many unanswered questions to be addressed first.[10] The Bank was interested— but only if its involvement could help salvage its increasingly recognized and problematic environmental and social track record from its past hydropower projects.

A Campaign against NT2 Emerges

As NT2 gained traction in 1995, so did an emerging opposition campaign. While many organizations eventually campaigned against NT2, two groups made it a particularly strong focus and were to be long associated as leaders of the opposition to it. One was the US-based International Rivers Network (IRN),[11] which has a long history of advocacy for rivers and against hydropower in developing countries, based on both environmental and human rights concerns. IRN had been at the forefront of high-profile campaigns exposing the social and environmental costs of World Bank projects in India, Central America, and elsewhere. In 1996, IRN campaigns director Patrick McCully published an influential book outlining the environmental and human rights case against large dams titled *Silenced Rivers*.[12] IRN'S initiation of a Mekong program in 1995, at a time when a frenzy of dam building in Laos was being planned (and some projects were already under way), was a logical progression for the organization.

The other NT2 opposition group, Towards Ecological Recovery and Regional Alliances (TERRA), was based in Thailand and emerged out of the Project for Ecological Recovery, a leading Thai NGO within the growing movement of opposition to large hydropower dams and deforestation in Thailand. In the words of one of its founders, Witoon Permpongsacharoen,

> One of the main reasons for our engagement was an ethical concern. The success of our movement had made hydropower projects more difficult to construct in Thailand. At a time when Thai leaders were supportive of turning former "battlefields into marketplaces" this led Thai companies and EGAT to propose projects in neighboring countries to export electricity back to Thailand. So we felt we had a responsibility to address the unintended consequences of our campaign and follow those Thai companies to those countries as well.[13]

TERRA members included both Thai campaigners and foreign volunteers. In July 1995, it launched a new regional environmental journal, *Watershed*, which followed and reported on NT2 from its first issue. While IRN and TERRA were at the core of the anti-NT2 campaign, in subsequent years the movement grew to encompass many other groups. TERRA and the Project for Ecological Recovery was well connected with other Thai NGOs that were willing to help with letters and public statements. Other key international groups active at this time included Probe International (a Canadian group with close ties to TERRA), Mekong Watch (a Japanese research and advocacy group founded in 1993 by former Japanese volunteers in Laos), Focus on the

19

Global South (a development policy institute based in Bangkok), and a broad coalition of European and Australian groups that shared similar development perspectives with IRN and TERRA.

Noticeable in their absence were any groups based in Laos. While an informal coalition of mainly international NGO staff based in Vientiane shared information and networked with IRN and TERRA concerning NT2 and other hydropower projects in Laos, they were not able, given the political constraints in the country, to formally oppose the project in any way. Some groups, most notably Oxfam and in particular its US and Australian affiliates, might otherwise have been more prominent in their opposition if not for fear of repercussions for their field offices in Laos (see chapter 3 on NGO engagement with NT2).

Rebranding NT2 as a Green Project

In 1993, independent of considerations about NT2, GoL established the catchment of the proposed project as one of Lao PDR's first national protected areas, and its largest—Nakai-Nam Theun National Biodiversity Conservation Area (NNT NBCA; now known in English as Nakai-Nam Theun National Protected Area [NNT NPA]). Due to the area's exceptionally rich biodiversity, it would soon be recognized as the most important protected area in the country—and, in fact, one of the most important in the world.[14] In 1994, the Wildlife Conservation Society (WCS) worked with the GoL to conduct the first wildlife and habitat field survey of the area and, recognizing the area's high importance, followed this with the preparation of a framework management plan for NNT NBCA. Further plans were put on hold due to the uncertainties over NT2.

The global biological significance of NT2's catchment soon provided an additional justification for NT2—that of being a "green" project, which would be a net plus for the environment by helping to conserve biodiversity, compensating for the project's operating losses.[15] In its subsequent framing of NT2, the World Bank considered effective protection of NNT NBCA as central to the project's success. Investment in conservation of this globally significant protected area, to be made by a proposed designation of US$1 million per year of project revenues, would both safeguard the reservoir from premature siltation and serve as an offset for biodiversity lost or degraded by the project, including on the Nakai Plateau, the proposed site of the NT2 dam and its large reservoir. The World Bank, the GoL, the International Union for the Conservation of

Nature (IUCN), and others came to believe that NT2 was the best, and perhaps only, way to protect this large and important area. In fact, however, the looming prospect of NT2 deterred other outside groups from getting involved in the conservation of NNT (see text box). And for nearly a decade, the prospect of NT2 inhibited conservation of one of the most endangered species in the world, the saola (*Pseudoryx nghetinhensis*; see chapter 7).

Placing NNT NBCA front and center was, at best, ironic, since according to the World Bank's own operational policy (OP) 4.04 on natural habitats, issued in 1995, the proximity of the protected area should have prevented the Bank from supporting NT2: "The Bank does not support projects that, in the Bank's opinion, involve the significant conversion or degradation of critical natural habitats."[16] Critical natural habitats are defined as "existing protected areas" and significant conversion is described as "the elimination or severe diminution of the integrity of a critical or other natural habitat caused by a major, long-term change . . . , for example . . . permanent flooding (e.g., by a reservoir)."[17]

Prime Minister's Decree 164 (PM 164), which established the new system of eighteen NBCAs in 1993, included maps showing the boundaries of the new protected areas. The map for NNT (figure 1.1) clearly shows the protected area extending across the eastern half of the Nakai Plateau (the half of the plateau most distant from human influence and so probably of highest conservation value) to a western boundary at the Nam Theun River (the protected area's eastern boundary was set at the international border with Vietnam). In 1995, a compilation of protected area fact sheets for Laos, issued by the IUCN and the country's joint Lao-Swedish Forestry Cooperation Programme, confirmed that NNT included the entire eastern half of the Nakai Plateau, to the Nam Theun River.

The river was a logical, recognizable border for the new protected area. It also posed (or should have) a significant problem for World Bank support of NT2, since a large and distinctive portion of the protected area, the Nakai Plateau, through which the river flowed, would be inundated by the NT2 reservoir—in apparent violation of OP 4.04. But it was a problem that was either not recognized (which would be an act of almost incomprehensible negligence by the Bank) or else was quickly rejected as inapplicable or quietly and willfully ignored. Bank communications that were publicly available at this time, as well as reports by the NT2 International Environmental and Social Panel of Experts (PoE) and other stakeholders from the late 1990s, gave little or no attention to this potentially deal-breaking issue.

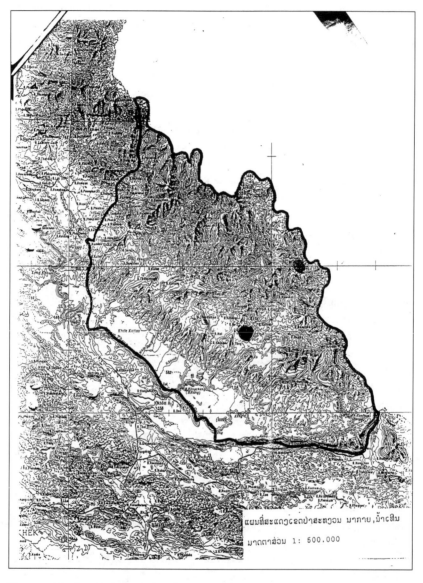

Figure 1.1. Map from the decree that established NNT NBCA in 1993. Here, the protected area extends southwest across the Nakai Plateau, to a western boundary at the Nam Theun River.

Given NNT's size, it could be argued that inundation of a comparatively small portion of the protected area, although it comprised thousands of hectares, would not constitute "severe diminution of the integrity" of the area. But the Nakai Plateau is home to a highly distinctive ecosystem, the like of which is found almost nowhere else in Indochina—a large river flowing slowly through open mixed grasslands, pine forests, and seasonal wetlands. Evidence of the plateau's significance was also noted in writing early on. WCS's report on the 1994 survey of NNT identified five habitats of "particular conservation importance," noting that all "are regionally threatened and occur in Nakai-Nam Theun NBCA as relatively large pristine stands." Two of the five priority habitats are found only on the Nakai Plateau—slow-flowing forested river and old growth pine mosaic.[18] A 1995 report prepared for the NT2 PDG by WCS, *Results of a Survey of the Terrestrial Wildlife in the Area to Be Affected by the Proposed Nam Theun 2 Hydroelectric Project*, states, "The Plateau's wildlife communities are of exceptional international importance to biodiversity conservation" and argues that inundation of the plateau would "lead to great reduction in internationally important populations of White-winged Duck and Blyth's Kingfisher, two Globally Threatened species, and River Lapwing, a species undergoing a National Historical Decline, and reductions in at least a further 49 species of conservation concern."[19]

Furthermore, it was commonly predicted (and borne out by events) that a major environmental impact of reservoir formation would lead to a significant reduction of the integrity of the rest of the protected area, above the plateau, by greatly facilitating access to the forests beyond the reservoir for illegal extraction of wildlife and timber.[20]

At the end of 2000, something happened, quietly, to remove the obstacle posed by OP 4.04. On December 29, 2000, the GoL issued a new Prime Minister's Decree, PM 193, stipulating "the establishment of the Nakai-Nam Theun NBCA, Corridor Areas, NT2 Project Reservoir Area, and Resettlement and Forest Area for people affected by the Project."[21] The decree shifted the western boundary of NNT from the Nam Theun River eastward to what would be the eastern shoreline of NT2's reservoir if the project went ahead. The decree noted that the 538-meter elevation topographic contour line marked the full supply level of the proposed reservoir, and this was defined and mapped as the new boundary of NNT, a boundary that remains today. With the stroke of an administrative pen, no part of the official protected area would be directly affected by NT2—putting the project in compliance with OP 4.04. NNT had been shrunk to make way for NT2.[22]

It is not clear if the GoL changed the NNT boundary on its own initiative or was quietly encouraged to do so by the project developers (NTEC/NTPC) and/or the World Bank. But even if it were claimed that the change did not violate the letter of the Bank's OP 4.04, it clearly violated the policy's spirit and intent. As a result of the maneuver, Bank involvement in NT2 did not result in inundating part of one of the world's most important protected areas; instead, it reduced its size by excising one of its most distinctive and important habitats.

Deterring to Conservation Investment

The World Bank and others promoted NT2 as the only viable option for well-funded support of NNT. But in fact, for more than a decade, between the mid-1990s, when the Bank's interest in the project intensified, and 2005, when the Bank approved it, other donors and institutions interested in supporting protection of NNT were deterred by the looming prospect of NT2. A combination of uncertainty over the dam's impact on the protected area and the promise of extensive support for the protected area from NT2 revenues sent them looking for other areas to support, even though NNT was recognized as the highest priority protected area in the country for management attention and investment.[23] For example, both the government of the Netherlands and UNESCO showed interest in supporting management of NNT at least as early as 1996, but then withdrew.[24] It could be argued that this was an incremental benefit of the NT2 project in that it allowed conservation investment to be directed to other parts of the country. The problem with this argument is that every other protected area in the country was less important than NNT.

During this time, conservationist Robert Mather was contracted to provide biodiversity survey and management planning technical assistance to a large, World Bank-facilitated project in Laos, the Forest Management and Conservation Programme, funded by an initiative known as the Global Environment Facility (GEF). Mather has observed that the World Bank/GEF project

> was supposed to support the setting up of management in four [N]PAs in Lao PDR. Naturally it being GEF, and the biggest and most prestigious project, the Lao Government fully expected that one of the four sites this project would cover would be

Nakai-Nam Theun—often considered the "Jewel in the Crown" of Lao protected areas (the other sites were Xe Piane, Xe Sap and Khamouanne protected areas). Then [name redacted] (the Task Manager), under clear instructions from Bank HQ, informed the Lao government that the project would prefer to work in Dong Phou Vieng (at that time a very small provincial protected area in Savannakhet province, that had no real justification for using GEF money). The unspoken reason was of course that they did not want to fund conservation work in NNT when they would shortly be funding the NT2 dam there. The Bank stuck to its guns, and Dong Phou Vieng was suddenly elevated from provincial to National Protected Area status, just to make it look good for the project.

So from my perspective, the [World Bank] was using its own agenda about the NT2 dam to divert important GEF funding away from where it should have been used to somewhere far less important for biodiversity conservation, which I thought was unethical and simply unfair. Effective conservation work could already have started much sooner than it did at NNT if it were not for the [World Bank's] conflict of interest.[25]

In sum, the NT2 project delayed investment in Laos's most important protected area during a critical decade when the region's illegal wildlife trade was beginning to intensify.[26] The trade would reach a catastrophic level by the time funding for NNT from NT2 revenues commenced. It is likely, for example, that tigers (*Panthera tigris*) were lost from the protected area, at least as a viable population, while protection of NNT remained in an NT2-induced limbo.

Hydropower and Logging

Logging of the Nakai Plateau's native pine (*Pinus merkusii*) commenced in 1990, at the time of the SMEC feasibility study. However, the signing of the NT2 MOU in 1993 coincided with a marked increase in large-scale logging of the plateau in the 1993–94 dry season.[27] In this regard, NT2 set a precedent that would be followed by other hydropower projects in the country. The signing of an MOU to explore project development, although it did not guarantee that a project would actually be built, was often immediately taken as a green light by logging interests, usually connected to the military, to log areas that might otherwise be off-limits. The rationale was often that the logging industry was seeking to avoid what had happened at Nam Ngum, where, in a time of war, the reservoir was filled before the forest in the inundation zone was cleared. This was widely viewed in Laos as wasteful of timber resources. As early as 1999 an independent report noted, "Dam proponents now justify the project on the basis that the Nakai Plateau is so degraded from logging that it is not worth saving."[28] PM 193 on aspects of NT2, issued in December 2000—almost five years before the World Bank approved its support for the project—makes explicit the link with logging. Article 10 of the decree states (unofficial English translation):

> The boundary of the reservoir at the water full supply level of 538 meters [above sea level] is determined for the purpose of proper reservoir clearing and removal of trees before filling the reservoir to ensure water quality and environment, and in the areas where there is difficulty in level determination and demarcation of logging areas, the rest of the trees will be cut and removed from those areas after filling the reservoir and when the actual inundated area will become known.

Given pervasively weak governance in the management of Lao forests and timber, the Nakai Plateau probably would have been logged with or without NT2. Nonetheless, the prospect of the proposed NT2 reservoir certainly provided an easy justification for the military-connected company that oversaw the logging, Bolisat Phattana Khet Phoudoi, to accelerate its activities on the plateau.

Delays, More Studies and Consultations

In October 1995 NTEC announced a delay in its construction timeframe due to difficulty in securing financing. Private financing depended on the World Bank providing a mechanism to shield investors from various risks on investment in Laos. Before considering this, the World Bank required a number of NT2 project studies. These were defined during a November 1995 World Bank mission and technical review, which resulted in a key aide memoire that defined the steps required by the Bank to move toward support for the project.[29] In response, NTEC contracted IUCN and the NGO CARE for environmental and social/resettlement studies, respectively. However, the GoL initially balked at paying for other studies mandated by the Bank on project alternatives and project economic impact. After a seven-month delay, the GoL eventually agreed to proceed with those studies.

The CARE report, released in July 1996, helped provide another rationale for NT2—improvement of the lives of the Indigenous Peoples whom would be resettled by the project. These communities were described as impoverished and faced with a deteriorating natural resource base. Project proponents promoted the idea that a carefully planned and implemented resettlement program would be the best way to make these communities more secure.

The controversies that ensued, including the conflicts among NGOs described in chapter 3, gained an unprecedented amount of international attention for a project in Laos. This included an Australian television documentary and articles in newspapers around the world.[30]

On October 1, 1996, EGAT made a startling announcement: it was canceling the 1995 power purchase agreement due to delays caused by NTEC's failure to secure sufficient project financing. EGAT argued that the delays would not allow NT2 to be operational by 2000 and thus could not be included in the 1500 megawatts of electricity imports from Laos to Thailand planned by that year.

This would prove to be a major interruption; it would be many years before a new power purchase agreement, which provided the economic basis for the project, was approved. At the time, however, the cancelation of the agreement barely dented the enthusiasm of the project's international proponents, who seemed to view it as a temporary setback or a negotiating ploy by EGAT. The next month the World Bank launched its NT2 Environmental and Social Project, financed by the Bank's International Development Association (IDA), for preparatory work on environmental and social aspects of the dam. This included initial funding for the PoE, as described in chapter 2. The PoE made its first visit to Laos in January 1997. Its first report makes no mention of the recent power purchase agreement cancelation.[31]

Under the auspices of the project, two major studies were commissioned: a study of alternatives to NT2, conducted by Lahmeyer Consulting, and a study of NT2's economic impacts, conducted by the US firm Louis Berger. At the same time, IUCN produced an environmental and social management plan for the catchment area and connecting corridors.[32] At this time potential impacts along the Xe Bang Fai River were not acknowledged or studied in any detail.

Presentations on these Bank-mandated studies, through a formal public participation process in Vientiane, began in early 1997. The studies of alternatives and economic impact both recommended that the project move forward. During this period, NTEC and GoL authorities also conducted local-level consultations, mainly with villages that would be directly affected by the project.

The lack of a power purchase agreement also didn't slow down the enthusiasm of Lao authorities and companies. Later in 1997, Bolisat Phattana Khet Phoudoi reported it had already cleared 500–600,000 cubic meters of timber from the reservoir area, mostly for export to Vietnam. Authorities also reported that they had already resettled fifty-one families, years before the project had any mechanisms in place to assist them.

A second project monitoring body, the International Advisory Group (IAG), made its first visit to Laos in May 1997. Whereas the PoE formally reported to the GoL, the IAG was established to assess social and environmental studies directly for the World Bank.

Facilitating Private Sector Investment

The World Bank's deep commitment to NT2 was due to the project's alignment with an evolution in Bank thinking and priorities—that a better way for governments of the world's poorest nations to generate revenue was to replace (or augment) reliance on handouts of aid (grants or soft loans) with income-earning commercial ventures and that the best way to do this was to involve the private sector. With NT2, this inspired the initiation of public–private partnerships through a facilitating mechanism known as build-own-operate-transfer (BOOT) and political risk loan guarantees.

Under BOOT, a concession is granted to a private developer to build, operate, and earn a share of income from a piece of infrastructure for a set period of time, after which ownership is transferred to the host government. In the case of NT2, NTEC's lead partner, Transfield, specialized in BOOT projects in Australia, and the prospect of implementing NT2 as a BOOT project in Laos is what made it attractive to the company in the first place. NTEC proposed a twenty-five-year concession period (preceded by a five-year construction phase). Such schemes are attractive to governments without the means to finance large infrastructure projects themselves. However, they have limitations, and in many places, experiences with BOOT have been decidedly mixed.[33] The agreements often fail to adequately take into account the value of the local resources (land, water, etc.) provided by the host government. They are also vulnerable to misappropriation of funds and resources and can create potential for disinvestment and lack of maintenance by the company as the transfer date approaches. In a detailed independent examination of NT2's BOOT arrangements, researcher Andrew Wyatt describes how the interests of the private investors and of the GoL differed substantially and how these differences were hidden or not acknowledged at the time.[34]

Another BOOT Perspective

In the late 1990s, I found myself in southern Laos, in the small provincial capital of Attapeu, preparing for a wildlife survey of a nearby protected area, Dong Ampham. On a sunny morning, at a small clapboard restaurant near the open air market, I met and started chatting with another Westerner. He was a Belgian, a hydropower engineer, who was working on preparations to construct a large hydroelectric dam on the wild Xe Kaman River. In fact, the proposed dam would inundate part of the protected area I was scheduled to survey. Like NT2, the project would be a BOOT scheme, with most of the electricity exported.

When he learned that I was a conservationist, he began to describe, with a somewhat defensive enthusiasm, what a *great* deal the BOOT scheme was for the government and people of Laos. "We design the dam, pay for it, build it and then give it completely to the government after twenty years!" He talked as though, if not vigilant, his company and investors risked getting the short end of this great deal for Laos.

I pointed out that Laos was *giving* him a river, millions of years old, to destroy and to make money from for twenty years. What value did he put on that? How many such rivers could he find in Belgium to dam? He left the questions hanging in the air and turned back to his noodle soup, and we moved on to other topics.

WILLIAM ROBICHAUD

In the case of Laos, such a public–private partnership could only proceed if investors were assured that their investments would be protected by the rule of law—something not taken for granted in Laos. The GoL was not considered credit worthy and was reputed to frequently "change the goalposts" when it came to investment rules, often after investors had already sunk considerable sums into a project. Lao PDR was governed more by decrees than the rule of law, and with minimal transparency. Such background did not give investors a sense of security for an investment that would have to endure for the length of the concession agreement—twenty-five years, which was longer than Lao PDR had been a sovereign nation.

In late May 1997, the World Bank approved a precedent-setting political risk guarantee. While intended as a mechanism the Bank could use globally, it was designed with NT2 in mind. In announcing the new mechanism, a World Bank statement indicated that NT2 was "a possible beneficiary" of the mechanism as a first test case.[35]

What Is a Political Risk Guarantee?

A political risk guarantee, sometimes referred to as a "sovereign risk guarantee" or "political risk insurance," is a form of insurance provided by governments or international financial institutions (IFIs) to large companies and commercial banks that wish to do business in countries that present an uncertain investment environment. The guarantee is typically part of a low-interest financing package. For donor country companies, loan guarantees for contracts or projects lower the cost of doing business with risky governments. In the case of NT2, the World Bank had to create an entirely new political risk guarantee mechanism, because Laos, as a highly indebted, low-income country, was not eligible for the standard guarantee mechanism provided under its International Bank for Reconstruction and Development branch, normally meant for middle-income countries. To help pay for the dam, the GoL would borrow money from the Bank's IDA branch, which offers inexpensive financing to the worst performing (or most highly indebted) governments.

Such guarantees impose financial penalties on a borrowing country that reneges on its contractual obligations to a project for the full concession period for what are defined as "political" reasons—mainly changes within a government after the companies have already made their investment and/or the project is operational. This includes changes in laws and regulations and project expropriation or nonpayment by the government or its state-owned enterprises. If any of these scenarios cause loss of investment, the guarantee is triggered and, in the case of NT2, the World Bank and ADB would reimburse the commercial lenders for losses up to the full amount of the guarantee. Then, through having the country's virtual "credit card," the World Bank would require the borrowing government (GoL) to repay the Bank for its costs in meeting the guarantee.

Criticisms of risk guarantees predate NT2 and include concerns about shielding companies from the cost of doing business and thus subsidizing their profits, all in a nontransparent manner. Investors frequently avoid public scrutiny by citing the need for commercial confidentiality.[36]

Independent researchers raised specific concerns about the World Bank and ADB risk guarantees in regards to Laos and NT2. This included criticism that these agencies were not sufficiently scrutinizing project viability and were too focused on subsidizing the companies and protecting them from the real costs and risks as they strove to demonstrate they could pull off a new model of public–private partnership. It was also noted that the guarantees only protected the outside lenders and companies. There was no equivalent mechanism to protect the people and the environment of the area should NT2's impacts prove more severe than anticipated and/or should the promised mitigation measures fail to protect the environment and restore the livelihoods of affected people.[37]

Despite this flurry of activity, as 1997 progressed, a gap emerged between World Bank enthusiasm for the project and the reality of a regional economic meltdown that was taking hold in Southeast Asia. This manifested as a stalemate when EGAT made no move to renegotiate the rejected power purchase agreement with NTEC.

By late 1997 the Thai and regional economy had imploded, as the Southeast Asian economic crisis deepened and a bubble in the financial sector burst. Despite the lack of a power purchase agreement and amid the expanding economic crisis in the region, as late as November 1997 a Bank mission to Laos expressed its strongest support yet for NT2. Its vice president at the time, Jean Michel Severion, stated, "We think that there is now a good chance that the poverty alleviation, environmental protection and macro-economic operations . . . will be met."[38] Staff indicated they hoped to proceed with the project within six months but noted they first had to wait for a new agreement to be signed. This proved overly optimistic.

The ensuing financial crisis brought economic growth and the demand for more electricity to a halt throughout Thailand. Other private sector hydropower projects under development in Laos, including Xe Pian-Xe Nam Noy, and Xe Kaman 1, were postponed or canceled.

In early 1998, the World Bank finally recognized economic reality and backed off its predictions of quick approval. In an interview with *Watershed* magazine, the Bank's Thailand country director predicted a three- to six-year delay in completion of the project. He also indicated that if NT2 didn't go ahead, the World Bank would be interested in reviving the original GEF conservation project for NNT.[39]

Table 1.1. Timeline of Key Events in the History of Nam Theun 2

1989–91	First NT2 feasibility study by Snowy Mountain Engineering Corporation
March 1993	PDG formed, signs preliminary MOU with GoL/EGAT
December 1993	NTEC formed, Transfield takes over lead role from SMEC
January 1994	Full MOU for NT2 development signed between NTEC, GoL, and EGAT
1994	TEAM Consulting prepares first preliminary social and environmental impact study
March 1995	Power purchase agreement signed between EGAT and PDG/NTEC
October 1996	Power purchase agreement canceled by EGAT due to delays in financing
November 1996	World Bank initiates social and environmental program in support of NT2
January 1997	First mission of PoE to Laos, public participation process initiated
July 1997	PoE endorses NT2
Late 1997–98	Regional economic crisis worsens, delaying project
September–October 2002	NTPC formed and concession agreement signed
July–October 2003	EdF unexpectedly withdraws from NTPC and then rejoins it a few months later
November 2003	Second power purchase agreement signed between EGAT, GoL, and NTPC
2004	ADB and other financial institutions recruited as potential cofinancers
August 2004	International technical workshops held
Early 2005	Formal appraisal process takes place, leading to World Bank approval on March 31
June 2005	Financial closure by World Bank and financial partners, construction commences
April 2008	Impoundment of reservoir begins following resettlement of local communities
March 2010	Generation and export of electricity to Thailand commences
December 2010	Official project grand opening
December 2012	XBF Downstream Compensation Program handed over to GoL
December 2015	PoE refuses to endorse the closure of the resettlement program due to sustainability issues; resettlement program extended for two more years

The dire regional economic situation continued into 2000. Changes occurred in the composition of NTEC when Merrill Lynch (US) bought out the distressed Thai shareholder Phatra Thanakit. During this time the World Bank did not completely give up on NT2 but rather "continued low-level participation through bridging activities."[40] IUCN and WCS continued their management planning in the protected area. It was an uncertain time for the campaigners who had been fighting against NT2. Aviva Imhof, then the Southeast Asia program officer for IRN, recalls, "In those years we referred to it as the 'zombie project.' It was sort of dead but subject to revival at any time." In June 1998, a coalition of Thai NGOs wrote to the Thai prime minister urging that the Thai government not buy electricity from NT2 due to the project's potential social and environmental damage. Then, in February 1999, the GoL announced that NT2 was the country's highest priority for electrical sales to Thailand and subsequently met with the Thai prime minister to discuss the possibility of reviving the project.

At this point the World Bank itself was cautious—and perhaps distracted by an ongoing process that was to have a major impact on the debate over large hydropower worldwide, a review of dams around the globe by the World Commission on Dams (WCD). Initiated in response to the sustained criticism of large dams by civil society groups, the WCD was organized with the support of IUCN and the World Bank and featured representatives from many sectors, including industry and civil society. The WCD report, released in November 2000, recommended major reforms in the way that large hydropower projects were planned and implemented.[41]

The "Zombie Project" Comes Back to Life

In August 2001, following its consideration of the WCD conclusions and recommendations and with the regional economy slowly recovering, the World Bank agreed with the GoL on a new NT2 decision framework, which was not made public until July 2002. The framework comprised three main elements: 1) a GoL commitment to implement the project in a "development framework," meaning that project revenues would be used for poverty alleviation and environmental conservation as well as to carry out Bank-mandated economic reforms; 2) agreement that the project would adhere to high technical, financial, and economic standards and conform to the Bank's safeguard policies; and 3) a requirement that the Lao PDR's development path and NT2 in particular be supported by both other financial partners and civil society.[42]

The first point provided a new justification for NT2—it was now to be defined, in addition to the other ways it had been characterized, as a contribution to nationwide poverty reduction. This was to be achieved through the allocation of the GoL portion of project revenues to specific poverty-focused programs rather than to the country's general funds. Through this decision framework, the Bank moved to position itself as supportive of large infrastructure projects mainly for their potential for poverty alleviation and environmental sustainability. The framework's last point implied that the Bank did not want to go it alone but rather wished to bring in other financial backers. This led to participation in the project for the first time by the ADB, which in 2003 signaled its interest in supporting NT2. A number of other multilateral and bilateral agencies were also approached to consider participation in it.

After a period of cautiousness, following criticisms of past large hydropower projects dating from the mid-1990s and through the WCD process, in February 2003 the World Bank endorsed a controversial new "high reward, high risk" strategy for water projects. This was in part a response to criticism from some borrowing countries that the Bank had become too risk-averse in its avoidance of large infrastructure projects.[43] It was also due to a fear of competition—mainly from Chinese institutions. *Doing a Dam Better* indirectly acknowledges this dynamic, noting that if the Bank had required too many conditions, the GoL would have been unable to meet them and "might have tried to develop the project with other partners."[44]

The year 2001 also saw a shuffling of the ownership structure of NTEC, signaling a revival of interest in NT2 by new parties. On September 19, 2001, the companies that comprised NTEC signed a shareholder's agreement, which brought significant changes to the consortium. Transfield reduced its equity share and within the next year exited the project completely, selling its shares to Électricité de France (EDF) and the Electricity Generating Public Company Limited (EGCO), a for-profit subsidiary of EGAT. The other two NTEC shareholders also sold their shares to EGCO.

The second half of 2002 saw a number of important developments. First, on August 27 NTEC was dissolved. A new company, the Nam Theun 2 Power Company (NTPC), replaced it and was incorporated in Laos. The lead contractor and developer was now EdF, holding a 35 percent share in the new company. The GoL stake in the project was represented by the Lao State Holding Enterprise, a subsidiary of EdL, and remained at 25 percent. The Thai company EGCO held another 25 percent and Italian Thai Development Public Company, a Thai construction company that planned to act as a project subcontractor, held a 15 percent share.

On October 3, 2002, the crucial concession agreement was signed between NTPC and the GoL. The agreement covered a five-year construction period following financial close and a twenty-five-year concession period, after which NT2 would be turned over to the GoL. The agreement included unprecedented measures for ensuring social and environmental mitigation. Many details in the agreement essentially substituted for Lao law, which was deficient in many areas for a project of this size and complexity. The agreement provided for the ongoing involvement and funding of the PoE as well as three important plans detailing NTPC's social and environmental obligations: an environmental assessment and management plan, a social and environmental management framework, and a resettlement action plan.

EDF Withdrawal and Reengagement

In July 2003, just as a new power purchase agreement was finally about to be signed, EdF made the stunning announcement that it was withdrawing from the project, sending shock waves through the communities of both project proponents and opponents. On the day of the announcement, IRN staff celebrated with champagne. It seemed as if the "zombie" had finally suffered a fatal blow.

A French parliamentary commission had recently found the state-run company's international operations to be failing and putting taxpayer funds at risk. EdF acknowledged that it was overextended internationally and said it would change its focus to the European electricity market. However, the withdrawal from NT2 put France in an awkward position, with the GoL taking the move as a diplomatic affront. The GoL gave NTPC three months to find a new lead developer, and EGAT demanded that a power purchase agreement be signed within a year. This set off a period of furious behind-the-scenes lobbying and negotiations.

In early August the World Bank issued a formal statement on the French withdrawal, implying that it was not giving up on NT2 and was waiting for NTPC to find another lead investor.[45]

The French bilateral aid agency Agence Française de Développement saw NT2 as not just a commercial venture but also as a development project linked to its growing overseas aid program in France's former colony. The GoL and the French government had a series of intense discussions. In the end, French participation became more about NT2's reinvention as aid—it was a political decision more than a commercial business decision. In October 2003 EdF, now apparently with the assurance of French government assistance to NT2 through Agence Française de Développement and the French import–export bank, announced it was back. A new power purchase agreement between NTPC, EGAT, and the GoL was signed on November 3, 2003.

Final Confrontations in a Long Campaign

The World Bank and its new NT2 financial partners then quickly moved toward NT2 approval, focusing on the complex financing package the project required, among other issues. One of these outstanding issues, on which both Bank staff and the campaign NGOs agreed, was the poor quality of past local level consultations. What had in fact been one-way information dissemination clearly did not meet Bank consultation standards, particularly in the post-WCD era. In response, the World Bank contracted James Chamberlain and Anek Nakhabut, a Thai consultant, to conduct a more thorough and authentic consultative process, which started in late 2004 and extended into early 2005. By all accounts the quality of these consultations were much better than that of earlier efforts. World Bank staff later informed Chamberlain that they proceeded with NT2 in part because of the confidence they had gained through this consultative process.[46]

Regardless, for some critics, the fact that these consultations, no matter how well done, came at such a late stage in the process, at a time when the project had such momentum and in the context of a decision already made (at least by the GoL), gave them little meaning.

In the face of renewed momentum toward approval of NT2, the long-running campaign against that approval was also revived. IRN and TERRA remained at the center of the effort. Environmental Defense, WWF Thailand, Friends of the Earth (including its French, Japanese and US affiliates), and other international groups that had not been prominent in early phases of the campaign now joined in.

This coalition was well represented during a series of international technical workshops on NT2 organized by the World Bank, NTPC, and the GoL in Washington, DC, Paris, Tokyo, and Bangkok during August and September 2004. These workshops, intended to inform civil society about NT2 and gain its support for the project, were widely denounced by coalition members as biased, superficial, and ineffective.

Over the following months the organizations opposed to NT2 made several intensive last-ditch efforts to stop the project. In late 2004, TERRA devoted an entire issue of its journal *Watershed* to NT2, which it entitled "No Time for Another Mistake." Many international groups lobbied their governments and

Figure 1.2. Thai villagers, many of whom were affected by the World Bank–supported Pak Mun dam project, protest in front of the World Bank office in Bangkok in March 2005, shortly before the Bank's board was to make a final decision on support to NT2. Photo by Premrudee Daoroung/TERRA.

World Bank representatives through meetings and letter-writing campaigns. This was particularly successful in the United States, as that country's World Bank executive director ended up casting one of the few no votes when NT2 finally came before the World Bank board. IRN commissioned independent studies of the resettlement action plan and of the impact assessment for the XBF River basin, which were released in early 2005. On March 14, 2005, Japanese groups released a letter to World Bank president James Wolfensohn, signed by 153 civil society organizations from 42 countries, urging the Bank to reconsider its support for NT2.[47] Thai organizations, including TERRA and WWF Thailand, organized protests in front of the Lao embassy and World Bank offices in Bangkok.

As NT2 moved toward final appraisal by the Bank, whether it was "WCD compliant" was one of the concerns raised by critics who saw the severe restrictions on civil and political freedoms in Laos as fundamentally at odds with WCD ideals of local participation, transparency, and accountability. Resettlement and the treatment of Indigenous Peoples in the country were of particular concern. By 2005 a series of reports by the UNDP, the ADB, and a number of NGOs had all pointed to serious humanitarian issues pertaining to the GoL's policies of internal resettlement of Indigenous communities and the resulting harm to the lives of the people affected.[48] Critics saw this as linked to a growing and pervasive resource grab of land and forests and also water for private sector hydropower for export that by 2005 was well under way in the country, often in the name of development. They questioned whether anything close to WCD standards could be achieved in such an environment.[49]

These efforts and concerns proved unable to deflect the momentum toward NT2 approval. In February 2005, a study commissioned by the Australian Agency for International Development recommended that the Australian government support NT2. With Australia on board, other countries and international lenders soon announced support as well.

Over the years of its planning, those campaigning against NT2 had confronted the project's redefinition and changing rationale on numerous occasions. In this final stretch, one particular justification for the project reemerged, one that was often spoken about but seldom acknowledged in written reports—the China factor. The argument was that if the World Bank and affiliated IFIs didn't support NT2, the Chinese would step in and fund it, with much lower social and environmental standards and protections. While this argument wasn't new, having been raised by Transfield's David Ivarach back in 1996, concerns over the rapidly emerging economic influence of China in the region added momentum to the project as it underwent the World Bank's final appraisal process in early 2005.

Project Approval

The World Bank was eventually able to assemble an impressive group of IFIs, bilateral agencies, and private banks to finance the US$1.297 billion price tag of NT2 (including contingency funding).[50] In addition to the Bank (both its IDA and Multilateral Investment Guarantee Agency), the ADB (which among other support also extended a political risk guarantee), and the European Investment Bank (which helped finance the Lao equity share through Lao State Holding Enterprise), other groups included:

- *multilateral and bilateral aid and export credit agencies* (COFACE [France], EKN [Sweden], GIEK [Norway], Nordic Investment Bank, Agence Française de Développement [France], PROPARCO and the Export–Import Bank of Thailand),

- *nine international commercial banks* (ANZ, BNP Paribas, BOTM, Calyon, Fortis Bank, ING, KBC, SG, and Standard Chartered), and
- *seven Thai commercial banks* (Bangkok Bank, Bank of Ayudhya, Kasikorn Bank, Krung Thai Bank, Siam City Bank, Siam Commercial Bank, and Thai Military Bank).

On March 31, 2005, at the end of its formal appraisal process, the World Bank's executive directors voted in favor of NT2. This stimulated a final period of preparations that resulted in the formal financial closure of the project on June 10, 2005, by all participating financial institutions, at which time an amended concession agreement was also signed. Fourteen years after the completion of the first SMEC feasibility study, NT2 was finally moving forward. The project had survived, overcoming numerous obstacles: diverse and intense opposition from international civil society, a regional economic crisis, temporary withdrawal of one of the project's major underwriters, an apparent violation of one of the World Bank's own operational policies, and a major reassessment of the value and risks of large hydropower by the WCD. The remaining chapters of this book examine if this perseverance was warranted.

NOTES

1. NTPC, "History of NT2," www.namtheun2.com/index.php/about-us/about-style-6.

2. Wikipedia, "Mekong River Commission," https://en.wikipedia.org/wiki/Mekong_River_Commission.

3. See Andrew Wyatt, "Infrastructure Development and BOOT in Laos and Vietnam: A Case Study of Collective Action and Risk in Transitional Developing Economies" (PhD diss., University of Sydney, April 2004), which describes a 1973 speech on NT2 to the Mekong Secretariat by Khamsing Ngonvorarath.

4. Ian. C. Porter and Jayasankar Shivakumar, overview, *Doing a Dam Better: The Lao People's Democratic Republic and the Story of Nam Theun 2*, ed. Ian. C. Porter and Jayasankar Shivakumar (Washington, DC: World Bank, 2011), 9.

5. Philip Hirsh, "Global Norms, Local Compliance and the Human Rights-Environment Nexus: A Case Study of the Nam Theun II Dam in Laos," in *Human Rights and the Environment: Conflicts and Norms in a Globalizing World*, ed. Lyuba Zarsky (London: Earthscan Press, 2002), 147-71.

6. World Bank, transcript of interview with Jamil Sopher, World Bank Group Oral History Project, 2005, 41.

7. At this point the PDG formally changed its name to NTEC. For some time both terms continued to be used, seemingly interchangeably. For clarity, we generally use NTEC.

8. Winnie Tan, Nam Theun 2 hydropower project World Bank mission briefing, unpublished meeting notes, NGO Forum on Laos, November 4, 1995.

9. "Nam Theun II Power Deal Signed," *Watershed* 1, no. 1 (1995): 5.

10. "Nam Theun II Power Deal Signed," 5.

11. In 2007 IRN dropped the "Network" in their name and became International Rivers.

12. Patrick McCully, *Silenced Rivers: The Ecology and Politics of Large Dams* (London: Zed Books, 1996).

13. Witoon Permpongsacharoen, personal communication to Bruce Shoemaker, 2016.

14. William Robichaud, Clive W. Marsh, Sangthong Southammakoth, and Sirivanh Khounthikoummane, *Review of the National Protected Area System in Lao PDR* (Vientiane: Lao-Swedish Forestry Programme, 2001), 60.

15. Joe Tobias, Peter Davidson, and William Robichaud, "Can Development Save One of South-East Asia's Last Wildernesses?," *Oriental Bird Club Bulletin* 48 (1998): 24–29, http://orientalbirdclub.org/nakainam.

16. The World Bank Operational Manual, Operational Policies: Natural Habitats, OP 4.04, September 1995, 1.

17. The World Bank Operational Manual, Operational Policies: Annex A, Definitions, OP 4.04, September 1995, 1–2.

18. Robert J. Timmins and Tom D. Evans, *A Wildlife and Habitat Survey of Nakai-Nam Theun National Biodiversity Conservation Area, Khammouan and Bolikhamsai Provinces, Lao PDR* (New York: WCS 1996), 5.

19. WCS, *Results of a Survey of Terrestrial Wildlife in the Area to be Affected by the Nam Theun 2 Hydroelectric Project* (Vientiane: WCS, 1995).

20. WCS, *A Preliminary Wildlife and Habitat Assessment of the Nam Theun 2 Hydropower Project Area* (Vientiane: WCS, 1995), 5.

21. "Prime Minister Decree on the Establishment of the Nakai-Nam Theun NBCA, Corridor Areas, NT2 Project Reservoir Area, and Resettlement and Forest Area for People Affected by the Project," December 29, 2000, unofficial translation by Bounsalong Southidara, January 19, 2001.

22. That the change was made quietly is indicated by the fact that in June 2001, more than six months after PM 193 was issued, the Lao-Swedish Forestry Programme published an update of its fact sheets pertaining to protected areas (under the title *Fact Sheets: National Biodiversity Conservation Areas in Lao PDR*). The update still listed the area of NNT NBCA as 353,200 ha and described its western boundary at the Nam Theun River. Interestingly, at the same time, the organization published another volume in the same series titled *Review of the Protected Area System of Lao PDR*. The review makes no mention of PM 193, but one of the columns in a table showing the sizes of the NBCAs is titled "Draft *Fact Sheets*," and in that column, the size of NNT NBCA is given as only 305,800 ha (3,058 square kilometers).

Curiously, PM 193 describes NNT NBCA as being 353,200 ha, the same size given by PM 164 in its decree establishing the area in 1993. But in fact, PM 193 reduced the size of NNT NBCA by more than 13,000 ha, or about 4 percent. PM 193 added two corridors to it (perhaps in attempted compensation for the area taken away), connecting it to two nearby protected areas. But the corridors are not considered legal additions to the protected area and are not as significant ecologically as the plateau and so do not resolve the conflict with OP 4.04.

23. Robichaud et al., *Review of the National Protected Area System in Lao PDR*, 60.

24. William Robichaud, letter to Alan Rabinowitz, March 2, 1996.

25. Robert Mather, email message to Bruce Shoemaker, August 18, 2016.

26. From 1999 to 2003, the World Bank supported the District Upland Development and Conservation Project in Nakai-Nam Theun through loans to the GoL. But the project's design and its implementation were checkered at best, and it is generally considered to have achieved little of lasting value in the protected area.

27. See "Speaking of Nam Theun 2 . . . Past, Present and Future (?)," interview with Satoru Matsumoto, *Watershed* 10, no. 1 (2004).

28. IRN, *Power Struggle: The Impacts of Hydro-Development in Laos* (Berkeley, CA: IRN, 1999), 64.

29. World Bank, *Aide Memoire to the Committee on Planning and Cooperation from the World Bank Technical Mission for the Nam Theun 2 Hydroelectric Project*, November 9, 1995.

30. Special Broadcasting Service (video recording), *Dateline: Dam Destiny*, Sydney, July 6, 1996.

31. PoE 1.

32. IUCN, *Environmental and Social Management Plan for the Nakai-Nam Theun Catchment and Corridor Areas*, May 1, 1998.

33. Charlie Pahlman, "Build-Operate-Transfer (B.O.T.): Private Investment in Public Projects . . . or Just More Public Subsidies for the Private Sector?," *Watershed* 2, no. 1 (1996).

34. Wyatt, "Infrastructure Development and BOOT in Laos and Vietnam."

35. Charlie Pahlman, "Where Investors Fear to Tread: Risks and the Nam Theun 2 Dam," *Watershed* 3 (1997), 53.

36. See for example Patricia Adams, "Patronage Canada," Probe International, April 2, 1997, https://journal.probeinternational.org/1997/04/02/patronage-canada.

37. Pahlman, "Where Investers Fear to Tread," 55.

38. "World Bank Up Support for Nam Theun 2 Despite Thai Economic Meltdown," *Watershed* 3, no. 2 (1998): 4.

39. "World Bank Still Upbeat on NT2, but Expecting Delays . . . While Thai Economic Crisis Hits EGAT and Thai NT2 Companies," *Watershed* 3, no. 3 (1998): 4.

40. Porter and Shivakumar, overview, 11.

41. WCD, *Dams and Development: A New Framework for Decision-Making* (London: Earthscan, 2000).

42. World Bank, *Decision Framework for Processing the Proposed NT2 Project*, July 2002.

43. See IRN and Friends of the Earth and Environmental Defense Fund, *Gambling with People's Lives: What the World Bank's New "High-Risk/High-Reward" Strategy Means for the Poor and the Environment*, June 2003.

44. Rosa Alonso i Terme, and Homi Kharas, "Lao PDR Gets Ready for NT2," in *Doing a Dam Better*, 41.

45. World Bank, *World Bank Statement on EDF's Withdrawal from Nam Theun 2 Hydroelectric Project*, August 12, 2003.

46. James Chamberlain, personal communication to Bruce Shoemaker, March, 2017.

47. Friends of the Earth Japan, letter from 152 civil society organizations to James Wolfensohn, March 14, 2005, 4–5.

48. See Ian G. Baird and Bruce Shoemaker, "Unsettling Experiences: Internal Resettlement and International Agencies in Laos," *Development and Change* 38, no. 5 (2007), which summarizes these key studies.

49. Aviva Imhof and Shannon Lawrence, "An Analysis of Nam Theun 2 Compliance with WCD Strategic Priorities," International Rivers Network and Environmental Defense, February 2005, www.internationalrivers.org/sites/default/files/attached-files/nt2wcdanalysis 2005.pdf.

50. Daryl Fields, NT2 project manager, personal communication to Bruce Shoemaker, January 23, 2017. While a figure of $1.45 billion is frequently cited as NT2's price tag, not all contingency funding was needed, resulting in this adjusted lower figure.

2

Independent Guidance and International Credibility

The Panel of Experts

DAVE HUBBEL and

BRUCE SHOEMAKER

This chapter explores efforts by the World Bank to develop a more successful model for large hydropower while building credibility and thus international support for the Nam Theun 2 hydropower project (NT2) through what was then a relatively new mechanism—a panel of experts who would not only provide advice but also hold specific powers to oversee social and environmental aspects of the project.

Background

By the mid-1990s, the World Bank's reputation as an institution that funded and implemented projects to alleviate poverty and contribute to sustainable development had, for many observers, including international media, been severely tarnished. This loss of reputation resulted in particular from its support for large-scale hydroelectric dams. Since the late 1980s, the Bank's political and financial support for big dams in Amazonia, Africa and Southeast Asia had been headline news around the world; its consequences included destruction of rivers and forests and the impoverishment of thousands of people dispossessed of their lands.

The Bank's history of supporting hydroelectric dams in the Mekong River basin had been equally controversial. In the early 1990s, its involvement in the

Pak Mun hydroelectric project in Thailand on one of the largest Mekong tributaries, and that dam's subsequent destruction of one the most productive inland fisheries in the country, had produced widespread protest. It was a defining moment when it became clear to local communities throughout Thailand that neither the Thai state nor an allegedly poverty alleviation institution like the World Bank would listen to their concerns or act in their interests. The movement begun at Pak Mun grew into the community-based Assembly of the Poor, which mounted sustained mass demonstrations of tens of thousands in front of government offices in Bangkok over a number of years. The Pak Mun debacle was widely acknowledged throughout the Mekong region. By 1994 it had become politically impossible for the Thai government, the Electricity Generating Authority of Thailand (EGAT), or the World Bank to propose new hydropower projects in Thailand.[1]

Laos, however, was different. In many ways it was the perfect place for the Bank to resuscitate its strategy of facilitating support for large hydroelectric dams. First, it was a "least developed country"[2] that fit well into the Bank's expressed commitment to alleviate poverty. The country's political environment also made it easier for the Bank to promote its new model without the criticism and controversy it would have faced in more open countries. By 2005, the authoritarian government of the Lao PDR (GoL) had repressed all criticism of its policies and development initiatives for two decades. There was no organized civil society—no local NGOs, no citizens' groups, no independent academics or media that monitored human rights were permitted. International nongovernmental organizations (INGOs) within the country could implement projects only in close cooperation with the GoL. These INGOs could critique development policy only in the most oblique and innocuous ways. In Laos, neither the World Bank nor GoL would face questioning by civil society about the planning, implementation and potential social and environmental impacts of a large dam. For local communities to raise critical questions regarding policies and development projects of the Lao People's Revolutionary Party was (and remains) a very risky undertaking.

However, as the Bank contemplated a large hydropower project on a Mekong tributary just a few hundred kilometers from the Pak Mun dam, Bank staff undoubtedly realized they would need to do better, not only to restore Bank credibility but also to fend off its critics and gain the international support needed to proceed with NT2. As Peter Stephens recounts in his contribution to *Doing a Dam Better*,

> NT2 followed a number of hydro projects that had failed, been withdrawn, or become entangled in controversy. These projects left the World Bank bruised

and confused, with some staff eager to do things better and other staff worried that hydro was too risky and time consuming. The unfortunate trail of projects had also created a presumption of guilt in the minds of many Bank-watchers: if these earlier projects had turned out poorly, surely NT2 would be the same.[3]

The absence of independent civil organizations in Laos was well recognized internationally. To gain international support for NT2, the Bank needed to demonstrate that the lack of opposition to the project within Laos was not due to the country's repressive political environment but rather because Lao citizens themselves believed the dam really was in their best interests. The Bank thus sought to procure alternative sources of endorsement perceived as independent. One way in which it attempted to do this was through a panel of experts that would monitor and possibly endorse plans relating to mitigation of NT2's social and environmental impacts.

The Establishment of the Panel of Experts

Following an appraisal mission by its staff to Laos, the Bank released the first document pertaining to its NT2 social and environmental project in November 1996, which outlined how the Bank would support project preparations. An international panel of experts intended to provide independent guidance on NT2 was to be commissioned that would consist of three specialists who could advise the Bank and the GoL about potential impacts of the project on the people and environment of the Nakai Plateau and other areas that would be affected.

"This body, which was called the International Environmental and Social Panel of Experts (PoE), had a significant and occasionally high profile role throughout the planning and implementation of NT2. It is thus curious that *Doing a Dam Better* barely mentions the group—offering only a general description of the Bank's view of the PoE's role:

> The World Bank's participation in NT2 led to creation of an Environmental and Social Panel of Experts that was instrumental in advocating, designing, and monitoring the implementation of environmental and social safeguards. Formation of an independent Panel was proposed early in the project preparation process but was not implemented until 1997, after the World Bank became a more active participant in the project.[4]

When the PoE first visited Laos in January 1997, its members included Tim C. Whitmore of Cambridge University, Lee M. Talbot of George Mason

45

University in Virginia, and Thayer Scudder of Cal Tech. All three were well known in their respective fields. Whitmore was a tropical forests specialist with years of experience in Malaysia and other countries. Talbot was an environmental biologist who had served as an environmental advisor to three US presidents, as head of Environmental Sciences at the Smithsonian and as director-general of the World Conservation Union (IUCN). His list of publications is impressive and includes nine books.

The inclusion of Scudder, an anthropologist, was a surprise to many observers. He was widely considered to be among the world's foremost experts on the impacts of dam resettlement on local communities, and he was critical of the way in which large hydropower had been implemented. Thus he was seen as an ally of the international movement for informed decision making about large-scale infrastructure projects. He was even a member and financial supporter of International Rivers Network (IRN) and had famously written, regarding a large African dam, that involuntary resettlement is "the worst thing you can do to people, other than kill them."[5] Scudder's presence on the PoE led to optimism among some NT2 skeptics that it would not support a poorly conceived project and that his participation would provide an ongoing opportunity to influence the PoE as it carried out its mission.

PoE accountability was initially somewhat confusing to observers. It was a creation of the World Bank through its International Development Association (IDA) and "mandated by the Bank's Safeguard policies."[6] But the Bank wanted the PoE to be independent, in the sense that it would be an advisory body to the GoL. Early PoE reports reflect some of the confusion in this regard.

According to its first two reports, its findings were to be "submitted directly to the Ministry of Industry and Handicraft and to the World Bank."[7] The third report from January 1998 states merely that its findings were to be "submitted directly to the Ministry of Industry and Handicrafts."[8] In reality, the PoE was committed to a transparent process and all of its reports have been widely distributed. The PoE's fourth report from January 1999 clarified the situation, stating that its findings were to be "submitted directly to the Ministry of Industry and Handicraft of the Lao PDR, and thereafter are to be made available for distribution to the World Bank, other cooperating organizations and the public."[9] All subsequent PoE reports repeated this commitment to openness and have been readily available (to English-speaking people with internet access), via World Bank and NTPC websites. In addition, the PoE members mailed out sixty to seventy hard copies of each report to interested parties.

The PoE's Quick Transformation
into Project Advocates

The PoE's first report to the GoL (and the World Bank), released at the end of its initial two-week visit on February 7, 1997, focused on project basics, acknowledging that resettlement of Indigenous residents of the Nakai Plateau would not be easy. It also recognized that management of the Nakai-Nam Theun National Biodiversity Conservation Area (NNT NBCA, now known as Nakai-Nam Theun National Protected Area [NNT NPA]) to the east of the proposed reservoir, would be a big challenge.[10]

In its second report, released six months later, the PoE dramatically and unexpectedly announced that it was placing "on record its considered and unanimous opinion that the Nam Theun 2 Project should be undertaken with the participation of the World Bank."[11] This unequivocal endorsement was made even though the members of the panel recognized that "many details still have to be worked out and that the development of management and action plans for environmental and social aspects of the project are still in an evolving stage.[12]

The PoE's endorsement after having existed for only a half year and after having spent just twenty-two days in Laos stunned observers who had hoped that it would seriously consider the substantive concerns being raised by NT2's many critics. For others it confirmed their suspicion that the PoE was no more than a sophisticated public relations ploy by the World Bank, which sought to portray NT2 as a new model of "global importance."[13]

The endorsement in the PoE's second report transformed the group from what some had expected would be a dispassionate monitoring body that retained a critical perspective into an unabashed proponent of the project. Strong support would be reflected in each review through the eighth report, which was published in February 2005, shortly before the Bank approved funding NT2.

Aviva Imhof, who for many years led IRN's NT2 campaign recalls, "The PoE's enthusiastic advocacy for the project caught us by surprise. It was as if they had lost all objectivity and had no interest in hearing our concerns. From that point up until NT2 was approved all they did was push the project. To us it seemed that they had abdicated their professional responsibility to be a neutral monitoring mechanism, something that was sorely needed given the political situation in Laos."

Jacques Leslie's 2005 book *Deep Water* surveyed the worldwide controversy over hydroelectric dams from the perspectives of a community activist, a spokesman for the dam industry, and a so-called neutral person between the factions. It provides some insights into why the members of the PoE, including Scudder, the "man in the middle," were predisposed to make the quick transition from neutral questioners to avid supporters of the project. Nearly a third of the book describes Scudder's search to find the "one good dam" that would justify his thirty-plus year involvement advising the World Bank and other institutions that financed large-scale dams, with their requisite resettlement of tens of thousands of people. Over the course of his long work with large dams, Scudder had been continually disappointed, as one after another failed to live up to its promises and resulted in severe, sometimes horrific, environmental and social problems. Leslie concludes that Scudder's "career could be read as a struggle to reconcile his belief in dams with the accumulating evidence of their failures."[14] Despite this legacy, Scudder remained hopeful that with better planning and implementation, with more "fine tuning," it was possible to build a dam that really would benefit local communities. Ever the optimist, in NT2 Scudder felt he had finally found the dam that could be done well, not ravage the environment, and not dispossess tens of thousands of their livelihoods. While acknowledging the possibility of failure, he—and presumably others in the PoE—believed that implementation of NT2 would be worth the risk, including to their professional reputations.

PoE members may also have been influenced by the well-known "culture of approval" within the Bank—the unrelenting pressure to get projects approved and implemented even in the face of massive odds of failure. In this case, the GoL's strong support for the project, the limited information available to it, and the dire rhetoric from the Bank and such organizations as the Wildlife Conservation Society about the prospects for conserving forests and wildlife in the eastern Nam Theun watershed without NT2 probably contributed to the PoE's rapid endorsement. PoE member Lee Talbot also made sweeping pronouncements about NT2, saying, "I know of no other dam project ever, anywhere, where the environmental benefit is so overwhelming."[15] Despite decades of collective experience, the PoE apparently succumbed to the pressure of the culture of approval in just six months.

PoE members disagree with this assessment and note that two of them were already well-known critics of the Bank's culture of approval. They believe that, given the knowledge at the time, their 1997 endorsement was justified, arguing that the dam would be built regardless of World Bank involvement and that its engagement provided a chance to avoid the increasingly apparent negative impacts of other private sector Lao hydropower projects. They also cite the uncontrolled logging taking place and the involuntary resettlement of Indigenous Peoples that was occurring, how these "were a death sentence for the cultures involved as well as to at least some of the people" and that these activities would likely continue unabated if the Bank pulled out. "We already recognized the globally important biological and cultural diversity of the watershed, and knew that it would be lost if the Bank's involvement stopped." Panel members also point out that "the environmental and human health conditions of the people both in the watershed and on the plateau were deteriorating rapidly" and that NTPC had made the commitment to improve living standards in the project area, as well as that the project had been granted $1 million per year for management and conservation of the protected area.[16]

Some of the arguments made by PoE members are debatable. For instance, the concern that if the World Bank didn't see to the building of the dam, the Chinese would have obscures the fact that at the time NT2 was conceived there was no structure in place in Laos for large-scale private investment. It was the NT2 experience, through both its political risk loan guarantees and the investment structures created in conjunction with the project, that enabled the subsequent barrage of private sector hydropower projects. In 1997, Laos was a very different place.

After the PoE's second report, it seems to have been drawn into a phenomenon known as "mission creep." As social scientist Larry Lohmann explains this process, when a simple engineering project is imposed on a complex social landscape, it produces a myriad of unforeseen impacts, which are then interpreted by the implementers as opportunities for more planning, more engineering, more technical management, and more development.[17] Having committed to the project, the PoE increasingly focused on providing detailed recommendations for implementation while restating its support for the dam. Only the PoE's third report in 1998 indicated that its members were becoming aware of the project's potentially severe social and environmental impacts. Still, the PoE did not want these complications to delay the project:

> The Panel wishes to emphasize that the actions recommended in this report are not to be used to further delay the World Bank appraisal and approval process. In most cases the Panel's recommendations should be incorporated in Project documents (e.g., the Watershed Management Plan and Resettlement Action Plan) which are currently under revision, and which the Panel will review when they are ready later in 1998.[18]

The deepening Southeast Asian economic crisis and lessening electricity demand in Thailand did not seem to have any impact on the PoE's enthusiasm, as reflected in its fourth report of 1999, which, while issuing twenty-three planning and implementation recommendations, notes its "strong support for the NT2 Project" on the grounds that "it sets new high standards for resettlement and environmental issues and has the potential to be a model of global significance."[19]

In early 2003, as momentum increased following a reshuffling of the private consortium behind the project, the panel's sixth report, while issuing twenty-five recommendations, repeats its appraisal from its fourth and fifth reports: "As in previous reports, the Panel reiterates its strong support for the NT2 Project." The panel added that it was convinced, however, that without the support of the World Bank "the effect will be to increase rather than decrease rural poverty, and to seriously degrade the globally recognized biodiversity values of the NNT NBCA."[20]

The PoE's seventh report in March 2004, this time with forty-one recommendations, again emphasizes support for what had been redefined, by the PoE and the Bank, as a "multipurpose project," with a core focus on poverty alleviation:

> The Panel continues to reiterate its strong support for the NT2 Project. . . . Especially gratifying is the extent to which the Project has become a multipurpose project for national development in which emphasis on poverty alleviation has begun to focus not just on specific projects but on their coordination and integration. Development initiatives proposed for the Xe Bang Fai River basin illustrate this trend.[21]

The eighth report was issued in February 2005. While continuing to issue implementation recommendations (twenty-three this time), the overriding focus was a strong recommendation that the World Bank approve funding for NT2. The Bank's board of executive directors approved funding NT2 on March 31, 2005.

The PoE during Project Construction, 2005–2010

In 2006, David McDowell, previously on the Bank-appointed International Advisory Group (IAG) (see text box) for NT2, joined the PoE, restoring it to a troika for the first time since the death of Tim Whitmore in 2002. McDowell, an international diplomat from New Zealand with a long history of public service, had also served, as had Talbot, as a director general of IUCN.

By the time its ninth report was issued in early 2006, the PoE no longer had to encourage the Bank to fund the project. Rather, it had become a component of a contractually mandated compliance mechanism agreed to (and funded) by the Nam Theun 2 Power Company (NTPC) and the GoL:

> In the past the Panel's primary responsibility has been to provide independent review of, and guidance on, the treatment of environmental and social issues associated with the NT2 Project. This responsibility remains but is now enshrined in the Concession Agreement as a contractual right—and applies to both the GoL and the NTPC. In addition, under the Concession Agreement the PoE is accorded compliance supervision functions in respect of the environmental and social activities and obligations of the parties. It is required to act independently of the parties and in a manner which best protects the environment and the interests of those impacted by the project.[22]

Although the World Bank had required oversight by panels of experts in contentious projects since the 1980s, the provision of a panel with authority to determine under what conditions the NT2 project could move forward was something new.

The mechanism by which the PoE was financed changed in 2004. Until then, the PoE had been funded through a grant from the IDA to the GoL. However, from 2004 to 2009, funding was paid through an IDA grant into a "special account" administered by NTPC, not the GoL. After 2010, funding was provided by NTPC, as specified in the concession agreement between NTPC shareholders and the GOL.

As NT2 construction proceeded, the PoE focused on monitoring implementation of the social and environmental aspects of the project. This resulted in long lists of increasingly detailed recommendations for everything from micromanagement of project road width to vast and complex development schemes along downstream portions of the Xe Bang Fai (XBF) River impacted by the dam.[23]

The PoE's eleventh Report, published in early 2007, focused on one major responsibility, noting that while construction was on schedule, "most of the social and environmental programs are behind schedule. The most time-bound of these, the program to resettle the eleven hundred households to be displaced by the rising waters, has fallen well behind [schedule] in terms both of physical relocation in permanent housing and livelihood development."[24] This worried the Poe because part 1 of schedule 4 of the concession agreement clearly stated that "reservoir implementation impoundment must not be commenced until all Resettlers have been relocated." The PoE observed that "the final judgment of when this point has been reached is in the hands of the Resettlement Committee 'on the advice of the Panel of Experts'": "In short, a substantial responsibility resides in the hands of the PoE in relation to the timing of the commencement of impoundment. The PoE, for its part, will not shirk this responsibility."[25]

In its thirteenth report of February 2008, two months before the NT2 dam was scheduled to be closed and the flooding of the Nakai Plateau was to begin, it voiced its ongoing concerns about the slow implementation of many of the social and environmental aspects, including resettlement plans, and noted that it feared it would be impossible for the impoundment to begin in April as planned owing to "*the number and magnitude*" of requirements set forth by the concession agreement that had "*not yet been met.*"[26] It added that it

> *accepts that delays beyond this date will involve risks, possibly involving postponement of impoundment until the next rainy season. A sustained drive to avoid these risks will require a major effort on the part of all parties and substantial additional funding. We trust and hope that this will all be forthcoming for we too want this project to meet expectations.*[27]

The report listed twenty-eight issues that urgently needed to be addressed if the PoE were to sign off on impoundment. These ranged from increasing biomass clearance in the 450-square-kilometer reservoir from 15 square kilometers to 30 square kilometers to recommending that "NTPC purchase at replacement cost for healthy stock approximately half of the 4,206 buffalos owned by resettler households" and that it "provide compensation for buffalos which have died since October 2007."[28] The PoE further noted that "buffalos are currently starving because of lack of grazing. . . . The problem is that insufficient grazing exists outside of the reservoir basin. . . . Villagers reported to the PoE that buffalos never died of starvation when they lived at the old village site."[29] The panel also required that the concession agreement stipulate that irrigation for each 0.66 ha farm lot be met "at the very latest" by the commercial operation date of 2010.[30]

The PoE returned to Laos in late March, just before impoundment was scheduled, and visited all the resettlement villages on the Nakai Plateau. In its subsequent fourteenth report issued on April 4, 2008, it explained that knowing "the impoundment date was important for the GoL and NTPC, as well as the project-affected people," it had conducted the follow-up mission to determine whether its recommendations had been carried out and announced that the conditions required by the concession agreement "*have been met or are sufficiently far advanced that we believe impoundment can proceed as planned on April 10.*"[31]

What could have been a high-profile showdown was avoided. In the thirteenth report, the PoE gave NTPC and the GoL a specific to-do list that had

Figure 2.1. Seated along the right side of the table, *left to right*, PoE members Lee Talbot, David McDowell, and Thayer Scudder interview Kri residents in the village of Ban Maka in Nakai-Nam Theun National Protected Area in January 2007. Photo by William Robichaud.

to be accomplished before it would allow inundation to commence. The parties agreed to accelerate development activities. The PoE's fourteenth report, issued the week before inundation was to begin, is conciliatory, emphasizing the progress made and avoiding detailed discussion of problems. The PoE effusively praised GoL for its effective responses, saying, "We believe there are few other governments that could mobilize and achieve such a set of actions in such a short time" and also complimented NTPC efforts.[32] The World Bank quickly applauded the PoE decision, noting that in its fourteenth report it "expressed its full support" for the beginning of impoundment of the Nam Theun River in April and listed "actions to be completed before the dam gate is closed in June 2008."[33]

In retrospect, given the slow speed at which social aspects of the project were addressed before and after this brief period, remarkable progress appears to have been made. NTPC and GoL authorities were certainly motivated to do what needed to be done to avoid confrontation. A flurry of activities to address the PoE's concerns ensued. This included the issuing of a decree from the prime minister's office that incorporated the initial ten-year control of the reservoir fishery by resettlers.

Ram Chopra, a career Bank official, noted in the first draft of a chapter for *Doing a Dam Better* that "once the Bank has approved the [project], the Bank's leverage declines."[34] These dynamics also affected the PoE. It retained some influence after its endorsement of the project, as its approval for reservoir inundation was required. However, after that 2008 approval its influence appeared to decline. Subsequent reports reveal its increasing worry about social and environmental aspects even as it continues to extol the project's potential. As information became available and problems multiplied, the PoE's recommendations increased in number and detail.

The PoE's Second Transformation

As NT2's social and environmental problems became more apparent and the deadline for completion of the resettlement implementation plan drew closer, the PoE's role as a contractually mandated institution regained importance. As it chronicled increasingly dire conservation problems in the NNT NPA and ongoing sustainability issues with the resettlement program, the PoE's criticisms grew stronger. According to a former NTPC consultant in 2015, "The PoE are no longer the compliant cheerleaders for the project that NTPC and the World Bank had become accustomed to. Instead they have become an annoying irritant, their visits to the country dreaded rather than welcomed."

The PoE's increasing disillusionment with NT2 culminated in surprising news on August 14, 2014, for all sides of the long debate. In a *New York Times* commentary piece by Jacques Leslie, Scudder formally came out against the project. After five decades of involvement with large dams, Scudder defined the project as his "final disappointment" and stated that "Nam Theun 2 confirmed my long-standing suspicion that the task of building a large dam is just too complex and too damaging to priceless natural resources."[35]

Subsequent PoE reports made it clear that all members of the PoE had developed serious reservations about NT2. In late 2015, much to the disappointment of NTPC and the World Bank, the PoE again used its enforcement powers by refusing to sign off on completion of the resettlement implementation plan due to concerns about its sustainability and effectiveness.[36] The World Bank, its financial partners and the GoL subsequently agreed to an extension of the plan through 2017. After nineteen years of service, at age eighty-six, Scudder, needing more time with his ailing wife, resigned from the PoE.

The PoE's Impact and Legacy

The PoE's evolution over the course of NT2's history left a complex legacy. It is best evaluated through a few key issues.

Initial Approval and Expert Narrative Control

Whether World Bank staff assumed that the PoE would favor NT2 or not, creating it was an astute move. Given the World Bank's poor reputation with large hydro projects, it made sense that Bank staff would have wanted to improve this time around and avoid more bad publicity. Had the PoE opposed the project, it would have provided the Bank good cover to withdraw. On the other hand, the support of the PoE for NT2 gave the Bank a way to manage information and to launch an unprecedented public relations campaign to build international financial support.

The PoE created a body of outside experts that could operate in a country where, as any person knowledgeable about the political, social, and natural environments of Laos knew, citizens who even obliquely questioned GoL's development projects risked intimidation, imprisonment, or deportation. PoE members were immune to this threat and had total access to everything affected by almost any aspect of NT2. In contrast, Lao and foreign nationals not sanctioned by the GoL and the Bank to access these areas would find it very difficult to do so and might even endanger themselves and the organizations with which they were affiliated if they tried.

By mandating establishment of the PoE and providing it exclusive access to project areas, the Bank was able—at least during the period when the PoE unconditionally endorsed its involvement in NT2—to use the PoE to monopolize "expert" information and thereby control the narrative about the dam. Others with detailed knowledge of the Mekong basin's Indigenous Peoples, communities, and riverine and forest ecology who were raising critical questions about NT2 were not acknowledged by the World Bank, the GoL, the Thai government, or NTPC. These individuals and organizations were labeled as uninformed or lacking a public mandate or "against dams per se," no matter how good such dams might be, and their views were discounted.[37]

The Bank used these rhetorical strategies to ignore IRN reports about impacts to the XBF fishery by independent researcher David Blake, a specialist with extensive experience in the Mekong region.[38] Another detailed critique of the Social Development Plan's agriculture and livestock components was ignored by the Bank.[39] Both reports provided more accurate predictions of what would happen than anything produced by the World Bank, NTPC, the consulting companies, or the contracted NGOs.

This raises the question of what counts as an expert. In the case of the PoE, expertise was defined as having a long record of involvement in resettlement and environmental programs elsewhere but not necessarily as possessing up-to-date, in-depth knowledge about Laos or the politics and ecology of the Mekong region. This may explain the initial naiveté of PoE members regarding the political realities of the country. These realities were readily apparent to other analysts with more experience in the region, and they significantly affected the outcome of NT2.

On Independence and Access to Information

The PoE's independence has been highlighted in all its subsequent reports. A general understanding of "independent" in this context would be the ability to provide advice and make judgments without interference or influence from individuals or agencies invested in a project like NT2.

To expect the PoE to not rely on the World Bank (directly or through the GoL) for financial support could be criticized as unrealistic. Still, in its early years, some critics did perceive a potential conflict of interest, since the PoE's lucrative consultancy arrangement would only continue if NT2 moved forward—and that would happen only if the PoE endorsed it.

While structurally this is of concern, there is no evidence that this was actually a problem. Although the PoE was funded by project investors—the World Bank through its IDA, and the GoL, and NTPC—all those who worked with and are familiar with the PoE's work are confident that financial considerations did not influence their views concerning NT2, and that they retained independence from the Bank and the other investors. This was demonstrated on numerous occasions.

One important aspect of independence is how and where information is accessed. The official record reflects overreliance on information provided by institutions with a financial stake in the project. While the acknowledgments section of the reports almost always mentions having met with "NGOs," not once in the nine reports published before project approval did the PoE list an independent noncontracted NGO based in Laos or elsewhere in the Mekong region. No independent researchers or other policy or academic institutions are acknowledged. The PoE did interact with people able to provide independent perspectives. However, they were almost never acknowledged in the way that project shareholders and contractors were. Asked about this omission in 2016,

Scudder explained that the PoE was concerned for the safety of independent researchers in the country.[40] This is understandable, at least for NGOs and other informants based in Laos. Other PoE members emphasize that independent sources consulted included "many well-informed and influential people of a variety of persuasions."[41] Still, PoE reports would have been strengthened had this been explained in each report and if more regional resource people had been cited.

Each PoE report also contains a references section that lists documents the panel reviewed. There are very few references to any documents not produced or funded by NTEC/NTPC, the World Bank, or the GoL (which used Bank funding or provided documents at the behest of the Bank). Only three or four of the dozens of documents cited could be considered to have independent authorship—that is, could be seen as a source that was not financed by the project investors, and whose terms of reference was not defined by them. This despite the fact that a number of independent reports and articles with great relevance to aspects of NT2 were produced by researchers, NGOs, and academic institutions during this time. The perception of PoE independence would have been strengthened had it been more apparent that PoE members were considering some of those independently produced documents, including critical ones.

A notable exception was the unnumbered interim report, dated March 2002, attributed to the PoE, but with just one author, Thayer Scudder.[42] This report focuses on downstream issues in the XBF River basin. It appears to have been a reaction to an independent report entitled *The People and Their River: A Survey of River-Based Livelihood in the Xe Bang Fai River Basin in Central Lao PDR*, published a few months earlier by the Canada Fund.[43] The study provided a comprehensive examination of people's nature-based livelihoods along the XBF—a river that would be heavily impacted by NT2. While it did not specifically consider the impacts of NT2, *The People and Their River* indicated that many economic and social aspects that affected more than one hundred thousand people had yet to be addressed by NT2 plans.

Public Access to Information

The PoE's willingness to disclose problems with project planning and implementation provided a much more rigorous system of oversight than there would have been had that role been left to NTPC or sporadic monitoring of NT2 by the World Bank. The documentation in PoE reports spans the last twenty years of NT2's development and thus provides an invaluable historical record. There are few such records available, either in Laos or in more open societies, for projects of this complexity and contentiousness.

One shortcoming, however, is the dearth of reports in Lao language. The PoE's eleventh report noted that "this current report and future PoE reports are to be translated into Lao to expand their accessibility."[44] However, that report and the two subsequent are the only ones available in Lao. All others, before and after, are available only in English. Despite the inability of Lao-based civil society to engage in public advocacy or criticism of NT2, Lao-language reports would have been useful resources for people within and outside of the GoL.

Impact on Project Implementation

The PoE's monitoring of the resettlement process on the Nakai Plateau and willingness to illuminate implementation problems and to offer recommendations for improvements, particularly in NNT NPA, is notable. These efforts are described in other chapters. The PoE played a significant role in keeping macrodevelopment and destructive projects (mines, roads, logging) out of the protected area and ensured that much of the promised assistance for resettlers was delivered according to plan. While PoE monitoring on the XBF was less consistent, it still drew attention to the issues with the Downstream Compensation Program there.

Conclusions

In retrospect, we believe that PoE endorsement of NT2 in July 1997 was premature. The PoE stated that it endorsed NT2 before the main plans for environmental and social mitigation, compensation, and resettlement were completed. As PoE members were the only people in Laos free to see and say what they knew about NT2, they had an essential responsibility to remain open minded and objective. World Bank staff were able to use the PoE endorsement to discount what emerged as very legitimate concerns raised about the soundness of NT2 by outside researchers and campaigners.

Still, PoE members deserve recognition for their willingness to critique the deficient aspects of the project in recent years. It is not easy for people as heavily invested in the success of a project as was the PoE with NT2 to acknowledge that a project has fundamental problems. For their integrity and their willingness to admit that what they hoped and tried to accomplish did not fully come to pass, PoE members deserve great respect.

There are many examples of the PoE delineating problems and insisting they be addressed by NTPC and the GoL. Some observers believe that these outcomes provide evidence of the PoE's effectiveness and justify such panels in future projects. However, the total NT2 PoE experience provides a broader lesson: perhaps the very need for an independent panel of this type is by itself a red flag. If such a panel is needed, then it may be that conditions for executing such a project do not exist in the country of concern.

If the World Bank believes it needs a mandate from a panel of experts because it is concerned about the sincerity of a government or the capacity of corporations to determine social and environmental impacts or to plan and monitor massive resettlement or project-related "environmental mitigation" programs, we would argue that it should not even consider involvement in so risky, complex, and destructive a project.

Furthermore, if the World Bank determines that an outside panel of experts is required to ensure minimal standards of transparency and accountability, and an adequate degree of public understanding of a project like NT2, this is a likely indicator that the people living in that country do not have the opportunity to freely express themselves or to gain access to the information needed to understand the project. If those basic structures do not exist, it is unlikely that the World Bank or any other outside institutions will be able to construct them. The Bank's money and the advice of independent panels are no substitute for an engaged local citizenry and a government accountable to its own people.

The International Advisory Group

While the PoE has become a longer-lived institution with a higher profile, another panel of international advisors, the International Advisory Group (IAG), also provided independent monitoring and advice for NT2 through the period of its planning and construction. Whereas the PoE was officially structured to advise the GoL, the IAG was established in 1997 to "provide an independent source of advice for World Bank president James Wolfensohn on potential issues and problems arising for the project."[45] Its mandate and its members changed over time. In 2006 it received a new terms of reference from the World Bank for the post-approval implementation phase of NT2. A key figure in the early years of the IAG, David McDowell, moved over to the PoE in 2006. Between 1997 and 2011 the

IAG produced ten reports at least as detailed and comprehensive as those of the PoE.

The IAG's first report, issued in August 1997, shortly after the PoE backed NT2, also endorsed the social and environmental aspects of the project stating, "On balance, our conclusion at this point is that the developmental, poverty alleviation and environmental benefits of the project outweigh the negative aspects."[46] The IAG reconfirmed its strong support for NT2 at various times, up through the period of NT2 approval by the World Bank in 2005. As it did with the PoE, the World Bank used the IAG's endorsement of NT2 in its public relations materials to help justify the project.

The IAG played an important role in gathering information on the social and environmental aspects of the project, including the extent to which it could be expected to contribute to poverty reduction. Its reports, like those of the PoE, were made publicly available.[47] The IAG played a significant role through its initial endorsement and ongoing monitoring of the project—it is an important part of the NT2 story. We regret not being able to give the IAG the attention that it deserves in this chapter and book.

The World Bank decided to terminate the IAG shortly after the completion of NT2's physical infrastructure. Its last report was dated June 2011. The IAG remained broadly supportive of NT2 up until the time of its dissolution. It is an open question as to whether in light of the social and environmental problems that have subsequently emerged, the IAG, should it have continued, would have followed a similar trajectory as that of the PoE in becoming increasingly critical of the project over time.

NOTES

1. In 2000 the WCD had selected Pak Moon as one of its key case studies—and had found that the World Bank's signature Thai project had performed poorly and that its purported benefits had not been worth its severe economic, social, and environmental costs.

2. As defined by the UNDP and World Bank. LDC status makes a country eligible for the IDA's grants and concessional loan lending mechanism.

3. Peter Stephens, "The Communications Challenge," in *Doing a Dam Better: The Lao People's Democratic Republic and the Story of Nam Theun 2*, ed. Ian C. Porter and Jayasankar Shivakumar (Washington, DC: World Bank, 2011), 121.

4. Duke Center for International Development, "Some Cross-Cutting Lessons," in *Doing a Dam Better*, 135.

5. Jacques Leslie, *Deep Water: The Epic Struggle over Dams, Displaced People, and the Environment* (New York: Picador, 2005), 108.

6. World Bank, NT2 project appraisal document, March 31, 2005, 31.

7. PoE 1:4; PoE 2:3.

8. PoE 3:3.

9. PoE 4:5.

10. PoE 1.

11. PoE 2:4.

12. PoE 2:4–5.

13. PoE 6:8.

14. Leslie, *Deep Water*, 215.

15. Quoted in Leslie, *Deep Water*, 219.

16. Lee Talbot, personal communication, email to Bruce Shoemaker, October, 2016.

17. Larry Lohmann, "Mekong Dams in the Drama of Development," *Watershed* 3, no. 3 (1998). See http://www.thecornerhouse.org.uk/resource/mekong-dams-drama-development.

18. PoE 3:6.

19. PoE 4:8.

20. PoE 6:9.

21. PoE 7:12, emphasis added.

22. PoE 9:12.

23. See PoE 8:25–26.

24. PoE 11:9.

25. Ibid.

26. PoE 13:8, emphasis in original.

27. PoE 13:10, emphasis in original.

28. PoE 13:23.

29. PoE 13:23.

30. PoE 13:15.

31. PoE 14:38, emphasis in original.

32. PoE 14:38.

33. World Bank, "Tunnel Closes and Nam Theun 2 Reservoir Begins to Fill," April 10, 2008. www.worldbank.org/en/news/feature/2008/04/10/tunnel-closes-and-nt2-reservoir-begins-to-fill.

34. Ram K. Chopra, "Private-Public Partnerships: Mobilizing Financing for a Large Infrastructure Project, Lessons from Nam Theun 2 Experience," 22, paper presented at "Nam Theun 2: Lessons-Learned Workshop, Vientiane," May 19, 2006. This workshop was organized by Ian C. Porter, country director for Lao PDR, World Bank.

35. Jacques Leslie, "Large Dams Just Aren't Worth the Cost," *New York Times*, August 24, 2014, www.nytimes.com/2014/08/24/opinion/sunday/large-dams-just-arent-worth-the-cost.html?mcubz=3.

36. In contrast to previous PoE reports, the World Bank issued a formal statement to this report in which it downplayed the criticisms made in the report and instead highlighted other World Bank and NTPC assessments of NT2.

37. See, for example, World Bank, project appraisal document, A-42.

38. David J. H. Blake, "Independent Technical Review: NT2 Impacts on Xe Bang Fai Fisheries," IRN and Environmental Defense, January 2005, www.internationalrivers.org /sites/default/files/attached-files/nt2fishimpacts.05.02.09.pdf.

39. IRN, *Agriculture and Livestock Development Plan* (Berkeley, CA: IRN, 2005). Due to the fear of reprisals within Laos, the author didn't sign the document.

40. Thayer Scudder, personal communication, email to Bruce Shoemaker, October 2016.

41. David McDowell, personal communication, email to Bruce Shoemaker, October 2016.

42. PoE 5.5.

43. Bruce Shoemaker, Ian. G. Baird, and Monsiri Baird, *The People and Their River: A Survey of River-Based Livelihoods in the Xe Bang Fai River Basin in Central Lao PDR* (Vientiane: Lao PDR/Canada Fund for Local Initiatives, 2001). Disclosure: the lead author of *The People and Their River* is also the second author of this chapter and a co-editor of this volume.

44. PoE 11:7.

45. IAG, "Nam Theun 2: Handing Over," report 10, June 2011.

46. IAG, *World Bank's Handling of Social and Environmental Issues in the Nam Theun 2 Hydropower Project in the Lao PDR*, report 1, August 19, 1997, 5, http://documents.world bank.org/curated/en/860761468276563271/pdf/multi-page.pdf.

47. IAG reports are available on the World Bank website (http://documents.world bank.org/curated/en/docsearch?query=IAG).

3

The Promises and Pitfalls of Nongovernmental Organization Consultation and Engagement

BRUCE SHOEMAKER and

DAVE HUBBEL

In its attempt to develop and portray the Nam Theun 2 hydropower project (NT2) as a new model for large dams, the World Bank engaged nongovernmental organizations (NGOs) that focused on conservation and development in the project's planning and implementation. This chapter reviews the history, controversies, outcomes, and lessons of this engagement and also includes some recent reflections by some of the individuals who had a role in NT2.

Traditionally, hydropower development has been the purview of private companies and government agencies. However, World Bank staff recognized not only that NGO engagement could provide crucial information and perspectives but also that their very involvement could foster a more positive image for the dam. *Doing a Dam Better* cites the consultation of NGOs with respect to impacted communities as one of the "salient positive features" of NT2.[1]

The suppression by the government of the Lao PDR (GoL) of local NGOs and the consequent absence of organized civil society meant that this type of engagement and information sharing could not be performed by local groups. So the Bank turned instead to international nongovernmental organizations (INGOs). This led to much conflict and controversy in Laos and abroad.

The importance of contracted INGOs in building international credibility for NT2 was highlighted in a 2006 "lessons learned" paper from a World Bank workshop held in Vientiane:

> The initial scope of such consultations was focused on the [Nakai] plateau and to a very limited extent, on the protected area. A basic socio-economic baseline was developed, but it was quite cursory and impressionistic. CARE and subsequently, in 1997–98, IUCN [International Union for the Conservation of Nature] were engaged to assist in the consultations and to provide some international credibility to the process.[2]

The Bank also encouraged other, noncontracted INGOs based in Vientiane to participate in both informal meetings with staff and a formal public participation process to review project plans. They were invited to attend a series of workshops held in early to mid-1997 to review external studies that had been conducted by private consulting firms on alternatives to NT2 and a project economic analysis of the dam and the environmental and social/resettlement studies that had been carried out.

The World Bank's apparent acceptance of INGO engagement as a substitute for the type of independent local civil society necessary to provide meaningful input on project plans was based on a shaky foundation. In the 1990s, most INGOs in Laos were new to the country. Their presence had been facilitated by the same opening of the country that would soon bring in hydropower developers and other private companies. Few were accustomed to working in a communist country. Some may have worked in China, but not in support of local communities confronted by the impacts of large infrastructure projects. A major impediment was that all INGOs, which in more open societies might directly support local communities and organizations, were required in Laos to partner exclusively with government departments. Their role was to implement the GoL's development vision and provide technical expertise and innovations, not to work directly with local communities or in any way challenge government policies. To expect such groups to represent the interests of communities unable to speak for themselves regarding a project supported by a government that had just recently allowed them to operate in the country was not realistic.

Among the newcomers was the US-based Wildlife Conservation Society (WCS), an affiliate of the Bronx Zoo. WCS's first memorandum of understanding (MOU) with the GoL stipulated that it would work with the Department of Forestry to conduct wildlife and habitat surveys of the new system of twenty protected areas, called national biodiversity conservation areas (NBCAs).

In early 1994, one of the first joint WCS–Department of Forestry projects was a survey of the Nakai-Nam Theun (NNT) NBCA, which included areas of the Nakai Plateau and the Annamite Mountains, areas of high conservation importance. WCS was thus well positioned in late 1994 when it was approached to conduct a detailed survey of the plateau for the developers, the Nam Theun 2 Electricity Consortium (NTEC), then known as the Project Development Group. The first NTEC-funded survey was completed in June 1995.[3] This was followed by a revised report issued in 1996.[4]

The WCS surveys of the plateau and NNT NBCA drew the attention of the International Rivers Network (IRN). In early 1995, IRN had made the Mekong River basin a priority for its work, due to its high global significance and the quick pace at which plans to build dams there were proceeding. In August and again in October 1995, IRN director Owen Lammers wrote to WCS's Asia program director, Alan Rabinowitz, to explain IRN's perspective and implore WCS to work with IRN to oppose NT2 and explore alternative strategies for the Nakai Plateau and NNT NBCA, which made up most of the project's catchment. During a visit to New York, Lammers had what seemed to him to have been a productive face-to-face meeting with Rabinowitz. But on December 15, 1995, in response to an article by Patrick McCully in IRN's *World Rivers Review*, Rabinowitz wrote to Lammers and called IRN's assertion that species such as tigers and elephants would be negatively impacted by NT2's reservoir untrue:

> IRN has blatantly published inaccurate and misleading information when it states that habitats for species such as clouded leopard, Asian golden cat, black bear, tiger, elephant, large-antlered muntjac, etc. etc. will be lost or affected by the dam. Once again and I repeat this for the last time to you, only the white-winged wood duck and probably some fish species are likely to be affected by the dam. All the other species mentioned in the article are long gone from the inundation area and are now only found in the forests of the upper watershed.[5]

The letter was startlingly inaccurate. Many species, notably elephants but also tigers, large-antlered muntjacs, and, in all, at least seventeen key species of medium or high global importance, were present in the inundation area and would be gravely affected, a fact well known to WCS field biologists.[6] Ironically, in 2001 WCS was to implement a project to manage elephant-human conflicts on the Nakai Plateau, conflicts that resulted from the flooding of the elephants' plateau habitat.

In November 1995, a World Bank meeting with concerned Vientiane-based INGOs had revealed many flaws and unanswered questions in NT2 planning. The Bank's visit resulted in the issuing of an important aide memoire, which called for additional studies and consultation in advance of any decision on NT2.[7] Bank staff then quickly moved to engage other Lao-based INGOs to assist in social and environmental aspects of the proposed project. Staff approached the Lao office of CARE International (headed by its Australian affiliate) to ask if it would conduct social and cultural surveys of Nakai communities slated for resettlement. One of CARE's focuses was ethnic minority and Indigenous communities, and it had already collaborated with the World Bank in Laos in writing a profile on Indigenous People for it. CARE agreed and contracted with NTEC to assemble a team to conduct the study. The team included James Chamberlain, an ethnolinguist, and Charles Alton, an agricultural economist, both with extensive knowledge of Indigenous Peoples in Laos and years of experience in the country as well as Latsamay Silavong, liaison with the Department of Forestry who would later become the Lao country director for IUCN, and Bounleung Philavong, a Lao CARE staff member.

CARE's involvement sparked a controversy within the NGO community in Vientiane. Since early 1995, a small group of NGO staff, including some Lao nationals, plus members of the Bangkok-based group Towards Ecological Recovery and Regional Alliances (TERRA), had formed the Rivers Group to share information regarding the rapid expansion of hydropower in the country. Participants included senior staff of the American Friends Service Committee, Community Aid Abroad, Oxfam Belgium, Canadian University Service Overseas, the Consortium, World Education, and a local group for Lao INGO workers, the Sustainable Agriculture Forum.[8] A leading active participant in the latter was Sombath Somphone, who was then forming the Participatory Development Training Centre, which for many years was the only quasi-local NGO in Laos. NT2 was a major focus within the Rivers Group. Due to the controversial nature of hydropower and in deference to GoL sensitivities, activities were generally low profile. CARE was not involved and its staff were unaware of the group.

Members of the group were dismayed to learn that CARE had agreed to work for NTEC. In their view, CARE seemed to be wading into an issue, hydropower, in which it had expressed little interest before, and they worried that CARE's study would be used by the Bank and NTEC to justify the project, regardless of the study results.[9] Members were disturbed that CARE hadn't consulted with other NGOs before accepting the work and saw its agreeing to undertake the study as undercutting solidarity and cooperation among the nascent NGO community in Laos. However, given the low profile the Rivers Group intentionally assumed and its insular nature, it is unclear how CARE staff were even supposed to know it existed.

At the time a common view among Rivers Group members was that CARE's work for NTEC was poorly considered but typical of large "entrepreneurial"-style NGOs. Such organizations, in the opinion of many group members, were acting more like consultants than NGOs and were likely motivated by the possibility of signing lucrative contracts either then or in the future to implement social impact aspects of NT2. Increasingly vocal criticism led CARE to organize a meeting for the NGO community on January 8, 1996. The well-attended gathering was contentious and did little to resolve the controversy. CARE's director made the point that the organization wasn't endorsing NT2 but saw its involvement as "an opportunity to bring the NGO viewpoint into the decision-making process."[10] Some attendees questioned whether hiring consultants more accustomed to working with large multi-lateral aid agencies than for NGOs was really a legitimate way to promote an "NGO viewpoint." The episode generated much debate about engagement by INGOs in a large infrastructure project with social and environmental impacts, particularly in a country with that severely restricted civil society and freedom of speech.

CARE's director at the time, Mike Carroll, a well-respected development worker with a long record of work in Laos, recalls,

> We felt we were influencing a corporation (NTEC), with strong support from the World Bank, to follow Bank operational directives regarding safeguarding the rights of Indigenous Peoples, including their documentation and pre-baseline poverty status. We worked with a senior sociologist and anthropologist at the Bank who shared our belief that NT2 needed professional external pre-baseline ethnicity and poverty assessments. CARE was able to bring to the effort recognized anthropologists and a resource economist fluent in Lao with nearly 60 years of combined experience in the country. We hoped the study could be a model for the GoL to use in the future since no such models existed in 1997.

Carroll did acknowledge, however, that CARE "could have done a better job communicating with other NGOs and involving the NGO Forum sooner rather than later in mutual consultations."[11]

Certainly, some of the criticism leveled at CARE at the time, including by the first author of this chapter, was overly strident and unfair. Chamberlain and Alton, relatively unknown to many NGO staff, despite their long track records in the country, were both to gain respect for their work on issues of ethnicity, poverty analysis, and impacts of internal resettlement. Despite the CARE team's credentials, however, the possibility that the World Bank might be using the organization to justify the project was a legitimate concern left unresolved.

The Bank's November 1995 aide memoire also requested help from the Lao program of the International Union for the Conservation of Nature (IUCN), known as the World Conservation Union, in planning and assessment of environmental aspects of NT2. IUCN is a hybrid INGO/multilateral organization of both sovereign states and NGOs.[12] In 1988, IUCN was the first conservation organization to establish a program in Laos. Its initial task was advising the GoL in establishing the national protected areas in the country. Among the largest and most important for biodiversity was the NNT NBCA, which included part of the Nakai Plateau and most of the Nam Theun river basin's catchment east of the plateau. For the World Bank to support a hydropower project that could severely impact an important protected area, which a well-known international conservation organization had helped establish, was risky. If IUCN had publicly opposed NT2, it would have been seriously awkward for the Bank. IUCN's support for the dam, or at the least its silence, was thus a critical component in preventing its governmental and nongovernmental members from opposing NT2. After a sustained delay due to GoL objections to paying for Bank-mandated studies, IUCN began to implement an environmental and social management and planning project in the NNT NBCA. Wildlife survey components were contracted to WCS and completed in July 1997.

Just one month after the meeting about the CARE study, the rift in the INGO community, both in Laos and internationally, deepened significantly. On February 7, 1996, Rabinowitz released an open letter to IRN on WCS letterhead: "As director of Asia Programs for WCS, I am giving my full support to the NT2 project as long as the World Bank remains involved and as long as the current plans for environmental protection and mitigation remain intact."[13] Rabinowitz detailed several reasons for the endorsement and concluded, "I view the currently proposed NT2 scheme at this point in time as the only way to help reverse the rapid decline of forests and wildlife in the NNT NBCA."[14]

The letter stunned many observers, including other WCS staff, to whom it came as a complete surprise, and caught the attention of the regional and international press. It also triggered a response from Lammers at IRN, who called WCS unprofessional for endorsing a project before its own studies were completed, when the Bank itself was still officially noncommittal.[15] WCS vice president John Robinson then entered the fray, denying that WCS supported NT2 per se; Rabinowitz's comments, he maintained, were just in support of the proposed biodiversity outcomes of NT2.[16] This statement was met with skepticism within IRN—staff saw it as an attempt at damage control. An exchange between Rabinowitz and IRN continued for several months and degenerated into barely disguised name-calling. The dialogue ended with bad feeling on both sides in October 1996.

Aviva Imhof, former Mekong campaign director for IRN, recalls Rabinowitz's endorsement as "a huge deal that had a major impact. By giving NT2 'NGO cred' it weakened and undercut our work . . . , [and] the Bank was able to point to WCS's involvement whenever environmental concerns were raised."[17]

Interviewed in 2016, Rabinowitz recalls, "The situation in Laos was dire. The Annamites were under siege—the wildlife trade was rampant, border controls were weak and the country had limited development opportunities. Having the World Bank step in, along with the prospect of significant funding for conservation, seemed like the best possible alternative. If the project was done right, it would be worth the sacrifice of the reservoir area on the Nakai Plateau."[18] An observer at the time who has asked to remain anonymous remarks, "I think Rabinowitz was, at least in part, cultivated and seduced by Transfield's David Iverach, an intelligent charmer. I suspect, but can't say for sure, that Iverach suggested to Rabinowitz to write the letter. I've heard that there were cheers of victory and jubilation in the NTEC office when the fax of Rabinowitz's letter came in."[19]

It was not just Western conservation groups that disputed WCS's position. Rabinowitz's critics included one of the most prominent environmentalists in Thailand, Veerawat Dheeraparasart. In response to the WCS endorsement of NT2, Veerawat authored an article titled "Why NT2 Won't Save Wildlife" in which he refuted Rabinowitz's claims point by point.[20]

In July 1996, CARE completed its report, which offered a detailed description of the livelihoods and cultures of Indigenous communities on the plateau and in the catchment. The report did not explicitly endorse NT2, but its conclusions certainly leaned in that direction: "Hence, with the proviso that World Bank criteria are adhered to in the formation of the development plan and in the approach to the Indigenous Peoples, carefully planned resettlement is not an entirely unwelcome solution."[21]

The report's description of deteriorating natural resources, population increases, and market forces leading toward uncontrolled resource extraction portrayed a bleak future for communities living on the plateau. The report's lead author later recalled, "Our cautious statement here was based on our desire to generate support for the survival of Indigenous Peoples which very obviously not going to come from any other sources[,] and to encourage/generate additional research."[22]

NT2 critics thought the report, and in particular the way it was used by project proponents as an unqualified endorsement of resettlement, understated the degree to which loss of forest resources on which local communities had depended was due to a massive increase in logging in NNT related to NT2 since the early 1990s. To those observers, the report symbolized the flawed logic behind NT2—logging in their minds was a major factor in the rapid loss of the resource base for local communities, and yet that loss was being used by proponents to justify the need for poverty alleviation by construction of the dam.

Imhof recalls,

> The CARE report set up a strong theme that persisted for years, which was that the people on the Nakai Plateau needed to be resettled in order to protect their livelihoods and that NT2 was the only way of doing this. The whole idea that people could be resettled in the same general location, but with far less land and natural resources, and that this would set them up for a richer livelihood was just preposterous! But at the time the idea had a big impact on people's thinking.[23]

IUCN director general David McDowell engaged in dialogue with IRN to convince it to abandon its opposition to NT2.[24] In a letter to IRN campaigns director Patrick McCully, McDowell pointed to a recent endorsement of NT2 by the International Environmental and Social Panel of Experts (PoE), stating,

> I do concur in the major conclusions. It seems to me that on this occasion the Bank may be getting it more right than wrong, though history will tell. So may I gently suggest that you have another look at Nam Theun and see if you agree, notably in the light of the limited alternative course of action available to the international community.[25]

By early 1997, the INGO community was split. Many environmental groups outside of the country were opposed to the project. WCS, IUCN, and CARE were working for the project and, rightly or wrongly, were perceived as supportive. Reaction among Vientiane-based groups, by contrast, was varied. Some tried to stay as far removed from the debate as possible. Rivers Group members remained skeptical but were limited in what they could do. Some dialogue occurred between members of the group and the GoL, especially with staff in its Science, Technology and Environment Office (STENO).

In February 1997, a parody of the state-run *Vientiane Times* entitled "NTEC Lao PDR Times" was anonymously published that made IUCN, WCS, and CARE targets of biting satire. A fake advertisement for CARE described it as an "NGO for Sale" able to provide, "the thin veneer of legitimacy being associated with an NGO can offer you." Alan Rabinowitz's enthusiasm for NT2 was also targeted. The paper took aim at a prime conservation argument—that the sacrifice of much of the Nakai Plateau for the dam would allow permanent conservation of the more intact upper watershed and habitat of the recently discovered saola—by quoting an IUCN survey team member supposedly found eating a "saola steak sandwich": "I know I shouldn't, I know it's wrong," mumbled the embarrassed IUCN team member between bites. "But by only agreeing to eat the deteriorated lower half of the Saola, we are confident that the pristine upper half of the rare animal can live on."

International NGOs and the Public Participation Process

There was also a sustained effort by the World Bank to secure NT2 consultations from other Lao-based INGOs. INGOs had been invited to the first NT2 presentation as early as 1991, but the process began in earnest with a November 4, 1995, briefing between fourteen Bank staff members and representatives of eighteen INGOs.[26] Many representatives, especially within the Rivers Group, requested that contact with the Bank be termed "informational briefings" not "consultations." Representatives stated they were not in a position to provide meaningful feedback because they had not been provided with enough information in advance (many project documents remained confidential past NT2 approval in 2005) and because it had not been made clear how their input would be used. They also did not want to be surrogates for Lao civil society. Shortly after the 1995 meeting, Rivers Group member Charlie Pahlman of Community Aid Abroad noted, "We didn't want the World Bank to be able to claim it had conducted in-country consultations when it had only met with international groups."[27] Pahlman, who later published articles on NT2 focused on national sovereignty and pitfalls inherent in the political risk loan guarantee and the build-own-operate-transfer (BOOT) ownership model for NT2, also expressed frustration at how the Bank and Nam Theun 2 Power Company (NTPC) expected all NGO consultation to be confined to narrow social and environmental aspects, even though NGOS were also concerned with many other issues, such as economics and national sovereignty.[28]

At the urging of the Bank and NTEC, INGOs were invited by the GoL to a series of presentations on the studies being prepared in support of NT2 in the first half of 1997. In December 1996, INGO representatives in Laos had met with Bank staff to discuss information sharing and consultation. The group followed up with a letter outlining what they saw as minimal standards for further participation.

The tension between the INGOs and the Bank came to a head during the first NT2 national consultation workshop, held January 27–29, 1997, meant to provide an overview of studies under way, which suffered from the very issues INGO had feared. The workshop had limited participation, as many refused to attend, citing short notice and lack of documentation on how their participation would be used.[29]

INGO staff in Vientiane found themselves in a bind. The GoL agencies with which they worked were under internal pressure to complete consultation so that the project could proceed; this put pressure on the INGOs to participate. Yet INGO staff were increasingly frustrated by the biased presentations of project consultants, who should have been impartial but who in reality had pro-dam perspectives. This was particularly true of Lahmeyer International, the principal firm contracted by GoL to study alternatives to NT2. Lahmeyer's leader, Bert Oud, was a strong advocate of NT2 and eventually worked as a consultant for NTPC.[30] That companies like Lahmeyer had a record of conducting studies and then implementing hydropower projects based on their studies was not lost on INGO representatives.

Six Vientiane-based Rivers Group-affiliated NGO staff (not including IUCN, WCS, and CARE) met with Linda Schneider, the Bank NT2 liaison, on March 27, 1997, to express dissatisfaction with the way consultations were structured. Their concerns included biased moderators, meetings being scheduled on short notice, and not enough information being supplied in advance of consultation sessions.[31]

During this period, NTEC, through David Iverach of its lead corporate partner, Transfield, reached out to international groups that were seen as potential critics of the Bank. His objective was to convince them that NT2 was different from past World Bank–supported hydropower debacles and thereby head off an international campaign against the dam. His outreach included a meeting in early March 1997 at the Lao embassy in Washington, DC, coordinated by the Bank Information Center, a research and advocacy NGO. Representatives of several US NGOs, as well as the US government's executive director to the World Bank, attended. A couple of weeks later Iverach met in Bangkok with staff of the NGO Focus on the Global South. He also met with directors of TERRA and its Thai affiliate, Project for Ecological Recovery, which had a history of working with communities affected by dam projects in Thailand. Despite Iverach's efforts, internal NGO documents make clear his outreach attempts were not successful.[32] Thai and international environmental NGOs remained skeptical of NT2.

In mid-1997 the GoL ordered the NGO Forum on Laos, an umbrella group of NGOs that had only been established the previous year, to disband. While no official reason was provided, it was widely perceived as a reaction to NGO engagement with NT2 over the previous period, dating from the CARE meeting, as well as a clear warning that the GoL would not tolerate opposition by Lao-based international NGOs to its hydropower development agenda.

By 1998, with the regional economy in free-fall from the Asian economic crisis, and with NTEC unable to secure a power purchase agreement with the only customer for NT2's electricity, the Electricity Generating Authority of Thailand (EGAT), NT2 faded in importance and the controversies dogging the INGO community in Vientiane dissipated and the pressures on them eased.

Subsequent INGO Role in Project Planning and Approval

In 1998, the IUCN Lao program was contracted by the World Bank to conduct a pilot study on integrated community development and conservation and to create a social action plan for NNT NBCA communities.[33] IUCN subcontracted WCS to assist with some components. IUCN incorporated results into an environmental and social management plan that was meant to serve as the guiding document for management of the NNT NBCA component of the NT2 project.[34] While not a formal endorsement of NT2, IUCN staff acknowledge that the resulting management plan did essentially recommend that the project go forward.[35] This was certainly conditional, and staff recognized that implementing the plan for NNT would be very challenging. Still, they viewed it as the most realistic way to secure protection and management of a valuable natural and cultural resource.[36]

In mid-2000, Stuart Chape, the outgoing IUCN country director, documented serious reservations about NT2, writing in an internal report that "the principles upon which IUCN entered the NNT NT2 process . . . are now compromised in three important areas." The report described the GoL's failure to follow through on the logging restrictions it had agreed to, a lack of commitment by the Bank and others to ensuring protection of a proposed "northern extension" for the NNT NBCA, and the Bank's failure to protect saola habitat. Chape saw the World Bank and PoE as having abandoned IUCN, questioning whether the partnership initially envisioned would be possible and raising concerns over the damage to IUCN's reputation in the campaign against NT2 by "anti-dam groups."[37] IUCN worked on a couple of small projects for NNT after that but soon phased out its engagement.

WCS remained involved in NT2-related projects on a longer-term basis. From 2000 to 2002 it implemented components of the Bank-funded District Upland Development and Conservation Project (DUDCP), sponsoring activities for local communities within the NNT NPA and conducting an eighteen-month study on elephant-human conflict on the Nakai Plateau, which examined what was likely to happen once the elephants' habitat was inundated.[38] Then in 2004, WCS was contracted by the Bank to research villagers' perceptions of wildlife in NNT NPA; the results of this study would be used to prepare the *Social and Environment Management Framework and First Operational Plan*.[39] In 2004 WCS initiated a five-year project, funded by NTPC, aimed at minimizing human-elephant conflicts that were expected as a result of the NT2 reservoir formation.

In late 2000, the World Commission on Dams (WCD), a Bank-funded initiative in which IUCN played a role and that many NGOs and dam industry groups participated in, released its groundbreaking report titled *Dams and Development: A New Framework of Decision-Making*.[40] The report leveled criticism at past hydropower projects and called for much higher social, environmental, and public consultation standards for any future dam construction. It recommended that future hydro projects have the support of local communities and civil society as a precondition of moving forward.

Although the World Bank did not endorse all the findings, it did respond to some of the report's key recommendations, including its strong recommendation that civil society have a voice in project planning. In 2002, the Bank released a decision framework outlining progress needed in three areas before it could support NT2.[41] The third pillar of this framework mandated "obtaining broad support from international donors and civil society for the country's development strategy and for Nam Theun 2 itself": "International civil society has a legitimate and strong interest in the project as well—particularly since local civil society is not developed and there are no local NGOs [in Laos]. Broad support from international NGOs, particularly those involved with environmental and social issues, provides much-needed comfort that the environmental and social issues relating to the project will be successfully managed in the event."[42]

Thus ironically, the Bank implied it could move forward with NT2 because it trusted the INGOs, while the INGOs agreed to take part because they trusted the Bank's judgment about the viability of NT2. They were depending on each other to overcome NT2's daunting social, environmental, and reputational risks.

While the Bank's decision framework document acknowledged that "anti-dam groups" were unlikely to cease opposing NT2, the Bank nevertheless held out hope of gaining support from other groups. Later, as a growing coalition of NGOs and other civil society organizations worldwide came out against NT2, it became increasingly important for the Bank to point to the presence of the few INGOs still taking part in NT2's planning and implementation.[43]

In January 2004, a coalition of NGOs wrote IUCN asking it to formally document its concerns regarding NT2, based on the project's failure to comply with WCD guidelines. While IUCN did not do this, it also made no further statements in favor of NT2.

WCS, while not renouncing Rabinowitz's endorsement and while continuing to contract with project stakeholders, was "very quiet" and "refrained from any sort of explicit advocacy for the project."[44] According to the WCS Lao program co-coordinator Arlyne Johnson, by 2004–5 WCS wasn't in favor of NT2 but saw it as inevitable and regarded its engagement in NT2 implementation as a means for recommending what actions should be taken to minimize the impact of the dam on wildlife and human-wildlife conflict."[45]

WWF in Laos and Thailand

In the early 2000s, World Wide Fund for Nature International (WWF) operated a Thailand program based in Bangkok and a separate Hanoi-based Indochina program for Laos and Vietnam. Reflecting their different operating environments, the Thai and Indochina programs approached NT2 in contrasting ways. In Laos, WWF avoided taking a stand on the dam. It did not participate in the planning or implementation of NT2 like WCS or IUCN did, but it also did not issue any statements opposing it. WWF Thailand, on the other hand, became outspoken in criticism of the project and joined local Thai NGOs opposed to NT2 at a meeting with the World Bank in Bangkok where they raised their concerns. In May 2003, WWF released a statement opposing NT2, citing Thailand's lack of need for NT2's electricity and the damage NT2 would cause to ecosystems of the Nam Theun and Xe Bang Fai River basins. WWF concluded that "there is currently no justification for the dam" and that the international donor community should instead provide resources to support alternative forms of economic development.[46] Staff of WWF Thailand further engaged in the campaign against NT2 by holding press conferences and participating with TERRA and other local groups in a protest at the Bank's headquarters in Bangkok. WWF Thailand is a species-focused conservation group with a Thai constituency, and so it was particularly alarmed by the threat posed to the Nakai Plateau elephants.

Robert Mather, who headed WWF Thailand, recalls that there was no coordinated strategy between Thai and Lao offices or with WWF International. Staff in Thailand felt strongly about NT2 and wanted to stop what they saw as an unnecessary and destructive project. According to Mather, the silence of the WWF Lao office was based on fears of repercussions from the GoL. Mather believes, however, that WWF Laos could have done more to oppose the project and that its "self-imposed censorship went considerably further than was actually necessary."[47]

In an attempt to gain support for NT2, the World Bank organized international technical workshops in late August 2004, with stops in Bangkok, Tokyo, Paris, and Washington, DC. Civil society participants found the workshops frustrating—their impression was that they were largely a public relations exercise, as Bank staff did not demonstrate a sincere interest in hearing their input. In particular, they noted problems with biased moderators, especially in Tokyo and Bangkok, and vague and incomplete answers at all locations. A summary by Shannon Lawrence of Environmental Defense noted that "the World Bank, the ADB, NTPC, and the GoL were unable or unwilling to substantively respond to concerns that were raised at the workshops" and had discouraged critical comments.[48]

In March 2005, shortly before the Bank and its partners made their final decisions about NT2, an international coalition of 153 groups from 42 countries, led by Friends of the Earth–Japan, wrote to World Bank president James Wolfensohn to urge the Bank to deny financing on the grounds that the project had failed to meet the conditions of the Bank's decision framework and, specifically, because it had failed to earn the support of international civil society, noting that nearly all questions raised at all four 2004 international technical workshops had reflected concerns about NT2 and that "at this stage, no international civil society organization has expressed public support or endorsement of the project, and even IUCN and the Wildlife Conservation Society have backed down from their earlier endorsements of Nam Theun 2."[49]

While the World Bank was successful in convincing an array of institutions and government-funded bilateral donors to get on board, it was not successful in gaining broad civil society support. In the end the Bank essentially abandoned that aspect of its 2002 decision framework. Having earned the support of a number of INGOs provided it considerable cover to do so.

The project appraisal prepared by Bank staff that served as the basis for approval by the board of executive directors on March 31, 2005, highlights the importance of the role of INGOs in project preparation: "The GoL and NTPC have conducted and documented more than 200 public meetings and consultations between 1996 and 2003. A review was undertaken of the consultation process during this period. Most of the activities were organized during 1996–1997 period, when the basic socio-economic and cultural research was being undertaken predominantly by CARE and IUCN."[50]

Following approval in 2005, both WCS and CARE remained active in the NT2 project. In early 2006, CARE began implementing a livelihoods restoration project for people who were losing land to NTPC's facilities. The vision was for a multiyear project. However, only a short preparatory phase was implemented. CARE pulled out, reportedly due to undisclosed disagreements with NTPC regarding implementation.[51]

WCS continued its NTPC-funded elephant mitigation program on the Nakai Plateau through 2009. Concurrently, it was contracted by an NTPC-funded GoL body, the Watershed Management and Protection Authority (WMPA), for a 2005–7 project to train WMPA staff to systematically monitor and evaluate the status of wildlife and the effectiveness of WMPA in controlling the threat of illegal hunting and trade in the NNT NPA.

By the time NT2 became operational in 2010, WCS's involvement had come to a close. Its first contract for WMPA had been required by the Bank, and when it ended, WMPA determined that the regular presence of international conservation groups was no longer necessary.

INGO Engagement in Retrospect

The involvement of INGOs in the official NT2 participation process in 1997 was fundamentally problematic. This excerpt of a 2004 critique of its legitimacy stands as a concise summary of the basic issues:

> Faced with a lack of Lao civil society organisations—but needing NGO participation in order to satisfy Bank policies—the participation of international NGOs working in the country was sought, and the few that attended became surrogates

for local groups. The lack of substantive criticism was taken as consensus, even though no Lao citizens dared to speak openly against the project and international NGOs did not want to risk getting expelled from the country by openly criticising the project.[52]

Interviews in 2016 with former staff of agencies that developed financial relationships with NTEC/NTPC share common themes regarding their thinking at the time: first, the weight of World Bank backing, including the Bank's social and environmental safeguards, represented the best hope for preserving biodiversity and improving the socioeconomic status of local communities; next, NGO involvement could make a difference; and finally, NT2 was inevitable and the project would be better as a result of NGO engagement. NGO endorsements of NT2, implicit and explicit, were all made with similar caveats—that this would require ongoing World Bank oversight to ensure that the high standards of the planning documents were met and that the GoL would fulfill its part of the agreements. Acknowledging that the project was ambitious, they held out hope that it could be realized with net positive social and environmental outcomes.

Not all conservationists in the region saw it this way. Robert Steinmetz, who helped lead WWF Thailand's opposition to NT2, recalls:

> It was deeply disappointing to see WCS and IUCN become enthusiastic supporters of the dam, willing to sacrifice the people, wildlife, and habitats of the Nakai Plateau for the promise of one million dollars for park management nearby. Money wasn't the major limiting factor for conservation anyway. But this alignment of big conservation NGOs became the jewel in the World Bank's crown. It bolstered their position, shut down discussion of alternative options, and provided a much-needed appearance of scientific credibility, which the Bank flaunted constantly thereafter to dismiss opposition to the dam.[53]

The decidedly mixed social and environmental outcomes described in the next chapters elicit a variety of reactions from INGO staff and consultants who were involved.[54] Asked in 2016 whether he would recommend that IUCN take on the role it did with NT2 in the future, John Baker, chief technical advisor for IUCN in 1998–99, replied "Never! At least not in the way we worked. In positioning ourselves as a contractor to the project, rather than an agency bringing its own resources to the table, we were viewed by the GoL as just another consulting firm out to make money on the project. This diminished IUCN's influence and helped set up the project for failure." Former IUCN Lao director Chape wrote in 2000 that IUCN was "being used as a 'prop' for the NT2 process" and confirmed in 2016 that despite good intentions of some Bank staff, he still believes the World Bank was using the organization to validate its approval of NT2.[55]

Alan Rabinowitz believes that his support for NT2 was justified given what he perceived as the stark alternatives, but he has expressed surprise at how the World Bank ended up managing the project. "The $1 million/year for conservation never should have just been turned over to the Lao government. Outside agencies should have been involved. Just turning the funds over to the government was a recipe for disaster."[56]

While it could be argued these groups helped NT2 turn out better than it otherwise would have, not everyone who worked for these groups believes it. When asked that question, Baker replied, "Perhaps . . . but from what I can tell only in a most minimal and passive way."

Johnson believes that in the midst of a challenging situation, WCS was able to make a contribution to conservation. In particular, she points to the way WCS managed elephant-human conflict on the Nakai Plateau and how WCS-trained Lao staff continue to support conservation in institutions such as WMPA and NTPC. She notes,

> Engagement requires having development institutions that care about and want to ensure conservation and limit the damage their large infrastructure projects will cause as well as having financing agencies willing to put into place binding agreements. In such instances, having conservation NGOs involved is a better alternative than using private consulting companies.[57]

Carroll, the former CARE director, reflects,

> In retrospect, I would not recommend that INGOs become involved in large infrastructure projects such as mining and hydropower or, for that matter, be used by large UN agencies or bilateral donors[,] as their project designs run the risk of being too large, complex, poorly designed by inexperienced external foreign consultants with little or no local language ability or in-country experience. If NGOs choose to be involved in such mega-projects, it is best for them to have a separate commercial consulting firm so that the NGO's core values are not compromised.[58]

Conclusions

Among those in the INGO community who participated in public consultation in Vientiane in 1996–97 and again at the international level in 2004, the overwhelming consensus in recent years is that their participation meant little, that they were being used in a stage-managed way to prop up a decision that had already been made. Recent revelations of shortcomings of key social and environmental objectives have only confirmed initial doubts. In the process, considerable wariness about the underlying objectives and agendas of large development institutions like the World Bank was generated.

The experience of NGOs with public consultations around NT2 suggests that representatives faced with decisions about such consultations ought to approach them with extreme caution to avoid unwittingly ending up participating in orchestrated events. It is especially important that the participation of INGOS not be used as a proxy for local engagement. Cooperation with large development institutions should only be considered following analysis of what the purpose is of such consultations and whom they will benefit.

The positives of the participation of organizations such as CARE, IUCN and WCS have to be weighed against the negatives, particularly the fact that their involvement lent momentum and credibility to a dam that has harmed the local environment and the livelihoods and cultures of the people in the area. In *Imperial Nature*, which focuses in part on NT2 and how the World Bank co-opted the language of "environmental sustainability" in a renewed hydropower development agenda, author Michael Goldman writes, "International NGOs have played an increasingly crucial role. Indeed, I would argue that they have propelled the process along in ways that private capital and the multilateral banks could not have done on their own."[59]

It can be argued that many of the current problems in NNT may well have occurred without NT2, or with an NT2 absent World Bank support. However, were that so, the Bank and its financial partners, as well as such contractors as CARE, IUCN, and WCS, would not be the subjects of this research. The record clearly indicates that involvement of a small group of INGOs—in their explicit or implicit endorsements of NT2 and by their taking money from project proponents to produce implementation studies—was used by the World Bank and NTPC not only to undercut opposition to the project mounted by a much broader coalition of international groups but also to circumvent requirements that the concerns of Lao citizens be heard. The Bank's project appraisal document, perhaps unintentionally, makes this revealing statement in regards to INGO participation in the local consultation process: "Limitations lay not so much in the willingness of people to speak out, but rather in the lack of a process wherein government and project officials would be explicitly responsive to what people were saying."[60]

This is a diplomatic way of saying that despite the INGOs best efforts and the Bank's use of them to justify the project, in reality there were no mechanisms in place for decision makers to respond to input from local communities affected by the project.

International groups contracted by various NT2 parties miscalculated the capacity and willingness of the Bank and NTPC to achieve the project's ambitious social and environmental goals. Taking money from project developers to pay CARE, IUCN and WCS to carry out studies and formulate plans that indicated approval of a dam also exposed them to criticism and, at the very least, created the appearance of a conflict of interest.

NOTES

1. Duke Center for International Development, "Some Cross-Cutting Lessons," in *Doing a Dam Better: The Lao People's Democratic Republic and the Story of Nam Theun 2*, ed. Ian C. Porter and Jayasankar Shivakumar (Washington, DC: World Bank, 2011), 135.

2. Nazir Ahmad, "Nam Theun 2: An Assessment of Stakeholder Engagement," 14, paper presented at the Nam Theun 2: Lessons-Learned Workshop, Vientiane, May 19, 2006. This workshop was organized by Ian C. Porter, country director for Lao PDR, World Bank.

One of the principal facilitators of these exercises, James Chamberlain, rejects the idea that this CARE/IUCN engagement should have been construed as "consultation." He also states that while the exercises were cursory they were not impressionistic and were based on recognized qualitative research methodologies.

3. WCS, *A Preliminary Wildlife and Habitat Assessment of the Nam Theun 2 Hydroproject Area* (Vientiane: WCS, 1995).

4. Robert J. Timmins and Tom D. Evans, *A Wildlife and Habitat Survey of Nakai-Nam Theun National Biodiversity Conservation Area, Khammouan and Bolikhamsai Provinces* (New York: WCS, 1996).

5. Patrick McCully, "World Bank Takes U-Turn on Supporting Critical Nature area," *World Rivers Review* 10, no. 3 (1995); Alan Rabinowitz, WCS, letter to Owen Lammers, IRN, December 15, 1995.

6. In regards to the seventeen species of global importance the report states, "These habitats are particularly important for large mammals, several species which probably occur at higher densities on the Plateau than elsewhere in the Nam Theun NBCA." A further thirty-seven key species had been found to be present on the plateau, "but their populations are unknown" (WCS, *A Preliminary Wildlife and Habitat Assessment*, 15).

7. World Bank, *Aide Memoire to the Committee on Planning and Cooperation from the World Bank Technical Mission for the Nam Theun 2 Hydroelectric Project*, November 9, 1995.

8. The Consortium was a collaboration of World Learning, World Education, and Save the Children-US and was directed at the time by Bruce Shoemaker.

9. In fairness to CARE, the country director had attended previous informational meetings between the World Bank and other resident NGOs in Vientiane.

10. Winnie Tan, "Information Sharing Meeting Concerning CARE's Involvement in the Proposed Nam Theun Hydro Dam Project," unpublished meeting notes, NGO Forum for Laos, Vientiane, January 8, 1996.

11. Mike Carroll, personal communication to Bruce Shoemaker, September 2016.

12. IUCN originally operated in Laos as a NGO. Around the time it became involved in NT2-related studies its status in the country was upgraded to that of an international organization.

13. Alan Rabinowitz, WCS, open letter to Owen Lammers, IRN, February 7, 1996, 1.

14. Alan Rabinowitz, WCS, open letter to Owen Lammers, IRN, February 7, 1996, 2.

15. Owen Lammers, IRN, open letter to Alan Rabinowitz, WCS, March 28, 1996.

16. John Robinson, WCS, letter to Owen Lammers, IRN, April 4, 1996.

17. Aviva Imhof, personal communication to Bruce Shoemaker, May 2016.

18. Alan Rabinowitz, personal communication to Bruce Shoemaker, July 2016.

19. Anonymous, personal communication to Bruce Shoemaker, September 2016. As noted in chapter 1, Transfield was the lead company in the NTEC.

20. Veerawat Dheeraprasart, "Why NT2 Will Not Save Wildlife," *Watershed* 1, no. 3 (1996).

21. James Chamberlain, Charles Alton, Latsamay Silavong, and Bounlieng Philavong, *Socio-Economic and Cultural Survey: Nam Theun 2 Project Area* (Vientiane: CARE International, 1996), 59.

22. James Chamberlain, personal communication to Bruce Shoemaker, February 2017.

23. Aviva Imhof, personal communication to Bruce Shoemaker, May 2016.

24. McDowell would join the PoE in 2006. See chapter 2.

25. David McDowell, IUCN, letter to Patrick McCully, IRN, August 25, 1997.

26. Winnie Tan, "Nam Theun II Hydropower Project World Bank Mission Briefing," unpublished meeting notes, NGO Forum on Laos, November 4, 1995.

27. Charlie Pahlman, personal communication to Dave Hubbel, November 1995.

28. Charlie Pahlman, "Where Investors Fear to Tread: Risks and the Nam Theun 2 Dam," *Watershed* 3 (1997): 1; Charlie Pahlman, personal communication to Bruce Shoemaker, 1997.

29. Bruce Shoemaker, director, the Consortium, letter to Somphone Phanousith, STENO, January 24, 1997.

30. In an official NGO response to the WCD report, written by Patrick McCully, Oud, who had served as an industry-affiliated WCD consultant, was termed a "NT2 fanatic." While at NTPC, Oud wrote a memo arguing how NT2 was compliant with WCD guidelines, attached as an annex to the PoE's fifth report.

31. Nico Bakker, minutes, meeting between Linda Schneider, World Bank liaison officer and representatives of some NGOs, March 27, 1997.

32. TERRA, internal memorandum regarding meeting with NTEC, June 1997), 2; "Iverach is selling a dam. NT2 is corporate profit, not development." See also Paul Lewin, Bank Information Center, email to Martin Dunn et al., April 4, 1997, and Kamal Mahotra, notes on informal discussion with NTEC representatives, Focus on the Global South, March 20, 1997.

33. World Bank, *Policy and Human Resources Development Fund Annual Report, Fiscal Year 1997*, vol. 1: *Resource Mobilization and Cofinancing*, January 1998. "In Lao PDR, a grant to prepare a Forest Management and Conservation Project included a design for community mobilization approaches that took into account the special socio-economic and cultural characteristics of Laos to secure the peoples' direct involvement in the conservation-oriented management of forestry resources" (12), http://s3.amazonaws.com/zanran_storage/www.worldbank.org/ContentPages/2019176.pdf.

34. IUCN, *Environmental and Social Management Plan Management Plan for the Nakai Nam Theun Catchment and Corridor Areas*, May 1998.

35. John Baker, IUCN chief technical advisor, 1998–99, personal communication to Bruce Shoemaker, May 2016, and Stuart Chape, IUCN country representative, 1993–2000, personal communication to Bruce Shoemaker, October 2016.

36. By 2004, the World Bank's own analysis indicated that IUCN's optimism was mistaken. See World Bank, *Implementation Completion Report (IDA-31860) on a Credit in the Amount of SDR 1.5 Million (US$2.0 Million Equivalent) to the Lao People's Democratic Republic for a District Upland Development and Conservation Project*, March 25, 2004. "The team . . . established the design based on studies carried out as part of Nam Theun II and projects being implemented by other institutions (such as the IUCN). . . . The IUCN effort had identified many of the requirements for success but was not sufficient when it came to the design of the delivery of agriculture support through the public institutions" (13–14), http://documents.worldbank.org/curated/en/285561468772480047/pdf/278810LA.pdf.

According to James Chamberlain, who worked on social aspects of the study, "The IUCN team was composed mainly of ex-Fiji and Indonesian wildlife and botanical people with no experience in Laos. We had very hostile internal disagreements over such things as swidden agriculture. These 'experts' actually proposed moving Brou villages from the NBCA to locations outside the boundaries to be combined with the Plateau resettlement, or, in the case of Vietics, to concentrated villages in one corner of the protected area. Their not so secret agenda . . . was to transform the NBCA into a national park—sans humans. I believe they thought that the World Bank could assist them in this endeavor." James Chamberlain, personal communication to Bruce Shoemaker, February, 2017.

37. Stuart Chape, *Nakai-Nam Theun NBCA and Proposed NT2 Hydropower Dam: A Status Report on Key Issues and Implications for IUCN*, IUCN, May 2000, page 7.

38. Chape, *Nakai-Nam Theun NBCA and Proposed NT2 Hydropower Dam* (10): "No economic analysis of the [DUDCP] project or of any of its components was carried out at appraisal. The intention of the project was to test a low-cost method of increasing incomes and food security, providing minimal social services and protecting the conservation area."

39. In 2002, the GoL relabeled national biodiversity conservation areas "national protected areas."

40. World Commission on Dams, *Dams and Development: A New Framework for Decision-Making* (London: Earthscan, 2000).

41. World Bank, *Decision Framework for Processing the Proposed NT2 Project*, June 2002.

42. World Bank, *Decision Framework for Processing the Proposed NT2 Project*, 5.

43. See for example Porter and Shivakumar, preface to *Doing a Dam Better*, xl, and the acknowledgments and praise of the Bank's "financial partners," which include "a number of civil society organizations"—a clear reference to the groups that accepted World Bank/NTPC funding to work on NT2.

44. Aviva Imhof, personal communication, email to Bruce Shoemaker, May 2016. Some former WCS staff reject the idea that WCS endorsed NT2. However, at no point did WCS formally renounce the endorsement by Rabinowitz made in the organization's name.

45. Arlyne Johnson, personal communications to Bruce Shoemaker, September and November 2016.

46. WWF, *WWF Position Statement: Nam Theun 2 Dam Project*, Bangkok, May 9, 2003.

47. Robert Mather, personal communication to Bruce Shoemaker, August 2016.

48. Shannon Lawrence, *The World Bank's International Technical Workshops on Nam Theun 2*, civil society summary, Environmental Defense, October 1, 2004, 1, www.internationalrivers.org/sites/default/files/attached-files/techwkspsum11.11.04.pdf. See also Lawrence's summary, "World Bank Hypes Nam Theun 2 as Project Deadline Looms," published in *World Rivers Review* 19, no. 5 (2004): 16.

49. Friends of the Earth Japan, letter from 152 Civil Society Organizations to James Wolfensohn, March 14, 2005, 4–5.

50. World Bank, NT2 project appraisal document, March 31, 2005, A190.

51. Adam Folkhard, personal communication, email to Bruce Shoemaker, June 2016.

52. Shalmai Guttal and Bruce Shoemaker, "Manipulating Consent: The World Bank and Public Consultation in the Nam Theun 2 Hydroelectric Project," *Watershed* 10, no. 1 (2004): 21.

53. Rob Steinmetz, personal communication to Bruce Shoemaker, August 22, 2016.

54. Note that all former INGO staff interviewed spoke as individuals, not as representatives of their former agencies.

55. Chape, *Nakai-Nam Theun NBCA and Proposed NT2 Hydropower Dam*, 9; Stuart Chape, personal communication to Bruce Shoemaker, October, 2016.

56. Alan Rabinowitz, personal communication, interview with Bruce Shoemaker, July 1, 2016.

57. Arlyne Johnson, personal communication to Bruce Shoemaker, September 9, 2016.

58. Mike Carroll, personal communication to Bruce Shoemaker, September, 2016.

59. Michael Goldman, *Imperial Nature* (New Haven, CT: Yale University Press, 2005), 194.

60. World Bank and MIGA, *Project Appraisal Document on a Proposed IDA Grant (Nam Theun 2 Social and Environmental Project)*, Report No: 31764-LA, March 31, 2005, p. A190.

Part Two

Social and Environmental Context and Outcomes

4

Ethnicity in the Nam Theun 2 Theater

A Sense of History

JAMES R. CHAMBERLAIN

What is terrible is to *have* thought. But did that ever happen to us?

Waiting for Godot

When we speak Semai and when we speak Malay, the truth is not the same.

Semai hunter-gatherer

This chapter examines historical and ethnic considerations that underlie social dimensions of the Nam Theun 2 (NT2) hydroelectric project. The dam is located in central Laos, a relatively little known area, but one that lies at the nexus of a multitude of ethnic and historical forces and domains, including Tai, Siamese, Vietnamese, Cham, Khmer, and Lao kingdoms, principalities, and diverse cultural types ranging from hunter-gatherers to sophisticated city dwellers. It is safe to say there are no other project areas in the entirety of the Asian continent that manifest this level of combined historical and ethnological diversity; it is unique in this sense, and when the worldwide biological importance of the watershed is added to this, it becomes even more so. Without a clear understanding of this background, as this chapter shows, social issues currently facing the project cannot be understood and will remain obscured. More than one hundred years ago

Spanish-American philosopher George Santayana wrote that "progress, far from consisting in change, depends upon retentiveness; . . . those who cannot remember the past are condemned to repeat it." Oft-quoted as it has become, in the case of NT2, truer words were never spoke.

Ethnically, the territory that stretches from the Song Ca River basin in Vietnam to points south, which encompasses the north-central Annamites, has a unique history, one that has been little studied and remains little understood. The territory does not correspond to modern political boundaries; it extends to the right bank of the Mekong and includes the basins of the Songkhram, Chi, and Mun Rivers, reaching the Tonle Sap in the south, and the basins of the Nam Theun, Nam Gnouang, and Xé Bangfay tributaries on the left bank. Apart from Bahnaric peoples, the earliest identifiable inhabitants were ethnic groups belonging to the Vieto-Katuic branch of Austroasiatic.

Many of these groups are still found in this territory. Nowadays of course, the various nation-states have crisscrossed the map with arbitrary political demarcations representing countries and provinces, but those working on the ground would do well to keep in mind Korzybsky's admonition that the map should not be confused with the territory. That is to say, lines on the maps of developers have little meaning for peoples who inhabit the diverse array of riverbanks and forests. Likewise of course, peoples and cultures and languages may have little meaning for developers once they have been mapped and put in their place, so to speak.

This chapter focuses on the ethnolinguistic reality of the areas in and around NT2. I discuss three aspects of this reality: the historical, anthropological, and linguistic background; the way ethnic groups were perceived and "processed" within the frameworks established by investors and developers leading up to the decision to proceed with construction, and the repercussions of these "best-laid plans."

Ethnic Groups in the NT2 Project Area

As in Russia, China, and Vietnam, the Lao system of ethnic naming follows the Marxist-Stalinist practice of establishing an ethnicity (tribe, nationality, etc.) as a discrete unit consisting of one name, one language, one people. In Laos, they appear currently as a list of forty-nine *xon phau*, or ethnic groups, which are further classed under four linguistic stocks, or *takun*. Although additional names of some 160 language groups are sometimes provided, called "xeng" ("bunch, cluster"), these are not broken into branches or subgroups. Thus, standard international academic practice for determining detailed ethnolinguistic phylogeny (stocks, families, branches, and subgroups) is not recognized in official documentation. Of the four ethnolinguistic stocks found in Laos, three are represented in the NT2 project area: Be-Tai (Lao-Tai), Austroasiatic (Mon-Khmer), and Miao-Yao (Hmong-Mien).[1]

Vieto-Katuic (Austroasiatic)

Vieto-Katuic is the name proposed by Gérard Difffloth to denote the next higher order of relationship between the two branches of Austroasiatic, Katuic, and Vietic.[2] The Katuic branch includes Brou (Makong, Puah, Charouy, Tri, So), Katang, Ta-Oy, Katu, and Kouay (Souay), which are spoken in Khammouane, Savannakhet, Saravanh, and Champasak Provinces in Laos, northeastern Thailand, central Vietnam, and northern and eastern Cambodia. Vietic speakers are found in Borikhamxay and Khammouane in Laos and (excluding for the moment Mường and Vietnamese) Nghệ An, Hà Tinh, and Quảng Bình in Vietnam (see figure 4.1).

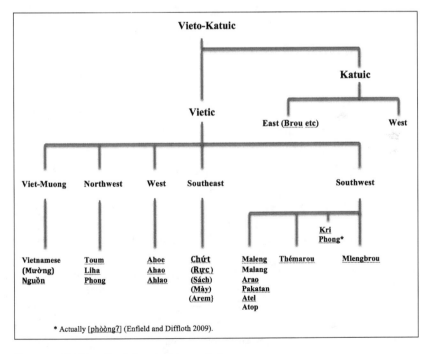

Figure 4.1. The Vieto-Katuic branch of Austroasiatic.

Figure 4.2. A Thémarou family at the village of Ban Vang Chang on the upper Nam Theun River, in 1996. The photo was taken shortly after this family, as part of a group of forty-three people, was taken out of the forest and resettled to the outskirts of this Brou village, for reasons that are unclear. They were told to construct houses, and this was the result. Photo by James Chamberlain.

Although the Annamite chain serves as a watershed divide, it has not been a barrier to human movement. Vietic peoples, the earliest inhabitants of the Nam Theun basin so far as has been detectable, are found on both sides of the chain. Their considerable diversity as measured by language attests to the age of their habitation.[3] The location strongly suggests that this was the homeland of proto-Vietic. From here, Vietic peoples, the ancestors of Mường who form a more homogenous group all the way to Hòa Bình and adjacent areas, moved northward into the present-day Vietnamese provinces of Nghệ An and Thanh-Hoa. The Mường have been well described by Cuisinier but their closest relative, the Nguồn, are found far to the south in Boualapha District in Khammouane Province, and Vietnam's adjacent Quảng Bình Province near the narrow corridor that links Nakai-Nam Theun National Protected Area (NNT NPA) and Hin Nam No NPA.[4] Thus it can be said that all subgroups of Vietic are represented in the NT2 project area.

An interesting aspect of the Vietic branch is its cultural typology, which ranges from urbanized living and wet rice paddy cultivation to swidden farming, emergent swidden farming, and two technologically distinct types of hunter-gathering, which can be loosely defined as primarily hunting (such as practiced by the Chứt, using crossbows) and primarily gathering (without crossbows).[5] No other branch of any language family in Asia contains this level of cultural diversity. It represents a unique microcosm of Southeast Asia that has persisted from the distant past to the present, but one whose value has gone largely unnoticed and unappreciated by developers and anthropologists alike.

Table 4.1 illustrates the spatial distribution of the various Vietic groups and reflects the importance of river valleys, as it shows that hunter-gatherers tended to live in the upper portions of rivers.

The Katuic branch is considered by Diffloth to consist of two main subgroups: Eastern and Western. Eastern Katuic includes Katu, Pacoh, Chatong, and Ngkriang, while Western Katuic includes the various types of Brou, Makong, Puah, Chry, Tri, Charouy, Thro (So) as well as the Kuay and Yoe languages of southern Laos, Cambodia, and Thailand.[6] A possible Central group would contain Ta Oy, Ong, Katang, and Yiir, but this is sometimes included with the Eastern group.

In the greater NT2 project area the Brou groups are mainly Puah and Charouy. On the plateau and in the protected area they are mainly Charouy. Puah and Charouy are not mutually intelligible. The names can be misleading, and so it is perhaps not surprising that both are sometimes referred to as types of Makong. Linguistically, however, the distinctions are well defined—consider, for example, the word for "rice," which is /dɔoy/ in Puah and /vaʔ/ in Charouy.

Brou settlement of the plateau is more recent, indicated by the homogeneity of their language from village to village. By comparison, the Vietic peoples' languages vary significantly by river valley to a degree where they are largely unintelligible across basins. Brou settlers probably arrived from the south, from Boualapha, Gnommarath, and Mahaxay Districts of Khammouane. It seems likely that the majority arrived subsequent to the Siamese depopulation raids that began some time after 1826, because the Brou who were transported to Thailand, where they are called So (/throo/), originated in areas other than Nakai. Many came from Boualapha, for example. But other groups who were long residents of Nakai, such as the Sek (/threɛk/) from the upper Nam Noy, were captured and sent to Thailand, where they can still be found today in Nakhon Phanom Province. Sek from Na Kadok village, who fled to avoid the Siamese, established the village of Na Vang in the interior of the catchment, but after it was abandoned, it was taken over by Brou.[7]

There are no records of early habitation of Vietic or Vieto-Katuic, at least that can be positively identified. Where they survive, they reveal that

Table 4.1. Geographical and Ecological Setting of Vietic Peoples in the NT2 Area

	North	Nakai-Nam Theun River System								South
	Khamkeut District	Sot and Mon Rivers		Nam Theun River		Noy and Pheo Rivers		One River		Boualapha District
		upper	lower	upper	lower	upper	lower	upper	lower	
Ethnicity	Ahoe Ahao Ahlao Liha Toum Phong Pakatan	Atop Atel Makang	Arao Malang Maleng To'e	Thémarou	Maleng (=> Bo)	Kri	Phòng?	Mlengbrou	Phòng?	Cheut
Cultural Type*	IV	I	II	I	II	III	II	I	II	I
Forest Type	dry evergreen/ semi-evergreen/ wet evergreen	wet evergreen	dry evergreen/ semi-evergreen	wet evergreen	dry evergreen/ semi-evergreen	wet evergreen	dry evergreen/ semi-evergreen	dry evergreen/ semi-evergreen/ wet evergreen	dry evergreen/ semi-evergreen	wet evergreen
Closest Contacts	Nghê An, Na Pè, M. Cham	Arao	Khamkeut, Nakai Plateau	Kri, Maleng	Nakai Plateau	Vietnam, lower Noy	Vietnam, Nakai Plateau	Phóng, Yooy	Nakai Plateau	Vietnam

Source: Chamberlain, "Eco-Spatial History."

*Cultural Types: I—Hunter-Gatherer, II—Emergent Swidden, III—Swidden (rotating villages), IV—Paddy and Swidden hunter-gatherers on the mainland spoke Austroasiatic languages: Aslian in southern Thailand and Malaysia, Pramic (Mlabri) in northern Thailand and Laos, and Vietic as described here. Charles Higham mentions an archeological site on the coast at Bau Tro just across the Annamite Range from Nakai[8] that uncovered evidence of a population of hunter-gatherers that dated to 2500 to 2000 BC and is geographically closest to the present-day location of the Vietic group Sách (the same ethnonym as the Tai-speaking Sek, who came from a nearby location and who now inhabit the upper reaches of the Nam Noy and Nam Pheo in NNT NPA).[9] There is really no good estimate of time depth for a hypothetical proto-Vieto-Katuic, though the prehistoric presence of hunter-gatherers in the same location is perhaps indicative. Unfortunately, bamboo-based cultures such as the hunter-gatherers of Nakai have left few traces for archeologists to pursue. That humans were present from early times is attested not far away, in the Nam Kata basin some 12 kilometers southeast of Lak Xao, where a human burial was excavated in a cave at Pha Phen, revealing a complete skeleton radiocarbon dated at 6190 BP.[10] Nearby caves and rock shelters yielded an assortment of other Neolithic and possibly Paleolithic remains.[11] There have not been other serious archeological surveys carried out in the NT2 area, either on the plateau or in adjacent zones.[12]

Be-Tai

Many ethnic groups in the NT2 area speak languages belonging to the Be-Tai sub-family.[13] These include Sek /threɛk/, Phou Thay, Nyo, Yooy, Bo, Kaleung, Mène, Pao, Kouan, Meuay, O, E, Khang, Yeuang, Kaleum, and Xam.[14]

Kam-Tai originated in the state of Chu under the Zhou Dynasty in China, but the Be-Tai and their language quickly split off, as they moved east, possibly around the sixth century BC, to establish the Yue kingdom on the coast around the mouth of the Yangtze River. Prior to the fall of Yue, some clans or strains of Yue, known as Luo-Yue (Lo-Yue) moved south into what later became southern Lingnan and Annam, and later moved west and southwest into northwestern Vietnam, Laos, Thailand, Burma, and Assam. Collectively, they are known to linguists as the Central and Southwestern Tai. Later, when Yue fell to Chu in 333 BC, many of the feudal lords and princes comprising the Ou-Yue fled south as well, along the coast, bifurcating at Guangdong, west into Guangxi and Guizhou and south into what later became Jiaozhi and Jiuzhen (present-day northern Vietnam). These included the ancestors of northern Zhuang and Pu-Yi in the first instance and Be, Sek, Nyo, and Yooy in the

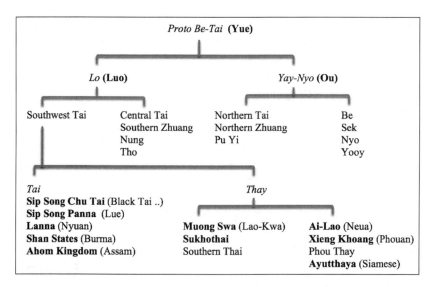

Figure 4.3. The Tai family tree in historical perspective.

second.[15] Linguists refer to these as the Northern branch of Tai. Many Tais from both branches became players in the NT2 theater.

What the family tree for Tai from a historical perspective might look like is represented figure 4.3.

Beginning in the Tang period, the eastern portion of the Tai-speaking area was well settled and firmly under Chinese or Sino-Vietnamese control, leaving little room for autonomy, despite many attempts. However, when the Tais expanded westward into less populated realms not under Chinese control, numerous polities evolved rapidly, as shown in figure 4.3, from smaller principalities and kingdoms into the nation states of Thailand and Laos. In the east the Tais were never able to attain this level of political status. Nevertheless the underpinnings of strong social organization and local administrative skills have always been present in the various Tai cultures, allowing them to politically dominate other less stratified societies. This is the essence of the interethnic relationships that have pervaded the NT2 area and all social aspects of the project itself.

Hmong (Hmong-Mien)

Originally there were not many Hmong residing in the NT2 area. The census of 1931 reports a total population of 802, and these appeared to be living primarily in the vicinity of Napè in Khamkeut.[16] Since this time, due primarily to in-migration from the north, the Hmong population of Khamkeut has increased dramatically to a degree where it exerts considerable local political influence and maintains a relatively high degree of local autonomy. Its relationship with Tai-speaking groups has become mostly symmetrical, but less aggressive Vietic speakers are in a decidedly one-down position and are no match for Hmong villages when competing for resources such as land or forest products. In addition, it has become common for Vietic groups to hire out their labor to Hmong in exchange for cash, rice, or opium.

Hmong villages are found only to the north of the boundary between Khamkeut and Nakai, although residents of the villages are known to make regular forays into NNT NPA to hunt. At one point in 1994 Hmong settlers intruded into NNT NPA and took up residence at the Brou village of Ban Na Vang, where they cleared large tracts for swidden cultivation. When the governor of Khammouane ordered the Hmong to leave, they refused, and a confrontation ensued. Four Hmong leaders were shot and killed by provincial militia before the group agreed to depart, accepting an offer of relocation to the roadside of Route 13 just north of Na Thone, now the site of a thriving market.[17]

Ethnographically, Hmong differ from other ethnic minorities of Laos in organizing their society beyond the level of the village, in their common ethnic consciousness, and in their establishment of an intricate clan network that spans the entire northern portion of the country. The boundary between Khamkeut District and Khammouane Province marks the southern side of this territory.

A Sense of History

It is in this north-central part of Laos that the many worlds of Southeast Asia come together—north and south, island and mainland, old and new, cultural and political. But events in the Khammouane-Khamkeut area of Laos can only be understood by examining those that occurred further north and on the other (coastal) side of the Annamites. The protohistory and history of the NT2 project area are highly complex; researchers attempting to study the region now need to reckon with it, as it was never understood by the NT2 players, government or foreign.

Arrival of Tais

The first Tais must have reached the area around twenty-one hundred years ago.[18] They would have been the ancestors of the Sek belonging to the Yay-Nyo (Ou-Yue) branch of our dendrogram (figure 4.3). It is not impossible that Li or Hlai peoples, who were found on the mainland coast at least as far south as Thanh-Hoá, preceded them, but there is no evidence to support this. Sek and their namesakes the Vietic Sách, however, resided in the Gianh River basin, and given their highly archaic linguistic features, the Sek must have split off from the mainstream very early on.[19] Their closest counterpart, the Mène, were originally located further north on the Chaha River, a tributary of the Sông Cả in Nghệ An.[20] Three hundred plus years ago Sek moved over the Annamites into the Nam Noy and Nam Pheo valleys of what is now the NNT NPA. Around the same time, another group of Sek, linguistically distinct from the first, established the gold mining village of Na Kadok in a place that is just a few kilometers outside the northern boundary of the NNT NPA. Many Mène, Meuay, and other Tai families moved onto the plateau in the early 1990s, especially into the Ahoe village of Sop Hia and the more commercial village of Tha Lang. Sek and Mène people share a interest in gold, and the Mène of the Chaha are still known for their prospecting skills to this day.[21] Other Mène fled into Khamkeut to escape the Ho-Cheuang uprisings, the largest group of which have been recently resettled at Keosènekham to the north of Lak Xao as part of the Theun-Hinboun Hydropower project development on the Nam Gnouang.

Chinese Colonizers
(Beginning in the Han Dynasty
206 BC–220 AD)

Chinese colonization of the area began with the Han arrival in 221 BC. Commanderies were established at the mouths of important rivers, Hồng, Mã, Cả, and southward, setting in motion a complex feudal dynamic with Chinese warlords governing Indigenous populations. The place of the Nyo and Yooy in this equation must have been considerable, although on this point histories are silent.[22] But whereas the Chinese occupied the coastal areas of Jiuzhen, the inland territories were not heavily populated and would have allowed eventually for an easy expansion northward by Mường (Mwai) peoples, perhaps to evade the Tais on the west, the Chinese to the east, and the Khmers to the south. Nevertheless, it was the Sinicization of this group that gave birth to Đại Việt, the first Vietnamese kingdom, at the end of the tenth century. This expansion must have happened prior to the arrival of the Central Southwestern Tais, as the Mường refer to Tais as Nyeo (< Nyo) and not Tai.

Contact with Khmers

Khmer influence in Khammouane-Khamkeut began at least as early as 722 AD, when Chenla sent an army to Nghệ An to assist a Tai chieftain in his revolt against the Chinese. Khmer interest in the area continued until well after the emergence of Đại Việt and lasted until the consecutive invasions of Nghệ An in 1128, 1132, and 1137. Although the Khmers were unable to defeat the Vietnamese forces, they remained in control of Khammouane until the late fourteenth century.[23]

Influences of Đại Cồ Việt

By the mid-twelfth century, the Tais to the north of Đại Việt, squeezed between the Chinese and Vietnamese, were conveniently prevented from exerting any autonomy, and so the only space for maneuver was to the west and southwest. Tais who earlier expanded west, the Lao Kwa of Louang Prabang, Nyuan, Lue, Shan, and Ahom, had already begun to establish their larger autonomous polities and statelets. The remaining Tai and Thay settled in areas adjacent to Đại Việt, home to the Nguru-hong of Sip Song Chu Tai, the Ai Lao of Houa Phanh, the Phouan of Xieng Khoang, and the Thays and Nyos of Nghệ An. All of these groups began to assert their autonomy vis-à-vis Đại Việt at a time when the latter was embroiled in struggles up and down the eastern mainland with Angkor and Champa.[24] They were not always successful but nevertheless continued their struggle. During the Mongol invasion of the 1280s, these Tai-Thay groups again tried to gain control of territory, only to become targets of increased Vietnamese attacks when the Mongols retreated. John Whitmore relates:

> In the mid-1330s, the Ai-lao became quite active on their southeast, coming half way down the Ca River of Nghệ An. The overconfident Vietnamese troops met unexpectedly strong resistance as the Ai-lao struck with elephants and horses, throwing the Vietnamese back. A decade later, the Ai-lao were still probing the border regions. A Vietnamese inscription from 1336 claimed trouble only with the "miserable" Ai-lao, other mountain groups (including the Bon or Phuan of Xieng Khwang) having "recently" submitted. The Ai-lao were led by their "obstinate" chief Bong, perhaps Souvanna Khamphong, believed to have been a grandfather of the first ruler of Lan Xang, Fa Ngum.[25]

Battles continued during the Ming Dynasty into the late fifteenth century, and in the end Đại Việt partially reinforced its authority, ceding Houa Phanh and Xieng Khoang to Laos while retaining control over Nghệ An, lending the Lao border between Houa Phanh and Nghệ An its peculiar shape. It is from these areas, especially southern Houa Phanh and Nghệ An, that the Tais who now reside in the NT2 areas of Khamkeut and Nakai originate.

Tai Migrations Beginning in 1875

Thereafter, Tai arrivals to the NT2 area can be dated with some certainty. The direct cause of migration was the Ho or Cheuang uprisings that began in Laos in 1875. The Ho were probably ethnic Zhuang (Tai) warriors fleeing the Tai-Ping rebellion (1851–64) in Guangxi province.[26] On horseback, in groups known as Black Flag, Red Flag and Yellow Flag Hos, they ravaged their way across northern Vietnam, picking up recruits from the White Tai under Deo Van Tri in Lai Chau. In Laos, they were joined by Khmu (Kha Cheuang), angry at their vassalage under the Tais. In the muang of Xam Tay (in present day Houaphanh Province, Laos) they were led by Phanga Thao Nyi—a reference to the mythic figure of Cheuang (or Cheuang Nyi Gran) whom the Khmu believed would rescue them from servitude and domination. One of his disciples named Thao Koet was the leader in southern Houa Phanh and Nghệ An and was particularly fierce.[27] In his wake whole villages of Tais from Houa Phanh and the Song Ca basin in Nghệ An fled south into Kham-mouane, into what is now Khamkeut District of Borikhamxay Province in Laos, where their descendants reside today.[28]

Upon entering Khammouane, the Tais (apparently not having learned their lesson from the revolt of the Khas further north) began to exert their in-fluence and eventually came to dominate the Vietic groups. That said, how-ever, it should be mentioned that even as late as 1906 the Chao Muong of Khamkeut was an ethnic Phong who had a reputation for fairness and the ability to balance the interests of Tai and Kha.[29] Some of the Vietic groups were labeled Puak, a name reserved for Mon-Khmer vassals under Tai fief-doms in Sip Song Chu Tai, and others were simply referred to as Kha. Some, remnants of the Nam Gnouang hunter-gatherers mentioned by Grossin, be-came attached to the Tai villages to whom they hired out their labor.[30] This pattern was repeated when the Tais moved into the Ahoe village of Sop Hia on the plateau and came to dominate that group politically.

Many other historical events have had direct bearing on the NT2 area, each of which could be pursued as a separate topic of research. A few note-worthy directions would include the influence of the Vietnamese court at

Huê; intrusions of the Siamese military; Khammouane under the French colonial administration; contacts with Neo Lao Hak Xat between 1945 and 1975; and post-1975, pre-NT2 programs and policies.

Ideally, a more comprehensive history of central Laos and Vietnam will be written in the future, in which NT2 will no longer be the disproportionate center of attention it is at the moment but rather a medium-sized footnote to the history of these countries.

The NT2 Demesne—What Did They Know?

The multidimensional aspects—ethnic, historical, ecological, and political—of the NT2 project area are difficult to fathom. Yet without such background it is hard to imagine how decisions were made with respect to the human factors of NT2. The territory is considerable, encompassing not only the Nakai Plateau and the adjacent NNT NPA but also the peripheral areas that surround the plateau and NNT NPA, the corridors linking NNT to Hin Nam No in the south and Phou Hin Poun NPA to the west, the Nam Theun River and its tributaries downstream from the dam where it abuts the impact area of the Theun-Hinboun hydropower project, and the area downstream from the power station along the Xé Bangfay all the way to the Mekong. Each microniche, each ethnic group and language, and each spiritual territory found within these expanses has its own history, origins, and sets of influences. Time and space do not allow for their details to be set forth, and in truth our knowledge is sadly lacking. So far we have only been granted a small glimpse of what lies beneath the surface.

What is inexcusable is that NT2's developers put a stop to research into all of these areas just as it was getting under way in 1995, 1996, and 1997 (the halcyon days, as it were, in retrospect), replacing it with the preparation of safeguard policy documents required by the World Bank and other international lenders.[31] Safeguard documents are not a substitute for in-depth research. In their completed form these documents are limited to superficial, rapid appraisal-style gathering of information. They may have been sufficient to assuage consciences and fulfill institutional requirements, but in the final analysis, they have led to a systemic institutionalization of intellectual poverty and to a sanctimony of conventional thinking that has pervaded the project since 1997. From the specialist's vantage point, the processes of preparation have taken Laos's amazing array of unique languages, cultures, and ecosystems and reduced them to mediocrity. Even if one cannot, as they say, stand in the way of *progress*, one can demand more of the process—that it be interested and curious and committed to documenting in the name of knowledge and human dignity what exists before it is gone forever. *There is no safeguard for this.*

I do not offer any evaluation here of the various social impact assessments and ethnic group development plans that have been carried out, other than to note the remarkable quality and color of the mapping. The assessments and plans were prepared by the Nam Theun 2 Power Company (NTPC) and evaluated by the World Bank and Asian Development Bank. Suffice it to say, the anthropological work on these documents appears rushed and does not bear evidence of immersion field work, leaving one wishing for pure ethnography, of which only brief snapshots are provided. *Anthropology, except in its most desultory form, is likewise not a requisite part of the safeguard process.*

We know least about the Vietic speakers, with the exception of the Kri of Ban Maka, whose language and culture have been studied intensely and masterfully by N. J. Enfield (not as an official part of the NT2 project.)[32] Of course, the Kri constitute only one of many groups in the NT2 project area, and we do not know to what extent they and their experience are representative. Also, prior to NT2, many Vietic languages had been studied by Michel Ferlus and Gérard Diffloth.[33] I have offered some ethnographic and ethnozoological notes along with the analysis of a Liha myth.[34]

In the NT2 project area, we know linguistically who is who, where people live, what they call themselves, and how they are known to outsiders. *We have them on the map.* We know a little bit about how people live and what they eat. But the regrettable conclusion is that after the first ten years of project preparation, little was still known about what these many diverse peoples think and how they feel. That would have involved learning peoples' languages and undertaking long-term research, something that was never considered (although it was recommended in the social action plan for the protected area). There was Enfield's ex parte work on Kri, which took place between 2004 and 2006, but it was carried out too late for inclusion in the planning process.[35] In hindsight, what could have set this project apart from others is the continuation of in-depth research from 1997 on; then indeed NT2 might have been labeled a better dam, as opposed to simply a bigger one.

Action or Lack Thereof

Where Vietic ethnic groups were concerned, attempts to carry out NT2 project preparation by following safeguard policies essentially failed.

According to one report, the World Bank's operational directive for Indigenous Peoples

> emphasizes participatory processes, requiring development of minority plans "based on consideration of the options preferred by the Indigenous Peoples affected by the project." It also emphasizes the importance of "ensuring genuine representation" . . . among people whose "social and economic status restricts their capacity to assert their interests and rights." . . . To achieve policy objectives regarding the Vietic Type I people, special measures should be devised for their protection, and to ensure that they are afforded opportunities to participate in the process of devising culturally appropriate benefits. . . . Specific arrangements for monitoring project-related impacts on Vietic Type I groups should be provided.[36]

This recommendation, however, was not followed and, in spite of convictions and ultimatums, in the end, alleged national sovereignty and expediency took precedence over safeguard mandates. The fact that the considerable efforts of the World Bank and NT2's International Environmental and Social Panel of Experts (PoE) did not convince NTPC or the government of the Lao PDR (GoL) to follow the safeguards with respect to vulnerable ethnic groups demonstrates that this is the reality. The World Bank was well aware of the risk. The record of the resettlement program run by GoL, according to Robert Mertz in a 2004 World Bank report,

> undermines the Government's credibility, confirms criticisms of its human rights policies, especially towards ethnic minorities, [and]. . . could also tarnish the reputation of the World Bank—guilt by association—unless we actively encourage the Government to improve its resettlement policy and practice—and are seen to be successful in doing so—not just with regard to future NT2-related resettlement on the Nakai plateau, but also by rectifying deficient past resettlement actions that have taken place in, or from, the NT2 Watershed. . . . [T]o shy away from this, would undermine our credibility with the international community and, most importantly, send a very dangerous signal to the Government that we are reluctant to stand up firmly when GoL actions contravene Bank policies in the context of the NT2 project.[37]

Thus there was a commitment, albeit short lived, on the part of the banks to resolve the problem of forced relocation of the Vietic group identified in the application of the safeguard process. The banks also clearly realized that the consultation process, as envisioned in the safeguard policies, would not work, especially for Vietic Type I groups. But in the end all was left in abeyance, and this contentious issue was allowed to conveniently fade from memory, like the vulnerable ethnic groups themselves, testifying to the ultimate unwillingness of the development banks to stand fast when, as Mertz puts it, government actions contravene bank policies. *Plus ça change . . .*

The next logical step in the avoidance of ethnolinguistic reality is denial and repression. With interest in ethnic minority issues waning, and no specialist staff in place at NTPC, in the banks, or in the government who could appreciate their situation, policies of homogenization came to dominate. We read in the 2015 report of the PoE that the combined percentage of the Nakai resettled population of Brou, Bo, and Ahoe has decreased (in only eight years!) from 67.4 in 2005 to 35.0 in 2013; according to the report, this does not reflect the true percentage of these groups but rather is an artifact of downplaying ethnicity on surveys. Tais, mostly from Khamkeut, now control the economies and local administration of Nakai, and inequalities increase wherever Brou, Bo, and Ahoe groups must compete with them. The historical pattern established by Tais in relation to Austroasiatic ethnic groups date back over twenty-five hundred years and have not changed. The various players in the project should have known this or should have arranged for the background research to have been carried out.

A short visit to the plateau resettlement hamlets of Nong Boua, Phonsavang, Sop Ma, and Sop Phène will confirm the inequality. Of course, all of the old haunts are gone, the shady sprawling old villages on the banks of the Nam Theun, full of fish, where an unhurried pace of life prevailed; these villages have been replaced by consolidated resettlements and row after row of unattractive monotony. These groups are vulnerable in the sense that their cultural practices are drastically at odds with the prescriptions of the resettlement plan.

Organizational mentalities have dominated the process, each one hesitating to presume on the other, their common evangelical goal being to *civilize the natives*. In this respect I am reminded of the master strategist B. H. Liddell Hart's maxim that "whoever habitually suppresses the truth in the interest of tact will produce a deformity from the womb of his thought."[38] The old shamaness Khamsone, ethnarch of the Ahoe in Sop Hia, knew this, and of the NT2 players said simply, "You can't believe them, they lie." She did presume. Now she has passed away. The Ahoe believe that after death they will be reborn as squirrels, haunting the forests that surround the NT2 dam site, the Ahoe spiritual territory. There is perhaps some comfort in the fact that this, finally, they cannot take away from her.

NOTES

1. Family names in parentheses are the official terms of the Lao government. The four *takun* are not typologically equivalent. Lao-Thai in international practice is Be-Tai, a branch of the Kam-Tai familiy belonging to the Kra-Dai stock. Hmong-Iu Mien (Hmong-Mien or Miao-Yao) is itself a stock (Iu Mien is the name of a specific language and is an error, as Iu simply is the Mien pronunciation of Yao). Mon-Khmer has been used as a sub-stock of Austroasiatic as distinguished from Munda. There are seven main branches in Laos: Kmunic, Palaungic, Pramic, Vietic, Katuic, Bahnaric, and Khmeric. Finally Chine-Tibet should be Sino-Tibetan, a stock, although only one Sinitic language, Ho, is indige-nous to Laos; the rest belong to the Lolo-Burmese branch of the Tibeto-Burman family, Khmeric.

2. Gérard Diffloth, "Vietnamese as a Mon-Khmer Language," in *Papers from the First Annual Meeting of the Southeast Asian Linguistics Society*, ed. Martha Ratliff and Eric Schiller (Arizona State University, Program for Southeast Asian Studies, 1992), 125–39.

3. The historical linguistic and dialectology principle is that diverse small areas are older than more homogenous larger ones.

4. Jeanne Cuisinier, *Les Mường: Géographie humaine et sociologie* (Paris: Institute d'Ethnologie, 1948).

5. See James R. Chamberlain, "Eco-Spatial History: A Nomad Myth from the Anna-mites and Its Relevance for Biodiversity Conservation," in *Landscapes of Diversity: Indige-nous Knowledge, Sustainable Livelihoods and Resource Governance in Montane Mainland Southeast Asia*, ed. Xu Jian Chǔ and Stephen Mikesell (with assistance of Timmi Tillmann and Wan Shum), (Kunming: Center for Biodiversity and Indigenous Knowledge, Yunnan Science and Technology Press, 2003).

6. Diffloth, "Vietnamese."

7. James R. Chamberlain, Charles Alton, Latsamay Silavong, and Bounlieng Philavong, *Socio-Economic and Cultural Survey: Nam Theun 2 Project Area* (Vientiane: CARE Interna-tional, 1996).

8. Charles Higham, "Hunter-Gatherers in Southeast Asia: From Prehistory to the Present," *Human Biology* 85, no. 1 (2013): 36.

9. See James R. Chamberlain, "The Origin of the Sek: Implications for Tai and Viet-namese History," *Journal of the Siam Society* 86 (1998).

10. Thongsa Sayavongkhamdy and Viengkeo Souksavatdy, "Excavations of Cave Sites at Pha Phen," in *Recherches Nouvelles sur le Laos*, ed. Yves Goudineau and Michel Lorrillard (Paris and Vientiane: École Français d'Extrème-Orient, 2008), 25–35.

11. Sayavongkhamdy and Souksavatdy, "Excavations of Cave Sites at Pha Phen," 26.

12. Colani apparently visited caves along the base of the Ak escarpment in Gnomma-rath, but I do not have the reference (Thongsa Sayavongkhamdy, personal communication).

13. Technically, Be-Tai and Kam-Sui are subfamilies belonging to the Kam-Tai family, one of three families that comprise the Kra-Dai stock together with Kra and Hlai (see

James R. Chamberlain, "Kra-Dai and the Proto-History of Southern China and Vietnam." *Journal of the Siam Society* 104 [2016]). Be and Hlai are both from Hainan Island but are not closely related.

14. The ethnonym Bo (/bɔɔ B3/) needs some explanation, as it has such a large population on the plateau. To begin with, it is not a homogenous term, and neither is it a very old one, apparently. Apart from on the Nakai Plateau, Bo are found along the Hinboun River and in at least one large village in Khamkeut near Napè. There are no people with this name that were transported to Siam in the nineteenth century. They appear on the 1931 Khammouane census (Pierre Grossin, *Notes sur l'histoire de la province de Cammon* [Hanoi: Imprimerie d'Extrême Orient, 1933], 61) separated into Thai Bo (pop. 146) and Kha Bo (pop. 180). The word "bo" is translated as "a mine" ostensibly in reference to the mining of salt on the plateau or to the mining of tin for the French in Phontiu in Hinboun District, the assumption being that these families were lumped together by outsiders under this name, which eventually became the accepted ethnic term, because they were engaged in these activities. The Bo at Sop Phène say they were originally Kha Maka, that is, Vietic from Ban Maka or Kri (older people still speak Kri), whereas the Bo of Sop Ma identify with the Bo of Hinboun, although earlier in 1996 they had also associated themselves with the Vietic Maleng group at Sangkhone on the Nam Sot.

15. Chamberlain, "Kra-Dai."

16. Grossin, *Notes sur l'histoire*, 61.

17. Na Vang villager, personal communication, interview, February 1996.

18. See Chamberlain, "Kra-Dai."

19. Beginning in the seventeenth century this river marked the boundary between north and south Vietnam. The French moved the border in 1954 slightly south of the seventeenth parallel.

20. Mène archaic features survive only as a substrat, though one that is readily apparent (James R. Chamberlain, "Mène: A Tai Dialect Originally Spoken in Nghệ An (Nghê Tinh), Việtnam—Preliminary Linguistic Observations and Historical Implications," *Journal of the Siam Society* 79 [1991]).

21. Frank Proschan, personal communication.

22. Chamberlain, "Kra-Dai"; Chamberlain, "Mène." Yooy today are found in Gnommarath along the foot of the Ak escarpment and in the village of Khon Kène on the Nakai Plateau, where they intermarried with Phong (phòòng?) (André Fraisse, "Les sauvages de Nam-Om," *BSEI* 24, no. 1 [1949]: 27–36). They are also known from Sakol Nakhon in Thailand, where they were taken by Siamese military in the nineteenth century. More importantly, they are cited by Charles Robequain (*Le Thanh Hoá* [Paris: G. Van Oest, 1929], 110), as having once resided in western Thanh Hóa close to the Nghệ An border.

23. Grossin, *Notes sur l'histoire*, 10ff.

24. John K. Whitmore, "Colliding Peoples: Tai/Viet Interactions in the Fourteenth and Fifteenth Centuries," paper presented at the Association for Asian Studies, San Diego, 2000, 7.

Space does not permit discussion of the role the Cham people in events of the twelfth century in Nghệ An and earlier further south. Interested readers may consult Vickery, "Champa Revised" (working paper no. 39, Asia Research Institute, Singapore, 2005). The Austronesian Cham arrived in the early centuries BC, possibly from Borneo, but as Vickery suggests, there is some problem with identity and Lin-yi may in fact have belonged to the Katuic branch of Mon-Khmer.

25. Whitmore, "Colliding Peoples."

26. Frank Proschan, "Cheuang in Kmhmu Folklore, History, and Memory," in *Tamnan kiaw kap Thaaw Hung Thaaw Cheuang: Miti thaang pravatisat lae Wattanatham*, ed. Sumitr Pitiphat (Bangkok: Thammasat University and the Thai Studies Council, 1996).

27. Proschan, "Cheuang," 196ff.

28. Note that until 1975 Khammouane Province included the district of Khamkeut, which has been reassigned to Borikhamxay under the current regime.

29. Paul Macey, "Etude ethnographique et linguistique sur les Kles Ks—Pong-Houk, dits: Thai Pong (Province du Cammon-Laos)." *Revue Indochinois* 5 (1906): 1411–24.

30. Grossin, *Notes sur l'histoire*, 62; James R. Chamberlain, "Vietic Speakers and Their Remnants in Khamkeut District (Old Khammouane)," in *Festschrift for Prof. Udom Warotamasikkhadit* (forthcoming).

31. Chamberlain et al., *Socio-Economic*; Charles Alton and Latsamay Sylavong, *Socio-Economic Technical Report* (Vientiane: IUCN, 1997); James R. Chamberlain, Charles Alton, Latsamay Sylavong, and Panh Phomsombath, *Cultural Diversity and Socio-Economic Development in the Context of Conservation: Environmental and Social Action Plan for Nakai-Nam Theun Catchment and Corridor Areas* (Vientiane: IUCN, 1997).

32. N. J. Enfield and Gérard Diffloth, "Phonology and Sketch Grammar of Kri, a Vietic Language of Laos," *Cahiers de linguistique—Asie oriental* 38, no. 1 (2009).

33. Michel Ferlus, "Sur l'origine des langues Việt-Mường," *MKS* 18–19 (1992): 52–59; Michel Ferlus, "Langues et peuples viet-muong," *MKS* 26 (1996): 7–28; Michel Ferlus, "Le maleng brô et le vietnamien," *MKS* 27 (1997): 55–66; Diffloth, "Vietnamese."

34. Chamberlain, "Eco-Spatial History"; James R. Chamberlain, *Nature and Culture in the Nakai-Nam Theun Conservation Area* (Vientiane: privately published, 1997).

35. Chamberlain et al., *Cultural Diversity*.

36. Daniel Gibson, back-to-office report, 2004, World Bank.

37. Robert Mertz, back-to-office report, April 2004, World Bank.

38. B. H. Liddell Hart, *Strategy* (London: Faber and Faber, 1954).

5

Broken Pillars

The Failure of the Nakai Plateau Livelihood Resettlement Program

G LENN H UNT,

M ARIKA S AMUELSSON, and

S ATOMI H IGASHI

NT2 proponents and the experts are under-estimating the diffi-culties that will be encountered by the ethnic communities now living on the Nakai Plateau. . . . [T]he [resettlement site] condi-tions are very different from those of [their] existing communities, in particular the quality of soils which is not suitable for agricul-ture and the lack of forests. Eventually many families resettled by the Nam Theun 2 project will abandon the resettlement sites. . . . So I think it will be very difficult for them. . . .They will be in a miserable situation.

Satoru Matsumoto,

community development worker on the Nakai Plateau

from 1992 to 1996 in 2004, shortly before project approval

I'm very worried about what will happen after the hand-over, and if they [the government] will continue to take care of us. Once the hand-over is done, we are allowed to sell our houses and lands, which I think many will do. There is not much for us here, no good soil to grow rice. But we cannot sell it now, so we must wait. Afterward, maybe people will move to the towns, but I think many will return to the forest. This place will be deserted.

resettled villager, Nakai Plateau, 2014

Prior to Nam Theun 2 (NT2), Indigenous villagers, representing many different ethnic groups with widely different cultural beliefs, practices, histories, and languages and all living on the Nakai Plateau, practiced diverse livelihoods, including paddy and upland rice cultivation, the raising of buffalo and other livestock, the collecting of non-timber forest products, riverbank gardening, and fishing on the Nam Theun River.[1] Poverty rates varied widely; those in villages farther from the Nakai District capital were generally poorer.

The flooding of 45,000 ha of land across the plateau to create the reservoir for NT2 resulted in the loss of the lands of approximately sixty-three hundred Indigenous Peoples from over eleven hundred households in seventeen villages and the relocation of sixteen of these villages (see figures 5.1 and 5.2). For those moved from their traditional lands to make way for the dam and reservoir, schedule 4, part 1, clause 3.1 of the concession agreement obliged the NT2 Power Company (NTPC) to restore resettlers' livelihoods in order to "ensure that Resettlers have their income earning capacity enhanced and achieve the Household Income Target, with adequate support being provided by the parties during the Resettlement Implementation Period" and to "materially improve Resettler livelihoods on a sustainable basis."[2] As part of its contractual obligation, NTPC produced a Social Development Plan before project initiation that proposed five livelihood "pillars" for resettlers: forestry, fisheries, agriculture, livestock, and off-farm activities.

Under the agreement, these pillars were to be implemented during a resettlement implementation period estimated to last nine years from project initiation in 2005, after which the project was contractually mandated to restore livelihoods to at least where they were preproject. However, in late 2015, the International Environmental and Social Panel of Experts (PoE), contractually mandated to make an independent assessment, determined that livelihoods had not been sustainably restored and that the resettlement implementation period would have to be extended for at least two more years. The lenders' technical advisory group (LTA), meant to advise international financial institutions (IFIs) on the project, reached a similar conclusion. The following sections examine each of the livelihood pillars and the reasons that restoring resettler livelihoods has proved much more challenging than envisioned by NT2 proponents.

While this chapter focuses on livelihood restoration, note that this is not the only form of assistance that has been provided to resettlers. NTPC has built significant infrastructure—roads, clinics, new housing, and schools—and has also provided support for education and health care. Those projects

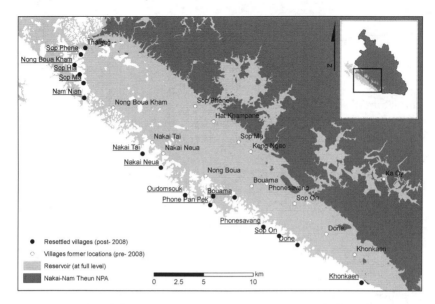

Figure 5.1. Locations of villages prior to inundation of the Nakai Plateau and of the new resettlement villages.

Figure 5.2. One of the NT2 resettlement villages, along the shore of the new reservoir in February 2012. Photo by William Robichaud.

Figure 5.3. World Bank online graphic representing the benefits of the NT2 project.

are relatively easy to quantify and have been well documented by NTPC and the IFIs in various reports and promotional materials (see figure 5.3) and therefore are not covered here.

In contrast, sustainable restoration of resettler livelihoods, ultimately much more challenging and important, has been ignored or downplayed in NTPC and World Bank communications. While NTPC and the government of the Lao PDR (GoL) have a plethora of information from various studies and reports on many aspects of environmental conditions and livelihood pillars, none have been made public. Thus, this chapter mainly relies on the biannual reports of the PoE, which provide an important project history, and on other limited independent research and field work that has been conducted in the resettled communities, including by this chapter's authors.

The Forestry Pillar

The most important component of the strategy to restore and enhance the livelihoods of the resettled communities, envisioned to provide a third of their income, was community forestry.

What Is Community Forestry?

Community forestry is a model in which local communities assume a significant role in the management and land use decisions of a designated forest area. Community forestry can take many forms. It can refer, for example, to groups of smallholders growing trees on individually titled land, cooperatives comanaging forests leased to them by the state, and even single communities managing large areas of natural forest under ancestral tenure as common property. There are three factors to consider in assessing the extent to which a community forestry effort is driven by local interests. First is the extent of rights locals have over variable forest products and services. Next is the extent to which locals drive decision making about forest management objectives and operations. Finally is how and to whom benefits of forest management (monetary and otherwise) accrue. Generally, the more rights and decision-making power local actors have, the more benefits are likely to end up in community hands and the greater the incentive will be for locals to invest in sustainable forestry and conservation. The model promoted in the NT2 context was based on experiences in the Maya Biosphere Reserve in northern Guatemala, where nine communities manage relatively large areas of natural forest (12,000–80,000 ha) under twenty-five-year concession contracts with the state for timber and a range of nontimber forest products. Over time, communities have established their own enterprises, which provide many employment opportunities in this remote region while driving broader economic development in participating communities. Fifteen years later, deforestation rates in community forests have dropped to virtually zero, while in nearby strict protection units, deforestation rates outstrip regional averages, which are some of the highest in the world.

Following the model set up by the World Bank in the 1990s in Laos through a forestry management and conservation project, resettled communities were organized into a village forestry association (VFA). They were to operate a full-fledged forest enterprise that would log within their allotted concession, process the wood, and then sell the lumber, generating sustainable income for the resettlers. A management plan was approved by the GoL and a 25,000 ha concession was awarded. The concession agreement stated that the area was to be "preserved for sole use of villager forestry development" for seventy years. NTPC agreed to purchase a sawmill for the community, and the GoL committed to closing private sawmills on the Nakai Plateau.

Well before the plans for the VFA were finalized in 2000, the World Bank's multiprovince forestry management and conservation project, on which the VFA concept was modeled, had already fallen apart. Once it was time to share benefits with villagers, officials simply refused to comply, forcing an early end to the project. A related but smaller-scale NGO project, supported by the World Wildlife Fund (WWF) in Sekong Province, likewise collapsed in 2005 because officials would not allow villagers to manage the forests.[3] By 2005, at the time of NT2 approval, the VFA model had been discredited within GoL and had no real political support. At the national level, the World Bank and other international donors had already abandoned attempts at instituting it and had accepted a "production forestry" approach instead in which the Lao state retained much more control—and a much higher percentage of logging revenues.[4]

The Origins of Failure

Around the year 2000, one of the coeditors of this book walked into a Vientiane restaurant and saw a Western acquaintance who worked for NTPC on the development of plans for social and environmental mitigation of NT2. He was visibly shaken and despondent. He said he had just come from a meeting at the NTPC office, where NTPC's liaison to GoL, a senior Lao functionary with close government ties, had heatedly declared that there was no way villagers in Laos, including villagers resettled due to NT2, would be allowed to manage timber. The most important of the five livelihood pillars for resettled villagers had just been knocked out, long before the project started. Yet the promotion of village forestry would continue for years—as either a charade or a wishful swim against the current, but destined for failure either way.

What followed was predictable. As early as October 2006, barely a year following project approval, the PoE was already reporting that "the forestry aspects of the project are not proceeding well."[5] Subsequent reports detail a growing litany of failures. These problems were originally described as short-term issues with planning and local capacities. In a 2009 report, while acknowledging that poaching was a problem, the PoE largely blamed the sector's lack of progress on planning that was "simply too ambitious to be achieved by a group of villagers with little managerial or commercial background in an enterprise like this."[6]

However, more fundamental barriers were at play. Many of these revolved around the unwillingness of GoL authorities to follow through with actions needed to give the sector a chance of success. By 2010 the PoE was referring to the "always troubled village forestry sector" and noted "villagers are angry about lack of enforcement of regulations supposedly protecting the timber set aside as a mainstay of their livelihood program and incomes."[7] The PoE struggled for years to close private sawmills on the plateau operated by the influential Phonesack Group and Bolisat Phattana Khet Phoudoi (Mountainous Areas Development Company; commonly known by its Lao acronym, BPKP), as well as illegal furniture and charcoal businesses. During each visit the PoE would be given assurances that the problems would soon be solved. But on its next visit the illegal enterprises would still be operating. By late 2010 the PoE found that per family revenue for the VFA was only half of what had been envisioned.[8]

One overriding fact could not be ignored: those tasked by GoL to implement the program were simply not on board with the concept of allowing villagers to control or significantly benefit from forestry activities. Evidence continued to mount. For instance, excessive taxation of the VFA seriously cut into revenues that were expected to go to the villagers. Officials also appeared unwilling or unable to control increased timber poaching by outsiders on the VFA forests.

In an effort to improve management, proposals were made as early as 2010 to convert the VFA, widely seen as dominated by a few influential local families and officials, into a limited liability corporation. Villagers would still supposedly earn dividends, but the management would be professionalized through a private partnership. However, the process took a couple of years, during which the situation continued to deteriorate.

In 2011, an attempt was made to bring in an international forestry NGO to assist. A representative of one group quickly determined that the conditions for a successful village forestry initiative did not exist. He later recalled,

> The VFA was not a community forestry operation and the political support necessary for it to become so was lacking. In reality, the body was a "Village Forestry Association" in name only. For all practical purposes, it was a government-run operation. Villagers were not involved in decision making about management or enterprise operations. Village heads invited to join in mission meetings were clearly uninformed about the workings of the VFA. Although the mission was not given the opportunity to interview a random sample of villagers, interviews with others indicated that the VFA was not seen as a body that is owned by villagers—indeed, forest areas in the concession were seen by resettlers as "owned by the VFA," which was perceived to be government-run, for the benefit of government officials and connected elites in the villages. . . . Even as a quasi-government operation, competing government interests were undermining the VFA, notably through excessive taxes. In 2010, the year before my visit, in a form of legalized corruption, the VFA paid some 42 percent of its income to taxes . . . this was only one of a number of strategies that was used by the GoL to undermine the VFA as it stood. The idea that it should evolve into a community-owned enterprise apparently was anathema.[9]

Not only were conditions absent for successful forestry initiatives such as those in Mesoamerica but there also seemed to be no prospects for improvement.

A formidable mix of social, ecological, economic, and policy obstacles stood in the way—the challenges of bringing people from different ethnic groups together to operate one enterprise, the low priority given villager-based forestry by project and local officials, the increasingly degraded status of the concession forest resource and, perhaps most importantly, the whole "community forestry" concept had been initiated from the outside rather by local communities. The same NGO representative noted,

> Even if there had been political will and sufficient finances available, building a successful community forestry enterprise along the lines initially envisioned would have been tremendously challenging, if not impossible. There was little enthusiasm from the IFIs and NTPC to take the steps necessary to make such assistance possible. There would have needed to be a major change of position by the Bank, the appearance of significant financing, and strong indication from all relevant GoL institutions that they were committed to the vision of building a genuine community forestry enterprise on the Plateau.[10]

The criticisms made in subsequent PoE reports are even stronger and reflect rapidly increasing disillusionment. In mid-2011 the panel wrote, "It cannot be said that the forestry sector of the project is in a sound position": "The wholesale and uncontrolled plunder of the reservoir's and the watershed's rosewood resources by anyone with a chainsaw, a boat or even a motorcycle does not foster a sustainable management or ethic and it is clear that a high proportion of Nakai resettlers is heavily engaged in the pillage."[11] The PoE avoided blaming the villagers for this situation and instead linked the lack of forest management and a functioning VFA as the reason villagers were cutting down valuable hardwoods, such as rosewood, in the protected area. The PoE noted that due to heavy taxation and subsequent low dividends from the VFA, villagers felt no sense of ownership of the forests.

In early 2012, the PoE found VFA conversion to a limited liability corporation still dragging on and expressed surprise at finding the private Phonesack Group sawmill still in operation long after it was to be shut down.[12] It again voiced concerns about the overtaxation of the VFA, stating, "The VFA was set up to build up the incomes of several thousand of villagers who had lost their land and houses through inundation, not to fill the GoL's coffers."[13] Its report also noted that NTPC had engaged a lawyer to see if the tax level was "excessive in the Lao context."

A year later the PoE again expressed frustration at how village forestry, meant to be the "flagship" of the entire resettlement program, had turned out: "To understate, the outcome has been disappointing, not least to the resettlers themselves."[14] The February 2013 report details numerous problems with the initiative: conflicts of interest, foot dragging, excessive taxation (termed "inequitable"), misgovernance, and lack of transparency. The PoE also pointed out the irony in the fact that just as the limited liability corporation had finally been secured along with a potential contract, there were "now serious doubts about the volume and quality of the remaining resource."[15] It noted the VFA's projection that if cutting continued at the current rate the resource would be exhausted by mid-2015. While private sawmills were finally closed, this may have been because they were running out of timber to process.

PoE visits in 2014 found little progress in resolving these issues—in some ways the situation had further deteriorated. A field report stated, "Village forestry is unquestionably the least successful of the five livelihood pillars. . . . Originally planned to provide a third of the resettlers' income, it has not come close to achieving that goal."[16] While the PoE pointed to some positive elements—an agroforestry initiative and the possibility that GoL would soon refund some of the excessive taxes previously collected, it acknowledged that the sustainability promised by the concession agreement was unlikely.[17] It also noted that village forestry lands, in violation of the agreement, were increasingly converted to other uses. After a late 2014 visit, the PoE reported that "no objective observer would contend that holding the NT2 forestry pillar upright is a sustainable exercise at the moment."[18] No dividends whatsoever, it stated, had been paid to villagers for more than two and a half years (since April 2012). It observed that the failure of the forestry pillar would be a major consideration when it decided whether or not to extend the resettlement implementation period beyond 2015. The December 2014 report distributes blame among government officials, the IFIs, and NTPC, noting: "GoL agencies that have been key players in the NT2 village forestry experiment . . . cannot escape a degree of responsibility," but "neither have the IFIs always fully pulled their weight."[19] While it gives credit to NTPC for its initial work, the PoE points to subsequent management and planning as "inadequate in the Lao context" and notes that NTPC's withdrawal, following the expenditure of allocated funds, was counterproductive.[20] It did not completely give up hope for the sector, but progress would only be possible if the GoL, the IFIs, and NTPC pulled together, which would presumably require new funding, energy, and commitment.

The PoE visited again in late 2015. Its report makes clear that few of the recommendations in previous reports had been followed and that the sector was still a failure. The report references the state of this sector as a major reason to extend the resettlement implementation period beyond 2015, explaining, "one reality is that the resettlers have been forced by this sectoral failure to seek elsewhere the income needed and have resorted to illegal or unwise practices to do so."[21] The report notes that sustainability in the forestry sector was "a long way off" and would require fundamental changes, most importantly the "high level political support" of the GoL—deemed unlikely any time soon.

The Fisheries Pillar

The Social Development Plan, also known as the resettlement plan, envisioned creation of a reservoir fisheries industry run by resettled villagers for the benefit of their own communities. The PoE has consistently held fisheries to be the best performing of all the livelihood pillars.[22] In 2010 it reported the total harvest by all resettlers to be 1,479 tons per year, just below the 1,575 tons per year catch the 2005 plan had predicted as the most likely harvest under a medium-scale catch scenario. Fisheries production has followed the typical reservoir scenario of extremely high numbers of fish after the dam was closed followed by a decrease and then stabilization of catch. The PoE reports that fisheries have been stable the last few years, and officials close to the project note that household catch averages 3–4 kilograms per household per day, of which 75 percent is sold, 20 percent consumed, and 5 percent preserved or processed.

In spite of this relative success, the fisheries pillar has been less productive than it could have been for resettlers due to several factors, some of which have also raised concerns about sustaining the fisheries. Reservoir fisheries are inherently fragile and need proactive care and management. The 2005 plan lists measures that must be implemented to mitigate risks that threaten sustainable fisheries: ensure water quality through pre-impoundment biomass clearance, guarantee exclusive fishing rights for resettled communities, and prevent introduction of exotic species. Despite the explicit warnings in the plan, NTPC and some GoL officials have been unable or unwilling to implement the policies and regulations needed to address these concerns.

Water Quality and Biomass Clearance

Healthy fisheries require good water quality. A common problem with flooding a large reservoir is that it ultimately inundates a large amount of biomass such as trees and shrubs, which then decay once the reservoir is filled, which leads to a decrease in water quality. Decomposition removes oxygen from the water, and in extreme cases results in anoxic conditions that cannot support aquatic life. In NT2 there was substantial biomass in the impoundment area. In the plan, NTPC noted that "water quality after inundation will depend largely on removal of vegetation. . . . From a fisheries management point of view it is vital to minimize, from the beginning, the risk of high level biodegradation and rapid deterioration of water quality, which will invariably have negative consequences for fish production and thus the livelihoods of reservoir fishers."[23]

The resettlement plan states that in order to ensure good water quality in the first few years after impoundment, biomass "must be removed as much as possible, particularly in those reservoir areas that will be permanently inundated during reservoir operation."[24] Yet this was only partially carried out. Throughout early PoE reports there was clear emphasis on the need to proceed with extensive biomass clearance. This was consistently delayed. Shortly before impoundment, the PoE once again demanded clearance of the biomass, recommending that "most of the additional 1,500 ha of biomass should be removed from the permanently inundated area."[25] The PoE went on to add that the Ministry of Finance

> states that because of time and financial constraints, their contractor is planning at this point to clear 1,500 ha out of 3,000 ha of biomass identified for clearance. *PoE considers this insufficient and gathers that there are resources available to clear a wider area.* Removal after impoundment will be more expensive and in some areas impossible and it appears that there will be time to achieve the additional clearance since many of the areas for clearance are in higher sections of the inundated area.[26]

In April 2008, as impoundment began, the remaining 1,500 ha of biomass had still not been cleared, leading the PoE to request that an "agreement be reached as a matter of urgency between the GoL and the NTPC on the remaining strategic areas of biomass for clearance and the contractor be engaged to undertake this work immediately since it will only be possible to do it up to around mid-May."[27]

Contrary to the PoE recommendations and those of NTPC as articulated in the Social Action Plan, the agency decided not to require clearance of the remaining biomass, which means that substantial leftover biomass in the reservoir will continue to degrade over the next decade or longer. According to a source long close to the project, at the time biomass clearance was pending, NTPC staff and Électricité de France (EdF), the largest NTPC shareholder, provided misleading information to the GoL's Science, Technology and Environment Agency in order to avoid the time and expense of full clearance. They reportedly stated that 70 percent of the biomass was underground, as in boreal or northern climates, with only 30 percent above ground and thus wasn't worth clearing.[28] Scientists working for the project dispute this claim pointing out that in tropical climates 60–70 percent of the forest is above ground.[29]

Whatever the reason for nonclearance, insufficient biomass clearance has had a direct impact on water quality. An environmental scientist on the project reports that due to the lack of full clearance,

> the reservoir continues to have a strong thermocline through most of the year. Thus most of the reservoir remains anoxic and only the upper 5–7m of depth is oxygenated. As a result, fish life and aquatic organisms are only available in the upper layer of good quality water. . . . There is some small improvement each year in water quality, but the majority of the reservoir volume remains devoid of oxygen, and thus devoid of fish life.[30]

A thermocline is generally a surface layer of warm water stratified above a layer of cooler water. The cooler water is anoxic, with little or no dissolved oxygen. Stratification is overturned during the cool dry season because the surface water becomes cooler than the deep water and moves to the bottom. This mixing can result in large fish kills as the anoxic water comes to the surface. A few minor fish kills of a few dozen have been recorded by NTPC scientists monitoring the reservoir fisheries, while Mekong Watch has reported villagers describing much larger fish kills, possibly caused by the mixing of the thermocline.[31]

NTPC undertakes monitoring at nine permanent locations in the reservoir to measure water quality under a variety of environmental conditions. The data are not publicly available, although recently NTPC/ Électricité de Lao (EdL) have published papers on reservoir water quality.[32]

Vincent Chanudet and his coauthors offer a picture of the scale of anoxic conditions from the lack of biomass clearance in the western portion of reservoir.[33] At a monitoring station at the NT2 dam wall, where there is a high concentration of decomposing vegetation, anoxic levels have remained consistently high, although there has been gradual improvement over time. In contrast, at the intake channel at the opposite end of the reservoir, which was more open before inundation, there has been significant improvement in dissolved oxygen. The data clearly show that biomass removal has a significant impact on water quality in the reservoir. Without data from other monitoring stations, we can only speculate as to the extent of anoxic conditions prevalent where biomass removal has not been undertaken. While the reservoir presently remains suitable for fisheries, it is likely it could have been far more productive had the recommendations of the Social Development Plan and the PoE prevailed over the consideration of short-term economic gains for project developers and contractors.

Enforcement of Exclusive Fishing Rights

The resettlement plan noted that providing those resettlers and other villagers who fished inundated stretches of the Nam Theun prior to the project with exclusive access to reservoir fisheries is an important tool to "avoid (i) over-fishing, (ii) fisheries conflicts, and (iii) unsustainable fishing practices."[34] It proposed limiting the number of fishers through a licensing system and hoped to achieve a high fish yield that would be sustained through a comanaged fisheries program.[35]

Excluding outsiders from fishing is not easy; it requires significant ongoing commitment. NTPC observed that the concept is against customs in Laos, so the GoL would have to play a key role in restricting outside access to reservoir fisheries.[36] Exclusive right to fisheries also contradicts the Forest Law, which states that "all lake and riverine systems are subject to unrestricted public access."[37] However, the legal basis of exclusive rights to resettled communities is contained in Prime Minister's Decree 24, which was issued following approval of the project and gave resettled communities exclusive fishing rights for ten years after dam closure. Following the overall failure of the other pillars to restore resettler livelihoods and in light of the present dependency of resettlers on fisheries, the PoE reports that in 2015 the GoL extended the legal basis for resettlers' exclusive rights by another ten years, a total of twenty years post-dam closure.[38]

Nonetheless, illegal fishing by outsiders continues to be a major threat. Since dam closure, almost every PoE report has noted with frustration the ongoing access outsiders have to the reservoir. Immediately following impoundment there were problems with two hundred contractors from the logging operation Phonesack Group, stationed in Oudomsouk, who were fishing from their base camp on twenty-five moored barges.[39] As the Nakai reservoir has since become well known for its fisheries, there have been numerous reports of outsiders moving to the area. The December 2015 PoE report again notes ongoing illegal fishing and fish marketing that by outsiders from neighboring provinces were reportedly engaging in in the Khamkeut portion of the reservoir.[40]

The resettlement plan warned that the "community feeling of ownership of the resources is crucial to the success of the fisheries management."[41] However, years after the creation of the Nakai reservoir, outsiders continue to fish illegally. Without strong enforcement of resettler rights, sustainability of reservoir fisheries is seriously threatened. In the PoE's words, there is "an urgent need to substantially improve the resettler fishers' feeling of ownership of the fish resource, and with it, recognition of their self-interested responsibility to watch for and report or apprehend those conducting illegal activities that undermine their livelihood."[42]

Neither the PoE nor other NTPC or World Bank reports have ever adequately explained the difficulty of enforcing fishing regulations on the reservoir. Was it an inherently impossible task, or did NTPC or GoL officials not take it seriously, or was it perhaps that some of those charged with implementation were more beholden to outside interests than to the well being of the resettlers?

Deliberate Introduction of Exotic Species

According to NTCP's 2005 plan,

There are at least 31 fish species presently living in the Nam Theun that are likely to establish populations in the Nakai Reservoir. This is a sufficient basis for a healthy fishery and there is no reason to introduce exotic fish species. The potential benefit for such an introduction is by far outweighed by the potential threat of diseases and decline in biodiversity.

This conclusion is based on Mourice Kottelat's comprehensive taxonomic survey of the Nam Theun/Nam Kading that he carried out in the 2002 dry season, before the dam was built, which the author then correlated with species recorded in the Nam Ngum and reservoirs in northeastern Thailand. As implementing agencies of the GoL commonly promote introduction of invasive species into native waterways, NTPC recommended that the District Agriculture and Forestry Office staff be trained and that awareness campaigns among the resettlement villages" be launched as "appropriate measures to control the introduction of exotic fish species in the first years."[43]

It is unclear whether the training took place. However, what is clear is that invasive species appeared in the reservoir within the first year. One of the coauthors of this chapter went to the site in August 2008, immediately after initial impoundment, and spoke with fishermen around the Thalang Bridge, who reported catching a variety of native species. Within a year, field reports from the reservoir were emphasizing the extent of introduced exotic species. In field notes from a 2009 visit, Mekong Watch reported a woman in Sop Hia village stating that she was catching mostly *pa nin* (tilapia) and *pa nai* (common carp or *Carpio carpio*) and that there was a lot of each.[44] Both are considered among the top one hundred worst invasive species in the world by IUCN.[45] In addition, NTPC researchers themselves have acknowledged other potential invasives such as the Siamese glassfish (*Parambassis siamensis*) (likely native to the Mekong but not previously found in the Nam Theun) that "will definitely influence the future evolution of the fish population in the NT2 Reservoir."[46] It is not clear how these exotic species will influence the reservoir fisheries and surrounding ecosystems, but there is concern that such species pose a threat to biodiversity and the environmental well being of the reservoir itself.[47]

The fisheries pillar is recognized as the only relatively successful livelihood pillar to date. However, the ongoing impacts of the expedient decision to avoid biomass clearance, combined with continued illegal fishing operations, have limited the fisheries pillar's potential to contribute to villager livelihoods. There also remain serious concerns, even among project-based scientists, over the introduction of exotic species into the reservoir. Combined with illegal fishing, this raises concern over whether reservoir fisheries will be able to provide sustainable livelihoods for members of resettled communities in the long term.

Finally, while a ten-year extension of the exclusive fishing rights granted to the resettlers is to be commended, questions as to what will happen once the reservoir is opened to full access abound. As NTPC has itself acknowledged, there are major challenges in other Lao reservoirs where fisheries have become overwhelmed through overfishing.[48]

The Agricultural Pillar

Of sixteen resettled communities, four—Ban Nakai Tai, Ban Nakai Neua, Ban Done, and Ban Khone Kaen—had relatively large areas of productive wet season paddy fields adjacent to the Theun River before those lands were inundated. They alone had a combined total of 80 ha of wet season fields, while 2 to 3 ha of paddy per village were recorded in four other villages. In the remaining eight villages the predominant rice production method was traditional rotational shifting cultivation of mainly upland glutinous rice (the main staple) and other vegetables.[49]

Since before the creation of the reservoir almost all households were engaged in some form of agricultural production, the agricultural pillar was meant to be a key component of the new livelihoods of resettled communities. The plan was to bring predominantly subsistence farmers into a cash economy where they would sell at least some produce for the purchase of rice and other necessities. Each household was to obtain 0.66 ha of land, including 0.5 ha of farmland and 0.16 ha of irrigated terraced rice paddy.

Early Challenges — Marketing and Pilot Villages

Once NT2 received approval, the project was supposed to quickly initiate support for communities in agricultural production in order to take advantage of the ready market for produce that the engineering and construction teams that would be on the plateau and in the nearby town of Gnommalath would create.[50] However, delays led to villagers not being resettled until just before impoundment in 2008, when the majority of construction work had already been completed and personnel had left.

In 2003, before the project was finally approved, NTPC established a pilot resettlement village called Nong Boua. An organic fertilizer factory and tree nursery were established, one of whose aims was "to demonstrate to other villages how a new village might look and function."[51] NTPC and GoL staff often took visitors to the pilot village for study tours, and at the 2008 annual stakeholders forum one chapter coauthor and other participants in the meeting were shown the "success" of the agricultural developments in the pilot village.

However, when another coauthor interviewed villagers in Nong Boua in April 2008, villagers indicated that while not all households had someone employed at a given time, all households took turns having at least one person working as paid staff for NTPC on the pilot farm or the fertilizer projects run by the company, so that all families could gain income from wages, which made the pilot village appear more sustainable than was actually the case.[52] Once NTPC no longer needed to hire resettlers in this capacity, the prosperity of the pilot village plummeted. Ironically, given its status as demonstration model, it is now considered the poorest of the resettled villages.[53]

Even before project approval, the agricultural agenda of the NTCP's plan had met with skepticism by outside observers. An independent review of the resettlement plan, commissioned by International Rivers Network (IRN) in early 2005, emphasized a number of concerns, including the poor quality of land allocated to resettlers. The report warned of high potential for a collapse in the agricultural sector that would necessitate a switch to traditional shifting cultivation methods. These methods would largely fail because the resettlers didn't have enough land to leave land fallow for as long as was required.[54] The following sections describe aspects of what subsequently occurred within the agricultural pillar and suggest that these concerns were justified.

Poor Quality of Land Allocated for Agriculture

During advance project consultations, villagers slated to be moved were asked if they wanted stay on the plateau or move down the escarpment toward Gnommalath. They chose to stay as close as possible to their ancestral lands on the plateau. This presented a challenge to project planners—how to inundate 430 square kilometers of the plateau (more than 40 percent of its area) and then find unoccupied places on the remainder for more than six thousand people to live and engage in "sustainable livelihoods." There was a reason that available sites had not been previously settled—they are unsuited to the types of agricultural production envisioned. NTPC itself noted the poor conditions in its plan: "erosion susceptibility, high acidity, poor nutrient content and high absorption of P [phosphorus]."[55] Soil quality was so poor that a 2004 version of the plan stated that projected modeling of dry season paddy "may prove to be an optimistic assumption" due to the limited area of soils with high clay content that are necessary to stop percolation losses in paddies.[56] This was later confirmed by a GoL official at the third annual NT2 stakeholders' workshop in Thakhek in October 2008 who stated that "paddy production (in Nakai) has no future."[57]

Rather than simply recognizing the basic unsuitability of the area for agriculture, planners promoted complex, and what would eventually be recognized as completely unrealistic, development solutions. Earlier versions of the plan highlighted the need to "maintain extensive additions of lime, organic and inorganic fertilizer, and rock phosphate to improve soil quality" in order to facilitate respectable yields. Just how much would be required was tucked away in obscure footnotes and annexes of the document. The NTPC estimated that in the first three years, 2–3 tons/ha of organic fertilizer would need to be applied. Subsequently, every resettled household would have to continue to add a *minimum* of 500 kilograms of organic fertilizer to their 0.5 ha agricultural field annually and possibly up to twice that amount.[58] The NTPC recognized that in the long run this fertilizer would need to come from livestock, making the success of the livestock pillar essential to the success of aspects of the agricultural pillar. The NTPC noted that at the beginning, the highly acidic soils would require two to five tons of lime per ha to neutralize aluminum, particularly during the first three years.[59] Finally NTPC noted the need for inorganic fertilizer to be applied at a rate of 50 kilograms/ha per year for irrigated paddy, maize, and vegetable crops, while acknowledging that resettlers would be unable to purchase such this fertilizer on their own once the project ceased its support after three years.[60]

Figure 5.4. Resettled villager preparing shifting cultivation field on marginal lands allocated by NTPC, in April 2008. Photo by Satomi Higashi.

The plan to provide high agricultural inputs to well over one thousand households quickly proved unrealistic, something the project developers likely knew but which was not noted in PoE and NTPC reports. Although villagers reported receiving fertilizer for three years, much of their lands were steeply sloped and unsuited to permanent cultivation, let alone paddy rice production. Once moved, resettlers immediately began preparing upland shifting cultivation fields in an attempt to secure a rice crop, their staple. The project provided supplemental rice for the first three years following resettlement. But once this support ended, problems with rice sufficiency began to emerge. By November 2010, the PoE was warning of increasing debt of villagers who had to buy rice through lenders.[61] It also cited a 2011 socioeconomic survey that reported that only 13 percent of resettler income was from agriculture and livestock on the plateau and that by early 2013 villagers were traveling to farm rice in relatives' fields off the plateau in Gnommalath and Mahaxay Districts because rice production was so difficult in the resettlement zones (figure 5.4).[62]

Failed Irrigation Systems

Irrigation systems have been highly problematic despite extensive planning that allotted each resettled household 0.16 ha of irrigated paddy. As early as 2012 the PoE reported that during the 2011–12 dry season only 4 percent of households were using irrigation systems.[63] The 2014 LTA report was scathing in its criticism of irrigation support for resettled communities, noting that irrigation had been installed at significant expense but had "almost no use."[64] The LTA noted that systems were subject to frequent failure and were "inadequate," as "water in shallow wells" was "unavailable for most of the dry season."[65] The December 2015 PoE report quoted NTPC data that at that time only 82 of 228 project irrigation systems were operational, just 12 percent of total irrigation areas.[66] While the report also referenced plans to repair broken systems, the history of failed irrigation schemes here and across Laos offers little hope that ongoing maintenance will be undertaken. Further, there is no certainty that irrigation will even be considered by communities with no familiarity with the technology. Uptake would require much extension support.

Defining and Protecting Property Rights

Provision of land was a fundamental element of the Nakai resettlement plan and particularly important for the agriculture pillar. The concession agreement stated that "no establishment of households other than bona fide resettlers should be permitted in the Resettlement Area."[67] To this end, participatory land use planning was completed in all resettled villages around the beginning of 2012 to give legal backing to village ownership.[68] Unfortunately, according to the December 2015 PoE report, both resettlers and outsiders have encroached on village lands. It notes both "outside speculative interest in acquiring land" and that presently "92 unauthorized resettlers are living in resettlement areas."[69]

Agriculture and New Households

The PoE has consistently emphasized the importance of the natural growth households of younger generations being incorporated into the agricultural program, in part because younger generations may adapt better than older generations to new technologies. In December 2015 the PoE reported that only 30 percent of new households owned their own housing or land on which to build in the future. Many are still sharing plots with their parents even though they are supposedly entitled to their own plots. In one of the four villages visited by the PoE during late 2015 in the northern part of the resettlement area, not one natural growth household owned its own land. In another village, the situation was termed "desperate," with thirty-four natural growth households sharing plots with parents, as they had not been allocated their own land.[70]

Overall Effectiveness of the Agricultural Pillar

The problems described in this section taken together have severely undercut the agriculture pillar. By December 2014 the PoE was reporting that the pillar was a "disappointing sector" with low utilization of household garden areas, irrigation systems, and gully dams that "nowhere near [justify] the work and resources put into them," especially given that the working of agricultural lands was "declining, not growing."[71] In 2014, the LTA carried out an independent evaluation so that it could advise on the upcoming planned closure of the resettlement program. It cited a "failure of the agriculture sector," with only 18 percent of resettlers making use of their allocated land. The report confirmed that "resettlers are returning to traditional shifting cultivation . . . [and] encroaching into village forestry association lands," thus undermining the already problematic forestry pillar and depleting upland soils due to insufficient fallow periods.[72] The December 2015 PoE report suggests increased use of agricultural lands through agro-forestry development initiatives, but statistics from the agriculture sector remain consistently low, and the future success of agriculture on resettler farms seems unlikely.[73]

The Livestock Pillar

Before resettlement, livestock was a principal and growing livelihood on the Nakai Plateau (see figure 5.4). While pigs and poultry made up the majority of livestock in the area, about half of the households on the plateau kept water buffalo as a critical part of their diversified livelihoods. The NTPC resettlement plan notes that buffalo are the "single most valuable traded product from villages on the Nakai in terms of value, and in 2002 this

Figure 5.5. Livestock grazing on dry season paddy fields on the Nakai Plateau prior to inundation by the NT2 reservoir. Photo by Satomi Higashi and Glenn Hunt.

trade earned Nakai villagers an estimated total of US$250,000."[74] Buffalo played a vital role in village livelihoods, both as assets and as an indicator of social standing. They also have great cultural importance, playing key roles in spiritual practices in many Indigenous villages. Buffalo could be readily traded to generate cash income in order to cover medical emergencies, buy rice during times of shortage, or pay for weddings and funerals. During a visit to one resettled village in 2004, one coauthor was told that a single adult buffalo could be sold for US$300–$400—a significant amount for villagers.

Before impoundment, Nakai communities would allow large herds of buffalo to graze along the flood plains of the Nam Theun River, where fertile soils provided a good source of forage. Buffalo were generally raised in a semi-wild manner, able to roam and graze at will, although somewhat accustomed to returning to their owners in the evening (figure 5.5). A 1998 livestock census by

Table 5.1. Household Ownership of Buffalo across Resettled Communities

Number of Buffalo/Household	Number of Households
0	678
1–2	121
3–5	122
6–10	113
>10	123

Source: Data derived from 1998 CARE census cited in *Social Development Plan*, 11.

an international NGO found that the villagers who would eventually be resettled owned 4,168 buffalo among them.[75] A breakdown of buffalo ownership in 1998 across all communities to be resettled is given in table 5.1. Two resettled Nakai villages, Nakai Tai and Done, each had over a thousand head of buffalo. Two more, Nakai Neua and Boua Ma, each had between three and four hundred. Five others each had between one and two hundred head.[76]

Planning for the Livestock Pillar

The resettlement plan acknowledged that impoundment of 45,000 ha of prime buffalo forage land would be a significant loss. Several alternatives for forage production were proposed, but all were viewed with considerable uncertainty, given poor soil quality near resettlement sites and the experimental nature of forage development in the drawdown zone. The 2005 independent assessment of the plan raised concerns about the overall strategy, pointing out that proposals such as development of fodder shrubs and urea rice straw were largely untested and that several components were highly dependent on success of the agriculture pillar.[77]

Livestock Postimpoundment

Before impoundment, villagers were required to ensure that their buffalo were on the western bank of the Nam Theun River, opposite the forests of Nakai-Nam Theun National Protected Area (NNT NPA), so that the animals could be tended in the resettlement areas. However, it was widely understood that the new resettlement zones did not have the carrying capacity for the large number of buffalo owned by resettlers. In February 2007, the PoE issued this stark warning: "As for livestock, lack of pasture (both grazing and browse) for large stock will require cutting the villagers' 5,000 head of cattle and buffaloes, which are their main bank account, to approximately 2,000 head."[78]

There was, however, no recommendation from the PoE on how this might be done. Villagers were apparently instructed to sell their buffalo to traders. Subsequent PoE reports suggest that the combination of buffalo flooding the market and their increasingly unhealthy state due to lack of sufficient forage depressed prices to the point where villagers ceased selling them. As the PoE had recognized, "insufficient grazing exists outside of the reservoir basin."[79] As waters began to rise, the situation became increasingly desperate. By February 2008, the PoE reported, "Buffalos are currently starving because of lack of grazing."[80] The LTA reported in 2014 that at least eight hundred buffalo died of starvation immediately after impoundment during 2008 and 2009.[81] In retrospect, it appears that NTPC and Nakai District authorities tasked with implementing the resettlement process either failed to understand and plan for the need to reduce buffalo numbers prior to impoundment or simply had no idea how to do so.

Subsequently, and contrary to what had been envisioned, high numbers of buffalo ended up in the NNT NPA, either left or moved there by villagers or trapped by inundation. While buffalo were dying of starvation in the resettlement area, they were thriving in the NNT NPA, so much so that the PoE recommended in numerous reports that they be captured or exterminated because of significant damage they were causing.[82]

Ongoing Problems

Years after initial problems in the livestock pillar first developed, fundamental challenges remain. There has been little progress in ensuring the contribution of this sector to sustainable restoration of villager livelihoods. As of May 2014, there was no improved pasture growing on the Nakai Plateau, and only 4.5 ha of "cut-and-carry fodder" (plants that can be cut and provided to livestock as animal feed) in gardens across the entire resettlement area. In 2014, NTPC hired an expert in tropical forages, Bruce Cook, retired from Department of Primary Industries and Fisheries, Queensland, Australia, to review livestock production in the resettlement area. While his 2014 report on pasture and livestock development has not been publicly released, it is referenced enough in PoE reports to allow one to ascertain that forage production in the drawdown area of the reservoir holds little promise. Cook also describes cut-and-carry fodder grown in resettlement areas as "not very successful."[83] Further, Cook notes that despite efforts of NTPC to create communal grazing areas in each of the resettler villages, communities were uninterested or unwilling to support such areas. Instead, most large livestock "feed on rather sparse grasses and other vegetation, often in the degraded forest areas" in village forestry lands and that some had even been returned to the NNT NPA.[84] The 2014 LTA report ominously warns of "a critical lack of pastures and grazing lands to support livestock numbers," observing that "sustainability of current livestock numbers and expected growth" is thus of "significant concern."[85]

A more recent PoE assessment of the livestock pillar does not bode well for its future. Although some villages have drawdown grazing areas that reportedly look promising, these appear limited to shallower margins of the reservoir in only a small number of villages. Overall, villages were unwilling or unable to expend time and effort on growing cut-and-carry forage production.[86] In addition, the LTA reports that the carrying capacity for livestock (about thirty-five-hundred head) will be reached around 2017–18. According to Cook, quoted in the PoE's 2014 report,

> current practices in relation to crop and stock management are seen as unsustainable and will continue to result in land degradation and weed invasion. Farmers will need to change their attitudes. On the other hand, seeking "cut and carry forage" in a closed system "is unsustainable by virtue of the relatively large amounts of nutrient that are removed from the forage system, particularly when the soils are depauperate in the first instance. Even if farmers did return manure from the livestock shed, which in my experience they do not, it would amount to only partial replacement.[87]

Cook goes on to state that without incentives for farmers to invest time, money, and effort, the result will be "widespread land degradation and entrenched poverty among the people." He adds that "there seem to be few prospects for beneficial change."[88]

Off-Farm Pillar

With its core focus on vocational training and tourism, the off-farm pillar is often the most neglected of the livelihood pillars, both by the project and by the resettlers, who see it as the most foreign and complicated alternative within livelihood diversification.

As dam construction and resettlement commenced, the off-farm economy boomed owing to an increase in employment for resettlers. Opportunities came from direct employment on the dam project as well as through the provision of goods and services to the project and its migrant labor force.[89]

Regional economic development and improved infrastructure, such as markets, roads, electricity, and telecommunications, have boosted local demand and provided resettlers with improved access to new income sources. In addition, training has been conducted by the project and small capital support has been provided to villagers to establish small businesses.[90]

The small businesses of the Nakai Plateau are varied, ranging from small shops and kiosks selling cooking supplies, toiletries, and gasoline to car repair shops and beauty salons. Weaving and tailoring are also common off-farm activities in the resettled communities. Other off-farm activities include fish and food processing, employment by the VFA, NTPC and its subcontractors, and other service enterprises.[91] There are also signs of growing tourism, especially in the northern area of the Nakai Plateau. Most resettlers involved in off-farm activities are self-employed.

Despite the expansion of the off-farm economy, in 2013 it comprised only 17 percent of resettlers' total income, a relatively small increase from 1998 when it was recorded at 13 percent.[92] Those engaging in it reported a earning a small profit, taking a small loss, or breaking even. However, no one reported substantial profit, and most described their income as "having enough to eat" and "having enough to survive," as most profits were used to purchase simple dietary staples, such as oil and chilies.

Diversification into off-farm activities centers on labor-intensive, low-return activities such as basketry, weaving, and other handicrafts. Many seem to have diversified into off-farm activities at the encouragement of NTPC and owing to the lack of agricultural productivity. However, many seem to enter these activities casually, not in pursuit of exploiting potential productivity gains.

Vocational Training

Some villagers have acquired skills through the vocational training program, the main effort by NTPC within the off-farm pillar. Roughly twenty-five to forty-five people are selected annually to receive vocational training in either Thakhek or Vientiane to acquire skills in fields ranging from carpentry and mechanics to hairdressing and tailoring.[93]

Vocational training has helped expand the rural off-farm economy to an extent, as some people have established small enterprises upon returning to their villages. However, impediments persist. For example, it is often difficult to recruit participants for prolonged training in distant locations, especially women, who tend to be hindered by household responsibilities. At the same time, vocational training participants state that training periods are too short; more time is needed to learn new skills from scratch and more comprehensive training is necessary if they are to compete successfully against others.[94] Some who have established a business have found success elusive because demand is low for many of the skills acquired in vocational training. As one vocational training participant remarked,

> I have this beauty salon, but not many people come. They don't have enough money to spend and they don't care about fixing their hair or looking nice. Maybe if there is a wedding or a big event, then they come. But this doesn't happen a lot. So I have a shop, but no customers.[95]

It was frequently reported that people opened shops when they first returned from training, but after a few months they were forced to close. Many try to open another business on a trial-and-error approach, so the period between opening and closing down a business is considered a short cycle. Others resort to offering services from their own homes.

Resettlers face other obstacles trying to enter the off-farm economy. One is lack of capital. Although the project makes a certain amount of credit available, many prefer to wait and save up on their own, primarily because they fear going into debt. Another is the simple lack of knowledge or experience in how to launch and manage a business successfully. Finally, lack of social networks can make it harder for resettlers to "get their foot in the door" within the off-farm economy. The need for social networks was seen as a high priority for villagers engaging in off-farm activities, as it can determine the success of a local business, by, for instance, establishing the "first followers" or by connecting it to suitable partners in the value chain, such as a wholesale supplier.

Vocational training has aided some resettlers by providing them with new skills, which removes one of the impediments to participating in off-farm activities. Nevertheless, few participants have been able to use newly acquired skills as their main source of income, and they continue to struggle to enter the rural off-farm economy. The PoE has been critical of the off-farm pillar, noting that it needs to conduct a more thorough analysis of what off-farm possibilities exist, and has highlighted as "most disconcerting" the limited funds set aside for vocational training.[96]

Tourism

NTPC's efforts to upgrade roads to Nakai has led to an increase in tourism. International backpackers rent motorbikes and drive on what has become known as the "southern loop" from Thakhek along Route 12 to Mahaxay for cave viewing, then up to the Nakai Plateau (where they stay a night or two) and on over the plateau to Lak Xao and the Khong Lor cave before heading back to Thakhek along Route 8. The loop is now one of the mainstays of backpacker tourism in southern Laos, and the PoE reports that about a thousand tourists cross the Nakai per month.[97] However, while the caves along Route 12 and the Khong Lor cave near Lak Xao are big draws, the reservoir and its dead vegetation hold little attraction. This tourism provides income to a small number of households in communities north of the reservoir, especially in Thalang, where two households in particular have independently established popular enterprises that provide accommodations, food, and other services.

The PoE has noted the potential of ecotourism to boost the off-farm pillar but has observed that training and preparation for such endeavors has not been prioritized. Despite its potential, the PoE to date has found the project's contribution to the tourism sector to be "minor."[98] While the development of a sealed road from Lak Xao to Nakai is expected to bring more tourists from neighboring countries, particularly Thailand, more effort is needed to provide services, infrastructure, and training of villagers and to develop an overall concept for tourism. This is no easy task in a reservoir that tourists have described as "reminiscent of a graveyard for trees" and in a NPA with severely compromised conservation value. Overall, the PoE describes a lack of cooperation among stakeholders—government bodies, NGOs, the private sector, district authorities and, most importantly, the resettled communities—in creating any sort of viable tourism development plan.[99]

While resettlers themselves seem to be positive and open to the idea of promoting ecotourism, indicating that they would even be willing to offer homestays for tourists, the project has largely failed to build opportunities apart from the general improvement of road infrastructure.[100] Without a concerted effort to develop tourism, Nakai will remain largely a rest stop for travelers on their way to other destinations.

Illegal Poaching of Rosewood

The most lucrative off-farm livelihood for resettled communities since construction of the dam began has been by far the illegal poaching of rosewood (*Dalbergia* spp.). The exact contribution of illegal rosewood to the incomes of resettlers is not publicly available (NTPC conducted a study in 2015, but it has not been released).[101] Nonetheless, it is clear that rosewood harvesting (and subsequently other species of valuable timber, now that the rosewood has largely been depleted) has been one of the main, if not the principal, income generators for resettled communities. Poaching began soon after resettlement, with the PoE first remarking on it in its February 2008 report.[102] Reports of resettled villagers engaging in poaching were subsequently recorded in 2009 and 2010, with the PoE quickly coming to the conclusion in February 2011 that "in reality the main sources of income at the moment appear to be from illegal and unsustainable collection of rosewood from the reservoir and the watershed."[103] In the same report the PoE described the "uncontrolled and wholesale plunder of the reservoir and watershed's rosewood" in which it was "clear that a high proportion of Nakai resettlers were involved."[104]

Independent assessments of the Nakai Plateau resettlement program conducted by an international NGO also recorded widespread participation in timber poaching among resettled villagers. A resident in one village close to the town of Nakai who was interviewed for one report stated that out of a hundred households in the village, at least sixty were engaged in rosewood poaching.[105] Ironically, villagers were using the boats supplied by the project to transport logs from the NNT NPA to their houses.[106]

The PoE was acutely aware that resettled communities were engaging in rosewood poaching on a large scale. A number of PoE reports state that statistical data gathered by NTPC hid illegal logging activities. In fact, it appears that NTPC strategically hid the contribution of the rosewood poaching to resettler income while at the same time claiming that this unsustainable income should be used to measure the overall success of the project. The NGO field research recorded a startling admission from an NTPC-commissioned survey team that was investigating village livelihoods. When the researchers questioned the team during a chance encounter in the field, one of the team members replied (switching to English so that accompanying GoL officials wouldn't understand) that "illegal logging is the main livelihood option, however, we can't ask that question to villagers, and we don't report on it."[107]

The poaching of rosewood became so commonplace that it was conducted more or less in the open. The PoE reported that "piles of the valuable hardwood can be seen in or under many village houses," and other researchers have confirmed this.[108] In March 2013, the PoE made the sobering observation that poaching of Rosewood trees (*Dalbergia* spp.) has been so widespread and open that the more valuable species are now exceedingly difficult to find, indeed, almost extinct. . . . While Rosewood will sprout from stumps, the poachers are digging out the larger roots, effectively removing that potential for regrowth.[109]

The illegal trade in rosewood has indeed "brought signs of apparent financial prosperity, . . . including new houses, motorbikes, tractors and abundant beerlao," but the practice is completely unsustainable from the point of view of village livelihoods.[110] While incomes rose, this was ephemeral and at the expense of the biodiversity conservation goals of NT2.

Conclusion

The NT2 livelihood restoration program outlined in NTPC's Social Development Plan was a highly ambitious model of diverse strategies, all aiming to contribute to sufficient, sustainable livelihoods for resettled communities on the Nakai Plateau. While the livelihood pillars were envisaged as independent within a diversified model, they were also understood to be linked in various ways to the other pillars, making the success of some dependent on the success of others. One of the sources for livestock feed was to be forage grown on irrigated farmlands; similarly, the manure from large livestock was to be used as natural fertilizer on farmlands. Thus the failures of some pillars have exacerbated the difficulties with others. While the fisheries pillar is currently the only one that has been somewhat successful, by itself it remains insufficient as a livelihood for all resettled families.

The failure of local authorities and NTPC to protect communal property resources and use rights has further undermined the livelihoods of resettled communities. This lack of enforcement appears to be a reoccurring theme in the project and underscores the inherent weakness of the Lao state to manage complex livelihood restoration. In addition to the fisheries sector, outside logging interests have dominated community forests, all under the gaze of project proponents and developers and despite the concerns expressed by external monitors, such as the PoE.

Even in the agriculture and livestock sectors, where security of land tenure is essential for long-term sustainability, the project has failed in its objective of protecting community lands from encroachment by outsiders, leading to the seemingly irreversible loss of village resources. From a technical aspect, the project has failed to competently implement the livelihood pillars.

Many of these failures were predicted by outside monitoring organizations.[111] The lack of political will to restrict access to the reservoir and community lands and give strong land tenure rights to resettled communities is in many ways emblematic of failures in other parts of the country, where extractive industries and land concessions continue to displace both Indigenous and non-Indigenous communities from their ancestral lands without appropriate compensation. Project lenders and proponents appear to have ignored or failed to understand the sociopolitical realities on the ground in Laos. This has led to undermining of NTPC's ambitious plans and to a failure to implement many of the PoE's core recommendations. It is as if the whole livelihoods initiative was planned and implemented in a vacuum, in the belief that planning and money could override the country's fundamental realities. That miscalculation has led to substantial wasted effort and ongoing difficulties for resettlers and has compromised other important NT2 priorities, in particular biodiversity conservation in the protected area.

One fundamental issue has plagued the resettlement initiative from the outset—the lack of sufficient high quality land for the resettlers. The considerable resources put into this program—money, materials, and technical expertise—taken together were still not enough to overcome that basic obstacle. The failure of the NT2 resettlement program raises doubts about the viability of resettlement in Laos in general. Almost all projects in the country that require resettlement face similar or even worse constraints on available land. A myth persists in Laos to the effect that because the overall population density of the country is low, there must be lots of available underutilized land on which people can be resettled as long as they have some external support. This is just not the case. If resettlement couldn't be successful on the Nakai Plateau, with all the resources the World Bank, the ADB, NTPC and other donors brought to bear, it casts considerable doubt on whether it can be done anywhere in the country, at least not without subjecting resettled people to extended periods of suffering and impoverishment.

In December 2015, the PoE, tasked with determining if the resettlement implementation period had sufficiently met the commitment to restore resettler livelihoods, refused to sign off on the program's closure, stating that "a substantial proportion of the Resettlement Objectives and Provisions has not been fully achieved as yet." The PoE then went on to recommend a two-year extension of the resettlement implementation period to the end of 2017.[112]

Whether an extension of two more years will be enough to turn around the failures to date remains to be seen. While the World Bank is likely to try to formally exit the project at the end of 2017, a face-saving program of additional assistance appears to be in the works, one that will require further years of aid agency support well beyond what was initially envisioned. It is difficult to imagine that the fundamental issues with several of the pillars can be resolved. In any case, even these problems were resolved, it will be far too late for the project to be seen as a positive model of resettlement, either in Laos or in other parts of the world.

NOTES

1. The first epigraph is quoted from "Speaking of Nam Theun 2 . . . Past, Present and Future (?)," *Watershed* 10, no. 1 (2004): 9.

2. NTPC, *Social Development Plan,* final draft, March 2005, vol. 1, appendix A-1:5.

3. Benjamin Hodgdon, "No Success Like Failure: Policy versus Reality in the Lao Forestry Sector," *Watershed* 12, no. 1 (2007): 43.

4. Personal communication, Benjamin Hodgdon to Glenn Hunt, March 2016.

5. PoE 10:21.

6. PoE 15:27.

7. PoE 17:17.

8. PoE 17:17.

9. Benjamin Hodgdon, personal communication to Glenn Hunt, March 2016.

10. Benjamin Hodgdon, personal communication to Glenn Hunt, March 2016.

11. PoE 18B:24.

12. PoE 19:15.

13. PoE 19:14.

14. PoE 20:29.

15. PoE 20:30.

16. PoE 22:17.

17. PoE 22:18.

18. PoE 23:12.

19. PoE 23:13.

20. PoE 23:12.

21. PoE 24:22.

22. PoE 23:10.

23. NTPC, *Social Development Plan*, vol. 2, 15:36–46.

24. NTPC, *Social Development Plan*, vol. 2, 15:20.

25. PoE 13:4.

26. PoE 13:19, emphasis in original.

27. PoE 14:42.

28. Anonymous, personal communication to Glenn Hunt, August 2016.

29. Vincent Chanudet, Stéphane Descloux, Atle Harby, Håkon Sundt, Børn Henrik Hansen, Odd Brakstad, Dominique Serça, and Frédéric Guérin, "Gross CO_2 and CH_4

Emissions from the Nam Ngum and Nam Leuk Sub-tropical Reservoirs in Lao PDR," *Science of the Total Environment* 409, no. 24 (2011); Maud Demarty and Julie Bastien, "GHG Emissions from Hydroelectric Reservoirs in Tropical and Equatorial Regions: Review of 20 Years of CH4 Emission Measurements," *Energy Policy* 39, no. 7 (2011). Although some on the project disputed EdF's claims, the Science, Technology and Environment Agency listened primarily to the developers.

30. Anonymous, personal communication to Glenn Hunt, May 2016.

31. Maud Cottet, Stéphane Descloux, Pierre Guédant, Philippe Cerdan, Régis Vigouroux, "Fish Population Dynamic in the Newly Impounded Nam Theun 2 Reservoir (Lao PDR)," *Hydroécol* 19 (2016): 344; Mekong Watch, Nam Theun 2 dam project site, field survey report, December 2010, 10, http://www.mekongwatch.org/PDF/NT2FieldReport Nov2010.pdf.

32. Chanudet et al., "Gross CO2 and CH4 Emissions"; Cottet et al., "Fish Population Dynamic"; Vincent Chanudet, Pierre Guédant, Wanidaporn Rode, Arnaud Godon, Frédéric Guérin, Dominique Serça, Chandrashekhar Deshmukh, and Stéphane Descloux, "Evolution of the Physico-Chemical Water Quality in the Nam Theun 2 Reservoir and Downstream Rivers for the First 5 Years after Impoundment," *Hydroécol* 19 (2016).

33. Chanudet et al., "Gross CO2 and CH4 Emissions."

34. NTPC, *Social Development Plan*, vol. 2, 15:22.

35. NTPC, *Social Development Plan*, vol. 2, 15:40–41.

36. NTPC, *Social Development Plan*, vol. 2, 15:40–41.

37. NTPC, *Social Development Plan*, vol. 2, 15:22.

38. PoE 24:18.

39. PoE 16:20–21.

40. PoE 24:19.

41. NTPC, *Social Development Plan*,15:36.

42. PoE 24:19.

43. "Laos to Release 2 Million Fingerlings to Boost Fish Stocks," *Vientiane Times*, July 3, 2008; Savannakhet Provincial Agriculture and Forestry Office, personal communication to Glenn Hunt, 2009; WWF staff, personal communication to Glenn Hunt, 2009; NTPC, *Social Development Plan*, 15:44.

44. Mekong Watch, NT2 field trip notes, unpublished, 2009.

45. http://www.issg.org/database/species/search.asp?st=100ss.

46. Cottet et al., "Fish Population Dynamic," 343.

47. NTPC, *Social Development Plan*, 15:44–45; Cottet et al., "Fish Population Dynamic"; Gabrielle C. Canonico, Angela H. Arthington, Jeffrey K. McCrary, and Michele L. Thieme, "The Effects of Introduced Tilapias on Native Biodiversity," *Aquatic Conservation: Marine and Freshwater Ecosystems* 15, no. 5 (2005).

48. NTPC, *Social Development Plan*, vol. 2, chap. 15.

49. NTPC, *Social Development Plan* , vol. 2, chap. 2:23–28.

50. NTPC, *Social Development Plan*, vol. 2, chap. 12.

51. NTPC, *Social Development Plan*, vol. 1, appendix C-2:1.

52. Mekong Watch, NT2 field trip notes, unpublished, 2008.

53. PoE 24:32.

54. IRN, *Agriculture and Livestock Development Plan for the Nam Theun 2 Hydropower Project: An Independent Analysis* (Berkeley, CA: 2005): 13.

55. NTPC, *Social Development Plan*, vol. 2, 12:20.

56. NTPC, *Social Development Plan*, April–May 2004 draft, vol. 2, 21:10.

57. Glenn Hunt, personal notes, NT2 third annual stakeholder forum, October 28, 2008.

58. NTPC, *Social Development Plan*, vol. 2, chap. 12, table 12.16, footnote a; 12:20.

59. NTPC, *Social Development Plan*, vol. 2, 12:7, 12:20.

60. NTPC, *Social Development Plan*, vol. 2, 12:20–21.

61. PoE 17:11.

62. Government of Laos, "Nakai Socio-Economic Survey," May 2011, cited in PoE 20:25–26.

63. PoE 20:26.

64. BNP Paribas/NTPC, *Resettlement Implementation Period—Closure Assessment: LTA Review Meeting—Findings*, November 5, 2014, 8.

65. BNP Paribas/NTPC, *Resettlement Implementation Period*, 16–17.

66. PoE 24:46.

67. PoE 24:15.

68. PoE 19.

69. PoE 24:15.

70. PoE 24:33.

71. PoE 23:15; PoE 23:16.

72. BNP/NTPC, *Resettlement Implementation Period*, 16–17.

73. This is partially attributable to the cessation of rosewood timber poaching due to overharvesting.

74. NTPC, *Social Development Plan*, vol. 2, 12:54.

75. NTPC, *Social Development Plan*, vol. 2, 2:18.

76. NTPC, *Social Development Plan*, vol. 2, 18.

77. IRN, *Agriculture and Livestock Development Plan*, 10–12.

78. PoE 11:11.

79. PoE 13:23.

80. PoE 13:23.

81. BNP/NTPC, *Resettlement Implementation Period*, 5.

82. PoE 13, 15, 17, 18.

83. Bruce Cook, cited in PoE 23:20.

84. PoE 23:21.

85. BNP/NTPC, *Resettlement Implementation Period*, 28.

86. PoE 23.

87. PoE 23:20.

88. PoE 24:37.

89. Most information in this section is based on Marika Samuelsson's 2015 paper "Livelihood Diversification into the Rural Nonfarm Economy: A Case of the Resettled Households of the Nam Theun 2 Hydropower Project," Department of Human Geography, Lund University, 2015. https://lup.lub.lu.se/student-papers/search/publication/5434849, which provides a more detailed description of this pillar than space allows here.

90. NTPC, *Nakai Resettlers' Reality: From the Past to the Future*, August 2014, 27, www.namtheun2.com/images/Document_for_website/Nakai%20Resettlers'%20Reality%20From%20the%20Past%20to%20the%20Future/Nakai%20resettlers%20reality%20-%20Final.pdf.

91. NTPC, *Nakai Resettlers' Reality*, 28.

92. NTPC, *Nakai Resettlers' Reality*, 33.

93. NTPC, *Nakai Resettlers' Reality*, 39.

94. Samuelsson, "Livelihood Diversification," interview no. 45.

95. Samuelsson, "Livelihood Diversification," interview no. 45.

96. PoE 24:41.

97. PoE 24:40.

98. PoE 24:45.

99. PoE 24:45.

100. Samuelsson, "Livelihood Diversification," 55.

101. Lilao Bouapao, "An Assessment of Income Sources," draft, NTPC, 2015, cited in PoE 24:5.

102. PoE 13.

103. PoE 18B:5.

104. PoE 18B:24.

105. Mekong Watch, NT2 field trip notes, unpublished, March 16–17, 2011.

106. Mekong Watch, NT2 field trip notes, unpublished, March 16–17, 2011.

107. Mekong Watch, NT2 field trip notes, unpublished, March 16–17, 2011.

108. PoE 19:10; Mekong Watch, NT2 field trip photo report, March 16–19, 2011.

109. PoE21A:5.

110. PoE21A:5.

111. See, in particular, IRN, *Agriculture and Livestock Development Plan*.

112. PoE 24:2.

6

Social Change in the Nam Theun 2 Catchment

The Kri Experience

N. J. ENFIELD

Much attention has been paid to the impact of the Nam Theun 2 (NT2) project on local people directly affected by the dam, such as those who were resettled to make way for the reservoir. This chapter examines some consequences of the project for people more distant from the project's center, in remote areas of the NT2 catchment, who have been affected less directly. We take a close look at what has happened to one group of people: the Kri.[1] Members of this group—around three hundred people—live far upstream in the NT2 catchment area, the management domain of the project's Watershed Management and Protection Authority (WMPA).

The Kri and Their Home Range

The Kri, who speak an indigenous language of the Vietic family, inhabit a small swath of territory in the upper reaches of the Nam Noy river, a tributary of the Nam Theun river. Nam Noy means "small river" in the Lao language. In the Kri language, the river is known as Ñrong. The eastern extent of Kri territory is at the Lao–Vietnam border adjoining Vietnam's Hương Khê District in Ha Tinh Province, the eastern edge of the Nam Noy river catchment. The downstream (westernmost) border of Kri territory is the Reew stream, just upstream from Teung, a long-established ethnic Sek village about an hour's walk from the Kri hamlet of Plùùnq (known in Lao and by government authorities as Maka Tai or "downstream Maka"), the furthest downstream of the Kri settlements.

Kri people live today in three separate hamlets, officially a single administrative unit known in Lao as the village of Maka (referred to by locals as downstream Maka, middle Maka, and upstream Maka). The village name Maka refers to an upper tributary of the Nam Noy. This stream, known as Mrkaa in Kri, is where the furthest-upstream Kri hamlet is currently situated. Upstream Maka is the most established and stable of the existing village sites and is the only settlement that is officially recognized by the Lao government. Other sites are regarded as temporary satellite settlements. At upstream Maka there is a Khammouane Province police post, which oversees the administration of Laos–Vietnam border traffic. An adult education hut was built by the provincial government in upstream Maka in 2003, and a permanent primary school building was built there (by Vietnamese laborers) in 2005. These developments represent a different approach to settlement than the approach traditionally taken by the Kri. The Kri are not accustomed to settling in one place for very long. Like many forest peoples, the Kri regard infrastructure as impermanent.

Social Ecology of the Kri in the NT2 Watershed

Like all upland peoples of Laos, the Kri live in a richly textured social context, maintaining regular contact with numerous other ethnic groups. Three distinct, broad ethnolinguistic categories are represented in the villages of the watershed. These groups are labeled Katuic (e.g., speakers of the Bru language), Tai (e.g., speakers of the Sek and Tai Mène languages), and Vietic (e.g., speakers of Kri, along with other endangered Vietic languages such as Thémarou and Ahlao). As described in the NT2 *Social and Environmental Management Framework and First Operational Plan*, in the "Ethnic Minorities Development Plan" section, Vietic groups were the earliest of the current inhabitants in the area. Other groups moved into the region in recent centuries. This document, following work by James Chamberlain, offers a "cultural typology" of Vietic groups, with four types distinguished by differences in livelihood:

Vietic I—small groups only recently or partially sedentary, with some difficulties adjusting to this lifestyle (classified as "most vulnerable"): includes Atel, Thémarou, Mlengbrou
Vietic II—originally collectors and traders who have become emergent swidden sedentists: includes Aro, Maleng, Malang, Mrkaang, To'e, Ahoe, Phong
Vietic III—swidden cultivators who are still moving between preexisting village sites: Kri

Vietic IV—combined swidden and paddy sedentism: includes Ahao, Ahlao, Liha, Phong and Toum.[2]

The Kri are the only group who were categorized as "Vietic III" in the time just prior to the NT2 project going ahead. With the recent adoption of paddy agriculture by some Kri families, and increasing government pressure toward sedentism, a shift to "Vietic IV" appears to be in progress.

The ethnic groups of the watershed maintain structured social relations with each other. From an anthropological perspective, such patterns of inter-cultural exchange are fundamental to the working of a larger society. People of different ethnicities in the watershed know each other. They know each other's names, each other's children, each other's houses. There are also kinship ties across different ethnic groups, with intermarriage not uncommon. During their travels in the watershed, villagers ensure that these relations of friendship and kinship are maintained.

Villages along the Nam Noy sometimes rely on each other for the supply of basic food, particularly during times of crisis. In 2006, I was there when many villages along the Nam Noy had their upland rice seedlings destroyed by overexposure to sunshine, due to later than usual onset of rainy/cloudy seasonal conditions. Replanting was required, and rice yields were delayed by about two months. Maka villagers had not been hit so hard, thanks to the cloudier conditions further upstream, and their paddy crops were harvested earlier than those in the villages downstream. The result was that during July and August 2006, the village of Maka had the best supply of rice along the entire river. Visitors from all along the Nam Noy came to ask Maka villagers for help. That they were able to get rice when they asked for it shows that the relationships in this area between people of different villages and different ethnicities and languages are not just perfunctory.

The various groups of the watershed also consult with each other for cultural, informational, and practical purposes. For example, the Sek have certain types of technical expertise, including expertise in paddy rice farming and experience in milling timber for building houses and river boats. In 2006, the chief of the Kri settlement of middle Maka (located where the Srô river meets the Nam Noy) paid two young Sek men to stay in his village for a number of weeks to mill wood for boat construction. In turn, Maka villagers offer their own special expertise in performing religious rituals for people from other villages. Villagers from downstream Nam Noy make journeys to Maka to consult Kri spirit mediums and have them perform rituals whose function is to resolve problems such as health or family issues. In another example, during a medical crisis in childbirth in Maka, villagers walked to the mostly Bru village of Vang Rae (about three hours' walk from Maka) to summon an expert midwife to come to upstream Maka to assist.

Alongside these more targeted types of intervillage consultation, there is also opportunistic consultation among villagers of different ethnicities in the course of villagers' travels through the area. For example, a person passing through a village may stop on someone's verandah for a rest and a chat. In these chance meetings, there will often be discussions of weaving techniques and fishing and hunting methods, an exchange of detailed up-to-date information about the condition of walking paths, sightings of wildlife, movements of transient traders, forest conditions, other issues of forest/village access, and reports of village news (illnesses, deaths, marriages, births). These examples show that the relations between different ethnic groups of the Nam Noy are substantial. People of neighboring groups have long depended on each other for real and often consequential assistance in many aspects of life.

There is also close interaction between Kri villagers and transient Vietnamese visitors in the watershed, who are of two main types: camper-hunters and hiker-traders. The camper-hunters hunt and trap in the forest, targeting animals valued in regional wildlife trade (e.g., pangolins, porcupines, turtles, bears, and, at least formerly, tigers), particularly in the uppermost areas of the protected area, away from villages. It has proven difficult for WMPA to prevent the movement of these camper-hunters, who enter the forest illegally from the Vietnam side and stay for extended periods in the forest, camping and setting snares for species of animal that fetch good prices in Vietnam. They also search with specially trained dogs, especially for pangolins and turtles.

Kri villagers seldom come into contact with camper-hunters. They say that they are afraid of the camper-hunters and will go out of their way to avoid them. By contrast, hiker-traders are well known to the Kri and are common houseguests. A hiker-trader is an itinerant peddler who walks from village to village in the watershed selling goods that he (they are invariably men) carries in a sack on his back, often trading them for goods to take back to Vietnam for sale there. The goods they take back to Vietnam include wild honey, domestic cats (particularly sought after as household pets are calico, or "three-color," cats), and illicit wildlife. At any given time, there may be dozens of Vietnamese hiker-traders within the watershed. On my field trips in the area I have counted an average of around two hiker-traders in any village per day (including the rare days when are there none at all), and I have counted as many as nine in a village at one time. Hiker-traders commonly enter Laos legally at the international border, crossing on the road from Hương Khê. They walk for a day down the Nam Noy, through the uninhabited upstream area of the NT2 catchment before arriving at the immigration police post at upstream Maka. They then gain access to the protected area, where they trade with villagers for up to three weeks, before returning to Vietnam. They sell a wide range of goods, including tools, cooking utensils, medicine, fish hooks, rope, clothing, alcohol, watches, jewelry, batteries, pico-hydro systems, washing powder, toothpaste, entertainment systems, and more. Residents of the watershed have long relied heavily on these men for supply of such items, which they would otherwise only be able to obtain by making long walking trips to the markets of either Nakai on the Lao side or Hương Khê in Vietnam. There are signs that this is beginning to change since the inception of the NT2 dam project: with the flooding of the reservoir and the upgrading or construction of foot trails to allow the use of hand tractors and motorcycles, it has become much easier to transport both essentials and luxuries into the protected area from the Lao side.

Traditional Knowledge of Biodiversity

Maka villagers are experts on many aspects of the biodiversity of the watershed. Kri people have an exceptionally broad and deep knowledge of the area's plant and animal life.[3] This is common to other ethnic groups in the area.[4] Residents are deeply knowledgeable about many aspects of the biodiversity of their environment because they have had firsthand experience with it, day in day out, year in year out, since they were infants. This knowledge is to a large degree encoded in their languages. Sustained field work on the languages of the watershed is therefore important not only for cultural and scientific reasons; it is also in the interests of conservation work. Characteristics of local languages and knowledge can provide important data points. For example, Maka villagers can recognize the saola (*Pseudoryx nghetinhensis*) from a photograph, but they do not have a native word for it (they use the Lao word), and they know little about its habits. Only a few villagers have ever seen this elusive animal in the forest. Since we know that the traditional home range of Maka people is well defined, this tells us something about the distribution of the saola itself.

Livelihood of the Kri in Transition

Until recently, the Kri rotated among village sites and agricultural activity within a well-defined traditional territory. This territory is centered on the banks of the Nam Noy and the lower reaches of its tributaries, from the Reew stream at Teung Village up as far as the streams of Klông Crùù, Caròòj, and Ting Tuu, on the way to the present-day border with Vietnam. Kri villagers have never permanently settled in any location beyond this territory. While other ethnic groups of the area will say when and how their group came to the area, the Kri, like other Vietic groups, say they have "always been here." Within this home territory, however, they relocate often. From a Kri perspective, any relocation is essentially a case of moving house, as opposed to moving village. This is because "the village" is not a traditional unit of social and domestic organization for Kri people.

Traditionally, a Kri family house would be abandoned by its builder/ owner about five years after construction, often, simply because it is disintegrating.[5] Kri houses are not constructed with the intention that they should be permanent or even particularly long lived. All components of the house are biodegradable; the Kri use forest products from the immediate vicinity (light timber, bamboo, rattan, fan palm leaves) as building materials. Rather than renovate or rebuild in the same spot, a house in disrepair would simply be left behind, as a family would often move to a new location anyway in search of new arable land. This sort of movement makes the organization of the Kri community quite fluid, with decisions being made mostly at the (extended) family level, not the village level.

The Kri practice shifting cultivation, but their traditional pattern of livelihood activity maintains a cycle of highly localized cultivation. They have not traditionally practiced pioneering shifting cultivation (or paddy cultivation). That is, they have not been in the habit of clearing primary upland forest in order to plant crops and gardens. To sustain their traditional practices, they have circulated among established village sites along the Nam Noy, the usual pattern being a movement of extended family groups every five or ten years. There is also a lot of local migration of individuals and families from settlement to settlement at all times. While busy cultivating, larger settlements traditionally break up into smaller groups, with families living temporarily at their swiddens.

In recent years, the villagers of Maka, like other upland minorities of Laos, have come under pressure from government authorities to establish permanent settlements. This pressure is ostensibly motivated by policies aimed at alleviating poverty. It is argued that sedentarization makes it easier and more efficient to deliver essential services to villagers. But there are clearly some trade-offs, and not all outcomes of sedentarization are positive. The trend toward Kri villagers concentrating in a tighter home range appears to be putting pressure on the local environment. If villagers are required to remain in one settlement, they will regularly need to find new cultivatable land within walking distance of the village. About one hour's walk to a swidden is normal, but if the walk becomes further than this, particularly if it is far uphill, villagers will prefer to reside in their swiddens for much of the agricultural cycle, at least during the intensive periods such as weeding, guarding from pests as crops mature, and harvesting. New land in these conditions can only be had by creating new upland swiddens on slopes and high hillsides near the village. This means cutting primary forest, a practice that the Kri had not previously engaged in. So, as a result of a policy that may have been intended to reduce environmental damage, villagers in the Maka area are beginning to engage in more damaging practices than they ever have previously.

Ever since the advent of WMPA oversight, there has been growing pressure to sedentarize. Maka villagers say they would prefer to continue their cycle of livelihood, circulating through familiar locations along the lowlands of the Nam Noy. But they are now forbidden by the authorities from regularly re-locating in the traditional manner. The Kri practices of cyclic migration are perceived to be destructive. But in fact because they involve cycling among previously cultivated sites within a strictly defined territory, these practices are sustainable (at least within a stable population) and not significantly damaging in the long term.

A small number of Maka villagers (in downstream Maka, near the Sek village of Teung) are successfully cultivating paddy rice—a new adaptation for the Kri—and others in the Kri community are also interested in adopting paddy farming. The key obstacle is expertise. Maka villagers have little experience with paddy farming, and they are not willing to take the risk of attempting to develop paddies without receiving ongoing supervision in the early stages of adoption. The Kri community of Maka is in close contact with the Sek community of Teung. It appears that villagers of Teung have supervised and trained Maka villagers in paddy rice agriculture.

Response to Development Efforts

An aspect of social change that has been accelerated by the NT2 project is village development work, much of which is funded and promoted by the NT2 Power Company through WMPA. This work has not always had the intended results, especially in cases where the activities were of low priority for the villagers. An example observed during research field work was a project to install latrines in Maka in 2005. Villagers were informed by the district administration that latrines had to be installed in the village for reasons of sanitation and health. Each family was supplied with a latrine kit, consisting of a ceramic toilet bowl, cement, large water bucket, and other pieces of equipment. One man from each household devoted several days to the project, first walking downstream to the village of Ka Oy to pick up the equipment and carrying it back up to Maka by foot (a three-day round-trip) and then installing the latrine (digging a large pit, mixing the cement for a concrete base, building a covering hut). This project failed. After the latrines were installed (with the help of a government team from Nakai district), they were never used.

The effort that villagers and district employees put in to this project showed no practical outcome. Worse still, the project took significant time and effort, which could have been expended on other livelihood activities. Prior consultation with villagers would have revealed that latrines are low on the Kri list of development priorities. There are more urgent needs, including food security, mother and child health, and transport access. The experience of latrines was a lesson. Because not every development activity can be done at once, the ones that are chosen should take into account local needs and desires, so as to ensure that the efforts of both villagers and development staff are not wasted.

Kri Resource Use in Transition

Traditional Kri resource use practices have posed little threat to the biodiversity of the NT2 watershed area. The Kri have never practiced logging. They do not mill wood for house construction or other purposes. They use smaller trees for light construction and firewood, and there is no indication that this demand has placed any burden on the general environment. Kri patterns of timber extraction are local to their villages, and their constant circulation within the broader territory over years has meant that ample time would pass for regeneration before an area might be exploited again. They would travel quite far to extract certain kinds of forest products, whose supply can be uncertain—for instance, rattan (*Calamus*) varieties and palm leaves (*Livistona cochinchinensis*) for roofing.[6] It is notable that the Kri have traditionally observed a highly restricted diet, proscribing the eating of all red meat, and most wildlife, as this is not that usual in the context of rural Laos. They are heavily reliant on fish for protein but seldom eat any of the common wild food sources for Lao villagers, whether at the small scale (insects, birds, bats, snakes, frogs, etc.) or the large scale (macaques, civets, muntjacs). This is beginning to change, as some villagers (men, for the most part) now do eat some red meat, such as wild pig. But even now, the Kri are not avid hunters. Finally, the Kri do not construct dams or engage in any other significant form of water control. Pico-hydro is used, as in other villages of the watershed, but this is a recent innovation.

Access to the Watershed

Prior to its legal status as a protected area, the NT2 catchment area had been well protected by sheer isolation. There was almost no access to the area other than by foot or by helicopter. Boats could enter the area from the plateau only with great difficulty, if at all, due to rocky rapids blocking access. The inundation of the NT2 reservoir has changed this significantly. Formerly, boat passage across the Nakai Plateau was slow, because of the serpentine shape of the Nam Theun river. Boats can now make a beeline straight across the reservoir from the district center to the edge of the protected area, and the rocky stretches of the tributaries that previously barred access have mostly been inundated. There were no roads, only a network of walking trails within the watershed. There were few hand tractors in the watershed (only seen in Sek villages such as Teung), which were brought in at great expense and trouble. Sek villagers purchased these tractors in the town of Nakai, dismantled them and carried them piece by piece, in multiple trips, up the rugged walking paths of the watershed, reassembling them once they were back in their villages. To operate these machines, used in paddy agriculture, every drop of fuel and oil had to be carried in on foot. Reportedly, General Chang (head of Borisat Phattana Khed Phudoi, a company that carried out extensive logging of the Nakai Plateau in the 1990s) offset these supply problems by occasionally delivering supplies and food to watershed residents by helicopter. He is reported to have donated two hand tractors to Teung village, flying them there in one of his helicopters.

Since the NT2 reservoir was flooded, delivery of goods, including major machinery such as tractors, has become a relatively simple matter. The number of hand tractors and motorcycles in villages of the watershed went from only a handful in 2006 to many dozens in 2011. This has obvious implications for changes in livelihood, sustainability, and environmental impact.

Transport and Communications in the Kri Context

Kri territory has not been directly affected by the flooding of the plateau, since it is far upstream of the project works and reservoir. There have been, however, a range of effects on the lifestyle of the population, as I have implied. With regard to transport and communications, inhabitants have always needed to make regular trips to the Nakai Plateau, for example, to visit the market, hospital, or district administration. When the WMPA was established, its main tasks were to "ensure the effective, long-term protection of the biodiversity and watershed values of the Nam Theun 2 catchment while at the same time safeguarding the well-being, traditional livelihoods and culture of its human inhabitants."[7] There were to be stringent restrictions on the amount of development activity within the watershed, since the protection of the watershed's unique biodiversity is a primary offset against significant environmental disturbance on the Nakai Plateau (flooding by the reservoir) and in downstream areas, both in the Nam Theun River (whose flow is interrupted by the dam) and the Xe Bang Fai River (whose flow is increased by reception of water from the Nam Theun after it is sent from the reservoir through the turbines of the powerhouse).

In the interests of meeting the WMPA's objectives, it was stipulated in the *Social and Environmental Management Framework and First Operational Plan* that no roads should be built inside the watershed. Instead, a network of "tractor trails" has rapidly been constructed in the middle and lower reaches of the watershed, linking the main boat landing at the Nam Theun (near the mostly Bru village of Tha Phai Ban) with other villages, including those over in the next valley to the south, along the Nam Noy. These trails might not technically be roads, but the same reasons roads were not ruled out for the NT2 watershed applies to the trails. They have transformed the speed and ease with which villagers can access the outside world and the reach and scope of resource extraction activities (e.g., they have increased the distance from the village that villagers can feasibly travel to clear forest for swiddens and have made it possible for them to transport more timber and rattan). The network of tractor trails protects neither the area's biodiversity nor the traditional livelihoods and culture.

In 2004, when I first did field work with the Kri, gaining access to the outside world from Kri territory was difficult. On the Lao side, the nearest point of access to a market was the Nakai District center. To get from Kri territory to the Nakai District center one first had to walk downstream following the Nam Noy for approximately fourteen hours (i.e., two days, with an overnight stay about half way—at the village of Vang Khuai, for example) until one came out of the watershed through a narrow descent onto the edge of the Nakai Plateau at the village of Ka Oy. From Ka Oy, most Kri villagers would walk another day across the plateau to reach the town of Nakai. The trip could be shortened by hiring a boat from Ka Oy and traveling down along the Nam Noy and the Nam Theun to one of the villages nearer to Nakai (e.g., Nikhom or Sop On). This cost money most villagers could not spare. From here, the walk was shorter, although again, if one had money, it was possible to get a ride with land transport such as a plough tractor or truck. If one had the funds for these forms of motor transport (and the luck to make the necessary connections), the entire trip from Kri territory to Nakai District took two full days, most of which was spent hiking. For most Kri people, however, the trip took three days, all by foot. So, a return trip from Kri territory to Nakai District center to buy, say, a 10-kilogram bag of salt, would entail six days' hike and a week away from home.

Note that the settlement at Nakai District center is only recent. Only twenty-five years ago (i.e., in many Kri people's living memory), one would have had to add yet another day's walk to get to Gnommalat, the next district center down the escarpment, closer to the Mekong.

Market and medical access on the Vietnamese side is a good deal closer and prior to the recent establishment of the Nakai District center, most of the traffic to and from the outside world was in and out of Vietnam. From the Maka area, in one long day (with about twenty stream crossings) it is possible to reach the first village on the Vietnamese side and then easily gain access (usually by motorcycle taxi) to the market at Hương Khê in Ha Tinh Province. Before there was a market in Nakai District center, Kri territory was a thoroughfare that all villagers along the Nam Noy used to reach the market in Vietnam by foot. Such trips by foot were common ten years ago, but now they are done by small boat. There has been an increase of boat usage most recently because of the increased availability of outboard engines and the fuel needed to operate them. Improved transport into the watershed, facilitated by the NT2 reservoir and the new tractor trails that WMPA helped build inside the watershed, means that fuel no longer needs to be carried in on people's backs. Residents of downstream villages (e.g., Sek villagers from Teung and Phong villagers from Poung) now regularly travel upstream by motorboat to buy supplies such as salt, bicycles, and tools from the Vietnamese markets, traveling through Kri villages on their way and upon return.

Prior to the flooding of the NT2 reservoir, there was an informal system of supply whereby residents of plateau villages closest to the points of access to the watershed maintained stocks of basic supplies, especially salt and fuel (the fuel mainly for the few hand tractors in the watershed). Watershed residents could access these supplies for less money and in a shorter amount of time. That is, a Maka resident needed only to go as far as Ka Oy if all he wanted was

Figure 6.1. Two Kri youths (at front and back of boat) transporting Vietnamese traders along the Nam Noy River. They were setting out downstream after processing at the Lao government's immigration checkpoint at Ban Maka, June 2009. Improved access into NNT (from both the NT2 reservoir, and on tracks built by WMPA), have made it easier to get boat motors and fuel into the protected area— thereby extending the reach of Vietnamese traders (including wildlife traders). Photo by N. J. Enfield.

salt. Since the flooding of the Nakai Plateau, it has become easier to get supplies such as salt, rice, fuel, and alcohol, the latter two bringing problems of their own. Alcohol abuse is a significant social and health problem in Laos. In the Kri case, the increased availability of alcohol has heightened the frequency of drinking bouts, which can last for days. These were traditionally restricted to special occasions, such as marriages and "new year" celebrations, but with greater access to inexpensive alcohol, drinking parties are occurring more often for no particular reason. These can be highly disruptive to village life, for reasons including diminished productivity and incidences of domestic violence.

In addition to making market access easier thanks to the well-stocked supply posts on the eastern edge of the reservoir, the new tractor trails also allow motorcycles to scuttle along them. If one has money to pay for boats, and one has access to a motorcycle, the trip from Nakai District center to Maka Village can now be completed in a few hours and without having to take barely a step on foot.

Conclusions

Kri people formerly had a relatively low-impact style of livelihood involving periodic movement from site to site within a limited home range. In the area of current Maka settlements, shifting cultivation was restricted to flat riverside land, which had usually been used previously for cultivation and then left fallow. But they do not have the same access to their ancestral lands along the Nam Noy as they used to. This is partly due to easier access in and out of the watershed and partly due to pressure from policies of the WMPA and the Lao government for villagers to settle permanently in consolidated village sites. Kri people have begun to move up onto the hillsides to clear forestland for upland cultivation.

Maka villagers have traditionally not made significant use of timber in their forest surrounds. Their main sources of building material are varieties of rattan and bamboo. But as development efforts have accelerated and the Kri are urged to live more sedentarily, their patterns of resource use are changing. Extraction of timber and other resources inevitably becomes more concentrated and thus less sustainable. Without access to their traditional range, the Kri are looking for arable land on higher ground, close to their fixed village base. In a new development, Kri people are making pioneering swidden fields on hillside and hilltop land, high above the valley in places that in the past would have been left alone.

Residents of villages in the Nam Noy area can cite obvious ways in which their lives urgently need improvement, including most importantly better access to medical care, land for cultivation, and the market for basic supplies such as salt. In these respects, Kri villagers say that the NT2 project has been beneficial to them. Today they enjoy increased access to the outside world, which has made their lives easier in various ways: more convenient transport, better access to infrastructure. But Kri villagers also recognize downsides of these major changes to their lifestyles. The rapid proliferation of consumer culture brings associated patterns of waste, pollution, and poor health from increased use of disposable luxuries, processed foods, and alcohol. These changes also lead an increased reliance on the outside world for everyday needs, which is turning villagers' attention away from the exploitation of renewable resources in their immediate environment and toward a focus on centralized market economies that demand cash. This in turn means that the Kri have a greater need for cash and may thus be more motivated to engage in unsustainable and illegal livelihood practices such as cutting and selling protected timber and wildlife trade. Both of these pursuits have also been significantly facilitated by better access to the watershed. In the context of an increasing reliance on a cash economy, it would be hard for any Kri villager not to be drawn into these activities.

A final effect of the rapid opening up of the watershed is an inevitable undoing of the tight social bonds that connect villages throughout the protected area. With each village now physically and socially linked more directly to the district center, Kri people will have less need and less opportunity to maintain the bonds that have for so long enriched, protected, and defined the broader interethnic community of the NT2 watershed.

The Kri experience has many lessons for anyone who would undertake a major development project that affects people's villages and homes. One lesson in particular stands out. It is that when planning such a project, it is absolutely crucial to attempt to see the project from the perspective of those project-affected people. It is telling that the *Social and Environmental Management Framework and First Operational Plan* frames the question of the Kri and other inhabitants of the catchment area as a matter of "ethnic minorities development," instead of, say, the "well being of catchment inhabitants." Kri people are of course aware of their political status as an ethnic minority, but this is hardly how they see themselves in daily life. They are, first and foremost, members of a community going about the business of raising their children, maintaining their social relationships, and trying to stay healthy, happy, and fed. And they are part of a complex web of economic and intercultural relations with numerous other villages and ethnic groups with whom they regularly come into contact. From their perspective, the activities and priorities of mainstream Lao government and culture are at the very fringes of their world. Any approach to working with them should not, therefore, be framed with those mainstream activities and priorities at the center.

To truly understand the threats and opportunities that a project like NT2 presents to project-affected people, to truly see things from their perspective, requires a significant investment of time, effort, and specialist skills (as is true of so many other elements of a major project, from modeling to surveying to finance). The point is not just to encourage empathy with affected people in the planning and execution of a project. Projects also need to get things right. A central project officer, being human, is likely to be unaware that his or her perspective on project-affected people is so skewed. We are naturally inclined to assume that others see the world in much the same ways as we ourselves do. But the fact is that ours is always just one perspective among many. This point is as simple as it is consequential. If questions of project planning and implementation are not genuinely posed and answered from the project-affected people's perspective, then the decisions that are made are unlikely to be truly in those people's interest and thus not in the interests of the project as a whole.

NOTES

This chapter is dedicated to Martin Stuart-Fox. Like any student of Laos, I owe Martin an enormous intellectual debt for his brilliant and pioneering scholarship. I also owe him a personal debt, for the warmth, support, and advice he offered a naive graduate student during my earliest visits to Laos, more than a quarter century ago.

I thank Bruce Shoemaker and Bill Robichaud for constructive commentary and careful readings of drafts of this chapter. The text explores issues that Bill and I have wrestled with in years of conversation.

1. For an introduction and overview of Kri-related issues, visit www.thekri.org.

2. James R. Chamberlain, *Nature and Culture in the Nakai-Nam Theun Conservation Area* (Vientiane: privately published, 1997).

3. As is to be expected, there are limitations: for example, while there are many species of bat in the Nakai Nam Theun National Protected Area, the Kri only have a single word meaning "bat" (*kreengq*) and no words for separate species. They are of course able to distinguish between, say, larger fruit bats and smaller insectivorous species by using various descriptors.

4. See Joost Foppes, *Domestication of Non-Timber Forest Products in the Nakai-Nam Theun NBCA*, District Upland Development and Conservation Project, June 2001.

5. Another important reason to move house is a death in the family. According to Kri cultural practice, when a family member dies (regardless of whether they die in the house or elsewhere), the house should be dismantled and rebuilt on another location. The floor of the house should be discarded.

6. See Jules Vidal, "Noms vernaculaires de plantes (Lao, Mèo, Kha) en usage en Laos," *BEFEO* 49, no. 2 (1959): 485.

7. See section 1.2. of NT2 WMPA, *Social and Environmental Management Framework and First Operational Plan*, April 1, 2005, to September 30, 2011, World Bank, January 2005, http://bit.ly/2iOoP1c.

7

Elusive Conservation in the Nam Theun 2 Catchment

WILLIAM ROBICHAUD

Always change a losing strategy.

Unknown

The Setting and the Hope

Almost any human endeavor, including a large hydropower project, is undertaken in a unique place, time, and culture. Appropriate alignment of the endeavor to its context will significantly influence its perceived success or failure. The place, time, and people need to be right.

The place of the Nam Theun 2 (NT2) dam is the Annamite Mountains and their foothills, along Laos's border with Vietnam. In terms of both biological and cultural diversity, it is one of the most remarkable areas in Asia. The Annamites' densely forested mountains and stream valleys are replete with species and languages found nowhere else in the world. In fact, it was here in 1992, just across the Vietnam border from the NT2 watershed, that arguably the most spectacular zoological find of the twentieth century was made, the scientific discovery of a new genus and species of large mammal, the saola (*Pseudoryx nghetinhensis*).[1]

Today, the portion of the Annamites that comprises the catchment of the NT2 dam is one of the most important nature reserves in the world, Nakai-Nam Theun National Protected Area (NNT NPA; formerly known in English as the Nakai-Nam Theun National Biodiversity Conservation Area, or NNT NBCA; figures 7.1 and 7.2).[2] Its high global conservation value derives from a combination of its location in the Annamites Mountains, its size (at more than 4,000 square kilometers with corridors, it is the largest gazetted protected area in Laos, Vietnam, or Cambodia), and the comparatively good condition of its forest cover (which is predominantly broadleaf evergreen or semiever-green forest). In fact, NNT NPA probably holds the world's largest nominally protected populations of several globally threatened species. Table 7.1 is a list for some of the best-known groups, amphibians, reptiles, and mammals (no birds are listed in the table; it is possible that some bird species meet the table's criteria, but none are yet known).

Understandably, the protected area became a central focus of environmental concerns about NT2. The World Bank endeavored to see that the project's likely impacts on NNT NPA were mitigated, and to frame better management and protection of Nakai-Nam Theun as an incremental conservation offset, to compensate for the area and significant biodiversity of the Nakai Plateau that would be put under water by inundation. Yet, despite extensive attention and resources given to the conservation of NNT under the NT2 enterprise, in late 2016, NT2's International Environmental and Social Panel of Experts (PoE) wrote, regarding management of Nakai-Nam Theun, that "continuation of the basically failed approach . . . will probably result in the [environmental protection] component of the NT2 project being determined to be unsatisfactory or in non-compliance."[3] Diagnoses of the causes of the disappointing results in NNT have tended toward the diverse and complicated, but the root problem, in fact, may be simple (if not simple to solve).

The World Bank's confidence in NT2's ability to deliver effective protection of NNT NPA was central to the Bank's approval of the project. There was a lot riding on this; once NT2 was completed, the shoreline of the new reservoir at full supply level would become NNT NPA's long western boundary, and the protected area would comprise nearly the entire catchment of the reservoir.[4] Its effective conservation could both benefit the long-term economics of the dam (by slowing siltation of the reservoir) and fulfill the Bank's own requirements that the project's environmental damage, particularly loss of biodiversity, be offset.[5]

In fact, according to NT2's proponents, if NNT NPA is not effectively protected under the aegis of NT2, the project and the new model it represents cannot be considered a success. The PoE wrote, "Success in managing and protecting the watershed [i.e., NNT NPA] is absolutely essential to the success of the NT2 Multi Purpose Development Project as a whole, and will be

Figure 7.1 A tributary of the Nam Theun River flows through the forest of NNT NPA. Photo by William Robichaud.

Figure 7.2. NNT NPA rises beyond the eastern shore of the NT2 reservoir, February 2012. Photo by William Robichaud.

Table 7.1. Some Threatened or Poorly Known Species That May Have Their Largest Nominally Protected Populations in NNT NPA

English Common Name	Scientific Name	IUCN Red List Status, 2017	Likelihood that NNT Holds World's Largest Nominally Protected Population
a frog not yet assigned a common English name	*Odorrana orba*	Data Deficient	high
a newt not yet assigned a common English name	*Tylototriton notialis*	Vulnerable	high
Indochinese box turtle	*Cuora galbinofrons*	Critically Endangered	moderate
Vietnamese three-striped box turtle	*Cuora cyclornata*	Critically Endangered as *C. trifasciata*, from which *C. cyclornata* was recently split as a separate species	presence of this turtle has not been confirmed, but is likely
pygmy slow loris	*Nycticebus pygmaeus*	Vulnerable	low
red-shanked douc	*Pygathrix nemaeus*	Endangered	high
white-cheeked crested gibbon	*Nomascus leucogenys* (sensu lato)*		high
Owston's civet	*Chrotogale owstoni*	Endangered	moderate
large-antlered muntjac	*Muntiacus vuquangensis*	Critically Endangered	high
similar muntjac species that may include Annamite dark muntjac and/or Roosevelts' muntjac	*M. truongsonensis/ rooseveltorum* species complex	Data Deficient	moderate?
saola	*Pseudoryx nghetinhensis*	Critically Endangered	moderate
Annamite striped rabbit	*Nesolagus timminsi*	Data Deficient	moderate?

*The IUCN Red List of Threatened Species divides this species into two, northern white-cheeked gibbon *N. leucogenys* (*sensu stricto*) and southern white-cheeked gibbon *N. siki*. The NNT gibbons are not sufficiently understood for them to be assigned to species.

Note: The table was compiled by the author in consultation with J. William Duckworth and Bryan L. Stuart.

important in affecting the reputation of those primarily involved with the Project."[6]

Protection of NNT from the impacts of NT2 was also required by the World Bank's own Operational Policy 4.04, which concerns natural habitats. Ironically, efforts to satisfy this operational policy seem to have significantly harmed NNT before the project started. One of the most important portions of NNT, the Nakai Plateau along the east bank of the Nam Theun River (which is home to, for example, Laos's largest population of Asian elephants, *Elephas maximus*) was excised from the protected area before the Bank's approval of NT2, in an apparent attempt to bring the project in line with the operational policy (for more on this and NT2's apparent noncompliance with the policy, see chapter 1).

The importance of ensuring that the project contributed to saving the remainder of NNT, combined with the absence of any examples of successful protected area management in Laos, prompted the World Bank to devise unprecedented measures to protect NNT. The most novel and prominent of these are as follows:

1. For the twenty-five-year concession period of the project, US$1M per year (indexed to inflation) of the dam's revenue will be used for protection and management of NNT NPA. The NT2 Power Company (NTPC) provides the annual payments, from the dam's revenue stream.[7] A lower level of preliminary funding was provided in advance of commencement of the dam's revenue flow, which in fact resulted in giving the protected area guaranteed funding for thirty-one and a half years.[8] Suddenly, thanks to NT2, NNT NPA became one of the most substantially and securely funded protected areas in the developing world.

2. To use these funds to manage NNT NPA, the World Bank required the government of the Lao PDR (GoL) to establish a new agency to manage the protected area. It was to be part of government but at least notionally external to the GoL line agencies that traditionally have responsibility for protected area management. This body, which was established by Prime Minister's Decree 25 in 2001 and commenced work in 2003, is the NT2 Watershed Management and Protection Authority (WMPA).

In addition to substantial and secure funding, WMPA was equipped with several other advantages that the World Bank hoped would engender success. It had a comprehensive management plan for the protected area, the *Social and Environmental Management Framework and First Operation Plan*.[9] The plan was prepared over several years by NTPC and runs to more than 350 pages.[10] Although the quality and suitability of the plan are debatable (for example, for a long time there was no Lao language translation of the plan), it was at least a comprehensive starting point. In addition, WMPA is supervised by two external monitoring bodies. One is the three-person PoE, contracted by the GoL, for which effective protection of NNT NPA has been a major focus. Two of the PoE's members, Lee Talbot and David McDowell, are former directors general of the International Union for the Conservation of Nature (IUCN). There is also an Independent Monitoring Agency, contracted by WMPA (which has raised doubts as to whether the agency is truly independent) and comprised of two international and two Lao members. Its sole remit is monitoring and guidance of WMPA.[11] WMPA was also given the guiding hand of a board of directors, drawn from senior levels of the GoL, and an executive secretariat to implement activities. Executive secretariat staff once numbered more than sixty, not counting dozens of part-time patrol rangers drawn from and based in villages in NNT. WMPA, although technically a GoL agency, was free and indeed required to pay staff salaries that are significantly higher than the standard for GoL employees, giving it at least the potential to attract talent. In fact, for a given staff level, WMPA probably pays the highest government salaries in the country. In the organization's early years, it also had up to four full-time, on-site international technical advisors at one time. Staff of the World Bank Lao office were also closely involved in monitoring and supporting WMPA's performance, which sometimes included intervening in and mediating sensitive political issues (such as efforts to keep illicit commercial logging and gold mining out of the protected area). In sum, few protected areas in Southeast Asia, if any, have as many material resources and advantages for successful management as WMPA.

Reality Met

Despite the substantial advantages arranged for protection of NNT through NT2, it is generally acknowledged that the experiment did not work. Commercial poaching of both timber and wildlife has continued largely unchecked.[12] In fact, cross-border poaching from Vietnam is so severe that in the 5–10 kilometer-wide band of NNT along the Vietnam border, very few wild animals larger than a few kilograms in size remain.[13] On a walk through even remote reaches of the protected area, one is as likely to encounter long lines of wire snares as some of the area's dwindling wildlife (figures 7.3 and 7.4).[14] Tigers (*Panthera tigris*) have probably been extirpated from the protected area (see figure 7.5) during the NT2 era, and it is at least possible

Figure 7.3. Village ranger in NNT NPA with wire snares removed during a patrol and expedition in 2009. Photo by William Robichaud.

Figure 7.4. A male large-antlered muntjac dead in a snare set by Vietnamese poachers in NNT NPA, in 2009. This rare species is endemic to the Annamite Mountains and is listed as Critically Endangered (the last stop before extinction) on the IUCN Red List. Photo by William Robichaud.

Figure 7.5. This is the first known photograph of a tiger in the wild in Laos, taken by a camera trap in NNT NPA in January 1999, as part of preparatory biodiversity studies for the NT2 project. It is also the last photograph of a tiger in NNT. By the time NT2-funded management and monitoring of the protected area began in 2006, the species was no longer detectable there, and is probably now extirpated from the protected area. Photo by William Robichaud/WCS.

that the critically endangered saola is also now gone (see text box on page 170).[15]

In response to criticism of its poor performance and at the direction of the GoL, WMPA experimented with changing its role. The organization had been established as a stand-alone implementation agency with a large staff. Then, in 2010, in an effort to better nest it within GoL structures and engage wider GoL assistance, it transformed into essentially a technical advisory body and funds manager; under this new arrangement, the implementation work of protected area management was delegated to relevant GoL agencies in the local districts and provinces. Ironically, WMPA was created at the request of the World Bank—at great expense—specifically to compensate for low conservation capacity in local government agencies, and yet the answer was now seen as delegation to those agencies. The restructuring coincided with the appointment of a new WMPA executive secretariat director who was soon widely viewed as unsuitable. He was eventually replaced, but only after several years at the helm. In addition, the local government agencies were not supported with significant numbers of additional staff to help fulfill their new responsibilities. These factors complicate assessment of the suitability of the new model of delegation to local agencies. In any event, the change did not result in better protection of NNT, and by all accounts, more likely the opposite.

The continuing poor results at protection of NNT and consequent disappointment are chronicled in the reports of the PoE, whose members were initially strong advocates of NT2 and put much stock in the project's promise of social and environmental benefits. Following are some of the PoE's progressively dire assessments:

February 2013: "For a variety of reasons WMPA has not been particularly successful in the past, most especially in terms of conservation of biodiversity."[16]

March 2013: "WMPA has been totally ineffective in protecting the watershed's biodiversity."[17]

May 2014: "In virtually every Report since 2001 the PoE has emphasized problems with the WMPA's performance in carrying out its mandates. . . . The situation has now become critical."[18]

December 2014: "In our extensive consultations in Vientiane, Thakhek, the Nakai Plateau and the watershed, we have found that there is a widespread lack of confidence and trust in the WMPA."[19]

October 2015: "[There are] extremely serious problems with WMPA."[20]

By late 2013, the situation had deteriorated to the point that the World Bank and the GoL's Department of Planning and Cooperation of the Ministry of Natural Resources and Environment commissioned a comprehensive, external review of WMPA. The findings of the review are summarized in a report released in 2014.[21] The report details considerable dysfunctions and identifies the core constraint on WMPA's effectiveness as a "muddled institutional management mechanism for the Watershed"; conservation leadership was "lacking," and the organization failed to address "the initial objectives." The report further identified eight factors that contributed to this core problem. Most of them concern institutional issues, and only one, "rapidly growing pressure on natural resources," is external to WMPA and its management arrangement.

That said, the pressure on NNT's resources is an important factor. WMPA's task is by no means easy. It faces immense challenges in protecting the large expanse of NNT, especially given the approximately seven thousand villagers living inside the protected area and the area's long, porous border with Vietnam, which is a conduit of intense poaching activity. Nonetheless, the general conclusion is that WMPA has fallen far short of expectations and has achieved much less than expected, given its abundant advantages. As the report of the organizational review put it, "Many protected areas managers worldwide would be happy to have this type of funding, furthermore as it is guaranteed over thirty years."[22]

Through the years, PoE reports identified similar internal problems with WMPA, namely, low staff capacity, ineffective management, misplaced emphasis (too much on development that was not linked to conservation and too little on conservation generally), and unsuitable organizational structure. Fixes to most were tried, to little avail. Finally, acting in part on the organizational review, in early 2014 the PoE, the Independent Monitoring Agency, the GoL, and NTPC insisted that WMPA undergo a more sweeping overhaul, stopping just short of a complete dissolution of the organization and abandonment of its model. The house was to be torn down to its frame but not replaced, only rebuilt. A long and convoluted process of restructuring ensued, which resulted in the contracts of most WMPA staff, including all of its senior managers, not being renewed. A high-level, interagency task force was formed to review WMPA's shortcomings and guide the restructuring. Its members include senior representatives of the GoL, staff of the World Bank and at least one well-respected Lao conservationist.

Unfortunately, by the second half of 2016, the long process of attempting to provide better protection for NNT by restructuring WMPA had ground to an unsatisfying halt. In its report issued in September 2016, the PoE wrote, "almost two years later virtually everyone that the PoE has consulted has emphasized that there have been no real results and that the restructuring, etc., must be considered a failure."[23] The ecologist Garrett Hardin once reminded us that some problems cannot be solved by the application of technical—or in this case, structural—solutions.[24]

More than two decades have passed since preparations began in earnest for NT2, with hopes and promises that the project would be a new model for the delivery of social and environmental benefits in the developing world. In that time, millions of words, literally, have been written about how to use NT2 to protect the exceptional biological richness of NNT NPA, in hundreds of pages of reports by the PoE and the Independent Monitoring Agency, in the *Social and Environmental Management Framework and First Operational Plan*, in survey reports, WMPA documents, and in enough emails to fill the reservoir to full supply level. Millions more words have been spoken in countless meetings and workshops. Yet there has been little to show for this, or for the millions of dollars expended (monies far in excess of the millions expended by WMPA—millions more have been collectively spent by other GoL agencies, the World Bank, PoE, etc.). NNT is little closer to effective protection from poaching than before most of those involved first heard the words "Nam Theun 2."

Sifting for Answers

In an article that biologists Joe Tobias, Peter Davidson, and I published in 1998 on NT2's role in conservation, we posed in the title the question "can development save one of South-East Asia's last wildernesses?"[25] The answer that has played out seems to be "no," and the next question to ask is, why didn't things go better in NNT? In particular, why has the WMPA model proved so resistant to success?

The root issue is probably not among those for which fixes have been tried: unclear mission, questionable leadership, inappropriate structure, weak staff, or the other real and valid problems identified by the PoE and the WMPA organizational review. Rather, PoE reports and the review can be read as a roll call of the consequences of a crucial issue that has gone largely unspoken: lack of motivation for biodiversity conservation. It is principally for lack of interest in its conservation mission that WMPA has not succeeded. Most other issues are peripheral symptoms of this, and cures are rarely found in the treatment of symptoms.

I served as one of WMPA's technical advisors for three and a half years, from 2006–2009. Of the approximately fifty staff at that time, only about five of them, or 10 percent, were truly interested in conservation, from the heart. The rest worked for the organization solely for the generous pay, or because the GoL had assigned them there. This lack of interest in the organization's core mission was paired with a near absence of any expertise in biodiversity conservation. The organizational review could find only one staff member with training in natural resources management. In the field of successful organizational culture and management, it is not considered good practice to assign responsibility for tasks to individuals who have neither interest in them nor the capacity to carry them out. Part of the constraint lies in the dearth of capacity for such work in Laos generally; but in addition, WMPA was structured to pay high salaries to attract competent professional conservation staff, and the high salaries spawned a patronage system by which some jobs went to poorly qualified civil servants with good connections.

But even WMPA's lack of enthusiasm for its mission is its own sort of symptom. It was formed as a new agency within a government that had not shown significant interest in nature conservation since it took the commendable, progressive step in 1993 to establish a system of national protected areas (including NNT). Consequently, WMPA is nested within a culture that does not encourage its goals and in fact often acts contrary to them. For example, the involvement of government staff in illegal logging and the wildlife trade has been well documented.[26]

WMPA also doesn't get much guidance or encouragement for its mission from the outside. Its funder, the engineering consortium NTPC, does not have biodiversity conservation as part of its core mission; in fact, its core mission, hydropower development, is generally destructive to biodiversity. Nor is biodiversity conservation part of the mission statement of NT2's chief architect, the World Bank. This is not criticism of NTPC nor the World Bank, just an acknowledgment of reality. Without doubt, there are individuals within these institutions and within the GoL who take conservation to heart and who have fought for NNT's protection. But as institutions they are poorly equipped to drive successful conservation. Where, at the heart of the effort to save one of the world's most important protected areas, was an organization whose mission, expertise, and passion lay mostly in conservation? Imagine building a large dam without engineers.

It is worth considering that most large hydropower projects, at least those with profiles similar to NT2, must achieve three goals to be considered successful: excellence in the construction and operation of the dam, excellence in supporting the livelihoods of people displaced or otherwise affected by the project, and excellence in protection of the dam's catchment (and also protection of a biodiversity offset, if agencies such as the World Bank are involved and if negative impacts cannot be mitigated near the source). These three undertakings require vastly different skill sets—engineering, social welfare, and biodiversity conservation. No one would dream, for example, of giving a conservation organization, such as the Wildlife Conservation Society (WCS) or World Wide Fund for Nature (WWF), overall responsibility for delivering all three, including construction of the dam. Yet it is common practice to give an engineering consortium, NTPC in this case, overall responsibility for building a dam and delivering the project's social welfare and biodiversity conservation outcomes—either as a supervising donor or as an implementing agency. A significant limitation of giving responsibility for conservation to a business consortium with shareholders is its core profit motive. Such a consortium is unlikely to embrace biodiversity conservation unless legally or contractually required to do so. Consequently, its foremost goal in the endeavor will be to minimize cost, not maximize results. Compare this to what gets a nonprofit conservation organization out of bed in the morning.

An environmental assessment of the likely impact of NT2 inundation predicted, accurately, that the greatest project-driven threat to NNT would be the ease of access that the new reservoir would provide to the protected area.[27] Before NT2, access from the outside to the interior of NNT was mainly either by foot or by boat going upstream along the Nam Theun River or some of its tributaries, which have their sources in the protected area. But boat access was difficult, due to rocky barriers and rapids along these rivers. Once inundation submerged many of these natural barriers, the reservoir and the inundated rivers that flowed into it were at high risk of becoming a poacher's highway. According to the NT2 concession agreement, NTPC had responsibility for mitigating this and for controlling entry into NNT from the reservoir—an engineering consortium with no previous experience or culture of protected area management and, more importantly, with no particular interest in it.[28]

As an institution, the World Bank has remained closely involved in NNT and WMPA as a committed, external problem solver. But the Bank is probably motivated more by a wish to prevent the NT2 experiment from failing (or to prevent it from being perceived as a failure) than to conserve wild animals and plants. The two are not the same. How many staff of the World Bank, NTPC, or WMPA waken and start the day thinking about the fate of red-shanked doucs or large-antlered muntjacs in NNT NPA? The number is certainly very small. This lack of interest is the core constraint, rather than any aspect of institutional structure in WMPA. Consequently, despite a decade of trying, the solution has not been found in the latter and never can be. Alignment with human nature awaits.

Although a dearth of motivation for conservation is a seemingly obvious and fundamental issue, it has rarely been discussed within the milieu of NT2 and NNT. Banks, government agencies, and engineering consortia tend to be more attracted to technical fixes. One exception came in 2005, about the time that WMPA was formed. Environmental Defense (now known as Environmental Defense Fund), compiled a review of NNT's comprehensive management plan, which was to be implemented by WMPA. The review noted:

> The management of the Nakai Nam Theun National Protected Area (NNT NPA) will be funded primarily by contributions from NTPC of US$1 million per year. The provision of substantial funding alone is unlikely to result in the sound management of NNT. The main constraint to improved management of the area is poor institutional commitment and a lack of secure property rights for local people, not funding. If funds are used inappropriately, greater environmental degradation and negative impacts on the livelihoods of NNT's residents are possible and perhaps even likely.[29]

Even earlier, in 2000, the World Bank funded, through a loan to the GoL, an initiative in NNT called the District Upland Development and Conservation Project (DUDCP). The project was intended as a test run and provider of lessons learned in anticipation of NT2's financial support for management of NNT and the founding of WMPA. The project did not go well.[30] In the lessons-learned report, Ramesh Boonratana, the project's wildlife consultant, identified lack of motivation in the implementing partners as a core issue: "Interest is the greatest motivation for learning and fulfilling ascribed responsibilities. One of the main reasons for failure in achieving the desired results in the training of field conservation staff is primarily due to the lack of interest in fieldwork amongst the members who are government staff."[31] Lessons were learned and reported, but not subsequently applied, and the project proved to be simply a harbinger of more disappointments to come. Application of learning can be difficult, and knowledge does not always overcome habit, institutional inertia, and the attractive ease of the status quo.

It is worth considering why the presence of motivated, long-term technical advisors to WMPA was insufficient to foster success. WMPA had at least six technical advisors, each serving various periods from 2005 to 2014, from diverse backgrounds (two Australians, one American, one Englishman, one Lao, and one Thai). Of course, the capacity and suitability of each varied, and none was perfect, but all shared a genuine commitment to WMPA's mission. Yet a lesson from the WMPA experiment is that the influence of technical advisors is decidedly limited. At least in the WMPA case, they were external to the organizational structure and were therefore often excluded from decision making, and unable to offer much input on key drivers of organizational success such as staff recruitment. Providing an organization with advice in fields in which it is not fundamentally interested can be whistling in the wind. This is not to say that WMPA's technical advisors did not do some good and make some positive contributions—most of them did. But their input could not change the endgame.

The Disappearing Endangered Species

That the NT2 project attempted to insert world-class conservation into an unsuitable political and institutional environment is reflected in the impact the project had, years before impoundment of the reservoir, on the protection of arguably the most important wildlife species for conservation attention in the project area, and indeed all of Laos (and one of the highest conservation priorities in the world), the saola. This distinctive hoofed mammal, in its own genus, was first discovered by science in Vietnam only in 1992 and was one of the most surprising zoological finds of the twentieth century.[32] The species is endemic to the Annamite Mountains, in which the NT2 catchment lies. After the discovery of the saola in Vietnam, the species' occurrence in Laos was soon confirmed, initially from horns found in villages in and near NNT.[33] The species occurs only in Laos and Vietnam.

In Vietnam, the discovery of this magnificent and rare species was celebrated with pride. But in Laos, a different attitude prevailed. The proximity of saola to the NT2 project area, at a time when the World Bank was evaluating if it should support NT2, was not welcome news to the GoL. From the time of the confirmation of saolas' occurrence in Laos in the mid-1990s, to World Bank approval of the NT2 project in 2005, some within the GoL feared that attention to the animal would put approval of NT2 at risk. This was despite the fact that it was known that saola had not been found on the Nakai Plateau or in any other areas that would be directly affected by the project. It inhabited only the upper reaches of NNT NPA, well beyond the NT2 inundation zone, and the protection of which was a hallmark promise of NT2.

Figures 7.6. Saola (*circled, left*) disappears from the cover of the Lao translation (*right*) of the book *Wildlife in Lao PDR: 1999 Status Report*

The World Bank saw successful saola conservation as both a pivotal benefit and requirement of the NT2 project. In fact, as part of the preliminary studies and preparations it mandated for its consideration of NT2, the Bank required preparation of a saola conservation action plan. As part of its involvement in NT2, WCS drafted an action plan in 1997, and revised it in 1999 with the International Union for the Conservation of Nature (IUCN), again under the aegis of NT2 and at the request of the World Bank.[34]

Neither version of the plan attracted much interest from the GoL, which subsequently made no move to implement it.[35] Despite encouragement to see and proactively use saola conservation as a positive rationale for NT2, GoL officials remained fearful that attention to saola might fan the flames of international opposition to the project.

The shadow that NT2 cast over saola conservation took a strange, Orwellian turn soon after the revised action plan was completed. In 1999, IUCN, WCS, and the Lao Department of Forestry's former Centre for Protected Areas and Watershed Management (CPAWM) jointly published a comprehensive review of the status of every species of vertebrate, except fishes, ever reported from Laos.[36] The book was an update and expansion of an earlier, slimmer work published by IUCN in

171

1993.[37] The new volume was a significant and valuable achievement. For the cover of the English-language edition of the update, IUCN assembled a collage of photos of Lao wildlife, including images of some of the country's most iconic and conservation-significant species. Included in this gallery was, naturally, a photograph of a saola—a beautiful camera-trap photo taken earlier the same year in Bolikhamxay Province (and the first wild photograph of the species in Laos), during a research trip in preparation for writing of the saola action plan. After IUCN published the English edition, CPAWM prepared a Lao translation. The Lao version was published about a year after its English counterpart. In general appearance, it is nearly identical to the English volume—same size, format, and so forth. Other than language, its cover differs in only one respect: the image of the saola is gone, replaced by a photo of a red muntjac (*Muntiacus muntjac*), a species common in many parts of Asia, including Laos, and of no conservation concern (and despite the fact that another species of muntjac was already pictured on the cover) (figure 7.6).[38]

Just a few years before millions of NT2 dollars would start flowing to support a government agency to conserve a key area of the saola's range, this was not a good omen. We can only hope that saola's disappearance from the cover of the book does not presage its disappearance from the forests of NNT.

Another Way—Engaging Motivation

Protected area management and the conservation of threatened biota are not easy. In our current Anthropocene epoch, they generally take extraordinary commitment and a high degree of competence. Given all that was riding on the NT2 endeavor, viewed from the outside it is surprising that a professional, motivated conservation organization was not engaged from the beginning to help manage NNT. In the early 2000s, as the World Bank worked to shape NT2 into a model they could approve, several conservationists urged it to involve conservation NGOs in the protection of NNT. The suggestion was rebuffed over concerns mainly about Lao sovereignty. Curiously, the Bank subsequently indicated that it understood the importance of such involvement, at least in principle. Its self-published volume on the history of NT2, *Doing a Dam Better: The Lao People's Democratic Republic and the Story of Nam Theun 2*, notes that "countries with limited human and financial capacity . . . need to rely on private developers to undertake responsibilities the government is unable to meet."[39] But the Bank took little action on this understanding in the conservation sphere. The only action it took, besides facilitating WMPA to hire a short-term, part-time biodiversity conservation technical advisor, was to require WMPA to contract WCS to help WMPA set up a wildlife monitoring program for the protected area. But WCS was not invited to give input on management decisions for the protected area.

Conservationists also lobbied the World Bank to at least introduce conditionality and thereby attempt to manufacture more motivation within the GoL for conservation, by linking disbursement of the dam's revenues—or at the very least, that portion of the revenues earmarked to fund WMPA—to performance in protecting NNT; but this, too, was rejected; again, on grounds of national sovereignty.

Three things are worth considering regarding sovereignty. First, concerns about national sovereignty did not, for example, stop NT2 planners from engaging international professionals to design and construct the dam. Why the implementation of conservation should have been treated differently is not clear, but the consequences are visible today in NNT.

Second, this is not about an arrogant bias that favors foreigners over Lao. It simply follows the motivation. That said, given the more engaged culture for conservation within international NGOs, higher salaries there than the government norm, and more opportunities for staff learning and development, many of the brightest, best-educated and enthusiastic Lao conservationists in the country work or have worked in the local Lao offices of international conservation NGOs. How much meaning does "international" have, when most of the staff of these organizations, increasingly including those in leadership positions, are Lao? To find some of the most dynamic, motivated Lao working in conservation, go to the offices of the international conservation NGOs, or the national nonprofit Wildlife Conservation Association. Motivation for the protection of nature lives there, and it is from that motivation that creative solutions, capacity, and success will flow. Of course, some outstanding and dedicated conservationists can also be found within GoL agencies. But the reality is that there are fewer there, and others who underperform are better tolerated and so more common. And even the most inspired conservation talent may have limited opportunity for influence within a political and administrative culture that does not place high priority on conservation.

Finally, using external expertise, in fact, aligns with Lao sovereignty. The GoL has expressed its sovereignty by choosing to not develop within its agencies significant capacity for biodiversity conservation or protected area management.[40] The GoL has seen fit to focus on other priorities, such as traditional economic growth. To expect it to now field large numbers of highly motivated and skilled staff for a challenging conservation project is its own soft shade of imperialism, in being clearly contrary to GoL priorities. It also sets up all involved for disappointment, frustration, and criticism—precisely the pattern of the past decade in NNT and WMPA.

Another justification for not engaging professional conservation institutions was the expressed wish to build Lao capacity for biodiversity conservation. This is laudable, but training (like advice) laid over lack of interest has little traction. Rather, start with interested and motivated people or institutions, and they will pursue and develop their own capacity and absorb capacity building from the outside. WMPA, in fact, has developed a capacity to do some things well, such as constructing tracks in the protected area. Unfortunately, much of what it did best was not conservation, and this simply reflects the government culture in which it operates. Additional training, funding, and restructuring are themselves unlikely to change this.[41]

The PoE said as much in its report in late 2016: "There is an urgent need to change the institutional culture of the Secretariat. Since the culture is determined by the staff and leadership, changing the culture requires changing the staff and most leadership."[42] I agree with the diagnosis, but not the prescription. Persistent tolerance of underperforming staff and weak leadership is not the cause of an unmotivated culture; *it is the result of it.*

In any case, if a fix were sought by simply changing staff at all levels, who would recruit, select, train, and lead the staff? Will it be government echelons that are highly motivated to achieve nature conservation and who possess a high level of knowledge of what that requires? If not, swapping staff is unlikely to lead to fundamental change. Even if such staff were selected from GoL ranks with the guidance of a conservation organization (as the PoE recommends) where will such highly motivated and qualified staff come from?[43]

The organizational review of WMPA also describes an overemphasis on rural development delinked from conservation, to the detriment of its core conservation mission. Again, this simply reflects GoL priorities. In one of the world's least developed countries, this emphasis on rural development is perhaps understandable—even if the country's long-term welfare, and its commitments under NT2, depend on sound environmental protection.[44]

What of the villagers who live in NNT, and engaging them? In the late 1990s, I conducted field surveys of a proposed northern extension to NNT NPA (the World Bank tried, unsuccessfully, to broker with the GoL the addition of this highly important extension to NNT as a condition of Bank approval of NT2). One day in camp, attempting to make small talk with my exceptionally capable Hmong guide, Khoua-cha, I thoughtlessly asked if he had ever attended school and if he could read and write. "No," he answered. After an uncomfortable pause, with a sweep of his hand toward the green canopy, he added, "But this forest is my school, and I've been studying here every day of my life." The residents of NNT are important—and potentially highly motivated—partners in conservation of the area's natural resources; they form the core of its patrol teams, for example. Linguist and anthropologist James Chamberlain (author of chapter 4 of this book) observed in his insightful, nuanced work *Nature and Culture in the Nakai-Nam Theun Conservation Area*, that "in Nakai-Nam Theun or elsewhere, we should first of all understand the ecological system as inclusive of ethnic or human diversity, and then, and only then, can development efforts begin to build on what is already there."[45] This is underscored by the fact that although the area we today call NNT has been inhabited by humans for hundreds, and perhaps thousands, of years, until the advent of the modern Lao state in the mid-1970s it retained approximately 95 percent of its forest cover.[46] Unfortunately, another consequence of weak institutional motivation for genuine conservation has been the sometimes poor quality of management's engagement with the residents of the protected area. Villagers need and deserve to be engaged with enthusiasm and integrity. Yet the DUDCP wildlife consultant's report observed:

> At the level of the patrolling and monitoring units, it is possible and feasible to draw manpower from the existing stakeholder communities and agencies to address the "lack" of human resources. At a higher level, however, there still need to be qualified and competent individuals. They are to provide the leadership, motivation, and guidance to the patrolling and monitoring units. By right, positions at this level should be assumed by the [NPA] staff, but given the current level of capacity, interest, commitment, and bureaucracy, they cannot and should not yet assume this role.[47]

Where Next?

Recent PoE reports and the WMPA organizational review discussed the engagement of a conservation NGO in support of NNT's management. The PoE, for example, recommended that "WMPA seek to establish an ongoing partnership or other relationship with a qualified international NGO" and that its board of directors "conclude an MOU with the Wildlife Conservation Society (WCS) to serve as a partner organization with the WMPA." The PoE noted that they and others who had pushed for a reorganization had "all strongly recommended" that WMPA find "a partner organization," one that could "provide the experience and expertise required to develop an effective organization" to make it possible for it "to carry out [its] mandate."[48] There was precedent for this, just downstream from NT2 in fact, at the Theun-Hinboun hydropower dam. There, the Theun-Hinboun Power Company simply contracted WCS to work with the GoL to deliver the project's desired conservation outcomes.[49] The results are generally considered to be much better than anything yet seen in NNT.[50]

In 2017, a solution to involve WCS in the management of NNT, which was strongly pushed by the PoE with support from the World Bank, was rejected by the GoL. The parties eventually resolved the impasse by agreeing to an alternative: that a consortium of four smaller organizations would be assembled to work with and support WMPA technically. This new NGO consortium was established in October 2017 under the name Nakai-Nam Theun Biodiversity Conservation Consortium (NNT BCC). The four founding organizations of the NNT BCC are: the Wildlife Conservation Association, a Lao civil society association established in 2013; Project Anoulak, a small French-registered NGO that, since its inception in 2013, has focused largely on wildlife research and protection in NNT; Agrisud International, a French-registered livelihood development NGO, which has operated in Laos since 2009; and Creative Literacy Laos, an Australian-registered NGO that was created in 2013 specifically to implement community education and conservation awareness activities in NNT.

The consortium has a five-year consultancy contract with WMPA. Most of the funding for engaging the consortium comes from the Lao Environment Protection Fund (from funds provided mainly by the World Bank), and a lesser amount from WMPA's large annual budget from NT2 revenues. The contracted services of the consortium are a blend of technical advice to WMPA, capacity building and some supervision and implementation of activities in a five year WMPA workplan. Importantly, the consortium also has some fiduciary power, as it is must co-sign with WMPA approval for WMPA's spending on implementation activities in NNT.

Whether this arrangement can reverse the course in NNT remains to be seen. In at least some substantial measure, it is already too late, coming as it does more than a decade after NT2 was approved and the dam's construction began. Much has already been lost from NNT, and much of that is probably beyond recovery or feasible restoration. Perhaps most importantly, this logical option was achieved only after years of intense pressure by the PoE, the Independent Monitoring Agency, and the World Bank. The NT2 model of using large infrastructure in the service of biodiversity conservation, within a context of limited desire for conservation, is clearly not suitable for replication elsewhere. Regardless of whether or not the arrangement with the new consortium can, against most precedent in Laos, deliver from this point forward, the overall NT2 model did not work as portrayed and promoted.

Given the considerable shortcomings and disappointments, it is interesting to speculate whether or not NNT NPA is still better off now than it would have been without the NT2 project. Of course this can never been known for certain. It is likely that WMPA's overemphasis on rural development, including its vigorous program of track construction in the protected area, have resulted in more harm than good to the biodiversity of NNT. On the positive side, the dedication and efforts of, in particular, the World Bank, PoE, and some partners in the GoL have been fundamental to keeping (or removing) large-scale pulses of degradation from the protected area (such as industrial logging and mining). This is important and should not to be forgotten. But it is likely that no participant in the project—be it the World Bank, the GoL, NTPC, or the external monitoring bodies—would dispute that protection of the area has fallen far short of the expectations and promises of the NT2 endeavor.

Proponents of NT2 hoped that the project would be transformative, and much was provided to try to achieve this.[51] It is unlikely that any future infrastructure project in the region will be endowed with as rich a concentration of preparation, funding, and external monitoring to achieve biodiversity conservation as NT2; still, with little result. But from this disappointment, perhaps NT2 can still be taken as transformative in other ways.

The World Bank attempted to carry out a large conservation project in an unreceptive environment. It probably meant well, but being a bank, it naturally saw a solution in financing; if WMPA was well funded, it could provide sufficient salaries to attract qualified, motivated staff. Unfortunately, it hasn't. Money cannot buy genuine motivation or gather it from a pool where little exists.

Fundamentally, it may be a nonstarter to use environmental destruction as a vehicle for environmental protection. Their stars do not align. As Chamberlain notes, after offering a critical analysis of the etymologies of the words "management" and "development," "For the Nakai-Nam Theun, then, what we are saying, at the most primitive level, is that in order to preserve ('protect') it, we must stomp on it, and make it submit to our authority, while at the same time converting its chaos into order."[52]

At the very least, as a starting point, if NT2 is to be transformative, it could be by bringing to an end the era of delegating nature conservation to engineering companies, development banks, and unmotivated government agencies. For such projects in the future, let engineers handle the construction, banks handle the financing, and government agencies the policy issues, and give the work of conservation to motivated conservation professionals. Anything else is folly. In fact, *Doing a Dam Better* identified the importance of this principle, in another context: "Just as communications specialists should not take the lead in designing bridges or drafting resettlement plans, it makes little sense for economists or engineers to drive the communication strategy."[53] Or, it can be added, the conservation strategy.

In some cases and countries, sufficient conservation professionalism to pair with development projects can be found in government agencies, and if so it should be embraced. If not, engagement of professional, qualified conservation organizations *from the outset, from planning through implementation,* will be necessary. It may not always work. Some NGOs may not wish to be associated with large development projects,[54] and others that do participate will always face an uphill struggle within a weak enabling environment. While professional conservation involvement is necessary, it alone is not sufficient. In Laos for example, much greater government commitment to conservation of the country's biodiversity is essential. Many of us who work in conservation believe that such a shift is possible and offer hope and encouragement that it comes soon.

For NNT, precious time has been lost, a window has already closed, and it remains to be seen what can still be redeemed. In his book that focused largely on the effort to save saola in NNT, environmental writer William deBuys observed of the area:

> Doucs still troop through its treetops, and the diligent searchers, with a modicum of luck, may yet hear the outlandish cry of the crested argus. The sambar, binturong and colugo remain. A cacophony of birds prevails. The large-antlered muntjac sounds its bark in the night. The python, although lamentably rare, keeps its place, and at least a few streams, like the Nam Mon, retain their otters. Surprising to relate, in a far corner of NNT, elephants continue to wear paths through the forest. Despite the riot of wildlife wealth, however, a theme of loss plays on.[55]

NOTES

1. Vu Van Dung, Pham Mong Giao, Nguyen Ngoc Chinh, Do Tuoc, Peter Arctander, and John MacKinnon, "A New Species of Living Bovid from Vietnam," *Nature* 363 (1993).

2. William Robichaud, "Nakai-Nam Theun National Protected Area," in *Evidence-Based Conservation: Lessons from the Lower Mekong,* ed. Terry C. H. Sunderland, Jeffrey Sayer, and Minh-Ha Hoang (Bogor, Indonesia: Council to Improve Foodborne Outbreak Repsonse, 2013), 110–24.

3. PoE 25:47.

4. Before the NT2 project, the boundary of NNT NPA extended all the way to the Nam Theun River. See chapter 1 for more on the change of the boundary.

5. PoE 21:5.

6. PoE 19:25.

7. Funding for management of Nakai-Nam Theun actually commenced before commercial operation of the dam, and support for the twenty-five-year concession period is not conditional on profitability.

8. Stephen Duthy to Robichaud, email, October 12, 2016.

9. NT2 WMPA, *Social and Environmental Management Framework and First Operational Plan,* April 1, 2005, to September 30, 2011, World Bank, January 2005.

10. The 2005 *Social and Environmental Management Framework and First Operational Plan* indicates that it was prepared by WMPA, but it wasn't. Things may have turned out better if it had been, but it was written by staff and consultants of NTPC, with some input from World Bank staff and consultants. This is another example of how with NT2, things were not always as they seemed.

11. Francis Lauginie, *Organizational Review of the WMPA, Inception Report: Main Observations and Recommendations,* working document, World Bank and the GoL Department of Planning and Cooperation of the Ministry of Natural Resources and Environment, 2014.

12. Camille N. Z. Coudrat, Chanthalaphone Nanthavong, Sengphachanh Sayavong, Arlyne H. Johnson, Jim B. Johnston, and William Robichaud, "Non-Panthera Cats in Nakai-Nam Theun National Protected Area, Lao PDR," *CATNews* 8 (2014).

13. Robert J. Timmins, personal communication, based on unpublished results from a field survey in 2015.

14. For an in-depth and lyrical chronicle of the catastrophic poaching problem in Nakai-Nam Theun, see William deBuys, *The Last Unicorn: A Search for One of the Earth's Rarest Creatures* (New York: Little, Brown, 2015).

15. Robert J. Timmins, personal communication, based on unpublished results from a field survey in 2015.

16. PoE 20:38.

17. PoE 21a:5.

18. PoE 22:39.

19. PoE 23:37.

20. PoE 24:72.

21. Lauginie, *Organizational Review of the WMPA.*

22. Lauginie, *Organizational Review of the WMPA,* 19.

23. PoE 25, 45.

24. Garrett Hardin, "The Tragedy of the Commons," *Science* 162, no. 3859 (1968).

25. Joe Tobias, Peter Davidson, and William Robichaud, "Nakai-Nam Theun: Can Development Save One of South-East Asia's Last Wildernesses?," *Oriental Bird Club Bulletin* 28 (1998): 24–29.

26. See, for example, Nick Davies and Oliver Holmes, "Revealed: How Senior Laos Officials Cut Deals with Animal Traffickers," *The Guardian*, September 27, 2016, https://www.theguardian.com/environment/2016/sep/27/revealed-how-senior-laos-officials-cut-deals-with-animal-traffickers.

27. Dersu and Associates, *Wildlife Management and Monitoring Plan*, Nam Theun 2 Power Company Ltd., 2007.

28. NTPC was so disinclined to patrol the reservoir that they essentially forced WMPA to accept delegation of this task to them, with funding from NTPC.

29. Environmental Defense, "Review of the Nakai-Nam Theun Social and Environmental Management Framework and First Operational Plan (SEMFOP-1) for the Nam Theun 2 Hydropower Project," Environmental Defense, 2005, 2.

30. William Robichaud, "Lessons Learned from the District Upland Development and Conservation Project (DUDCP), Nakai-Nam Theun National Biodiversity Conservation Area, Lao PDR: A Report to the World Bank," DUDCP, October 2003.

31. Ramesh Boonratana, "DUDCP: Draft Lessons Learned, Wildlife Expert's Contribution," DUDCP, unpublished report, 2003.

32. Dung et al., "A New Species of Living Bovid from Vietnam."

33. George B. Schaller and Alan Rabinowitz, "The Saola or Spindlehorn Bovid *Pseudoryx nghetinhensis* in Laos," *Oryx* 29, no. 2 (1995).

34. William Robichaud, *Saola Conservation Action Plan for Lao PDR* (Vientiane: WCS, 1997); William Robichaud, *Saola Conservation Action Plan for Lao PDR,* rev. ed. (Vientiane: WCS and IUCN, 1999).

35. In 2004, WWF-Laos revised the action plan in preparation for finally translating it into Lao and supporting the GoL in its implementation of the plan. But the GoL did not approve the translation exercise or implementation; again, almost certainly due to a perceived risk that attention to saola posed to NT2. The World Bank was already under pressure from some international conservation organizations to reject the project, and the GoL feared fueling the opposition's arguments.

36. J. William Duckworth, Richard E. Salter, and Khamkhoun Khounboline, comps., *Wildlife in Lao PDR*, 1999 status report (Vientiane: IUCN/WCS/CPAWM, 1999).

37. Richard E. Salter, *Wildlife in Lao PDR: A Status Report* (Vientiane: IUCN, 1993).

38. Since the publication of *Wildlife in Lao PDR: 1999 Status Report*, the red muntjac has been split into two species, southern red muntjac (*Muntiacus muntjak*) and northern red muntjac (*M. vaginalis*). According to the 2016 IUCN Red List of Threatened Species, the conservation status of each is Least Concern.

39. Teresa Serra, Mark Segal, and Ram Chopra, "The Project Is Prepared," in *Doing a Dam Better: The Lao People's Democratic Republic and the Story of Nam Theun 2*, ed. Ian C. Porter and Jayasankar Shivakumar (Washington, DC: World Bank, 2011), 90.

40. The reason the GoL has not developed more capacity for biodiversity conservation is not shortage of funding. For example, the total value of timber exported from Laos in 2014 is estimated at more than US$1.6 *billion*—and most of that revenue was illicit and did not pass through the national treasury. This is more than three times the total of all official foreign aid to Laos that year. See Denis Smirnov, "Assessment of Scope of Illegal Logging in Laos and Associated Trans-Boundary Timber Trade," WWF, June 2015, https://app .box.com/s/lol9on4su2pg3zqnu3lkqpr7hjpzoiem.

41. Boonratana's report from the NNT DUDCP project notes: "Although the NNT NBCA staff have undergone several formal and informal training and capacity building programs since the NBCA was established, yet none of the knowledge and skills acquired have been translated to meaningful activities. This is mainly because of a serious lack of interest and commitment" (3).

42. PoE 25:46.

43. PoE 22:45.

44. The GoL's drive to get Lao PDR removed from the United Nations Development Program's list of least-developed countries is a significant driver in the overexploitation and destruction of the country's natural resources.

45. James R. Chamberlain, *Nature and Culture in the Nakai-Nam Theun Conservation Area* (Vientiane: privately published, 1997), 5–5.

46. William G. Robichaud, Anthony R. E. Sinclair, Naa Odarkor-Lanquaye, and Brian Klinkenberg, "Stable Forest Cover under Increasing Populations of Swidden Culti-vators in Central Laos: The Roles of Intrinsic Culture and Extrinsic Wildlife Trade," *Ecology and Society* 14, no. 1 (2009).

47. Boonratana, "DUDCP," 20.

48. PoE 24:73; PoE 25:46.

49. Alex McWilliam and Ray Victurine, "Aligning Business Success with Conservation: A Case Study from the Lao PDR," paper presented at the Fifth International Conference on Water Resources and Hydropower Development in Asia, Colombo, Sri Lanka, March 11–13, 2014.

50. William Robichaud, *Motivation for Payment for Ecosystem Services in Laos: The Essential Alignment* (Bogor, Indonesia: International Centre for Forestry Research, 2014).

51. The final chapter of *Doing a Dam Better* is titled "NT2: A Transformative Endeavor."

52. Chamberlain, *Nature and Culture in the Nakai-Nam Theun Conservation Area*, 5–2.

53. Peter Stephens, "The Communications Challenge," in *Doing a Dam Better*, 118.

54. Some hope as well as a forum for collaboration between large infrastructure projects and conservation organizations can be found in the Business and Biodiversity Offsets Programme. See http://bbop.forest-trends.org.

55. deBuys, *The Last Unicorn*, 312.

8

Troubles Downstream

Changes in the Xe Bang Fai River Basin

IAN G. BAIRD,

BRUCE SHOEMAKER, and

KANOKWAN MANOROM

Introduction

Well over 150,000 people live in the lower and middle Xe Bang Fai (XBF) River basin, an area that has been heavily impacted by changes brought about by the Nam Theun 2 dam (NT2). This chapter examines NT2's impacts in the XBF basin and the effectiveness of the efforts to mitigate impacts and compensate for losses. In particular, we summarize our recent field-level research and contrast it with baseline data about river-based livelihoods collected in 2001, well before NT2 was constructed. Our chapter is based on our 2015 article "The People and Their River, the World Bank and Its Dam: Revisiting the Xe Bang Fai River in Laos" and, to a lesser extent, on our 2017 article "The World Bank, Hydropower-Based Poverty Alleviation and Indigenous Peoples: On-the-Ground Realities in the Xe Bang Fai River Basin of Laos." Both of these articles provide more detail on our research than is possible to provide here.[1]

The Xe Bang Fai and River-Based Livelihoods in Laos

In early 2001, Shoemaker and colleagues conducted a detailed study of river-based livelihoods in the XBF basin. The study was one of the first of its kind in Laos to describe the essential livelihood links that people—those living both right along the river as well as some distance away—have to their rivers. The resulting book, *The People and Their River: A Survey of River-Based Livelihoods in the Xe Bang Fai River Basin in Central Lao PDR*, documents the importance of the XBF and its associated tributaries and wetlands for local livelihoods, explaining, for example, how flood regimes along the XBF and its tributaries were crucial for the productivity of fisheries and rice and vegetable agriculture.[2] The study also details the fragile ecological balance of the river basin—one that provided great livelihood benefits but that also made downstream communities particularly vulnerable to changes in river flows. As the study explains,

> The Xe Bang Fai River and its tributaries form a complex hydrological system that has not been well studied and is little understood by outsiders. But it is clear that the people . . . have adapted to the specific environment of the area and have a sophisticated knowledge of the complex inter-relationships of diverse ecosystems in the basin. Consequently, local communities have long-established mechanisms that allow them to sustain and benefit from their natural resources while living within their natural environment. It should be noted however that this fragile balance is threatened by certain activities occurring in the basin—activities that are often not undertaken in support of, or in accordance with, the livelihood activities and natural resource management systems of local communities.[3]

The study was released as Nam Theun 2 Power Company (NTPC) was preparing various social and environmental studies for NT2. At the time, NTPC had not allocated any significant funding for downstream impacts; the focus was on resettlement and biodiversity conservation associated with the proposed reservoir and adjacent protected area. Earlier in 2001 the International Environmental and Social Panel of Experts (PoE) had raised concerns about the lack of focus on downstream areas: "One of the NT2 project's most serious impacts on livelihood can be expected in the densely populated (over 50,000 people) Xe Bang Fai basin where greatly increased river flows from the powerhouse can be expected to alter fish behavior, fishing technology, and access to river bank gardens."[4]

This was occurring amid controversy over the ongoing impacts of the World Bank–funded Pak Mun Dam on river-based livelihoods nearby in Thailand.[5] Additionally, the Asian Development Bank (ADB) had recently been forced to accept, after a long period of denial, that its Theun-Hinboun hydropower project, another trans-basin diversion project located close to NT2, was causing serious harm to downstream communities.[6] The negative downstream impacts of dams in the Mekong basin have continued to receive attention but in many cases, including that of NT2, not to the degree they deserve.[7]

The *People and Their River* study caught the attention of World Bank staff and the PoE. Its findings made clear that the NT2 developers had overlooked many issues relating to how people were linked to and dependent on the natural flows of the XBF. In contrast to NTPC's estimate of 50,000 potentially impacted people, *The People and Their River* estimated that 120,000–150,000 people derived significant livelihoods benefits from the XBF.[8] At the same time, groups such as International Rivers Network (IRN) and others were campaigning on NT2 and pressuring the World Bank to uphold high standards of consultation, compensation, and mitigation as recommended by the World Commission on Dams (WCD). As a result of this pressure, the World Bank required the developers to pay more attention to the XBF by funding fisheries studies and preparing a compensation plan. The PoE eventually acknowledged that NTPC's initial estimate of impacted people in the XBF basin was a gross underestimate. In 2010, 155,000 people living in one hundred riverside and fifty-six "hinterland" villages were listed as project impacted.[9] Most of the inhabitants of these villages, mainly rural lowland rice farmers, are ethnic Lao or Kaleung, but the statistic includes significant numbers of ethnic Phou Thai and Brou people.[10]

Water began flowing from the Theun basin into the XBF in 2010. In subsequent years, relatively brief visits by outside advocacy groups revealed serious concerns about the impacts of NT2 along the river.[11] Throughout this period the official line from NTPC and the World Bank was that impacts to the XBF were "less than anticipated" and that compensation efforts had been successful in restoring and improving local livelihoods. Still, a succession of PoE reports indicated not all was well along the XBF.[12] However, PoE visits to XBF villages had tended to be only for a day or two once every two years, the most recent of which was conducted in late 2012. A more in-depth independent assessment was needed.

Revisiting the Xe Bang Fai

Thirteen years after the original study, almost five years after NT2 became operational and following the termination of a Downstream Compensation Program funded by NTPC for impacted communities in the XBF basin, we returned for an assessment of the situation.

Two of the three authors of the 2001 book were able to participate in this new study, and a third researcher from Ubon Ratchathani University in Thailand also joined. The entirely Lao-speaking team conducted field work for approximately three weeks during December 2013 and January 2014. The team visited twenty-six villages in seven districts and two provinces in the XBF basin—many of which were visited during the 2001 study—and interviewed people from a number of other communities in the basin, totaling well over one hundred people, about half of whom were women (see figures 8.1 and 8.2). In order to allow for frank discussions at the village level, our research team chose an informal approach and had neither officials of the government of the Lao PDR (GoL) nor NTPC staff join our study. This approach has some limitations but was necessitated by the strict controls that often accompany officially sanctioned village visits in Laos. Despite these limitations, it is the most in-depth independent study of the situation in the XBF to have taken place since the completion of NT2. In a relatively short time we were able to gain a detailed understanding of the overall circumstances in the XBF basin in relation to NT2.

Downstream Impacts in the Nam Theun-Kading River Basin

While our research has focused on the XBF, it is only one of two large river basins that have been impacted by NT2. As a trans-basin diversion project, NT2 takes large amounts of water out of the Nam Theun-Kading River and sends it into the XBF. While the XBF has faced dramatic increases in the volume of water and been subject to related changes in the hydrology and water quality of the river, the Nam Theun-Kading River, having lost most of its volume of water downstream from the dam, has also been fundamentally altered, though in a very different way. This has undoubtedly resulted in serious ecological and livelihoods impacts, especially considering that the Nam Theun-Kading River was historically much larger than the XBF basin in terms of flow volumes.

Unfortunately, however, no independent assessments of the impacts of NT2 along the approximately 160 kilometers of the Nam Theun-Kading downstream of the NT2 dam to the river's confluence with the Mekong have ever been conducted. The situation is complicated by the presence of the Theun-Hinboun hydropower project, completed in 1998, and located approximately 75 kilometers downstream

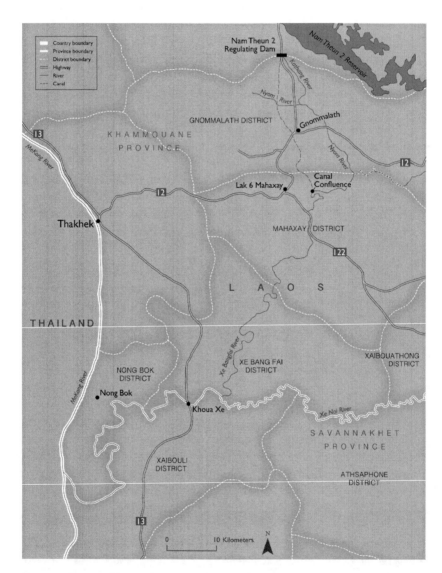

Figure 8.1. Portions of the XBF River basin affected by the NT2 project.

from NT2. Theun-Hinboun is also a trans-basin diversion dam, transferring water from the Nam Theun into the Hinboun River. Theun-Hinboun has had serious troubles of its own, and, since 2012, the Theun-Hinboun expansion project has further increased the amount of water diverted into the Hinboun, causing additional downstream impacts along that river.[13] According to NTPC, "there have been no major impacts following construction of the dam" to the forty communities it identifies as being located on the Nam Theun or to the tributaries in the area between the NT2 dam and the Theun-Hinboun project area.[14]

Given the propensity for NTPC to downplay negative impacts of NT2 in other locations, this statement is worthy of skepticism. It is difficult to believe that the dewatering of the Nam Theun and the blockage of fish migration have not had significant impacts on the ecology of the river and local livelihoods. However, this has not yet been examined in detail by outside investigators. Further research is called for, to look at both the specific impacts NT2 has had on the Nam Theun downstream and the cumulative impacts of NT2, Theun-Hinboun, and Theun-Hinboun expansion projects on the Nam Theun-Kading basin.

Findings

In early 2014 we encountered a drastically changed XBF. The additional water from NT2, which more than doubled its previous dry season flow, had dramatically altered the river's ecology and, in doing so, fundamentally changed its relationship to local communities. The World Bank and ADB have acknowledged that significant changes to the river have occurred, stating that "some characteristics of the water in the XBF have been affected by the project, including volume and flow rates, PH, temperature and color."[15] Indeed, there is little that has not changed, and these changes are particularly acute with respect to fisheries and aquatic ecosystems, rainy season flooding and rice production, riverbank vegetable gardens and water supply and quality, all of which are detailed in "The People and Their River" and summarized in what follows.

Impacts on Fisheries and Other Aquatic Resources

Historically, there have been hundreds of fish species in the XBF basin.[16] The overwhelming majority of people we interviewed have observed that NT2 has led to a severe decline in the diversity and quantity of fish and other aquatic life in the XBF and its associated tributaries and wetlands. Fisheries in some tributaries, such as the Xe Noi (figure 8.1), have been negatively impacted as well. The head of a village along the Xe Noi stated that "fish migrate up from the XBF, but over the last few years fewer fish have come from there."

The PoE reported a decline in fisheries in the XBF of 35 percent in 2010 and 25 percent in 2011.[17] Changes in water flow and quality have also made those fish that remain in the river more difficult to catch. Villagers report that some important migratory fisheries have virtually disappeared. Large fish have become much rarer.

Our findings suggest that villagers are finding it much harder to maintain their food security and income from XBF fisheries. All villagers interviewed living below the NT2 powerhouse near the Nam Kathang reported that changes in water hydrology, quality, and temperatures have led to a severe decline in fisheries in all seasons. Heavy impacts are also evident far downstream, at the XBF's confluence with the Mekong, where local fishermen reported that many species no longer enter the XBF in significant numbers, staying instead in the Mekong. Traditional fishing methods have been abandoned. Villagers universally reported that fisheries have declined in all seasons.

NT2-related hydrological changes have impeded the ability of villagers to catch fish and collect other aquatic resources. Women, especially widows and those in poorer families, often count on being able to collect aquatic animals and catch smaller fish using scoop nets in dry season shallows, along sandbars and near rapids. Increased dry season flows have eliminated or drastically reduced access to these resources for women. One woman told us, "We used to catch small fish in shallow areas of the river, but now there are many fewer fish and the water is too deep for us." Changes in water quality and quantity have resulted in the loss of shellfish and some types of aquatic plant life, such as the edible algae known as *nye* in Lao.

People in villages several kilometers from the XBF previously kept boats at the river and would go there frequently to fish.[18] They do this much less frequently now. A villager located 10 kilometers away from the river remarked, in a typical comment, that, "it is not worth the effort to go to the XBF. There are not enough fish to justify the trip." Villagers still fish a bit, though. In the area of Dang Village, in Mahaxai District, upstream from where water from NT2 enters the XBF, people reported catching more fish on days when the river level drops due to power generation fluctuations, as fish presumably move

Figure 8.2. Villagers boating on the XBF River in Mahaxay District. Due to dramatic hydrological changes in the river caused by water releases from NT2, seasonally inundated bushes have died along the edge of the river. Photo by Ian Baird.

Figure 8.3. A woman collects shellfish in a wetland adjacent to the XBF River. Since the advent of NT2, this activity has become much more challenging in many locations due to the increased river levels and the disappearance of many shallow areas. Photo by Kanokwan Manorom.

up above the confluence from more impacted downstream areas. Generally, however, fishing has become much more difficult. In 2001, we found an overall abundance of wild fish in many parts of the basin, and learned that this was especially the case during the rainy season. Villages such as Keng Pe in XBF District were the sites of thriving fish markets with traders coming from Thakhek daily to purchase fish from local villagers. In Keng Pe, the XBF fishery was the single most important livelihood resource for the villagers.[19] The market no longer exists.

Impacts on Wet Season Rice Cultivation

A delicate balance had long prevailed for rainy season rice farmers along the flood-prone XBF.[20] The annual flood was both an asset—bringing in essential nutrients for the soil—and a potential threat if too severe or long lasting. While flooding might destroy significant amounts of the rice crop every few years, this was balanced by high productivity in other years. Changes in river hydrology brought about by NT2 appear, however, to have upset this balance in significant parts of the basin, both upstream and downstream near the NT2 canal confluence as well as further downstream and in some tributaries. We observed large areas of abandoned rainy season rice fields in a number of villages during our investigations—for instance, along the road between the new and old Mahaxai District centers. From Gnommalath down into Nong Bok and Xaibouli Districts (figure 8.1), almost all the villagers we met reported that increased levels of flooding since 2011 have made rainy season rice farming more challenging and riskier—or, in some places, impossible. This has led to significant declines in wet season rice cultivation.

The extent to which NT2 exacerbated an unusually severe rain event in 2011, the first full year of the dam's operations, is uncertain.[21] In any case, it undoubtedly added to the perception of flooding risk among downstream communities. In some places villagers did not plant rainy season rice in 2012 and 2013 due to the trauma of the extraordinary flooding of 2011, even though some might have successfully done so. However, in other areas villagers reported that their rice fields did flood excessively in all three years. While NT2's concession agreement specifies that NT2 is supposed to stop or reduce operations when natural flooding is occurring along the XBF so as not to increase the impact of flooding, some villagers believe that the level at which water is to be cut off is too high and that they have therefore suffered increased flooding in their fields due to NT2 even when the water level does not trigger a shutdown.[22]

To our knowledge, NTPC has not conducted any follow-up studies since NT2 became operational in order to determine whether the water shutoff level is indeed appropriate.

Riverside Vegetable Gardening

Riverbank gardening has long been an important supplemental source of food and income for Lao villagers, including in the XBF basin.[23] We observed a dramatic decline in the number and size of such gardens, which are now confined to the upper parts of the riverbank. Fluctuating dry season flows caused by NT2 have greatly affected the ability of villagers to garden along the lower banks. Gardens are now smaller than they used to be and are significantly harder to water, since they must now be located further away—above the riverbed—to avoid the flooding and to stay out of the range of fluctuating waters in the dry season. In some places gardens have been relocated to the banks of smaller streams, near homes within villages, or along dry season rice fields. In many places villagers reported that dry season vegetable gardening has declined. Growing vegetables higher up requires more external inputs, such as chemical fertilizer and electricity to pump water from the river, or more labor to haul it manually. NTPC recognized these potential impacts; surveys determined that 3,180 households along the XBF were eligible for compensation specifically for the loss of riverbank gardens.[24]

Impacts on Water Quality and Supply

In 2001, Shoemaker and colleagues observed that villagers all along the XBF used its water for drinking, washing, bathing and other domestic tasks.[25] We received many reports of severe water quality problems during the first two years of NT2 operations. A high percentage of villagers along the XBF below the NT2 confluence developed skin rashes and many have stopped bathing in the river completely.[26] Some women wash clothes in the river and take water home for domestic use, but we did not meet any villagers who reported drinking river water. While hand pump wells were provided to villages located along the XBF, many reported that the well water was not suitable for drinking.[27] In many villages 15–30 percent of wells have broken down. Some villagers reported that they did not have the technical knowledge or parts to fix the wells that have been provided. Over time water quality has improved substantially, although NTPC recognizes that problems persist.[28]

The Downstream Compensation Program

The NT2 concession agreement obliged NTPC to allocate a maximum of US$16 million for a Downstream Compensation Program, meant to assist people negatively impacted by the project.[29] An additional US$2.3 million was eventually provided.[30] While planning began in 2005, the program only became fully operational in 2010. Intended to reach 155,000 people in 156 villages, it started activities in 77 villages in 2010. Another twenty-three were added in 2011, and the remaining fifty-six "hinterland" (located off the river) villages were only just included in 2012, the final year of the program, as it was officially handed over to the GoL on December 31, 2012.[31] In 2010, NT2's PoE had praised it as "a model not only for other river basins in Laos but also around the world."[32] The panel's assessments in more recent reports, however, have been much less effusive.

The Promotion of Irrigated Rice Cultivation

One of the most visible and capital-intensive development interventions supported by the Downstream Compensation Program, as well as complementary World Bank and ADB projects, has been pump irrigation for dry season rice farming (*na seng*). This involves the provision of electrical pumping stations and related infrastructure needed to bring XBF water into rice fields. The implicit rationale is that the benefits of pump irrigation will more than make up for project-related losses of fisheries and wet season rice farming. Project proponents have long seen such development as an important potential benefit of NT2.

Dry season pump irrigation has, however, a problematic history in the XBF basin, Laos, and the wider region. This was noted in the 2001 study, which found that diesel pumps provided by a GoL program for dry season rice farming were uneconomical and unpopular with XBF farmers:

> Most villagers view *na seng* as a supplement to—not a substitute for—the main rice crop grown during the rainy season. . . . [T]hey do not see irrigated dry season rice cultivation as either a panacea or replacement for their rainy season crop. . . . While *na seng* continues to be promoted heavily by government and international development institutions, in reality its expansion and whole economic basis are increasingly problematic.[33]

Those diesel pumps were largely abandoned within a few years. A later study found that dry season wet rice pump irrigation has been much less successful than was originally hoped, largely due to high costs.[34]

Our discussions with farmers for this study reinforce the earlier concerns about pump-irrigated *na seng*. When various costs are figured in—electricity for pumping water, fertilizer (much more is needed than for wet season rice) and, in some cases, labor and opportunity costs (due to the tight timeframe required to coordinate planting in adjacent fields)—the economic gains of *na seng* remain marginal, especially compared to rainy season rice farming (*na pi*). This is true even if diesel pumps are replaced with more cost-efficient electrical pumps. Some villagers also reported that *na seng* cultivation has caused soils to decline in fertility, which has led to reductions in *na pi* productivity and has forced farmers to add fertilizer in the rainy season, which was previously rarely required.[35] Following the 2011 flood event, many villages received subsidized electricity for one or two seasons. That has now ended, and farmers must pay full price for electricity, rapidly changing the economic calculation.

The vast majority of farmers we interviewed indicated that whenever they have a choice, they prefer *na pi* over *na seng*. Villagers from Dong Kasin Village in Nong Bok District, for example, have the option of conducting *na seng* in new locations near the XBF. But since their long-established rice fields located further away have not flooded in recent years, villagers have rejected *na seng* and are exclusively cultivating *na pi*.

Nevertheless, cultivating rice remains very important for villagers for economic and cultural reasons, and many communities still cultivate a lot of rice during the dry season. in villages where irrigation projects have recently been introduced, there is more initial enthusiasm and interest in *na seng*, and an increase in it can be observed there. A few women had positive comments about its potential. This initial enthusiasm may well be short lived. In many locations in the XBF basin the cultivation of *na seng* is already declining significantly. Overall, the situation seems to be a repeat of what the 2001 study found: dry season irrigated rice cultivation is much more popular with government agencies and international development organizations than with farmers.

Village Development Funds

As a step toward providing compensation for the loss of fisheries and other aquatic resources, the Downstream Compensation Program established village revolving loan funds, valued at US$250 per family, in project villages adjacent to the XBF.[36] Money can be borrowed for a limited number of "productive activities," such as buying inputs for lowland rice cultivation, raising animals, or aquaculture. Loans must be repaid with interest, often 6 percent per year. Individual villagers were not able to choose between receiving cash compensation and establishing village loan funds. Many reported that they would have preferred direct compensation; they have more confidence in their own abilities to use such funds for their own benefit than in the potential of participating in the loan program. There is never a point when villagers can withdraw money from the fund permanently.

The funds are supposedly overseen by village committees, but they are kept in banks at district centers and controlled by the district-level government. District-level women's unions were given initial responsibility for management of the program despite reservations expressed by the PoE, which stated that doing so without proper technical support and follow-up would be a "recipe for disaster." Later, a new provincial institution, the Rural Development and Poverty Eradication Office, established village revolving funds committees to manage the money.[37]

Microfinance and these types of village revolving funds have, at best, a mixed track record, both in Laos and internationally. Typically it is the poorest people—those most dependent on communal resources such as fisheries and the collection of aquatic resources—who suffer disproportionately from the loss of natural resources. They are, however, the ones least likely to be able or willing to take advantage of microfinance or village loan funds.[38] Practitioners familiar with microfinance in Laos report that such is the case in Laos. The funds are often unsustainable and the capacity of district-level institutions to manage them varies widely and has declined in recent years in many places. At the very least, ensuring even short- to medium-term success requires a transparent process (in which villagers retain control over the funds) and an extended commitment to support, training and monitoring—all features that were lacking in the prematurely terminated Downstream Compensation Program.[39]

In villages we visited, it appeared that the loan funds are used most by better-off villagers and hardly at all in Indigenous villages. Indigenous Brou villagers, and other relatively poor people, have in general been reluctant to take advantage of the funds out of fear of not being able to pay back the principal and interest. In some Brou communities, we were informed that almost no one had dared borrow money from the funds. In villages where people have taken out loans, some interviewees reported being threatened with jail or the loss of their land when they had difficulty making repayments. Many villagers express skepticism about the future of these funds.

The Downstream Compensation Program's
Overall Structure and Approach

Rather than recognizing and respecting the rights of impacted villagers to be compensated for project-specific impacts, the Downstream Compensation Program positioned itself as a rural development project, a common approach for many infrastructure projects in Laos. Compensation implies the rightful redress of lost assets or livelihood opportunities due to external causes. Development aid is more about providing people with new opportunities and may imply some level of risk—time and energy if not financial investment. Much of the "compensation" provided to impacted villagers through the program came in the form of development schemes, some of which entailed substantial risk and failed to benefit many of those most impacted by NT2. For instance, some villages were provided with chickens to raise. All those interviewed who were familiar with this initiative said it had failed. Either the chickens had died of disease or were quickly sold or consumed due to the high cost of buying feed. Villagers referenced various attempts to release nonindigenous fish into the XBF to revitalize fisheries and reported that they all had failed. Some World Bank reports and the PoE have expressed great optimism about efforts to introduce "submergence-resistant rice" (*khao ton nam*) and "floating rice" (*khao loi*) to flood-prone villages.[40] However, the relatively few villagers we met who were even aware of the attempted introduction of these rice varieties reported that they had been unsuccessful; even these new flood-resistant varieties of rice could not survive long periods of flooding. Many program inputs were for rural infrastructure, such as primary health centers or toilet construction. While these inputs have value, they do not address or sufficiently compensate for the livelihood and food security losses people have experienced. Other than these problematic program components and some short-term training and inputs on crop production, aquaculture, and other potential income-generating opportunities, no substantive direct compensation was provided for the loss of fisheries and related aquatic resources, even though this is one of the most visible and acute impacts of NT2.

The concession agreement between NTPC and the GoL is for a twenty-five-year period. However, the Downstream Compensation Program was based on the assumption that single, one-time development interventions would be sufficient to compensate for long-term ongoing impacts. As noted, the value of village development funds, or cash payments, was the equivalent to one-time contributions of US$100–250 per family. But while impacts related to water quality have lessened, other negative impacts will continue for the life of the project and beyond. Many villagers also received one-time cash payments for the loss of dry season riverside gardens. Interviewees expressed varying degrees of satisfaction with these payments, but it was frequently reported that compensation was barely sufficient to cover even one or two years of losses in revenue from vegetable garden production, let alone losses over the twenty-five-year project span. There were many reports of failures to compensate all of those impacted and a general perception that the compensation process was nontransparent and inadequate. Even before costs for consultants, studies, and project management are subtracted, the total expenditures per impacted person by the program averaged only US$119. Over the twenty-five-year life of the project this is well short of US$5 per impacted person per year.

The Indigenous Brou People of the Xe Bang Fai Basin and the World Bank

The World Bank's focus on poverty has led to increased attention on Indigenous Peoples who, while consisting of 4.5 percent of the world's population, make up about 10 percent of the world's poorest people. The World Bank has developed safeguards for ensuring that the projects it supports result in the fewest possible negative impacts on Indigenous Peoples and that there are appropriate plans in place to mitigate impacts and provide appropriate compensation when there are impacts.[41]

Although the GoL does recognize ethnic difference within Laos, it does not accept the concept of Indigenous Peoples and considers all citizens of Laos to have equal rights and to be equally "Indigenous."[42] Despite this, however, the World Bank remains obliged to apply its worldwide safeguard policies for Indigenous Peoples in Laos. The Bank has generally defined all those who speak languages in the Hmong-Iu-Mien, Tibetan-Burman, and Austroasiatic families as Indigenous Peoples in Laos, at least for the purposes of applying its policies. Virtually all of the over six thousand people relocated from NT2's reservoir area on the Nakai Plateau, including many ethnic Brou people, were defined as Indigenous with respect to the Bank's policies. Curiously, the Bank took a very different approach in the XBF River basin.

As part of the planning process in advance of project approval in 2005, the World Bank investigated the status of those people living downstream in the XBF basin who were potentially vulnerable to negative impacts. While the vast majority of people living downstream in impacted areas speak languages in the Tai-Kadai family and therefore would not be considered Indigenous, there are also thousands of ethnic Brou people who speak an Austroasiatic language. While spread out in both their own and mixed communities within the larger non-Indigenous population, their total numbers may well exceed the number of Indigenous Peoples on the Nakai Plateau. At the time these communities were being assessed, an anthropologist working for NTPC argued that the Brou in the XBF basin did not need to be recognized as Indigenous because they were, according to him, more assimilated into lowland cultures than the communities on the Nakai Plateau. James Chamberlain, a recognized expert in ethnicity issues in Laos who had also worked as a consultant in relation to NT2, objected to this characterization. The World Bank, however, ignored Chamberlain's advice and failed to recognize the Brou in the XBF basin as Indigenous.[43] This decision was expedient for the Bank and NTPC—it meant that they did not need to spend time identifying Brou people and communities within the much larger population of the basin. It also meant that important World Bank safeguards regarding Indigenous Peoples did not have to be applied.

There are compelling reasons for these people and communities to be recognized as Indigenous. An earlier World Bank–commissioned independent assessment of NT2's 1996–97 public consultations had pointed out "in some of the villages on the Xe Bang Fai, many of the villagers do not speak Lao fluently."[44] While most Brou engage in capture fisheries and other livelihood activities similar to those of non-Indigenous Peoples, they have a number of vulnerabilities and have been historically, culturally, and economically marginalized in comparison to the dominant ethnic groups. During our field work in 2014, it was clear that project-impacted Brou peoples we met in the XBF basin still have a strong sense of their own ethnic identity and have significantly lower economic and formal education levels in comparison to more dominant groups. But beyond that, the very idea that one's Indigenous identity could be stripped away on the say-so of one project-affiliated foreign advisor who decides that a group of people is "assimilated" would be regarded as completely unacceptable by almost anyone involved in issues of Indigenous rights and identity today.

This lack of recognition is particularly disturbing given the disproportionally severe impacts ethnic Brou in the XBF basin have faced since NT2's completion. Due to their lack of land and other economic assets, the Brou are among those most dependent on communal resources, such as rivers and associated wetlands, including associated nontimber forest products (NTFPs) linked to these habitats, for their livelihoods and were thus more greatly harmed by changes to the XBF as outlined in this chapter and our article on the topic. They are also among those least able to benefit from the Downstream Compensation Program—in particular the microfinance and dry season irrigation components. They are particularly vulnerable to GoL policies related to internal resettlement and village consolidation under which predominantly Indigenous communities are resettled and incorporated into larger communities tending to be dominated by lowland groups. These policies have generated considerable international human rights concern, and both the World Bank and the PoE have advised against the implementation of such resettlement policies in NT2 project areas.[45] However, during our field work Brou villagers reported that GoL officials were citing the negative impacts of NT2, in particular the perceived increased risk of flooding, erosion, and a need to develop "new livelihoods," as justification for pushing communities to relocate, in some cases into village consolidation sites the GoL had already prepared. These impacts, however, remain under-recognized. Having failed to even acknowledge the existence of Indigenous Peoples in the XBF basin, it is then of course easy to overlook them while assessing impacts and the effectiveness of compensation programs.

Villager Views and the Grievance System

The vast majority of villagers interviewed believe that the changes to the XBF brought about by NT2 have had a significant negative impact on their communities. In some cases, the combined impact of fishery losses, the loss of rain-fed rice fields, and the loss of riverbank gardens appears to have led to severe declines in villagers' well being.

Overall, the risky short-term development interventions, many of which are proving unsustainable, and the minimal one-time payments provided by the Downstream Compensation Program have not adequately addressed the short-term or long-term needs of impacted communities. Over 90 percent of the villagers we interviewed stated that the compensation provided by NTPC has not come close to making up for their project-related losses. Some even mockingly laughed at the notion that they have received fair compensation. While there are exceptions, the predominant opinion is that NT2 has made them worse off overall. This view prevails from villages close to the NT2 power station all the way down to the XBF's confluence with the Mekong and along some tributaries.

NTPC and the World Bank have long promoted their "grievance process," which they claim is closely linked to NT2's accountability approach. James Adams, vice president of the World Bank's East Asia and Pacific region, stated, in November 2010 that "local consultations and international workshops have been undertaken to an unprecedented degree for Lao PDR, and the availability of public information has been considerable."[46]

In discussing the XBF in 2004, a NTPC representative stated that "the project would work through the relevant government committees, and that the grievance mechanism would let the villagers go from the village level to the district level to solve their problems."[47] The World Bank, ADB, and NTPC continue to claim that the grievance process is functioning well: "The Project's grievance mechanism is still active in the downstream area, and Project Affected Persons can submit any complaints they may have to the relevant grievance committees."[48] At the NT2 visitor's center in Gnommalath District, an information board explains NT2's grievance process as follows: "A grievance process was set up to review possible mistakes or oversight in the compensation process. When legitimate grievances were found, extra compensation was quickly made available. As construction drew to a close, lives returned to normal."

We could find no evidence of a grievance process as an actual effective working mechanism at the village level. Almost no one interviewed had anything positive to say about it. Apart from village leaders and local officials, most had either never heard of the process or did not think it existed. Not one interviewee thought it could lead to a more just level of compensation or that it would result in specific issues being addressed. In eight villages — ranging from the Nam Phit canal down to the Mekong confluence — individuals specifically mentioned that district officials had told them they could get into trouble or be arrested for complaining too much about the project. The common understanding was that NT2 was "a government project" and that it could be dangerous to criticize it openly. Our findings suggest that the mechanisms the project has set up to measure villager views and to log their complaints is not compatible with the realities of the authoritarian Lao political system.

Insufficient Resources and the Externalization of Costs

The PoE has stated that the "funding disconnect" associated with the Downstream Compensation Program is primarily linked to the original concession agreement. Unlike in the case of assistance for resettled people on the Nakai Plateau, there were no provisions in place should the funding allocated prove insufficient to restore the livelihoods of impacted people. Even in

2010, as the program was beginning large-scale implementation, the PoE was already raising concerns over insufficient resources: "The sustainability of an innovative program, the livelihoods of over a hundred thousand impacted people and the reputation of all those involved are at stake. Completing the Downstream work is fundamental to the overall success of the NT2 project."[49]

Despite the PoE's recommendations for a more robust Downstream Compensation Program, the World Bank and ADB declined to increase funding or require a reappraisal of costs, despite, as the PoE stated, that "it was always in the cards that the sum provided would not suffice to carry out the objectives of the Program."[50] The PoE subsequently expressed its concern over a World Bank/ADB May 2011 aide memoire which stated that the "handing over" of the program needed to be "accelerated" because funding was rapidly being depleted. The PoE predicted that such a rapid handover was destined for failure and that more should be done: its reading of the concession agreement was "that morally and ethically the Company, the Government of Laos and the IFIs [international financial institutions] continue to have an obligation to see the livelihood restoration process completed."[51]

Originally intended to run for five years from project commencement, once the allocated funding was spent, at the end of 2012, NTPC ended the program. While the GoL was supposed to continue implementation until April 2015, the lack of ongoing external funding quickly ended almost all program activities.[52] We found almost no indication of any substantive ongoing follow-up by the GoL. The overwhelming consensus among villagers was that the program had ended.[53] While the World Bank and ADB were strongly supportive of this early termination, the PoE was not, stating that there is an "inherent incompatibility between the limited funding provision and the requirement to 'at least restore livelihoods of Project Affected Persons in the downstream areas on a sustainable basis.'"[54]

Having failed to obligate NTPC to cover the full costs of compensation during concession agreement negotiations, the World Bank and ADB have instead supplemented the program with further public resources through additional NT2-related grants and loans.[55]

Conclusions

Our study, uniquely informed by baseline data from before NT2 was approved, found the situation along the Xe Bang Fai to be much worse than has been portrayed by project proponents. Specifically, our findings suggest that NT2 has caused serious downstream impacts and that many significant impacts are ongoing. NTPC has been unable to fully mitigate the impacts of the added water being released into the XBF. While many of these impacts had been predicted years earlier, insufficient attention has been given to research on them, particularly regarding fishery declines, the economics of wet versus dry season rice cultivation, and the ongoing effects of the loss of riverbank vegetable gardens.[56] While NTPC has acknowledged declines in XBF fisheries, it has not yet publicly released its detailed fisheries studies. No comprehensive independent evaluations of the Downstream Compensation Program and related mitigation measures have been conducted.

The assumptions, structure, and inordinately short timeframe of the Downstream Compensation Program were clearly inadequate and inappropriate. NTPC, the World Bank and other donors have not done nearly enough to protect and restore the livelihoods of those in the XBF basin harmed by NT2. There is also little evidence that the GoL, a NT2 shareholder that receives royalties and taxes from the project, is using project revenues to alleviate the impacts of NT2 in affected XBF villages.

There is a long track record of neglecting downstream impacts in the rush to develop large-scale hydropower in the region. Unlike in the case of earlier projects, however, the World Bank and the developers were well aware of the likely impacts of NT2 prior to project initiation, and they vowed to address them. The up-front acknowledgment of potential downstream impacts and extensive planning for mitigation and compensation were precedent-setting features of NT2 and an improvement over earlier projects. But in its approach toward facilitating private sector investment in NT2, the World Bank failed to ensure that the concession agreement obligated those investors to pay the full costs of mitigation and compensation for downstream communities.

Costs that should have been the responsibility of NTPC have instead fallen on the public. Both the World Bank and the ADB have had to provide additional financing to try to improve the livelihoods of impacted communities. More importantly, impacted communities have had to bear a high cost. Villagers are in effect subsidizing the profits of NTPC through their ongoing livelihood losses. NTPC's approach to mitigating and compensating for downstream impacts in the XBF River basin have fallen well short of what was envisioned. As a result, the expectations and predictions of NT2 being a positive new international model for better addressing the downstream impacts of large hydropower projects have not been met. In the end, the World Bank and its partners proved themselves to be more concerned with expediently facilitating private sector involvement and maintaining good relations with their client government than with the well being of the people and communities and river ecosystems impacted by their project.

NOTES

1. Ian G. Baird, Bruce Shoemaker, and Kanokwan Manorom, "The People and Their River, the World Bank and Its Dam: Revisiting the Xe Bang Fai River in Laos," *Development and Change* 46, no. 5 (2015); Kanokwan Manorom, Ian G. Baird, and Bruce Shoemaker, "The World Bank, Hydropower-Based Poverty Alleviation and Indigenous Peoples: On-the-Ground Realities in the Xe Bang Fai River Basin of Laos," *Forum for Development Studies* 44, no. 2 (2017).

2. Bruce Shoemaker, Ian G. Baird, and Monsiri Baird, *The People and Their River: A Survey of River-Based Livelihoods in the Xe Bang Fai River Basin in Central Lao PDR* (Vientiane: Lao PDR/Canada Fund for Local Initiatives, 2001).

3. Shoemaker, Baird, and Baird, *The People and Their River*, xviii.

4. PoE 5:29.

5. Tira Foran and Kanokwan Manorom, "Pak Mun Dam: Perpetually Contested?," in *Contested Waterscapes in the Mekong Region: Hydropower, Livelihoods and Governance*, ed. François Molle, Tira Foran, and Mira Käkönen (London: Earthscan, 2009), 55–80.

6. ADB, Theun-Hinboun hydropower project, aide-mémoire, November 1998; Bruce Shoemaker, *Trouble on the Theun-Hinboun: A Field Report on the Socio-Economic and Environmental Effects of the Nam Theun-Hinboun Hydropower Project in Laos* (Berkeley, CA: International Rivers Network, 1998); Jerome Whitington, "The Institutional Condition of Contested Hydropower: The Theun Hinboun–International Rivers Collaboration," *Forum for Development Studies* 39, no. 2 (2012).

7. François Molle, Louis Lebel, and Tira Foran, "Contested Mekong Waterscapes: Where to Next?," in *Contested Waterscapes in the Mekong Region*; Claudia Kuenzer, Ian Campbell, Marthe Roch, Patrick Leinenkugel, Vo Quoc Tuan, and Stefan Dech, "Understanding the Impacts of Hydropower Developments in the Context of Upstream–Downstream Relations in the Mekong River Basin," *Sustainability Science* 8, no. 4 (2013).

8. Shoemaker, Baird, and Baird, *The People and Their River*; PoE 5.

9. The number of villages included in the program varies between 150 and 159 in various NTPC and PoE reports; see PoE 5:24–25.

10. Shoemaker, Baird, and Baird, *The People and Their River*.

11. International Rivers to Nam Theun 2 Power Company," letter dated February 12, 2012; Ikuko Matsumoto, International Rivers, and Toshiyuki Doi, Mekong Watch, to Robert Zoellick, World Bank, and Haruhiko Kuroda, Asian Development Bank, letter dated September 10, 2012, regarding the July 7, 2010 update on the Lao PDR Nam Theun 2 Hydroelectric Project, www.mekongwatch.org/PDF/NT2letter24Sep2010.pdf ; "Can

Nam Theun 2 Really Alleviate Poverty? Compensation Delayed over Two Years, Villagers Burdened with Debt," Mekong Watch Press Release, Tokyo, December 10, 2010.

12. PoE 17; PoE 18B; PoE 19.

13. Whitington, "The Institutional Condition of Contested Hydropower," 254; Ian G. Baird and Keith Barney, "The Political Ecology of Cross-Sectoral Cumulative Impacts: Modern Landscapes, Large Hydropower Dams and Industrial Tree Plantations in Laos and Cambodia," *Journal of Peasant Studies* 44, no. 4 (2017): 776.

14. NTPC, "Rivers and People: Nakai Dam to Theun-Hinboun," poster on display at NT2 Visitors Center.

15. World Bank and ADB, *Nam Theun 2 Board Update: Project Progress during 2012*, December 31, 2012, 23, http://documents.worldbank.org/curated/en/872361468045088739/Nam-Theun-2-Board-update-project-progress-during-2012.

16. Maurice Kottelat, "Fishes of the Nam Theun and Xe Bangfai Basins, Laos: With Diagnoses of Twenty-two New Species (Teleostei: Cyprinidae, Balitoridae, Cobitidae, Coiidae, and Odontobutidae)," *Ichthyological Explorations of Freshwaters* 9, no. 1 (1998).

17. PoE 19:22.

18. Shoemaker, Baird, and Baird, *The People and Their River*, 7.

19. Shoemaker, Baird, and Baird, *The People and Their River*, 44.

20. Shoemaker, Baird, and Baird, *The People and Their River*, 44.

21. Baird, Shoemaker, and Manorom, "The People and Their River," 1091.

22. MEE Net, "Know Your Power: Toward a Participatory Approach for Sustainable Power Development in the Mekong Region," conference report, Chulalongkorn University, Bangkok, January 18–19, 2012; Teresa Serra, Mark Segal, and Ram Chopra, "The Project Is Prepared," in *Doing a Dam Better: The Lao People's Democratic Republic and the Story of Nam Theun 2*, ed. Ian C. Porter and Jayasankar Shivakumar (Washington, DC: The World Bank, 2011), 58.

23. Shannon Lawrence, "The Nam Theun 2 Controversy and Its Lessons for Laos," in *Contested Waterscapes in the Mekong Region*; Shoemaker, Baird, and Baird, *The People and Their River*, 23–24.

24. World Bank and ADB, *Nam Theun 2 Board Update: Project Progress during 2011*, March 23, 2012, 13, http://documents.worldbank.org/curated/en/211891468300318225/pdf/676790BR0P07640CR0IDA0SECM201200159.pdf.

25. Shoemaker, Baird, and Baird, *The People and Their River*, 39.

26. Matsumoto and Doi to Zoellick and Kuroda, 9.

27. Matsumoto and Doi to Zoellick and Kuroda, 6.

28. World Bank and ADB, *Nam Theun 2 Board Update: Project Progress during 2012*, 23.

29. See PoE 18B:6 and World Bank and ADB, *Nam Theun 2 Board Update: Project Progress during 2012*, 25.

30. PoE 19:19.

31. World Bank and ADB, *Nam Theun 2 Board Update: Project Progress during 2012*, 25.

32. PoE 17:24.

33. Shoemaker, Baird, and Baird, *The People and Their River*, 56.

34. Chu Tai Hoanh, Thierry Facon, Try Thuon, and Ram C. Bastakoti, "Irrigation in Lower Mekong Basin Countries: The Beginning of the New Era," in *Contested Waterscapes in the Mekong Region*.

35. See Baird, Shoemaker, and Manorom, "The People and Their River," 1094.

36. Families in villages included in the program that have links to the XBF but are located some distance from it were eventually provided with the equivalent of US$100 each in cash compensation.

37. PoE 18B:15.

38. Lamia Karim, *Microfinance and Its Discontents: Women in Debt in Bangladesh* (Minneapolis: University of Minnesota Press, 2011).

39. Ng Shui Meng, former UNICEF Laos Women's Development Program Officer and Jacqui Chagnon, development consultant and former country representative of American Friends Service Committee, personal communication to Bruce Shoemaker, January 2014.

40. PoE 17:12.

41. World Bank, "Indigenous Peoples Overview," September 16, 2016, http://www .worldbank.org/en/topic/indigenouspeoples.

42. Ian G. Baird, "Translocal Assemblages and the Circulation of the Concept of 'Indigenous Peoples' in Laos," *Political Geography* 46 (2015).

43. James Chamberlain, personal communication to Ian Baird, 2015.

44. Barbara A. K. Franklin, A Review of Local Public Consultations for the Nam Theun 2 Hydroelectric Project, World Bank, September 1997.

45. Ian G. Baird and Bruce Shoemaker, "Unsettling Experiences: Internal Resettlement and International Agencies in Laos," *Development and Change* 38, no. 5 (2007); PoE 19:33–37.

46. James W. Adams, preface to *Doing a Dam Better*, x.

47. NTPC, Xe Bang Fai compensation framework discussions, minutes, December 16, 2004, 6.

48. World Bank and ADB, *Nam Theun 2 Board Update: Project Progress during 2012*, 23.

49. PoE 17:22.

50. PoE 17:25; Patchamuthu Illangovan and Anthony Jude, "Response of the World Bank and ADB to International Rivers Concerns Regarding the Nam Theun 2 (NT2) Project," October 22, 2009, 7.

51. PoE 19B:27.

52. World Bank and ADB, *Nam Theun 2 Board Update: Project Progress during 2012*, 25; PoE 22:36.

53. According to the World Bank's 2016 implementation status and results report for NT2, the GoL's Resettlement Committee tasked with carrying on the Downstream Compensation Program after the "handover" closed the program in 2014 after declaring that villager livelihoods are fully restored.

54. PoE 18B:6.

55. Baird, Shoekmaker, and Manorom, "The People and Their River," 1100.

56. David J. H. Blake, "Independent Technical Review: NT2 Impacts on Xe Bang Fai Fisheries" IRN and Environmental Defense, January 2005; Tyson R. Roberts, "Fluvicide: An Independent Environmental Assessment of Nam Theun 2 Hydropower Project in Laos, with Particular Reference to Aquatic Biology and Fishes," unpublished report, Bangkok 1996.

9

Revenues without Accountability

National Poverty Alleviation and Nam Theun 2

BRUCE SHOEMAKER

Beyond the promotion of biodiversity conservation and improved livelihoods for affected communities at the local level, a key rationale provided by the World Bank and its financial partners for their support of NT2 was its potential for raising the revenue of the government of the Lao PDR (GoL) to be used for national-level poverty alleviation.

This rationale was first proposed in August 2001, when Bank staff met with GoL authorities to outline a new "decision framework" that the Bank would use in assessing whether or not to support the project. The first of three key aspects of the framework was "implementation of a development framework characterized by concrete performance that aims at poverty reduction and environmental protection."[1] The document specified that satisfying this would require "a serious start and demonstrated progress" by the GoL in implementing two programs in the country—the International Monetary Fund's (IMF) poverty reduction and growth facility and the World Bank's poverty reduction strategy paper (PRSP), along with a commitment to channel the GoL's portion of NT2 revenues into the poverty reduction efforts outlined in the PRSP, as well as for biodiversity conservation efforts.[2]

International financial institutions such as the World Bank, IMF, and Asian Development Bank (ADB) had come under fire in the late years of the twentieth century for their perceived neglect of poverty and by 2000 their repositioning as organizations focused on poverty reduction was well under way. The prescriptions contained in the PRSP, such as privatization and strict controls on government expenditures, have been linked, however, to earlier World Bank/IMF programs that favored overall economic growth at the expense of equity.[3] A 2003 paper by staff of the Bangkok-based Focus on the Global South, based in part on what had happened in Vietnam and Laos, contended that "little has changed in the substance, form and process of World Bank and IMF programs. 'Poverty' is used as a window dressing to peddle more or less the same Structural Adjustment Programs (SAPs) that led them [aid recipient countries] into a state of chronic economic crisis to begin with."[4]

Still, as recounted in *Doing a Dam Better*, the PRSP was the basis for the GoL's 2003–4 national growth and poverty eradication strategy of which "NT2 was an integral part."[5] In May 2002 the World Bank had helped the GoL set up a new Poverty Reduction Fund oriented toward investment in rural infrastructure. While the fund was initially to be supported by the World Bank through concessional loans, the idea was that once NT2 came on line, the portion of the project's revenues going to the GoL would be used for poverty reduction through the fund and other programs, particularly in the fields of health, education, agriculture, and rural infrastructure.

Worldwide, NT2 was the second large World Bank–supported resource extraction project to attempt to ensure that project revenues were specifically allocated for poverty alleviation. The previous one had been the Chad-Cameroon pipeline in west Africa. That project, which was promoted (as was NT2) as a new model, also involved the export of energy (in that case oil rather than electricity) and was implemented in a very poor country with an authoritarian government and high levels of corruption.

The World Bank's attempt to set up strict controls on how project revenues from the Chad-Cameroon pipeline were used are widely acknowledged to have failed. The Bank ended up being forced to withdraw from what became an embarrassing debacle.[6]

Using the same rhetoric of poverty alleviation and the promotion of good governance, and with the benefit of its experience with Chad-Cameroon, the World Bank instituted a Revenue and Expenditures Management Program (REMP) with the GoL as part of its financing agreement for NT2. Ensuring the accountability of the governmental institutions responsible for implementing the REMP in Laos, as in Chad-Cameroon, was difficult. Transparency International annual reports have continually rated Laos in the bottom tier of nations worldwide in terms of the perception of corruption.[7] One might thus think that the failures of Chad-Cameroon would have prompted the Bank to develop more rigorous financial monitoring mechanisms for NT2. Bruce Rich, in examining NT2 for his 2013 book on the World Bank, *Foreclosing the Future*, summarized how this was not the case, citing a March 16, 2005, technical brief by Adrian Fozzard, senior public sector specialist at the World Bank: "The project's anti-corruption measures were a major step backward from what had been attempted in the Chad-Cameron venture. There would be no independent financial oversight or separate bank accounts to ensure that profits actually went to poverty alleviation and environmental programs. The Bank did not require the use of any external independent financial auditors. Instead, the revenue to the Laotian government from the dam funds would be treated just like any other government income."[8] Instead, the Bank's technical brief on revenue and expenditure management for the project explained that "NT2 revenues will be co-mingled with other public resources and managed following standard [Lao government] budget execution procedures." In fact, "it will not be possible to identify individual transactions financed by the NT2 revenues"; instead the Bank would figure out a "method for determining additionality [i.e. how much extra, additional money was really going for poverty social and environmental programs because of the project] . . . with the NT2 financing partners *three years after project commissioning and thereafter as deemed necessary.*"[9]

Doing a Dam Better acknowledged that Laos posed a problem for the World Bank: "In an environment in which the state audit organization was weak," the IMF program "had already gone off track, partly over the deadlock over the independent audit of the Bank of the Lao PDR," and because "the budget was opaque, the World Bank needed a mechanism to demonstrate clearly how the revenues from NT2 would be spent."[10] But when the GoL objected to the type of strict controls that, based on experience in other countries, the World Bank deemed necessary, Bank staff, despite their doubts, essentially accepted a GoL proposal to instead "strengthen its existing systems through an improved public financial management system with appropriate transparency and accountability rather than earmarking and tracking specific NT2 resources." Rather than insisting on the type of accountability mechanisms that were clearly called for, the Bank accepted the GoL's vague promises of good behavior in management of NT2 revenues.

NT2 Revenue Management in Practice

External communications from the World Bank as well as the Nam Theun Power Company have continuously promoted NT2's poverty alleviation benefits. From the start, much of this has been a distortion, in particular the oft-cited US$2 billion in revenues for the GoL to be used for this purpose. The $2 billion figure (specifically, an estimated $1.95 billion over twenty-five years) refers to nominal value, a figure that doesn't take inflation into account.[11] A more accurate figure of NT2's value to the GoL at its inception was its "net present value" which, it was estimated, would not exceed US$250 million.[12] While this is still a considerable amount, it is not the huge windfall that has often been portrayed.

Despite the framing of NT2 as first and foremost a poverty alleviation project, World Bank staff have had difficulty ascertaining where project revenues are actually going. The few documents that are publicly available suggest that there are major issues with the REMP. The inability to confirm that NT2 revenues are in fact having an impact on poverty in Laos is one of the main factors that led the Bank's own internal evaluation team, for multiple years, to give NT2 a "moderately unsatisfactory" rating.[13] The Bank's mid-2015 implementation status report for NT2, a public document that might be expected to show the project in as positive a light as possible, had this to say:

> The Revenue and Expenditure Management Program (REMP) was intended to channel NT2 revenues to finance priority poverty reduction and environmental management programs. While audits confirm that the revenues have been received in the Government Treasury and a significant proportion of NT2 revenues have been allocated to eligible sectors, implementation of the revenue and expenditure management arrangements is not yet consistent with related obligations. The government has partially met requirements related to the conduct of Public Expenditure Reviews, peer audit reviews and reporting on NT2 revenue allocations and expenditures, and has not met obligations regarding public disclosure, NT2 revenue allocations and expenditures and regarding public consultations. The World Bank is working with Government to address these issues and restore compliance with the REMP requirements."[14]

The Bank's July 2016 status report retained the "moderately unsatisfactory" overall rating. The report notes that neither the required financial statements of NT2 revenues nor audits of the program have been made available by the GoL to the World Bank.[15] Despite requests as this chapter was being prepared, World Bank staff were not able to provide any details regarding how the Bank will measure any improvements in the program in the future.[16]

Many observers in Laos concur that there is little evidence of the GoL having significantly improved its basic services for poor communities following the addition of NT2 (and other hydropower) revenues in recent years.

Government counterparts to foreign aid projects in the health, education, and agricultural/economic development sectors seldom have funds of their own and tend to be completely reliant on foreign aid budgets. When this author was first in Laos in the early 1990s, the inability of the central government to pay teachers, health care workers, and other civil servants their minimal salaries on time was a chronic problem. Despite all the foreign investment projects since completed, many of which were justified as ways to give the GoL the resources to better serve its people, these chronic problems remain. In October 2013, long after NT2 revenues had started flowing, news reports were detailing the fact that the GoL was in fiscal crisis, at least three months behind on paying its teachers and in the process of eliminating an important monthly allowance for all of its civil servants.[17] An internal GoL auditing agency, the State Inspection Authority issued a report in 2015 documenting widespread embezzlement of government funds, including the loss of US$123 million between 2012 and 2014.[18] By early 2017 this process had implicated hundreds of, in many cases high level, government officials, who were forced to return misappropriated funds.[19] Despite an overall high level of growth, government officials in 2016 were forced to admit it would be impossible to meet the GoL's long-promised goal of being poverty free and able to graduate off of the United Nations list of least developed countries by 2020. The goal was redefined as a "long-term objective."[20] Recent reports note that despite some progress the country still lags behind on other essential millennial development goals with 44 percent of Lao children still stunted due to poor nutrition.[21] This suggests growing inequity and that the commitment to poverty alleviation as a central component of the country's development strategy in practice may not be nearly as robust as it has been portrayed.

An astounding, albeit inadvertent, admission by the GoL of the insignificance of NT2 in contributing to its poverty alleviation efforts was the June 2017 authorization of funding for the third phase (2017–19) of the Poverty Reduction Fund. The fund was established to channel revenues from NT2, and presumably other hydropower projects, into nationwide poverty alleviation—and to thus break the cycle of dependence on outside donors for large portions of the GoL's annual poverty alleviation programming budget. Yet only $6 million of the fund's $54 million budget is to come from GoL revenues. Seven years after NT2 began generating revenue the Poverty Reduction Fund remains, in large part, an international donor subsidized program.[22]

In September 2017 the World Bank issued a new report on the REMP. While the report details some recent progress, in particular the completion of some, but not all, of the long-delayed financial and audit reports for the program, the Bank is still not able to demonstrate a clear link between NT2 revenues and poverty alleviation. Instead, some general indicators of poverty in the country are provided. Most notably, the report reveals that income from NT2 to date has contributed just 1 percent on average to the GoL's total revenues per year since project commissioning.[23] This is in sharp contrast to the projections presented in a World Bank briefing paper prepared in advance of project approval in March 2005 that stated, "NT2 revenues will account for between 3 and 5 percent of total revenues in the period to FY2020."[24] Other reports have claimed NT2 revenues would range from 3 percent of GoL revenues in an Australian government review to 7–9 percent in an independent examination of the project.[25]

In addition to the question of how much of NT2's revenues are appropriately accounted for and channeled into poverty reduction programs is the issue of whether or not those programs actually address the main drivers of poverty in the country. The Poverty Reduction Fund focuses on rural infrastructure (roads, health clinics, irrigation) on the assumption that people are poor because they lack government services and access to markets. However, a series of ADB-funded participatory poverty assessments in Laos found that much rural poverty in the country is "new poverty" relating to the loss of land and the natural resource base on which rural communities have long depended.[26] These dynamics have been exacerbated by government policies relating to internal resettlement, land and forest allocation, and land concessions granted to foreign companies, policies that have received a certain amount of direct and indirect support from the same financial institutions promoting NT2 as a poverty reduction mechanism.[27]

Conclusions

In sum, whether or not NT2 has had a significant, positive impact on poverty reduction in Laos remains unknown, although there is considerable anecdotal evidence that it has been much less successful than anticipated. Despite rhetoric claiming that hydropower revenues would help the GoL provide better services to its people, whether increased income to the GoL is having a positive impact on the quality of life of the rural poor majority of the country has not yet been demonstrated. Given its enormous and ongoing impact on project affected people and the environment, the fact that, in relative terms to the country's overall budget, NT2 is contributing only a small fraction of what was initially projected is also a point of considerable concern.

The inability of the World Bank to provide hard evidence of NT2's poverty alleviation benefits is particularly disturbing given that NT2 is first and foremost a scheme to export electricity to Thailand. That is, the beneficiaries of the electricity NT2 produces are not primarily the people of Laos. Laos was already producing more than enough electricity for its own needs without NT2. Given this, the only real justification for building NT2 in Laos, with all of the social and environmental impacts it has entailed, would have been very real and measurable benefits for the Lao population as a whole. The World Bank and its financial partners had a special responsibility and obligation to clearly demonstrate that NT2 revenues really were making a difference in meeting the expectations of poverty alleviation used to justify Bank involvement in the project.

To date, however, this has not been the case. In the absence of better information, claims that NT2 is a successful model of poverty alleviation worthy of replication are without tangible basis and cannot be taken as anything more than wishful thinking.

NOTES

1. World Bank, "Decision Framework for Processing the Proposed NT 2 Project," June 2002, http://siteresources.worldbank.org/INTLAOPRD/Resources/NT2_Decision_Framework.pdf.

2. World Bank, "Decision Framework for Processing the Proposed NT 2 Project."

3. See, for example, Charles Abugre, *Still Sapping the Poor: The IMF and Poverty Reduction Strategies*, World Development Movement, June 2000.

4. Jenina Joy Chavez Malaluan and Shalmali Guttal, *Poverty Reduction Strategy Papers: A Poor Package for Poverty Reduction*, Focus on the Global South, Bangkok, January 2003.

5. Rosa Alonso i Terme and Homi Kharas, "Lao PDR Gets Ready for NT2," in *Doing a Dam Better: The Lao People's Democratic Republic and the Story of Nam Theun 2*, ed. Ian C. Porter and Jayasankar Shivakumar (Washington, DC: World Bank, 2011), 36–37.

6. Lydia Polgreen, "World Bank Ends Effort to Help Chad Ease Poverty," *New York Times*, September 10, 2008, http://www.nytimes.com/2008/09/11/world/africa/11chad.html.

7. Transparency International annual reports can be found at www.transparency.org. There are numerous accounts of corruption in Laos, including within the Ministry of Finance. See, for example, Richard Finney, "Former Lao Finance Minister Named in Corruption Probe," *Radio Free Asia*, January 8, 2016, http://www.rfa.org/english/news/laos/corruption-01082016142933.html.

8. Bruce Rich, *Foreclosing the Future: The World Bank and the Politics of Environmental Destruction* (Washington, DC: Island Press, 2013), 126.

9. Adrian Fozzard, *Technical Brief, Revenue and Expenditure Management*, Nam Theun 2 Hydroelectric Project, The World Bank, Washington DC, March 16, 2005, 11, emphasis added. http://web.worldbank.org/WBSITE/EXTERNAL/COUNTRIES /EASTASIAPACIFICEXT/LAOPRDEXTN/0,,contentMDK:20395394~pagePK:141137~ piPK:141127~theSitePK:293684~isCURL:Y,00.html.

10. Alonso i Terme and Homi Kharas, "Lao PDR Gets Ready for NT2," 39.

11. Ian C. Porter and Jayasankar Shivakumar, "Overview," in *Doing a Dam Better*, 7.

12. "Nam Theun 2: No Time for Another Mistake," editorial, *Watershed* 10, no. 1 (2004): 2.

13. World Bank, *Nam Theun 2 Social and Environmental Project: Implementation Status and Results Report*, June 30, 2015; World Bank, *Nam Theun 2 Social and Environmental Project: Implementation Status and Results Report*, July 11, 2016.

14. World Bank, *Nam Theun 2 Social and Environmental Project: Implementation Status Report*, June 30, 2015, 3.

15. World Bank, *Nam Theun 2 Social and Environmental Project: Implementation Status Report*, July 11, 2016, 9.

16. Daryl Fields, World Bank NT2 program manager, personal communication, September–November 2016.

17. Joshua Lipis, "Lao Teachers Face Three Months of Late Wages," *Radio Free Asia*, October 10, 2013, www.rfa.org/english/news/laos/teachers-10102013185425.html.

18. David Hutt, "Little Laos Tackles Big Corruption," *Asia Times*, February 16, 2017, www.atimes.com/article/little-laos-tackles-big-corruption.

19. Brooks Boliek, "Lao Officials Are Returning Money They Earned through Corruption," *Radio Free Asia*, January 24, 2017, www.rfa.org/english/news/laos/lao-officials-are-re turning-money-01242017144051.html.

20. Xinhua, "Laos Strives to Graduate from Least Developed Countries," June 29, 2016, http://news.xinhuanet.com/english/2016-06/29/c_135475835.htm.

21. World Bank, Lao PDR overview, April 2017, www.worldbank.org/en/country /lao/overview.

22. "Remote Communities Benefiting from Poverty Reduction Efforts," *Vientiane Times*, June 28, 2017, http://www.vientianetimes.org.la/FreeContent/FreeConten_Remote .html.

23. World Bank, *Nam Theun 2 Hydropower Project Update: Revenue Management*, 2. The discrepancy appears to be a combination of GoL NT2 revenues being somewhat less than projected ($28 million in 2016 rather than a predicted $33 million) and the total GoL budget being higher than projected.

24. Jeff Ball, Jim Elston, Majorie Sullivan, and Andrew Walker, *Review of Nam Theun 2 Hydroelectric Dam: Final Report to AUSAID*, February 21, 2005, 4.

25. Teresita Cruz Del Rosario, *The State and the Advocate: Development Policy in Asia* (London: Routledge, 2014), 18.

26. James Chamberlain, *Participatory Poverty Assessment: Lao PDR* (Vientiane: National Statistics Center, 2001); James Chamberlain, *Participatory Poverty Assessment: Lao PDR* (Vientiane: National Statistics Center, 2006).

27. For an overview of a series of reports and studies on this issue, see Ian G. Baird and Bruce Shoemaker, *Aiding or Abetting? Internal Resettlement and International Aid Agencies in the Lao PDR*, Probe International, August 2005.

Part Three

Nam Theun 2's Wider Legacy

10

Nam Theun 2 and the Transformation of Institutions and Public Debate in Laos

SARINDA SINGH

Changes in formal and informal domestic institutions in Laos, including in its limited civil society, have followed in the wake of the Nam Theun 2 (NT2) project, and public debate has reflected these changes. Proponents of NT2 argued that the project would transform institutions shaping public debate, not only in the project-affected area but also across all of Laos. While challenging the government of the Lao PDR's (GoL) one-party system was never on the agenda, NT2 proponents hoped that through strengthening the national legal and regulatory framework, the country would move toward more inclusive and socially and environmentally responsible development. NT2 was presented as an expansion of public involvement in development projects through publicly accessible project information, public consultations with project-affected communities, international workshops, stakeholder workshops, and national legislative reform. Certainly these were noteworthy for both World Bank–supported infrastructure projects globally and for hydropower projects in Laos.[1] Yet changes in political restrictions in Laos over the last decade have revealed the importance of other economic, political, and social conditions that were overlooked by NT2 proponents. These proponents exaggerated or overestimated the nationwide impact of reformed formal institutions and ignored informal institutions even though the latter are often more important in Laos, as in many developing countries.

International academics and activists have widely discussed NT2 in relation to international civil society but have given far less attention to the effects of NT2 on domestic social and political institutions. Likewise, in works promoting NT2, the World Bank emphasizes the importance of broad public engagement but then mostly treats civil society outside Laos.[2] Thus, the Bank appears most concerned with civil society as a public relations issue. The emphasis on international civil society is understandable given its broader relevance to global development and Bank-supported projects worldwide and in light of the relative geopolitical insignificance of Laos. However, the Bank's use of NT2 as a global model for socially responsible development is only justified if domestic trends in Laos support the Bank's claims.

Significantly, Martin Stuart-Fox noted just prior to the World Bank's approval of NT2 that "Laos is virtually devoid of civil society."[3] Laos has relatively limited overt political violence or civil strife, as public debate is effectively restricted "by the GoL's intolerance of criticism and fear of this intolerance."[4] Alongside this long-standing "culture of fear" has been a shift in political ideology from socialism to developmentalism: "development is now the dominant rhetoric and vision of the Lao state."[5] Together these trends mean that in contemporary Laos, questioning development is usually seen as a form of political opposition.[6] Residents of Laos cannot, therefore, question hydropower, especially NT2, as that would be taken as criticism of the Lao state.[7] Hence, the fact that public protests about hydropower projects are never reported in the Lao media is certainly not indicative of flawless implementation. Given this, it is important to attend to overt and covert forms of public debate, and the varied formal and informal institutions that enable or restrict such debate. While Laos has seen massive transformations in the decade since NT2 commenced, including shifts in public debate, these owe mainly to other economic, political, and social conditions and much less to NT2-imposed reforms to formal institutions. This chapter reviews Ian C. Porter and Jayasankar Shivakumar's edited volume *Doing a Dam Better* in light of the nature of public debate in Laos, key informant interviews I have carried out, and observations I have made while working in Laos over the last fifteen years.

Formal and Informal Institutions Shaping Public Debate

The notion of institutions directs attention to institutional trends across rural and urban contexts in Laos, as well as in domestic and international contexts. This chapter uses the term "civil society" for international civil organizations. "Public debate" here refers to the public as a social group that discusses, either overtly or covertly, any shared concerns. Habermas's concept of public sphere also applies, as well as such related terms as "political space," "public voice," and "political culture."[8]

An authoritarian one-party state governs a small and largely rural populace in Laos. Laos is consistently ranked low in global assessments of governance and civil liberties by the World Bank and others.[9] At the same time, there is limited overt state-sanctioned violence in Laos compared to other Asian countries.[10] Protests and open dissent are rare and largely unreported in national media. While Laos currently lacks the massive formal regulatory infrastructure of its much larger neighbors, less obvious social controls abound.

The fact of less obvious forms of social control relates to the distinction, highlighted in this chapter, between formal and informal institutions.[11] Formal institutions refer to codified mechanisms and procedures that the state oversees, such as official meetings, policy documents, and news announcements in the state-controlled media. While Laos's legal frameworks have certainly expanded over time, they are still marked by a lack of clarity, consistency, and enforcement. The authority of the party usually overrides international conventions and formal citizen rights granted by the Lao constitution.[12] Likewise, the state maintains tight regulatory controls on the mass media and, compared to neighbors, the Lao media has very limited capacity, distribution, and content. The education system is similarly constrained in contributing to public debate.[13] Laos has about seventy officially approved international nongovernmental organizations (INGOs), all of which work with government partners to support national development priorities. In 2009, a decree was passed permitting the establishment of domestic nonprofit associations. In addition, some organizations have permission to operate as social enterprises, nonprofit businesses, and training organizations.[14] Actors who might in other countries identify as members of civil society usually emphasize their technical contributions to business and development in negotiations with the GoL.

Informal institutions include social norms that are not explicitly outlined in legal frameworks but that are commonly referred to in private conversation and observed in practice. Personal connections are crucial—those without money, family, or organizational backing are unable to negotiate in the same way as those with these connections. Thus, nonpolitical civil associations can be established without official approval, but their survival depends on personal connections with authorities, and at times they are quietly shut down.[15] Other informal institutions include various forms of censorship of news, meetings, and reports, such as self-censorship, official censorship, and the use of politicized euphemisms (e.g., "neighbors" for China and Vietnam). For example, the host of Laos's first and only talkback radio program, which included much public debate about land concessions, deliberately excluded hydropower as a topic of conversation, as it was too politically sensitive.[16] Notably, the host's prior experience as a journalist with state media provided him with contacts and insight as to the bounds of politically acceptable topics. The GoL also has an ambivalent view of INGOs, despite their working closely with government partners, and all INGOs must subordinate advocacy to national development goals. Complex administrative processes (e.g., visas, memorandums of understanding, reporting obligations) can be selectively tightened and relaxed depending on money and connections. In a similar manner, government positions are rewarded less by low salaries and more by informal perks—ranging from ubiquitous project per diem to project equipment and vehicles and the rumored millions accumulated by national leaders.[17]

Informal institutions are ubiquitous across Laos, but they are usually implicit in practice and most apparent in domestic and rural contexts. One such institution is the social norm of suspicion of foreign interference. For example, during my field work near the NT2 dam site, I was invited to a celebration for party members, and interrogated by the then-governor of Nakai District, Khammouane Province. "You aren't from an NGO, are you?," he asked, when I said I was a PhD student. Another official laughingly supported me, reassuring him that "she's not the same as John!"—an INGO worker then based in Vientiane who was interested in villagers' concerns about NT2 and with whom after that I was careful not to be seen with in Nakai. Another country director of an INGO I had worked with previously warned me not to be seen with her in Nakai given the district governor's antipathy to the organization's work on elephant conservation, an officially approved part of NT2 but largely as a result of World Bank pressure.[18] Such experiences conveyed the social norm of suspicion of INGOs and foreign interference, despite the reports produced by NT2 proponents on the importance of engaging with civil society.

These examples also illustrate how informal institutions are often more important than formal institutions in Laos. The dissemination and implementation of national laws, including laws created to secure World Bank approval of NT2, is often contested by authorities, who dispute their applicability whenever they challenge vested interests.[19] Similarly, informal restrictions that prevent Lao citizens from voicing their concerns or questions about NT2 have been well documented despite the heavy rhetoric touting participation.[20] Yet all institutions are negotiations in practice; neither formal nor informal institutions are immutable or rigidly enforced, and the GoL is not a homogenous monolith. For instance, at times officials have used religious rituals informally alongside formal village meetings to combine persuasion with coercion.[21] Institutions for public debate are highly dependent on context.

Crucial to understanding development projects in Laos are the divides between rural–urban contexts and domestic–international contexts. Access to information, the extent of ethnic diversity, and the level of literacy differ widely depending on context. For instance, newspapers and reports online and that emanate from Vientiane and that are written in English as well as meetings that take place in Vientiane can be much more open and critical than reports that emanate from rural locales and that are written in the Lao language and meetings that take place in such locales. This context dependency of institutions shaping public debate within Laos was vastly underacknowledged by NT2 proponents, who primarily focused on formal institutions in international and urban contexts and overlooked informal institutions.

NT2's Minimal Role in Transforming Public Debate in Laos

This section examines *Doing a Dam Better* to consider how NT2's proponents presented the project internationally as a model for positive, nationwide expansion of public debate in Laos. While public debate did widen post-NT2, this project was not a primary cause of the expansion, and restrictions on public debate have subsequently reemerged. Most egregiously, *Doing a Dam Better* discusses concerns about international public relations and concerns about "reforms . . . in the political space" as though these are equivalent.[22] Furthermore, *Doing a Dam Better* pays little attention to the differences between formal and informal institutions and also includes inaccurate assertions about livelihoods and public consultations.[23] Given the ample literature on NT2, these gaps and inaccuracies can only be seen as the deliberate conveyance of misinformation in a strategic attempt to save face, which resulted from the prioritization of international public relations over serious engagement in the domestic context.

At the time, NT2 was the only hydropower project in Laos to publicly share information, and the World Bank promoted other information-sharing efforts. For example, in the lead-up to NT2's approval, the Bank provided discreet funding for Stuart-Fox's informative analysis of political reform in Laos.[24] The World Bank also pushed the GoL to conduct other initiatives that would have the specific effect of enabling people from all around the country to participate in decisions regarding the project, including information sharing, consultation with project-affected communities, the holding of international stakeholder workshops, and the drafting new national laws (see figure 10.1). *Doing a Dam Better* reports a major shift in the World Bank toward serious engagement with Laos's domestic context:

Figure 10.1. Public consultations between GoL staff and villagers in NNT NPA in late 2006. Such initiatives emerged from conditions set by the World Bank that had to be met if NT2 was to be approved and influenced formal institutions for public debate across Laos. Photo by Sarinda Singh.

Criticism regarding the government's poor governance record and the notion that affected persons might not feel free to openly voice their concerns in the Lao political and cultural context did not figure prominently in the first phase of World Bank involvement, from 1994 through 1997. It was not until the second period of involvement, after international civil society organizations voiced their concerns, that the World Bank took these criticisms more seriously.[25]

Doing a Dam Better also lauds changes in the GoL

The government's commitment to the communications plan, based on a genuine commitment to transparency backed up by actions, was a turning point for NT2. . . . One of the most important aspects of the strategy was to build the capacity of the government to undertake communications and consultations, not just for the NT2 project but also for all future development projects.[26]

Support from the World Bank did result in better interaction between INGOs and the Lao state than had been the case for other hydropower projects in the country.[27] Yet NT2 proponents focused primarily on formal institutions in international and urban contexts that give a distorted view of opportunities for public debate in Laos. For example, the authors of *Doing a Dam Better* ignore their own caution about the importance of the "Lao political and cultural context" and disingenuously claim that "reviews of the [workshop] transcripts indicate that those who attended the sessions were not constrained in terms of the views they expressed." In fact, I reported the exact opposite of the same event, about which a foreign INGO codirector privately observed, "These high-level meetings are all the same; this is not a forum for discussion."[28]

NT2 proponents also argued that the project would be socially transformative, not only in the project affected area but across all of Laos. Project developers did not envisage major political change coming out of the project, but it was hoped that NT2 would open up a range of new opportunities for public involvement than had been the case with other development projects in the country. According to the editors of *Doing a Dam Better*,

> NT2 has had a major impact on the [GoL], the hydropower industry, the World Bank and other financial institutions, civil society groups, and others closely following hydropower development. . . . It is a cornerstone of the growth and poverty reduction strategy of a poor country that is rich in natural resources. It reflects a shift in the mindset of the political leadership and government of Lao PDR, which undertook bold reforms and at the same time signaled the desire to engage more closely with the global community and to open up space for dialogue at home.[29]

NT2 was presented as catalyzing nationwide changes in Laos and was touted as an example of the GoL's new development priorities. Thus, *Doing a Dam Better* argues that

> the willingness of the government to participate in a consultation and public information process on NT2 was a milestone that indicated its commitment to environmental and social safeguards and to transparency. World Bank staff considered the consultation process remarkably open and wide ranging in the Lao context. Although some stakeholders criticized the way in which this process was carried out, it demonstrated the government's willingness to go beyond its normal limits in informing the public of the consequences of a major infrastructure project.[30]

Some observers who are critical of NT2 nevertheless concur with the World Bank's assessment of the participatory process, suggesting that Lao decision makers did indeed make a "conscious" commitment to "the reformist template of [NT2]."[31] However, a more common alternative view is that the GoL—or the majority of Lao decision makers—begrudgingly accepted certain

World Bank conditions for the sake of this project alone, which the Bank considered nonnegotiable due to intense international civil society pressure.[32] In this view, the GoL's "normal limits" were capable of being pushed for the sake of an international "public" concerned with NT2, not for the sake of a domestic public. As civil society members report, "This progressive legal framework was pushed on the Lao authorities in relation to this NT2 project, but was not meant to be fully applied to any other project. . . . Once trying to use the decree on compensation for those affected by a development project, I was told by a provincial governor that this only applies in Vientiane."[33]

NT2 was intended to be a global, regional, and national model but instead became a unique exception. As Fleur Johns reports, "A specially designed jurisdictional field was demarcated around [NT2], . . . the legal features of which do not correspond to the situation of any other company, individual, or agency in [Laos]."[34] Related to this, NT2 has certainly paved the way for other privately funded hydropower projects in Laos, but it has not, irrespective of formal institutions, provided a model for information sharing, participation, and consultation. For example, Johns describes how NT2 "'failed forward' into a successor, . . . the Xayaburi project," which drew on the same economic rationale but lacked "the wide-ranging reform agenda that accompanied Nam Theun 2."[35] Similarly, Boer and his coauthors argue that "around Xayaburi, few remnants of the audit, consultation and reporting architecture erected around [NT2] are still in evidence."[36] Lao officials privately note that NT2 is seen as overly complicated, slow, expensive, and onerous, especially when compared to other projects whose funders have imposed less stringent conditions.[37] Thus in the post-NT2 era, "Laos is largely following a private sector investment path which maintains sovereignty of decisions within the country and draws on the close relationship with China to implement projects through less publicly accessible processes than is required by international finance institutions."[38]

Finally, NT2 proponents assert the role of this project in expanding public debate in Laos through changes to both formal and informal institutions. Yet the emphasis on NT2 as part of a transformed Laos is misleading because project proponents tend to ignore the greater importance of other conditions that contribute to changes in public debate. Patchamuthu Illangovan in his contribution to *Doing a Dam Better*, "NT2: A Transformative Endeavor," maintains, for example, that

> there have been some noteworthy developments to date, such as the civil society decree, the media law, and the growing acceptance of more open criticism of

government policies and actions by members of the National Assembly and the general public. Citizens are demanding more accountability from government; their voices will only get louder as the nexus between politics and business interests in natural resources becomes more intertwined, increasing the risk that benefits will accrue to the few rather than to all Lao people. The government is beginning to respond to some of these concerns by opening the space for civic participation. NT2 is showing the way as an example of how a natural resources project can be developed to benefit the vast majority of the people.[39]

But why are Lao citizens demanding more accountability from the government? Why is the GoL beginning to respond to some of these concerns? And to what extent are these changes attributable to NT2? These questions are the focus of the following sections, which consider changing public debate in Laos in more detail.

Before I move on, however, it is important to note that these domestic changes are also related to changes in the World Bank and in international civil society. Notably, consultants who worked on NT2 in Laos reported that after its approval, the World Bank's emphasized public consultation because it was concerned about international public relations.[40] *Doing a Dam Better* does emphasize the links between transparency, communications, and public relations, but the overall focus is on the latter two issues internationally rather than domestic engagement in Laos.[41] The current priorities of the World Bank are reflected in its bowing under pressure—reportedly from donors and the GoL—to urge the International Environmental and Social Panel of Experts (PoE) to complete its work according to the concession agreement, despite the persistent problems with livelihoods in resettled villages and management of the Nakai-Nam Theun National Protected Area detailed in other chapters of this book. A recent PoE report indicates it has continued to push managers for a "new initiative . . . [that] amounts to a recognition of the realities on the ground."[42] One PoE member, Thayer Scudder, has even publicly abandoned his previous support for mega-dams after the continued failures of NT2's programs, arguing that the GoL "wants to build 60 dams over the next 20 or 30 years, and at the moment it doesn't have the capacity to deal with environmental and social impacts for any single one of them."[43]

Changes in Public Debate in Laos

While NT2 was hugely significant for Laos, it did not instigate a new era of socially responsible development, as is often claimed by NT2 proponents. Instead, a range of other economic, political, and social conditions are crucial to understanding shifts in public debate in the last decade. Much development and scholarly work has sought to understand the relations between changing economic, political, and social conditions. For instance, in neighboring Thailand the rise of the "middle-income peasant" has fundamentally changed the national political landscape: the rural populace no longer simply seeks to satisfy basic subsistence needs but to develop more productive connections to the Thai state.[44] The World Bank echoes some of these ideas in relation to NT2.[45] However, NT2 proponents underemphasized the complexity of change and overemphasized the trickle-down benefits of national economic growth.

Certainly, Laos's domestic economic, political, and social conditions are closely linked to national, regional, and global changes, as well to the domestic conditions of a small population with very limited education. Yet in works promoting NT2 the World Bank disingenuously underestimates the importance of all these. Expanding public debate in post-NT2 Laos was due to a growing economy as well as to the massive expansion of land concessions that have come to threaten the livelihoods of many and thus have motivated critical public debate despite the threat of state reprisals. Since 2012, informal and formal institutions to control public debate have once again been restrengthened. This indicates how NT2 *coincided* with, rather than *caused*, the expansion of public debate, many gains of which have now been lost. Thus, if the nationwide changes to formal institutions lauded by the World Bank had been effectively implemented, they would likely have mitigated the social and environmental impacts of land concessions. But instead NT2 "failed forward," not only into subsequent hydropower projects but also into myriad other domains of social and environmental governance.

From Repression to Expanding Public Debate . . .

The most comprehensive assessment of political reform in Laos in the early 2000s concluded that "greater political openness, either in the form of freer political debate or in how the Party functions, is not on the agenda, let alone any move towards multi-party democracy."[46] In 2004, the Tenth ASEAN (Association of Southeast Asian Nations) Summit hosted by Laos in Vientiane marked a certain degree of economic and political opening. Yet one Western ambassador described the complex negotiations he had to undertake to arrange his prime minister's attendance even though the logistics were relatively simple and described the Lao state as "inept, inefficient, and opaque."[47] At the time, this pessimism seemed well founded. The Asian economic crisis of the late 1990s saw turmoil as foreign investment in Laos dropped from US$2 billion in 1995 to US$20 million in 2000. At the height of the crisis, the only public call for a multiparty democracy since the revolution — a peaceful public demonstration by a small group of Lao university students in October 1999 — was quickly quashed and the leaders fled abroad or continue to be detained.[48] Foreign observers then bemoaned the underdeveloped potential of abundant natural resources held back by Laos' political system.[49] Despite this, there were subsequent changes in Laos prompted by broader economic conditions.

From 2005 to 2012, Laos saw 6–9 percent annual economic growth driven by investments in hydropower, mining, light industry, agribusiness, and tourism. Laos' rapid economic growth has benefited many Lao citizens, prompting a reevaluation of its status by some foreign observers. For example, a *Wall Street Journal* article in 2012 proclaimed Laos as "Southeast Asia's newest boom economy."[50] Likewise, the World Bank's Economic Monitor asserted that "with development soaring in construction, manufacturing, mining and services, Lao PDR's economic outlook in 2012 is positive."[51] An opening of public debate was also widely reported at this time. According to Christopher Roberts, for example, "Officials from both foreign embassies and international aid agencies generally indicated that the human rights situation has improved significantly and, according to one foreign ambassador, the Lao Government is willing to talk about any issue."[52] The expansion of public debate in Laos was enabled by changes in both formal and informal institutions.

Many important donor-supported reforms of national legal frameworks have contributed to changes in formal institutions in Laos. For instance, the United States supported Laos's accession to the World Trade Organization in October 2012.[53] Multilateral and bilateral donors have supported the Lao National Assembly, encouraging, for example, increased "public dialogue" through meetings and a public hotline.[54] In 2009, a decree made it possible for nonprofit associations to register for government approval. These associations were initially a part of efforts to standardize trade across ASEAN by, for instance, establishing requirements for professional science and engineering associations to be formed in Laos, but they subsequently received support from international donors and civil society.[55] The decree saw cautious optimism from a range of observers, including NT2 proponents, who viewed it as evidence of "a step closer to pluralistic and open public space in Laos."[56]

These changes in formal institutions coincided with changes in informal institutions that also expanded opportunities for public debate. For example, the National Assembly has many limitations—including the fact that nearly all of its representatives are members of the Communist Party—but it has also provided a forum for some public discussion.[57] At a 2011 National Assembly meeting, Khampeui Phanmalaythong, then head of the Academy of Social Sciences, questioned the need for Marxism-Leninism in the Lao education system. While he lost his position as director of the academy the following year, his speech marked an unprecedented high point in public debate.[58] Multiparty democracy disappeared from public debate in Laos, but not public debate itself, which turned to other pressing concerns.[59]

Most significantly, the massive expansion of land concessions across rural and urban Laos—conservatively estimated to cover 5 percent of Laos's land area, and having increased fiftyfold from 2000 to 2009—has prompted expanding nationwide public debate about land conflicts and corruption.[60] While low-level corruption due to low government salaries is ubiquitous and a social norm, high-level corruption increasingly became a target of critical commentary within post-NT2 Laos.[61] The surprise resignation of the Lao prime minister in late 2010 was partly forced by opposition within the party to his stated intention to tackle rampant corruption, land concessions, and resource extraction.[62] The national importance of these topics was seen in the popularity of Laos's first and only talkback radio program run by Ounkeo Souksavan from 2007 to early 2012, when the Ministry of Information and Culture revoked permission to air the program. Observers noted, "Social justice, overt corruption and land grabs were daily fare on 'Talk of the News,' a rarity in Laos's authoritarian context."[63] Though broadcast only in the Vientiane area, it provided an anonymous forum for Lao residents to share experiences across the country.[64] This expansion of public debate did not translate into substantial action, but it was still a positive change.[65] Similarly, in mid-2012, the *Vientiane Times* newspaper had a front-page article titled "Who Will Help the People if the National Assembly Won't?" This piece diplomatically avoided any mention of land concessions, but it clearly articulated the expectations the public had for their elected representatives and expressed frustration with inaction on public complaints.[66]

Laos's national leaders have explicitly acknowledged the political importance of land conflicts and corruption, observing that they "often cause disputes between the public and government officials" and allowing that, alongside economic growth, ensuring that citizens are able to voice their concerns is crucial to expanding public debate more generally within Laos.[67] The forms and impacts of land concessions are highly varied, but their nationwide prevalence and initially low political sensitivity compared to hydropower meant they could be part of domestic public debates in a way that NT2 could not. Hence, while NT2 did help expand public debate as well as instigate institutional changes within Laos up to 2012, it was not a major direct contributor to this process. For instance, INGOs and nonprofit associations could participate in formal working groups with GoL partners on land issues, but only private developers could participate in the only domestic working group for hydropower.[68] Similarly, despite the fact the NT2 helped expand public debate in post-NT2 Laos up to 2012, it itself could never be questioned on radio, in newspapers, or in the National Assembly. Notably too, Laos's hydropower plans have provoked much regional and global controversy, but they are justified on the grounds that they are necessary to combat poverty, and this line of reasoning "continue[s] to resonate with much of the population."[69] The prior political sensitivity of hydropower in general, and NT2 most especially, meant that these topics were strictly censored and excluded from discussions in the public sphere, thus limiting and constraining their contributions to expanding nationwide public debate.

. . . And Back to Restricted Public Debate

By late 2012, cautious optimism about increasingly open public debate in Laos had once again faded. As reported in international media since then, a number of interrelated events have coalesced to "[raise] alarms that a nascent liberalization of the communist-ruled country could be sliding backward."[70] While this section focuses on the domestic context, this slide is linked to regional and global shifts. For instance, with Laos seeing much economic investment from sources that do not stipulate onerous social and environment conditions, the World Bank and other Western donors have much less clout now than they did a decade ago.[71] Significantly, positive assessments of Laos's economy have ceased since late 2013 in the wake of massive debt accumulation, in part due to corruption and weak economic regulation that has forced more focus on previously underemphasized governance issues.[72] Even the state media acknowledge that the impacts from declining royalties, unpaid taxes, and misappropriated funds—at least US$150 million was reported lost to corruption between 2012 and 2014—"could harm Laos considerably."[73]

In the lead-up to these economic woes, a watershed event was the still unexplained disappearance of Sombath Somphone, a leading Lao community development worker, on December 15, 2012, after he was stopped at a police checkpoint in Vientiane. Somphone had long worked with government partners and had received international awards recognizing his work as founder of the Participatory Development Training Centre in 1996. His disappearance has been widely addressed by international human rights groups, civil society, and foreign governments. His Singaporean wife, Ng Shui-Meng, obtained footage from police closed circuit cameras and continues to work internationally for a thorough investigation. Short official statements denied involvement of the GoL but also provided no details pertaining to investigations regarding his disappearance and declined all offers of foreign expert assistance. This resulted in the EU issuing a second resolution in January 2014 stating that "the lack of reaction by the GoL raises suspicions that the authorities could be involved in his abduction." Despite this intense international scrutiny, updates on Somphone's disappearance from domestic media are restricted to brief official statements and do not mention alternative views from international sources.

Speculation about Somphone's disappearance has centered on his role as cochair of the Ninth Asia-Europe People's Forum in late 2012, a civil society forum that brings together heads of states from Asia and Europe. Like any other activity in Laos, this was supported by INGOs but required close cooperation with and permission from the GoL, especially the Ministry of Foreign Affairs. The forum was officially opened by Laos's deputy prime minister and foreign minister Thongloun Sisoulith on October 9, 2012, after a year's work with his ministry to secure official approval for keynote speakers and the discussion topics.[74] At the time, the forum, which attracted nearly 950 participants from forty-seven countries, was deemed a success for Laos; according to the party organ, "This event was without a doubt the largest civil society event ever organized."[75] It was also the first to include Lao nonprofit associations. However, concerns lingered about restrictions on the participation of Lao attendees by Lao officials at the event and about the consequences Lao attendees faced for speaking their mind. As later reported by Shui-Meng,

> The security apparatus of the state was uncomfortable with the opening up of the state, and uncomfortable with civil society opening up in Laos. The government was shaken by the fact that so many people came for the forum and that open questions were raised. . . . We found a lot of security people taking notes at every panel during the forum. Villagers came out and expressed ideas and were harassed on the spot. When they returned to villages, they were arrested, roughed up, and released. . . . Sombath knew that there was some risk involved—the Lao government was ambivalent to civil society meetings.[76]

Other INGO representatives present at the forum similarly reported that village, district, and provincial authorities harassed their Lao staff both at the meeting as well as later in their homes.[77]

On December 7, 2012, two months after the forum, the country director of the INGO Helvetas, Anne-Sophie Gindroz, was expelled from Laos.[78] In November 2012, she had written a private letter shared with five development partners at a round table implementation meeting, a kind of meeting that seeks to facilitate engagement between development partners and the Lao state. Notably, Helvetas was crucial in supporting and organizing the forum, and Gindroz's letter noted that INGOs most active in organizing it were not invited to the round table. Just one week later, Somphone disappeared.

Though there is no official statement linking these events, observers of Lao politics note the likely connections.[79] For instance, Shui-Meng noted that there was a need to make an example of a both Lao citizen and a foreign citizen; the disappearance of Somphone and the expulsion of Gindroz has been very effective in stifling public debate. She observed: "Fear was palpable. . . . No one will be critical of what the government does. After news that he had disappeared, a number of civil society leaders left the country. As a leader of community development, it sends a clear message to the rest of civil society. . . . Within Lao officialdom, no one wants to hear his name, no one wants to be reminded of his disappearance, and no one dares to talk openly about him."[80] Restrengthened restrictions on public debate have had wide-ranging impacts in Laos, including on hydropower. Remarking on the repercussions, a recent article on the Mekong River Commission commented that "the disappearance of Sombath Somphone . . . had a chilling effect on bureaucrats who must toe the government line on dam construction [and] . . . anyone publicly opposed to the government's massive infrastructure plans—aimed at developing hydropower and turning Laos into a net exporter of electricity—'can simply disappear like Sombath Somphone.'"[81] Many in Laos report that censorship has increased, that controversial topics are avoided, and that project activities are increasingly monitored and restricted, especially for more advocacy-oriented INGOs and topics like corruption, villagers' complaints, and resource management.[82] For example, one foreign researcher reported in early 2013 that "the political landscape has shifted dramatically in the last few months here in Laos, and it is proving to be quite difficult for me to collect data at the subnational and village levels." Simultaneously, land concessions have become much more politically sensitive than they were a decade ago, joining hydropower as off-limits to public debate.

The GoL's intention to restrict formal institutions is apparent in draft changes to laws for INGOs and nonprofit associations, which have been criticized by international observers.[83] Even more apparent since Somphone's disappearance is increasing informal restrictions on donor-supported initiatives, even for activities that already have government approval. For example, since 2012 the Land Issues Working Group, which had previously been viewed by the GoL as a nonpolitical technical group, has been classified as "politically dangerous."[84] Radio host Ounkeo Souksavan, a former Lao coordinator of this group, fled Laos to live in the United States after his radio show was canceled. Gindroz, explained that at the time she was expelled from Laos, she had been the chair of the Land Issues Working Group, which, she notes, "explains why the group has backed off from any sensitive work" and has disengaged from "community level action."[85] Many other former Lao participants in the group left the land management sector to seek employment in other less controversial areas, and Lao participants stopped attending meetings without the presence of a senior government representative to informally signify approval.[86] Offering justifications reminiscent of those offered for restrictions in pre-NT2 days, government officials increasingly talked about the undue influence of foreign (Western) organizations, particularly in relation to INGOs, that could be working against the Lao state.[87]

These informal restrictions on public debate are indirectly linked to NT2. At the ASEAN People's Forum held in Malaysia in April 2015, which was intended to provide civil society an opportunity to address ASEAN leaders, participants from Laos were tightly constrained. Reportedly, Laos sent proxies to push their interests at the meeting, who unsuccessfully sought to exclude Somphone's name from its report. Many from Laos declined to participate: "[They] fear retribution for criticizing government policy. . . . [They] will talk mostly about gender roles only, but not other issues such as land rights, the impact of hydropower dams . . . and enforced disappearance, because they are afraid for their safety."[88] Laos was supposed to be the host of the next Asia People's Forum in 2016 as part of its new chairmanship of ASEAN, and the international community wondered whether it would follow through. Then, in October 2015, Laos officially declined to host this meeting, claiming lack of time and resources and foreign criticism of the GoL. Maydom Chanthanasinh reported that "foreigners would like to use the ASEAN Peoples Forum to criticize ASEAN governments, and ASEAN governments do not agree."[89]

It is important to note in connection with NT2 that Chanthanasinh, who is now the representative for Lao civil society organizations in ASEAN, is a retired government official who was formerly involved with NT2 but who was removed by donor pressure due to his notoriety in Laos. At the time the World Bank was considering approval for NT2 in 2004–5, he was project director of NT2 in the-then Ministry of Industry and Handicrafts. Prior to that, he was vice president of Laos's then-largest company, the development company

Bolisat Phattana Khet Phoudoi, which was run by the military and became internationally controversial for illegal logging, threatening donor support for NT2.[90] The World Bank pressured the GoL to remove Chanthanasinh, and other notorious officials. A consultant then working on NT2 commented on their exclusion from the international workshops held in 2004, mostly due to World Bank pressure: "It was good, as they would have had no credibility and this would have undermined the whole project."[91] So a retired official previously excluded from NT2 by international pressure nominally represents Lao civil society at international forums but in fact restricts the activities of Lao participants. In the lead-up to the Communist Party Congress in January 2016, Lao's then-president emphasized the country's success in "maintaining national security and stability . . . jointly made by our [Lao] People's Revolutionary Party and people."[92] This statement prioritizing stability is telling and is clearly apparent in the restrengthening of restrictions on public debate in Laos since 2012. Maintaining stability motivates the GoL's protection of its political authority, and the newfound wielding of this authority illustrates the inaccuracy and irrelevance of NT2 proponents' statements about the transformation in relations between the GoL and its citizens. More recently, a notable dashing of the World Bank's aspirations for social responsibility through NT2 was the approval in June 2016 of Prime Minister's Decree 84, Compensation and Resettlement of People Affected by Development Projects. This replaced Decree 192 with the same title, which was declared in July 2005 as a condition for World Bank support for NT2.[93] While Decree 192 closely followed international financial institution policies, Decree 84 weakens many original provisions intended to improve the legal rights of project-affected people around the country.[94]

Conclusions

NT2 had wide-ranging effects on formal and informal institutions that shape public debate in Laos. NT2 was unique in promoting the idea of opening up space for public debate across an authoritarian country. Yet NT2 proponents who deemed the project a catalyst for socially responsible development focused on formal institutions in international and urban contexts while ignoring informal institutions and the context dependency of all institutions, giving a misleading representation of public debate in Laos. Many changes have occurred in Laos since NT2 officially commenced in 2005, but little change in the status of public debate can be directly attributable to NT2-related reforms such as information sharing or public consultation. Significantly, public debate about land concessions increased post-NT2, but public debate about hydro-power projects did not. Hydropower has consistently been a highly politicized topic, and any questions about it are liable to be taken as opposing national development and as criticism of the Lao state.

The massive changes in Laos have prompted widespread optimism about the country's future. Many observers who focused on the international and urban contexts were effusive about the outstanding economic growth and other changes in Laos.[95] Restrictions were eased on formal and informal insti-tutions that shape public debate within Laos. But in retrospect, this optimism was premature. Laos is certainly not unique in this respect, given the recent global economic downturn, as well as concerns about high-level corruption and increasing political restrictions in many countries in East and Southeast Asia.[96] Yet even before these recent global and regional shifts, increasing public debate about land conflicts and corruption had challenged Laos's economic rise. These debates are indicative of the challenges of managing economic growth and equitable distribution of benefits across the nation.

NT2 proponents predicted the project would instigate major changes in the way the GoL approached all future resource development projects. Despite such assertions and some indirect impacts via post-NT2 economic growth, NT2 has had little direct effect on shaping these public debates. Instead, it was land concessions that prompted unprecedented levels of public critical debate. Land concessions rapidly expanded during NT2's approval and are now preva-lent nationwide, but they were initially less politically sensitive than hydro-power. However, since 2012, Laos has seen renewed restrictions, particularly through informal institutions, which prioritize strict political control over all other goals. This account shows the complex interplay of economic, political, and social conditions at national, regional, and global levels.

These changes, of course, are not the responsibility of the World Bank. But the Bank and other NT2 proponents are responsible for biased or inaccu-rate representations of NT2 and its transformative potential in Laos and globally. NT2 proponent forecasts of the economic, political and social change that would flow from this project was overly simplistic. Their focus on formal institutions in international and urban contexts downplayed the obvious sig-nificance of informal institutions in domestic and rural contexts in Laos. Given that Laos has many similarities with other developing countries, the World Bank's claims can only be seen as strategic misinformation; like the GoL, the Bank can be seen as prioritizing its stability over serious commitment to trans-forming development.

NOTES

This chapter was produced with the support of an Australian Research Council Discovery Grant (DP1096157) and the School of Social Science, University of Queensland.

1. Mara T. Baranson, "Reflections on Implementation," in *Doing a Dam Better: Lao People's Democratic Republic and the Story of Nam Thuen 2*, ed. Ian C. Porter and Jayasankar Shivakumar (Washington, DC: World Bank, 2011), 153.

2. Baranson, "Reflections on Implementation," 153.

3. Martin Stuart-Fox, "Politics and Reform in the Lao People's Democratic Republic" (Asia Research Center working paper 126, Murdoch University, 2005), 29.

4. Sarinda Singh, *Natural Potency and Political Power: Forests and State Authority in Contemporary Laos* (Honolulu: University of Hawaii Press, 2012), 9–10; see also Martin Stuart-Fox, "Laos," in *Countries at the Crossroads: An Analysis of Democratic Governance*, ed. Jake Dizard, Christopher Walker, and Vanessa Tucker (New York: Freedom House, 2011), 325–46.

5. Anne-Sophie Gindroz, personal communication, 2016; Singh, *Natural Potency and Political Power*, 6.

6. Singh, *Natural Potency and Political Power*, 6.

7. Ian G. Baird, Bruce Shoemaker and Kanokwan Manorom, "The People and Their River, the World Bank and Its Dam: Revisiting the Xe Bang Fai River in Laos," *Development and Change* 46, no. 5 (2015); Sarinda Singh, "World Bank-Directed Development? Negotiating Participation in the Nam Theun 2 Hydropower Project in Laos," *Development and Change* 40, no. 3 (2009).

8. Stuart-Fox, "Laos." See also Warren Paul Mayes, "Unsettled Post-Revolutionaries in the Online Public Sphere," *Sojourn* 24, no. 1 (2009).

9. See, for example, World Bank's Ease of Doing Business Index, Transparency International's Corruption Index, and Reporters without Borders Press Freedom Index.

10. For example, journalists, trade unionists, community activists, and academics are not typically subject to violence from the state. See Dizard, Walker, and Tucker, *Countries at the Crossroads*.

11. Singh, *Natural Potency and Political Power*, 5–12.

12. See, for example, Steeve Daviau, "Organisations à but non lucratif: Timide émergence de la société civile en République démocratique populaire lao," *Canadian Journal of Development Studies/Revue canadienne d'études du développement* 30, nos. 3–4 (2010): 3–4, and Stuart-Fox, "Laos."

13. A foreign scholar of Laos reported that there are three excellent Lao historians: two are now recluses; the third coproduced the first modern national history book in Lao language but was forced out of a government position and into exile (anonymous, personal communication, 2015).

14. "Lao PDR Approves Decree for Non-Profit Associations," International Center for Not-for-Profit Law, May 21, 2009, www.icnl.org/news/2009/05-21.html.

15. For example, a popular student club at the National University of Laos that provided environmental education in schools in Vientiane in 2005 was eliminated after a year because it did not have official approval. It had been an extension of officially approved project activities conducted by an INGO in rural areas (see also Mayes, "Unsettled Post-Revolutionaries in the Online Public Sphere").

16. Ounkeo Souksavan, personal communication, 2011.

17. See, for example, AFP, "Luxury Home Building by Lao Leaders Raises Eyebrows among Citizens," *Radio Free Asia*, January 23, 2015, www.rfa.org/english/news/laos/politi cians-build-luxury-homes-01232015162351.html; "Exiled Democracy Activist Hits Back after Slur from Lao President," *Radio Free Asia*, December 9, 2015, www.rfa.org/english /news/laos/laos-president-12092015174707.html; and Sarinda Singh, "Developing Bureaucracies for Environmental Governance: State Authority and World Bank Conditionality in Laos," *Journal of Contemporary Asia* 44, no. 2 (2014): 326, 330–32.

18. Singh, *Natural Potency and Political Power*, 41–42.

19. See, for example, Benjamin Hodgdon, "Frontier: The Political Culture of Logging and Development on the Periphery in Laos," *Kyoto Journal* 69 (2008): 61; Sarinda Singh, "Contesting Moralities: The Politics of Wildlife Trade in Laos," *Journal of Political Ecology* 15 (2008): 6–8.

20. See Baird, Shoemaker, and Manorom, "The People and Their River"; Sarinda Singh, "World Bank-Directed Development?"

21. Sarinda Singh, "Religious Resurgence, Authoritarianism, and 'Ritual Governance': *Baci* Rituals, Village Meetings, and the Developmental State in Rural Laos," *Journal of Asian Studies* 73, no. 4 (2014).

22. Patchamuthu Illangovan, "NT2: A Transformative Endeavor," in *Doing a Dam Better*, 159.

23. For example, the World Bank lauds "increasingly participatory local consultations continue across the various project areas, as livelihood options are tested and refined" (Baranson, "Reflections on Implementation," 153). But see PoE 23:4 on continued problems with developing sustainable livelihoods for resettled villages on the Nakai Plateau, and see Baird, Shoemaker, and Manorom, "The People and Their River," on maintaining livelihoods for downstream villages on the Xe Bang Fai.

24. Singh, "World Bank-Directed Development?," 495.

25. Duke Center for International Development, "Some Cross-Cutting Lessons," in *Doing a Dam Better*, 139.

26. Peter Stephens, "The Communications Challenge," in *Doing a Dam Better*, 123.

27. Singh, "World Bank-Directed Development?," 495–96.

28. Nazir Ahmad, "Working with Stakeholders," in *Doing a Dam Better*, 112; Singh, "World Bank-Directed Development?," 495.

29. Ian C. Porter and Jayasankar Shivakumar, overview, *Doing a Dam Better*, 1–2.

30. Duke Center for International Development, "Some Cross-Cutting Lessons," 141.

31. Fleur Johns. "On Failing Forward: Neoliberal Legality in the Mekong River

Basin," *Cornell International Law Journal* 48, no. 2 (2015): 374. This view draws on the "neoliberal thesis"—the theorized connections between economic and political freedom—as well as the ostensible financial success of NT2. Johns (359) suggests that "from a financial perspective" NT2 has been "highly successful." But other studies for mega-dams around the world conclude that "estimates are systematically and severely biased below actual values" (Atif Ansar, Bent Flyvberg, Alexander Budzier, and Daniel Lunn, "Should We Build More Large Dams? The Actual Costs of Hydropower Megaproject Development," *Energy Policy* 69 [2014]).

32. Singh, "World Bank-Directed Development?," 504.

33. Anne-Sophie Gindroz, personal communication, 2016.

34. Johns, "Failing Forward," 370.

35. Johns, "Failing Forward," 360.

36. Ben Boer, Philip Hirsch, Fleur Johns, Ben Saul, and Natalia Scurrah, *The Mekong: A Socio-Legal Approach to River Basin Development* (London: Routledge, 2016), 161; Johns, "Failing Forward," 363.

37. See also Johns, "Failing Forward," 364.

38. Boer et al., *The Mekong*, 72.

39. Illangovan, "NT2," 159–60.

40. Anonymous, personal communication, 2015.

41. As the Duke Center for International Development acknowledges in its contribution to the volume, "World Bank senior management believed that the elaborate structure of oversight and monitoring groups was necessary in NT2 because of the project's high visibility and the potential criticism from international civil society organizations" ("Some Cross-Cutting Lessons," 143).

42. PoE 23:4.

43. Jacques Leslie, "Large Dams Just Aren't Worth the Cost," *New York Times*, August 22, 2014, www.nytimes.com/2014/08/24/opinion/sunday/large-dams-just-arent-worth-the-cost.html?mcubz=3.

44. Andrew Walker, *Thailand's Political Peasants: Power in the Modern Rural Economy* (Madison: University of Wisconsin Press, 2012).

45. Illangovan, "NT2," 159–60.

46. Stuart-Fox, "Politics and Reform," 2.

47. Anonymous, personal communication, 2004.

48. Stuart-Fox, "Laos," 327.

49. See, e.g., Robert Horn, "Laos' Old Guard Masks Future Prospects," *Asia Today International* 18, no. 7 (2000).

50. Patrick Barta, "Make Way for Southeast Asia's Newest Boom Economy," *Wall Street Journal*, October 26, 2012, http://blogs.wsj.com/searealtime/2012/10/26/make-way-for-southeast-asias-newest-boom-economy.

51. World Bank, *Lao PDR Economic Monitor*, May 2012, 1.

52. Christopher B. Roberts, "Laos: A More Mature and Robust State?" *Southeast Asian Affairs* (2012): 160.

53. World Trade Organization, "Laos's WTO Membership Terms Agreed," September 28, 2012, www.wto.org/english/news_e/news12_e/acc_lao_28sep12_e.htm.

54. UNDP in Lao PDR, "New Project to Strengthen National Assembly," June 6, 2014, www.la.undp.org/content/lao_pdr/en/home/presscenter/pressreleases/2014/06/30/new-project-to-strengthen-national-assembly-.html; http://www.sdcmekong.org/2014/07/new-project-launched-to-strengthen-the-lao-national-assembly.

55. See Learning House for Development, www.lao-cso-network.org/history.html.

56. Daviau, "Organisations à but non lucratif," 419.

57. This undermines claims that this body has a mandate independent of the party. For example, a provincial official who was not a party member was privately critical about Laos's elections: "The Party has already chosen who will get the position, so it doesn't matter who the majority [of the] people voted for, the Party-chosen people will still get the position" (anonymous, personal communication, 2011); Stuart-Fox, "Laos."

58. www.youtube.com/watch?v=9°5cejwNl1c&feature=results_video&playnext=1&list=PLC01FFC6C828E3E10; see also Simon Creak and Keith Barney, "Distressing Developments in Laos," *New Mandala*, December 23, 2012, http://asiapacific.anu.edu.au/newmandala/2012/12/23/distressing-developments-in-laos.

59. Previously, a minority of educated, urban elites used the concept of democracy to express dissatisfaction with the Lao state, especially during periods of turmoil like the Asian Economic Crisis when urban incomes were especially impacted (Grant Evans, personal communication, 2011).

60. Oliver Schönweger, Andreas Heinimann, Michael Epprecht, Juliet Lu, Palikone Thalongsengchanh, *Concessions and Leases in the Lao PDR: Taking Stock of Land Investments* (Bern: Centre for Development and Environment, University of Bern, 2012), 9, 20.

61. See, for instance, "Lao Officials Slam Corruption," *Radio Free Asia*, February 11, 2009, www.rfa.org/english/news/laos/laocorruption-02112009175322.html. On low-level corruption, see, e.g., Singh, "World Bank-Directed Development," and Singh, "Religious Resurgence, Authoritarianism, and 'Ritual Governance.'"

62. Martin Stuart-Fox. "Family Problems," *Inside Story: Current Affairs and Culture from Australia and Beyond*, January 19, 2011, http://inside.org.au/family-problems.

63. See "Off the Air in Laos," *Asia Times Online*, February 22, 2012, www.laolandissues.org/2012/02/22/off-the-air-in-laos, and "Land Issues Top Public Concerns," *Vientiane Times*, July 13, 2012, www.laolandissues.org/2012/07/13/land-issues-top-public-concerns.

64. A few months after the cancelation of this pioneering radio program, Laos participated for the first time in UNESCO's World Press Freedom Day, but government officials did not publicly discuss this program (Rojana Manowalailao and Dieter Schlenke, "The First Ever World Press Freedom Day Celebrated in Myanmar and Lao PDR," UNESCO Bangkok, May 9, 2012, www.unescobkk.org/news/article/the-first-ever-word-press-freedom-day-celebrated-in-myanmar-and-lao-pdr; Ian G. Baird, "Land, Rubber and People: Rapid Agrarian Changes and Responses in Southern Laos," *Journal of Lao Studies* 1, no. 1 [2010]).

65. Unlike neighboring mentors China and Vietnam, Laos had not seen the prosecution of any senior officials for corruption, despite the introduction of an anti-corruption law in 2005, until only very recently (e.g., "Former Lao Minister Named in Corruption Probe," *Radio Free Asia*, January 8, 2016, www.rfa.org/english/news/laos/corruption-010820 16142933.html).

66. Souksakhone Vaenkeo, "Who Will Help the People If the National Assembly Won't?" *Vientiane Times*, July 13, 2012, www.laolandissues.org/wp-content/uploads/2012/07 /Vientiane-Times-July-13-2012.pdf.

67. "National Assembly Members Tackle Land Disputes," *Vientiane Times*, November 14, 2012, www.rightsandresources.org/en/news/vientiane-times-national-assembly-mem bers-tackle-land-disputes; see also Marwaan Macan-Markar, "Carving up LAOS: Land Disputes Rattle the Government," *Edge Reviews*, April 11, 2013, www.sombath.org/en /2013/04/carving-up-laos-land-disputes-rattle-the-government.

68. IFI, "Hydro Advisory Overview," http://www.ifc.org/wps/wcm/connect/Lao_ EXT_Content/Sustainable_HydroPower/Sustainability_HydroPower/Hydropower+Devel opers+Working+Group.

69. Simon Creak, "Laos in 2013: International Controversies, Economic Concerns, and the Post-socialist Rhetoric of Rule," *Southeast Asian Affairs* (2014): 155–57; see also Singh, "World Bank-Directed Development," 501–2.

70. Thomas Fuller, "With Laos Disappearance, Signs of a Liberalization in Backslide, *New York Times*, January 10, 2013, www.nytimes.com/2013/01/11/world/asia/with-laos-dis appearance-signs-of-a-liberalization-in-backslide.html?r=0; see also "Call for Laos to Con sult NGOs on Restrictive Guidelines," *Radio Free Asia*, December 8, 2014, www.rfa.org /english/news/laos/roundtable-12082014171921.html, Amy Killian, "On the Path to Political Opening, Laos Stumbles," cogitASIA, April 22, 2013, http://cogitasia.com/on-path-to-po litical-opening-laos-stumbles, Creak and Barney, "Distressing Developments in Laos," and Macan-Markar, "Carving up LAOS."

71. Anonymous, personal communication, 2015.

72. IMF, "IMF Executive Board Concludes Article IV Consultation with Lao People's Democratic Republic," February 26, 2015, www.imf.org/external/np/sec/pr/2015/pr1578 .htm; Creak, "Laos in 2013."

73. Almost 150 Million USD Lost to Corruption in Laos, *Xinhua*, July 22, 2014, www .shanghaidaily.com/article/article_xinhua.aspx?id=231097 (see also "Civil Sector Workers in Laos Lose out to Corruption and Rising Cost of Living," *Radio Free Asia*, July 23, 2015, www.rfa.org/english/news/laos/civil-sector-workers-lose-out-to-corruption-and-ris ing-cost-of-living-07232015164600.html); "Govt Mobilises Funds for Flood Victims," *Vientiane Times*, August 29, 2016, www.vientianetimes.org.la/FreeContent/FreeConten_ Govt_mobilises.htm.

74. Lucy Duncan, "The Disappearance of Sombath Somphone: An Interview with Ng Shui Meng," American Friends Service Committee, May 7, 2014, www.afsc.org/friends /disappearance-sombath-somphone-interview-ng-shui-meng.

75. "Ninth Asia-Europe People's Forum Opens in Laos," *Communist Party of Vietnam Online Newspaper*, October 17, 2012, http://en.dangcongsan.vn/news-and-events/ninth-asia-europe-people-s-forum-opens-in-laos-152318.html.

76. Duncan, "The Disappearance of Sombath Somphone."

77. Anonymous, various, personal communication, 2015.

78. "NGO Director Expelled," *Radio Free Asia*, December 7, 2012, www.rfa.org/english/news/laos/expulsion-12072012153813.html; "Joint Letter on the Expulsion of Helvetas Laos Country Director, Ms. Anne-Sophie Gindroz," *Forum-Asia*, December 24. 2012, www.forum-asia.org/?p=15694; Creak and Barney, "Distressing Developments in Laos."

79. Similarly, Somphone Kantisouk, who was outspoken about rubber plantations, disappeared a decade ago in Luang Namtha Province. His foreign business partner immediately left Laos (Bertil Litner, "Fear of Foreigners in Laos," *Asia Times*, February 2, 2008, www.atimes.com/atimes/Southeast_Asia/JB02Ae01.html). If it weren't for foreigners, no one would know about these disappearances.

80. Personal communication, 2015; see also Duncan, "The Disappearance of Sombath Somphone."

81. Luke Hunt, "Why the Mekong River Commission May Be in Peril," *Diplomat*, October 10, 2015, http://thediplomat.com/2015/10/why-the-mekong-river-commission-may-be-in-peril.

82. "Into Thin Air: Southeast Asia's Growing Ranks of Disappeared," *AFP*, December 11, 2014, www.worldaffairsjournal.org/content/essay-southeast-asias-growing-number-disappeared.

83. rsbtws, "UN Special Rapporteurs: Draft CSO Decree Would Violate International Law," *Sombath Somphone*, September 13, 2015, www.sombath.org/en/2015/09/un-special-rapporteurs-draft-cso-decree-would-violate-international-law; "Laos Restrictions Threaten Development, say Non-Profit Groups," *South China Morning Times*, September 17, 2014, www.scmp.com/news/asia/article/1594490/laos-ngo-restrictions-threaten-development-say-non-profit-groups; Freedom House, "Laos," https://freedomhouse.org/report/freedom-world/2015/laos.

84. Anonymous, personal communication, 2015.

85. Anne-Sophie Gindroz, personal communication, 2016.

86. Anonymous, personal communication, 2015.

87. Anonymous, personal communication, 2015; see also Creak, "Laos in 2013," 163–64.

88. "Laos Civil Society Pressured to Drop Rights Issues from ASEAN," *Radio Free Asia*, April 22, 2015, www.rfa.org/english/news/laos/forum-04222015150409.html.

89. "Laos Refuses to Host Meeting of ASEAN Civil Society Groups," *Radio Free Asia*, October 12, 2015, www.rfa.org/english/news/laos/refuses-10122015173336.html.

90. Singh, *Natural Potency and Political Power*, 133–39.

91. Singh, *Natural Potency and Political Power*, 139.

92. "Laos Touts 40 Years of Stability, but Critics Decry Debt, Corruption and Poverty," *Radio Free Asia*, December 2, 1015, www.rfa.org/english/news/laos/laos-anniversary-12022015171027.html; see also "Selection of New National Leaders in Laos Indicates

Tilt to Vietnam," *Radio Free Asia*, January 22, 2016, www.rfa.org/english/news/laos/Laos-elect-01222016112729.html.

93. Land Issues Working Group, laws and regulations, www.laolandissues.org/links/laws-and-regulations.

94. These provisions include recognizing customary land tenure rights, providing assistance during livelihood transition, land certification, and a grievance redress mechanism, and allowing independent monitoring and public participation (Mekong Watch, "Comparison between PM Decree No. 192 and Decree No. 84," unpublished report, shared via the Land Issues Working Group email list, July 11, 2016).

95. For example, the World Bank in its *Economic Monitor*, the contributors to *Doing a Dam Better*, and Roberts in "Laos."

96. Michael Vatikiotis, "Graft Games," *New Mandala*, July 4, 2016, www.newmandala.org/graft-games.

11

Nam Theun 2, the Xe Bang Fai, and Thailand's Electricity Network

IAN G. BAIRD and

NOAH QUASTEL

We arrived at Mahaxay Town, adjacent to the Xe Bang Fai River (XBF), in Khammouane Province, central Laos on December 31, 2013.[1] It was the height of the "cold season" and according to news reports we saw at the time, people throughout the region, as far away as Bangkok, were wearing sweaters, knit hats, and scarves. We had journeyed to conduct field studies to trace the downstream social and ecological effects of the Nam Theun 2 (NT2) dam.[2] Water levels in the XBF were unusually low, and the ecology of the river had clearly been altered. The low water levels revealed seasonally inundated bushes and trees along the riverbed that were dead or dying (see figure 11.1).

However, by January 6 water levels began to rise. In Keng Pe, downstream of Mahaxay, comments from one villager helped us to better understand the situation. The XBF was nothing like it used to be before NT2 started operating, he told us. "I am not sure why, but we notice that water levels in the XBF tend to go down on the weekends and then back up during the week."

More clues came as we began our field work. While in the field in the XBF basin in Khammouane and Savannakhet Provinces in January 2014, the first author heard an ethnic Lao employee of the Nam Theun 2 Power Company (NTPC) state that "the water is low now because Thailand is not buying as much power as they usually do. When Thailand needs less power they phone up the operators of the dam and ask that less electricity be sent to them. Since

Figure 11.1. Dead seasonally inundated perennial vegetation in the XBF River on January 1, 2014, exposed when the water level fell due to cold weather and reduced air conditioning usage in Thailand. Photo by Ian G. Baird.

the weather is cold now, Thailand needs less power and so less water is being released." Another factor contributing to weak electricity demand in Thailand and the corresponding low water levels we observed was the New Year holiday, as offices and factories that consume large amounts of electricity were closed.

In this chapter, based on our 2015 article, "Rescaling and Reordering Nature–Society Relations: The Nam Theun 2 Hydropower Dam and Laos–Thailand Electricity Networks," we discuss the ways that the flow and the ecology of the XBF are now linked to Thai electricity consumption and how NT2 operates as part of regional electricity networks.[3]

Through the 1990s Thailand was rapidly industrializing, and NT2 was designed to serve as a new source of energy for the country's expanding electricity system (figure 11.2). At the time it was assumed, as public documents and debates over NT2 suggest, that NT2 would provide electricity to Thailand at a constant rate most days of the week and throughout the year. However, that is not in the end what happened. Power is drawn from NT2 according to decisions made by managers of the Electricity Generating Authority of

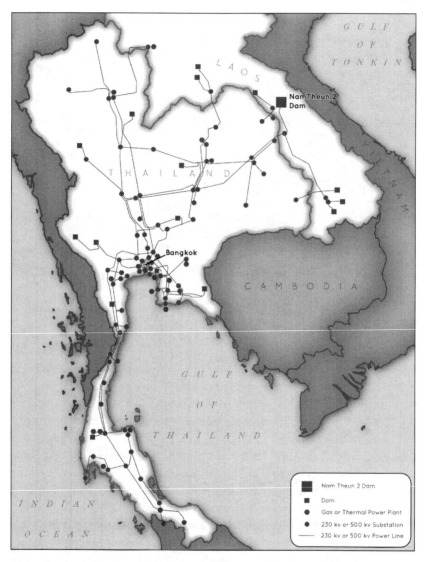

Figure 11.2. Map of the electricity grid in Thailand and the grid's link to the NT2 hydropower project in central Laos.

Thailand (EGAT). The dam is being opened and closed, and water released into or withheld from the XBF, in response to power needs in Thailand. A major driver and amplifier of these fluctuations is the use of air conditioning in Bangkok, more than 800 kilometers from the dam.

Environmental Flows

The use of NT2 to supply a variable load has had significant impacts on the XBF. Ecologists now recognize that large hydropower dams can have severe downstream ecological and social impacts and use the term "environmental flows" to refer to the relationship between ecosystem health and hydrological systems.[4] Research into environmental flows, however, shows that if water is released more regularly and in ways that mimic a river's natural daily and seasonal water flows downstream impacts can be reduced.[5] Attention to environmental flows suggests the need for comprehensive strategies to assess all the impacts, both positive and negative, of different hydrological regimes affected by the operation of dams or related forms of infrastructure.[6] Operating dams on irregular schedules and thus changing water release patterns can greatly influence environmental impacts downstream. However, appropriate dam management could mitigate the negative ecological and social downstream impacts caused by NT2.[7]

By the late 1990s the importance of environmental flows was well understood by dam experts and organizations concerned with dams. The World Commission on Dams (WCD) called for, among other initiatives, a review of existing and proposed dams to provide for a requirement that environmental flows be taken into account.[8] The World Bank chose not to follow WCD guidelines, but its own *Water Resources Sector Strategy* report nonetheless explicitly cites the importance of flows and argues that "well-conceived water infrastructure should . . . develop operating rules that specify ecological flows for the benefit of downstream riparians."[9]

Attention to environmental flows can, however, mean reduced profits, especially where dams serve electricity systems with varying load. Dam operators generally release water at various times of the day, making use of dam reservoirs as energy storage facilities—indeed dam reservoirs remain one of the few cost-effective solutions to the storage problem endemic to electricity system management. Batteries are very expensive, and utilities usually rely either on forms of hydro storage or natural gas peaking plants to handle variable load.[10] Managers may fill reservoirs (and cut downstream water flows) to create stores of potential energy, which allows for strategic commercial decisions concerning when to switch from storage to generation mode. A downstream-sensitive hydrological regime can directly impact electricity managers' abilities to make such strategic calculations. Thus, ignoring or prioritizing environmental flows involves significant trade-offs between profits for the owners and operators of the dam, the use value of the river for downstream communities, and broader societal and global concern with the human right to livelihoods, cultural heritage, biodiversity and ecosystem integrity.

Creating NT2's Flow Regime

At the time NT2 was proposed and the power purchase agreement and concessions agreement were drafted, there was little discussion of NT2 being used to handle Thailand's variable load. NT2 was planned and built with a broad willingness to sacrifice downstream ecologies and associated livelihoods in the XBF, and planning around NT2 showed a relative lack of concern for environmental flows; public consultations and the environmental assessment process did not include discussion of seasonal changes or the possibilities for linking downstream impacts to decisions concerning when to store or draw power on the dam. The initial power purchase agreement did, however, contemplate lower power use on Sundays: this was even built into the material configurations of the dam complex through the inclusion of a small regulating dam downstream of the main turbines. The agreement was designed to allow EGAT widespread flexibility, and considerable faith was put in the compensation process and Social Development Plan to remedy the damage that might be caused by varying downstream flow.

The agreement grants EGAT "full dispatch flexibility," which it represents as key to maximizing benefits to EGAT.[11] While the agreement contains typical "must-take" provisions for independent power producers, these provisions are formulated very differently from the way they normally are. EGAT is sold potential energy stored in the dam (rather than output as determined by NTPC). For the most part this is sold on a yearly basis, allowing EGAT wide discretion to take energy only when it serves its purposes. EGAT has the flexibility to decide when to dispatch and which generating unit to dispatch.[12] Primary energy is made available by NTPC between 6 a.m. to 10 p.m. on any weekday (Monday to Saturday inclusive), and EGAT buys 4,406 gigawatt hours per year.[13] While the exclusion for Sundays is not explained in the PPA, it is implied that it relates to variation in Thai demand, because offices and factories are normally closed on that day. EGAT has, however, the flexibility to dispatch power from NT2 as it requires—not only on Sundays but throughout the week and from week to week—subject only to certain operational constraints.[14] EGAT also retains the option to buy further "secondary energy" on top of primary energy or to buy energy at other times (e.g., after 10 p.m. or on Sundays) if the NT2 reservoir holds sufficient water. The overall structure of the power purchase agreement thus "allows EGAT to transfer water/energy from the low demand and generation cost period (typically November, December, January) to the high demand and generation cost period (typically March, April, May). Therefore, NT2 significantly contributes to one of the main objectives of any utility, i.e. keeping the generation cost as low as possible."[15] EGAT can thus ask for generation to be slowed down or sped up, and our observations of river flow on the XBF corroborate that EGAT regularly makes such requests. Short of a very high threshold for avoiding flood conditions, EGAT does not demonstrate concern over significant downstream impacts in Laos.[16]

The initial designs for NT2 and the concession agreement did take into account certain concerns about downstream effects. Early modeling indicated that seasonal flooding in the XBF would change, and in extreme cases could increase by a half meter toward the Mekong confluence. The proposed solution to these fluctuations was to rely on the NT2 reservoir to reduce seasonal flooding immediately downstream of the dam and to increase the planned size of the regulating pond below the power station. In addition, the power station would be shut down when necessary to limit flooding in the XBF. A 27-kilometer downstream channel would prevent additional serious downstream impacts associated with discharging turbinated waters into the Nam Kathang River.[17] These measures were adopted in the environmental assessment and management plan. The regulating dam and pond would limit the rate of increased discharge into the XBF to a maximum of 20 cubic meters per second so that the discharge would be more consistent. NTPC would also have to follow rules in declaring energy available. So as to prevent flooding, it would not, for instance, exceed maximum water releases into the XBF River. Thus, the plan claims the project includes "provision of predictable and consistent environmental flows."[18]

However, little attention seems to have been paid to designing the regulating pond in a way that would take into account environmental flows on the XBF in light of the possibility that EGAT would regularly change how much power it drew from the dam. The understanding was that the regulating pond would "continue to release water regularly during one full day when the operation of the Plant is stopped."[19] There appears to be no inclusion in the concession agreement (or power purchase agreement) of management plans to ensure environmental flows in the XBF would be safeguarded on a daily, weekly or monthly basis outside of those provisions. Nor was any planning undertaken for how to manage when NT2 operates as both a storage facility and low-cost form of load-following or peaker plant involving extended periods of low-water flow interrupted by more rapid water release, a circumstance clearly allowed by the power purchase agreement.

A close reading of the Social Development Plan shows that for NTPC, the solution to the problem of flows was to treat downstream fisheries as fungible — it was predicted they would be destroyed, but this loss would compensated by cash payouts. While in theory there was to be a process of consultation and informed consent by project-affected villagers, there were major linguistic and conceptual barriers to putting this process into action. There also appears to have been systematic distribution of misinformation — villagers were only told there would be a decrease on Sundays, not that there would be large-scale fluctuations on a weekly and monthly basis as well. In reality, consultation appears not to have guided the dam's operation. Instead, the central tool was cost-benefit analysis calculations of adequate compensation levels. The cost-benefit analysis worked on the assumption that the powerhouse would be shut down from late Saturday through Sunday, and that the consequent changes in water flow "cannot be fully regulated by this Pond."[20] At best the pond would ensure a "slow and relatively benign drawdown" and "the maintenance of a minimum flow."[21] As a result, "it is predicted that the NT2 discharges into the Xe Bangfai will cause a collapse in the aquatic food chain."[22] NTPC did not seek to overturn or shift the terms of the power purchase agreement in its Social Development Plan but instead took the approach of aiming for a full program of cash compensation for loss and mitigation through new fisheries development.

The concession agreement thus avoids interfering with EGAT's commercial decision making as to when to draw energy. As the Environmental Assessment and Management Plan states with respect to downstream XBF impacts, "The mitigation plan is expected to completely mitigate these losses, leaving households of the XBF at least as well off as without the Project."[23] However, strict limits were placed on funds made available for the Downstream Compensation Program in the XBF basin.

NT2's Link with Bangkok Air Conditioning

Bangkok is by far the largest city in Thailand and accounts for approximately one-quarter of the country's electricity demand. Thailand has a hot, humid climate. In fact, Bangkok is the hottest capital city in the world, in

Figure 11.3. Siam Paragon Mall, one of the largest malls in Bangkok, and one of the highest energy-consuming pieces of infrastructure in Thailand, April 21, 2007. Photo by KhunBhun. Available at flickr.com, used under Creative Commons Attribution Only licensing. https://creativecommons.org/licenses/by/2.0.

terms of average temperature (28 degrees Celsius).[24] Residents and businesses have been quick to parlay new wealth secured via economic development into air conditioning and refrigeration businesses. While still absent from most villages in Southeast Asia, air conditioning is a marker of modernization and new urban wealth. In earlier times government buildings in Thailand were not allowed to use air conditioning, but by the early 1990s that changed.[25] Bangkok's commercial buildings are now largely air conditioned, and this accounts for a majority of their heavy electricity consumption.[26] Shopping malls in Bangkok can have a very large electricity demand due to air conditioning. For example, in 2011 the huge Siam Paragon mall consumed nearly twice as much electricity as the entire northern Thai province of Mae Hong Son with a population of over 250,000 (123 gigawatt hours of electricity for Siam Paragon, 65 gigawatt hours for Mae Hong Song) (figure 11.3).[27] Using government

statistics and independent studies of building energy consumption, we calcu-
lated that electricity demand from Bangkok air conditioning exceeds the total
output of NT2.

However, air conditioning is not needed 24/7. A department store with a
2.5-megawatt load or an office with a 2-megawatt load may have little to no
energy consumption at night but ramp up to full-load use during business
hours.[28] Thailand's peak consumption occurs in the early afternoon of the
sunniest days (excluding Sundays) of the hot/dry season (April is, on average,
the hottest month of the year).[29]

The limited available public information on EGAT imports and sales indicate that EGAT is using Lao hydropower projects to satisfy these varying
loads. NT2 is a significant portion of Thai electricity imports (at 39 percent of
total capacity from abroad).[30] EGAT has financial motivations for relying on
imported power to meets its varying load: the Thai electricity system is highly
reliant on natural gas generation from independent power producers using
combined cycle plants.[31] These are designed for base load generation.[32] While
they can be put on standby and ramped up when needed, this is an expensive
option, with estimates beginning at 15 cents US per kilowatt hour.[33] Alterna-
tively, NT2 power at 1.88 baht (or 4.7 cents US) is much cheaper.[34]

Conclusion

EGAT's use of NT2 to supply variable and peak power is
wreaking havoc on the hydrological flows of the XBF River. Indeed, energy
usage in Thailand, and in particular the capital of Bangkok, is now fundamentally linked to the ecology of the XBF. The use of air conditioning, although it
has become an important facet of Thai modernization, needs to be considered
in light of disruptions to access to fish protein and loss of income by people
who depend on the XBF basin for their livelihoods. The Thai–Lao regional
energy network now appears highly biased toward serving high consumption,
while disregarding the impacts of distant production. Yet these environmental
and social impacts are not only a problem for affected villagers or parties to
agreements but circulate through the electricity network. Thai consumers,
EGAT, the GoL, and the international banks that supported NT2 remain
connected to problematic and unequal relationships with distant others.

Finally, there is wide scope to use solar photovoltaic power, which is an
excellent match with Thailand's daily load profile—air-conditioning demand
and solar output coincide with hot, sunny weather.[35] Worldwide panel costs

have fallen dramatically in the last decade and are increasingly grid competitive.[36] By 2016 solar energy became the cheapest form of energy in poorer countries, making it increasingly attractive to developers.[37] These changes would allow for a much more ecologically and socially benign electricity network—one that relied less on hydropower dam development in Laos. And one of the benefits of such a system, we suggest, is that there would be changes in how Thai electricity consumers relate to NT2 and the villagers who depend on its ecological flows.

NOTES

1. The "we" refers to Ian G. Baird, Bruce Shoemaker, and Kanokwan Manorom.

2. See Ian G. Baird, Bruce Shoemaker, and Kanokwan Manorom, "The People and Their River, the World Bank and Its Dam: Revisiting the Xe Bang Fai River in Laos," *Development and Change* 46, no. 5 (2015); see also chapter 10 in this volume.

3. The article was published in *Annals of the Association of the American Geographer* (105, no. 6 [2015]).

4. Brian D. Richter, Sandra Postel, Carmen Revenga, Thayer Scudder, Bernhard Lehner, Allegra Churchill, and Morgan Chow, "Lost in Development's Shadow: The Downstream Human Consequences of Dams," *Water Alternatives* 3, no. 2 (2010).

5. Megan Dyson, Ger Bergkamp, and John Scanlon, eds., *Flow: The Essentials of Environmental Flows* (Gland, Switzerland: IUCN, 2003).

6. Richter et al., "Lost in Development's Shadow."

7. Dyson, Bergkamp, and John Scanlon, *Flow*; Brian D. Richter and Gregory A. Thomas, "Restoring Environmental Flows by Modifying Dam Operations," *Ecology and Society* 12, no. 1 (2007): art. 12, www.ecologyandsociety.org/vol12/iss1/art12/; Angela H. Arthington and Stephen R. Balcombe, "Extreme Flow Variability and the 'Boom and Bust' Ecology of Fish in Arid-Zone Floodplain Fivers: A Case History with Implications for Environmental Flows, Conservation and Management," *Ecohydrology* 4, no. 5 (2011).

8. WCD, *Dams and Development: A New Framework for Decision-Making* (London: Earthscan, 2000), 30–31.

9. World Bank, *Water Resources Sector Strategy: Strategic Directions for World Bank Engagement,* January 1, 2004), 10.

10. Bruce Dunn, Haresh Kamath, and Jean-Marie Tarascon, "Electrical Energy Storage for the Grid: A Battery of Choices," *Science* 334 (2011): 928–35.

11. NTPC, EGAT power purchase agreement, summary for public disclosure, March 2005, 9, www.namtheun2.com/images/Document_for_website/Summary%20of%20 CA%20&%20PPA/041006%20-%20EGAT%20PPA%20%20Summary%20for%20 Public%20Disclosure.pdf.

12. NTPC, EGAT power purchase agreement, 22.

13. NTPC, EGAT power purchase agreement, 15; Robert Vernstrom, *Nam Theun 2 Hydro Power Project Regional Economic Least-Cost Analysis*, final report, World Bank, March, 2005, 19, http://siteresources.worldbank.org/INTLAOPRD/Resources/RELC-2005-final.pdf.

14. NTPC, EGAT power purchase agreement, 17.

15. NTPC, EGAT power purchase agreement, 9.

16. Witoon Permponsacharoen, director, MEE Net, personal communication, May 23, 2014.

17. ADB, *Summary Environmental and Social Impact Assessment: Nam Theun 2 Hydro-electric Project in Lao People's Democratic Republic*, November 1, 2004, 37, http://documents.worldbank.org/curated/en/524881468266127390/pdf/383810LA0IDASECM2004107920k01PUBLIC1.pdf.

18. NTPC, *Environmental Assessment and Management Plan*, March 1, 2005, 2:12, http://documents.worldbank.org/curated/en/221591468090579103/pdf/E3850v9orev0EAMP0March005.pdf.

19. NTPC, *Social Development Plan*, final draft, March 2005, vol. 3, 8:4.

20. NTPC, *Social Development Plan*, vol. 3, 8:4.

21. NTPC, *Social Development Plan*, vol. 3, 8:4.

22. NTPC, *Social Development Plan*, vol. 3, 4:40.

23. NTPC, *Environmental Assessment and Management Plan*, 2:32.

24. "The Hottest Places on Earth," www.express.co.uk/pictures/galleries/2803/The-HOTTEST-places-on-earth/Bangkok-in-Thailand-61160.

25. Surapong Chirarattananon and Juntaken Taweekun, "A Technical Review of Energy Conservation Programs for Commercial and Government Buildings in Thailand," *Energy Conversion and Management* 44 (2003): 744.

26. Chirarattananon and Taweekun, "A Technical Review of Energy Conservation Programs"; Surapong Chirarattananon, Pipat Chaiwiwatworakul, Vu Duc Hien, Pattana Rakkwamusuk, and Kuskana Kubaha, "Assessment of Energy Savings from the Revised Building Energy Code of Thailand," *Energy* 35 (2010).

27. Adam Pasick, "Bangkok's Lavish, Air-conditioned Malls Consume as Much Power as Entire Provinces," *Quartz*, April 6, 2015, http://qz.com/376125/bangkoks-lavish-malls-consume-as-much-power-as-entire-provinces.

28. Chirarattananon et al., "Assessment of Energy Savings," 1749.

29. Peter du Pont, *Nam Theun 2 Hydropower Project (NT2): Impact of Energy Conservation, DSM, and Renewable Energy Generation on EGAT's Power Development Plan*, Danish Energy Management, Bangkok, March 24, 2005, 42, http://siteresources.worldbank.org/INTLAOPRD/Resources/DSMmarch2005.pdf.

30. EGAT, power purchase agreement, 2014.

31. EGAT, power purchase agreement.

32. Saara Kujala, *Improving Power System Efficiency with Fast Flexible Power*, Wärtsilä Singapore, 2012, http://pennwell.sds06.websds.net/2012/bangkok/pga/papers/T2S3O1-paper.pdf.

33. Vernstrom, *Nam Theun 2 Hydro Power Project Regional Economic Least-Cost Analysis*, 35.

34. ADB, *Summary Environmental and Social Impact Assessment*, 20.

35. du Pont, *Nam Theun 2 Hydropower Project(NT2): Impact of Energy Conservation, DSM, and Renewable Energy Generation on EGAT's Power Development Plan.*

36. Kadra Banker, Michael J. Pathak, and Joshua M. Pearce, "A Review of Solar Photovoltaic Levelized Cost of Electricity," *Renewable and Sustainable Energy Reviews* 15, no. 9 (2011).

37. David Nield, "Solar Power Is Now the Cheapest Form of Energy in Almost 60 Countries," *Science Alert*, December 23, 2016, www.sciencealert.com/solar-power-is-now-the-cheapest-energy-in-the-world#.

12

Overpowered

Limiting Liability within Thailand's Nam Theun 2 Electricity Deal

GRÁINNE RYDER and

WITOON PERMPONGSACHAROEN

An important part of the Nam Theun 2 (NT2) story involves neighboring Thailand, where cash flows from Thai electricity ratepayers to the Nam Theun 2 Power Company (NTPC) and where public opposition to Thailand's NT2 power deal first began. In this chapter, we critically review the World Bank's economic rationale of NT2 as defended in *Doing a Dam Better* in light of published data from Thailand's power industry. We also examine the implications and legacy of the NT2 model for private and public interests.

Without Thailand, NT2 would not have been built. The Electricity Generating Authority of Thailand (EGAT), a state-owned power monopoly, agreed to buy most of the dam's power output.[1] EGAT subsidiary Electricity Generating Public Company (EGCO) owns one-third of the Nam Theun 2 Power Company (NTPC). Ital-Thai, one of Thailand's largest construction firms, was an equity investor and a major contractor for the dam's construction.[2] Seven Thai commercial banks provided long-term loans to NTPC.[3] Ultimately NT2 financing depended on the Thai government's political commitment to importing hydropower from Lao PDR.[4] The World Bank's rationale for financing NT2 rested on two contentious claims about Thailand's power industry: first, that Thailand needed NT2's power to meet the country's electricity needs from 2010 onward; and second, that NT2 would constitute a "competitive least-cost" addition to Thailand's power system.[5]

Dam without Demand

Doing a Dam Better partially concedes that NT2 power was not needed as of 2003, the year EGAT signed the power purchase agreement with NTPC and nearly two years before the World Bank approved financing, stating "Electricity Generating Authority of Thailand (EGAT), the main purchaser of power from NT2, had a large surplus of electrical capacity. . . . [B]y the World Bank's calculations, Thailand had a capacity surplus of about 3,500 megawatts over the 15 percent reserve it needed for power system reliability."[6] That capacity is equivalent to roughly three and a half times the installed generating capacity of NT2.

Normally, anything over a 15-percent reserve margin in a power system is considered overinvestment, which means power consumers are paying for too many power plants.[7] *Doing a Dam Better* acknowledges public concern about EGAT's imprudent demand projections but concludes that NT2 output would be needed eventually, if not right away: "The World Bank projected that [Thailand's] surplus would be gone by 2006 and the system would need additional capacity to meet its energy requirements and reliability criteria. The 920 MW net of power for Thailand produced by NT2 would be fully utilized within less than one year from the projected commissioning date."[8]

But that claim was also wrong. When NT2 began supplying power to EGAT in 2010, EGAT's surplus generating capacity stood at 29 percent of the power system (see table 12.1).[9] Subtracting the required 15-percent reserve margin, this amounts to 2,558.5 megawatts of excess capacity equivalent to roughly two and half times the installed generating capacity of NT2. While electricity demand slowly increased, the amount of generating capacity added to the system increased at a faster rate. This overinvestment in capacity was driven by government policy: first, a return-based incentive structure rewarded, rather than penalized, EGAT for erring on the side of overinvestment; and second, the private sector was encouraged to invest in power plants selling power to EGAT.

By 2015, EGAT's total surplus capacity had ballooned to 42 percent or 11,492.7 megawatts. Subtracting the required 15-percent reserve margin, this amounts to 6,935.8 megawatts of excess capacity in the Thai power system, or nearly seven times the installed generating capacity of NT2. Thailand's

Table 12.1. EGAT's Peak Demand and Generating Capacity Data

Year	Peak Demand (Megawatts)	Installed Capacity (Megawatts)	Total Reserve Margin (%)	Excess Capacity Above 15% Reserve Margin (Megawatts)
2005[10]	20,537.5	26,450.2	29	2,832.0
2010[11]	24,010.0	30,920.0	29	2,558.5
2015[12]	27,345.8	38,838.5	42	6,935.8

actual surplus capacity is even higher, but EGAT does not include the country's very small power producers in its official capacity figures. As of 2015, these producers—which range from 3-kilowatt solar installations to minipower plants under 10 megawatts —had reduced the country's peak demand by an estimated 1,000 megawatts.[13]

Dam Stalled

The Bank's claim that Thailand would need NT2 eventually might have had more credibility in the 1980s, and even early 1990s, when the country experienced high electricity demand growth due to rapid industrialization.[14] But by the late 1990s, NT2 had stalled due to the Asian financial crisis and a corresponding drop in Thailand's economic and electricity demand growth.[15] *Doing a Dam Better* doesn't quite explain that when the World Bank restarted NT2 discussions with the government of the Lao PDR (GoL) in 2001, its economic rationale for NT2 had all but disappeared due to partial privatization of Thailand's power generation business and the deployment of advanced generating technologies.[16]

Globally and across Southeast Asia, gas-fired combined-cycle gas turbine (CCGT) plants had become the generating technology of choice because of the abundance of cheap natural gas, their lower capital costs (about one-third to one-half the unit cost per kilowatt of NT2), faster construction times, greater reliability and operating flexibility, high fuel-efficiency and versatility, and fewer environmental risks (compared to coal, nuclear, and big hydro).[17] *International Water Power and Dam Construction* reported this trend as the "gas-fired threat to Southeast Asian hydropower."[18]

To take advantage of this advanced generating technology and finance rapid expansion, the Thai government invited private investment in power generation in the early 1990s. Its so-called independent power producers and small power producers were licensed to supply the Thai power grid under terms set by EGAT. Independent power producers were mostly CCGT plants with capacities of 700 megawatts s or higher. Small power producers—ranging from 2 to 150 megawatts in capacity—were generating electricity either through nonconventional sources such as wind, minihydro, or fuels from agricultural byproducts (e.g., bagasse) or using cogeneration to produce both power and steam for industrial customers and power for EGAT. Clearly, Thailand had plenty of commercially viable alternatives to hydro imports from Lao PDR, and NT2 proponents knew it. The Asian Development Bank (ADB) in its 2001 assessment of Lao PDR hydro potential reported that "low gas prices, improvements in combined cycle gas turbine plant efficiency, competition among [independent power producers] in Thailand, and excess capacity reserves [had] together resulted in a virtual hiatus in interest from new investors, and in the rate of development of Lao export [independent power producers] hydro power projects."[19]

While NT2 was stalled, Électricité de France (EdF) started building a 715-megawatt CCGT plant in Vietnam with financing from commercial lenders and political risk insurance from the World Bank and ADB.[20] The price of power from EdF's plant was 4.1 US cents per kilowatt per hour, less than the average price negotiated for NT2 power in 2003, which was 4.7 US cents per kilowatt per hour.[21]

Without NT2, both the World Bank and ADB knew that CCGT plants would have been the technology of choice for power industry investors in Thailand.[22] World Bank power sector experts had earlier advised EGAT to introduce competitive procurement and avoid power plants larger than 300 megawatts, noting that "technological changes had virtually eliminated the traditional cost advantage of very large plants."[23] By 2005, about 30 percent of Thailand's total power supply was already coming from large-scale gas-fired producers and nearly 8 percent from eighty-four small power producers, seventeen of which were using natural gas.[24]

Doing a Dam Better does raise the question of why the World Bank backed NT2 given Thailand's success with CCGT plants: "why build a project like NT2, with all of its in situ impacts and long-distance transmission, when Thailand had a large, successful, and economic program of electricity production from CCGT plants based on inexpensive supplies of natural gas?"[25] *Doing a*

Dam Better doesn't claim NT2 was better than or competitive with CCGT plants, only that NT2 "was priced to be competitive" with the expected future cost of Thai gas-fired producers.[26] And as gas prices increased, NT2 power became a cheaper supply for EGAT than Thai gas-fired producers. This is likely to remain the case unless or until gas prices decrease, given that the purchase price for NT2 power is fixed even if the dam's actual costs go higher than budgeted. Back in 2005 however, neither NT2 nor gas-fired CCGT plants were Thailand's least-cost option.

Least-Cost Sideshow

World Bank operations guidelines require Bank staff to prepare appraisal documents demonstrating that proposed projects are "least-cost" compared with alternatives, including the alternative of doing nothing. If projects fail the least-cost test, then public debt or costs could be expected to exceed the value of benefits derived, and the project should therefore be abandoned in favor of more economical investments.[27]

For NT2 to be a "least-cost" option for Thailand, the Bank would have had to first demonstrate a demand and then show that the project could compete on price against electricity produced by other sources and against the price of electricity saved by demand-side management or energy-efficiency investments. A simple price comparison shows that NT2 was not Thailand's least-cost alternative at the time of the Bank's decision to finance NT2 (see table 12.2).

A technical review by Thailand's National Economic and Social Advisory Council also found a number of errors and omissions in the Bank's NT2

Table 12.2. Price Comparison between NT2 and Alternatives[28]

Average price for NT2 power	4.7 US cents per kilowatt per hour[29]
Negotiated price range for Thai small power producers in 2001–2002	4.38–5.4 US cents per kilowatt per hour[30]
Weighted average cost of demand-side management/energy efficient/renewable energy projects not included in EGAT's 2004 power development plan	3.7 US cents per kilowatt per hour[31] 1.56 Thai baht/kilowatt per hour

economic analysis that discredited its conclusion that NT2 was "least cost" and necessary to meet Thai demand.[32] Among these flaws, the Bank considered only conventional large-scale thermal stations and gas-fired CCGT plants as viable alternatives to NT2.[33] Excluded were demand-side management, energy efficiency measures, renewable energy and cogeneration (combined power and heat), all of which have demonstrated economic advantages over large-scale supply expansion.

A separate study from 2004 commissioned by the World Bank confirmed this deficiency in the Bank's "least-cost" analysis. Prepared by one of Thailand's leading energy experts, Peter du Pont, the study concluded: "A careful accounting of the realistic potential of DSM [demand-side management], energy efficiency, and firm renewable energy resources within Thailand indicates an achievable amount of 1,499 MW of DSM/EE and firm RE resources—beyond what is included in [Thailand's] existing power development plan (PDP)—at a commercial cost less than NT2."[34] In total, the Bank's "least-cost analysis" had excluded a total of 5,841 megawatts of viable capacity in Thailand that was available for a cost that was less than or competitive with the agreed 2003 price of NT2 power.[35]

Doing a Dam Better acknowledges that Thailand's potential for demand-side management was greater than what the Bank assumed in its least-cost analysis (928 megawatts) but defends the Bank's bias for more supply over demand-side management as necessary to "guard against insufficient supply."[36]

The World Bank's bias mirrored that of EGAT's. Despite its excess capacity, EGAT's 2004 power development plan called for an additional US$24 billion investment in new generating capacity, including NT2—which was equivalent to twenty new large-scale power plants to be built over the next decade.[37]

Thai groups, independent energy experts, and media publicly challenged EGAT's expansion plans and its assumptions about demand growth and alternatives.[38] Thailand's National Economic and Social Advisory Council came out with an alternative power development plan that excluded planned large-scale hydro imports and coal-fired plants and instead recommended investments in demand-side management (1,500 megawatts), industrial cogeneration (2,500 megawatts) and renewable energy (2,200 megawatts)—all for about 60 percent less than the cost of EGAT's plan.[39]

Given the chronic excess capacity situation, Thailand's cheapest alternative to NT2 was first the no-build option, followed by investment in demand-side management to curb Thailand's demand growth. Had demand warranted procurement of new generating capacity, gas-fired CCGT plants and cogeneration using a variety of renewable fuels would have made more economic and environmental sense than NT2.

For the World Bank, its least-cost analysis and the public debate around Thailand's best electricity options were immaterial once EGAT signed the power purchase agreement in 2003. NT2 was the Bank's opportunity to develop its new "business" approach to hydro finance that would attract and protect private capital from risk and public accountability.

Risky Dam Business

When the World Bank and ADB first began promoting private investment in large hydro dams in the early 1990s, the ADB identified no less than ten categories of hydro-specific risk in its client countries that would have to be regulated by a project's contracts and agreements and allocated to the parties to them before private investors would consider risking their capital.[40] These risks included hydrological risk (risk of water shortages reducing power output and revenue), ecological risks (environmental changes affecting the dam's operations and lifespan), the risk that project-affected people might attempt to stop or delay the project, increased or unanticipated project costs and delays, and uncertainties directly related to cash flow (currency convertibility risk, reduced revenue risk due to sluggish demand, insolvency risks, and disaster risks).[41] In the past, the Bank's client governments and state utilities typically absorbed the financial losses associated with large dams as public debt; prospective private investors, on the other hand, had to be assured of profits and minimal risk of losses.

Delays due to public opposition and escalating demands for compensation were a major concern with the last hydropower dam financed by the World Bank in Thailand in the 1990s. An investigation by the World Commission on Dams found that the Bank-financed Pak Mun Dam ended up costing more than its limited seasonal power benefits. Construction costs went over budget by 68 percent; resettlement and compensation costs increased by 182 percent. A decade later, dam-affected communities had still not recovered from the loss of their fisheries and other riverside livelihoods.[42]

One year after Pak Mun's completion, Thailand's then–foreign minister, Kasem Kasemsri, told the *Nation* (one of Thailand's English-language newspapers) that buying power from NT2 was a good idea because it would not have to deal with the negative consequences of building another dam in Thailand.[43] For Lao PDR, *Doing a Dam Better* notes that the social and environmental impacts of NT2 posed "severe and perhaps the most visible risks."[44]

Limited Recourse Financing

NT2's financing is referred to as "limited recourse" financing, which means simply that investors, owners, and lenders have no legal recourse to the assets of the project sponsors in the event of financial losses or breach of contract. The first step in developing NT2 financing was limiting recourse, or financial liability, of project sponsors by establishing NTPC as a "limited liability" or special-purpose company under Lao PDR law in 2002.[45] The purpose of the limited liability company is to separate the company's assets from those of the company shareholders in order to protect shareholders and investors from the company's debts or other financial obligations. In this arrangement, the company shareholders' financial liability is limited to a fixed sum, most commonly the value of those shareholders' investments in the company. And if a company with limited liability is sued, the claimants are suing the company, not its owners or investors.[46]

As the ADB explains, limited recourse financing is based on "project risks and cash flows, in which guarantees from, or recourse to, project owners are limited. Equity investors link with debt providers to finance power projects on a package basis. Hence, a major plant can be constructed without relying entirely on the financial capabilities of the project owners."[47]

What is crucial is "to minimize risk and uncertainties related to the factors which will make or break the financial viability of the proposed project."[48] Financial risks are assessed and then allocated to the various project participants through a series of contracts and agreements.[49] The primary contracts used in limited recourse financing are the power purchase agreement agreement; the concession agreement; funding agreements; engineering design contracts; construction contracts; and operations and maintenance contracts.[50]

In theory, a limited recourse arrangement allocates financial risk to the party best able to manage or reduce those risks. Plant construction risk, for example, is typically taken by the head construction contractor, in this case EdF International. In the event EdF International could not fulfill its obligations, it would be liable for up to US$100 million.[51] For EGAT, it has effectively assumed demand risk for NTPC, but it cannot be held responsible for rising costs.

Guaranteed Cash Flow

The key contract governing NT2 cash flow is the EGAT power purchase agreement.[52] This document sets out the terms for power purchase and cash flow to NTPC, which is needed to obtain commercial loans and equity capital. Once the agreement was signed by EGAT in 2003, Thailand's demand uncertainty and competitive threats were no longer relevant to financiers because the project's cash flow was guaranteed by state-owned EGAT and set out in a detailed schedule of payment.[53]

Doing a Dam Better claims the EGAT power purchase agreement will generate $1.95 billion in revenue for the GoL over the project's twenty-five-year concession period. However, according to the Bank's project appraisal document, the agreement is expected to generate a total cash flow of US$1.289 billion (before debt service and taxes). About half of that (US$563 million) will flow back to commercial lenders, a third (US$397 million) to private sponsors (Ital-Thai, EdF International, and EGCO), and the remainder to the GoL—US$329 million.[54]

The power purchase agreement has advantages for both power seller and buyer: NTPC is guaranteed a return on its investment, and EGAT is protected from possible energy price increases. EGAT is obliged to purchase electricity from NTPC at agreed tariffs on a "take or pay" basis. This means that regardless of demand, EGAT must purchase 100 percent of NT2's available output (totaling 5,354 gigawatt hours per year on average). This arrangement ensures that the revenue flow to NTPC is kept within a narrow range of 90 to 110 percent of the annual average revenue, despite fluctuations in demand for power or hydrological inflows (which may vary 50 to 160 percent of the average).[55]

Exclusive Water Rights, Limited Liability

Another critical NT2 contract is the concession agreement, which grants NTPC the right to develop, finance, build, own, operate, and transfer NT2 to the GoL at the end of the twenty-five-year concession period. The agreement also grants NTPC exclusive rights to all of the flows of the Nam Theun and other affected rivers and limits the resettlement and environmental management budget to less than 10 percent of the project cost: US$90.5 million for expected impacts upstream and downstream, and another US$10 million for unanticipated impacts.[56]

NTPC's website explains that the agreement "defines, incorporates and costs all the environmental and social obligations, including compensation principles and payments . . . that are to be strictly followed by the Project Company and the GoL."[57] This document was not released for public review prior to the Bank's decision to finance, but a summary is posted on the NTPC website. One critical clause of public concern offers NTPC protection from the threat of reduced income or increased project costs arising from any future change in GoL law.[58] In that event, the agreement entitles NTPC to seek financial compensation from the GoL. This clause alone makes it difficult for the public to hold the NTPC or GoL liable for uncompensated damages or advance a less destructive operating regime.

Limited Public Accountability

Only short summaries of the concession agreement and power purchase agreement were publicly released on the NTPC website, and only in the year leading up to the Bank's decision to finance NT2. The complete contracts, all secretly negotiated by project participants, were not subject to public review or independent regulatory scrutiny in Lao PDR or Thailand, although *Doing a Dam Better* claims the World Bank was committed to transparency and public disclosure of NT2 project information throughout the course of its involvement.[59] But when a June 24, 2003, letter signed by forty NGOs in twenty-one countries asked the World Bank to release the entire NT2 concession agreement for public review, the response from Robert Mertz, a financial analyst for the World Bank's East Asia and Pacific Region, was no. According to Mertz's September 9, 2003, letter to Shannon Lawrence at Environmental Defense, the World Bank's disclosure policy "prohibits us from disclosing documents which have been provided to the Bank on a confidential basis." The Bank's refusal to uphold the public's right to know how the dam's environmental risks, costs, and liabilities have been assessed and allocated does not bode well for the affected public. Only through public disclosure can developers, prospective investors, and the public test whether the proponents' assessment of costs and risks are accurate and, more importantly, acceptable to directly affected people or not.

Public Subsidies

Doing a Dam Better lists all the sources of public and private financing for NT2, which includes a US$20 million World Bank grant to cover NTPC's resettlement and environmental mitigation programs, as well as low-interest loans, ADB and World Bank loan guarantees, and Multilateral Investment Guarantee Agency political risk insurance.[60] Without support from the World Bank and other government-backed financial institutions, international commercial lenders would not have risked their capital on NT2 due to the inherent risks associated with large hydro dams, political uncertainties about a cross-border power project, and the GoL's lack of creditworthiness and capacity.

NTPC is one-quarter owned by the GoL, an aid-dependent communist regime that lacked the legal and financial framework required for private capital investment. At a 2002 symposium in Lao PDR, one of the GoL's NT2 lawyers, Paul Cargill, explained the situation: "We all know where and what Laos is. . . . When [investors] look for the Lao legal system (being the laws themselves and the courts that apply and interpret those laws), they see an underdeveloped system which does not give them comfort that once they put their money in they can get it out."[61]

Political risk insurance was a key part of the package for commercial banks. To protect NT2 lenders against the risk of currency inconvertibility, expropriation, war and civil disturbance, and breach of contract in Lao PDR, as well as the risk of the termination of the power purchase agreement in Thailand, the World Bank's Multilateral Investment Guarantee Agency provided up to US$200 million worth of political risk insurance.[62] In the event NTPC fails to service its loans to international commercial banks, due to any of the conditions cited by agency, either the agency or the World Bank (or ADB) will step in to cover NTPC loan repayments.

Risks and Rewards

Four months after NT2 began supplying power to EGAT, the only private shareholder in NTPC, Ital-Thai, sold its 10 percent stake in NT2 for a profit of US$45 million.[63] This profit on shares was in addition to the US$125 million contract awarded to Ital-Thai for NT2 construction works.[64] To put this in perspective, Ital-Thai's profit on share sales is almost three times the total budget allocated for addressing downstream impacts and US$5 million more than the project's $40 million budget cost overruns.[65]

The NT2 finance deal has "buoyed the hydropower industry worldwide" according to *Doing a Dam Better*.[66] And no wonder. With NT2, the Bank has managed to reconfigure what investors widely regarded as an "unbankable" megaproject into a safe, guaranteed investment for private investors and commercial banks. As British researcher Nicholas Hildyard has shown with respect to private equity investment in large power and infrastructure projects globally, this reconfiguration is "less about financing development (which is at best a sideshow) than about developing finance."[67] Under the NT2 finance model, profits and revenues are contractually separated from costs and liabilities, and thus no dam is too risky or too environmentally damaging not to build.

In the next decade, EGAT plans to significantly increase its reliance on large hydro projects in neighboring countries. The largest project to date, a US$3.8 billion, 1285-megawatt hydro dam on the Mekong mainstream in northern Laos, got under way in 2012 with a similar contractual framework as NT2 but financed entirely by Thai commercial banks.[68] EGAT has also diverted its state monopoly revenue into private equity investments made by its newest subsidiary, EGAT International (EGATi).[69] In 2015, Thailand's Ministry of Energy approved EGAT's transfer of roughly half a billion US dollars to fund EGATi's equity investments in power projects outside Thailand, including the 7000-megawatt Mong Ton hydropower project in Myanmar.[70]

Conclusions

Public concerns about the NT2 model are legion: inflated private profits made possible by limited liability for social and environmental costs; EGAT's conflict of interest as power buyer and investor; limited public accountability for risks and rewards set out in project contracts; and no regulatory oversight to protect the public interest or win public consent either in Thailand or Lao PDR. A 2010 World Bank report flags a few of these problems as "governance challenges" in Lao PDR that if not resolved could prevent Laotians from benefiting from hydro development.[71] What neither the World Bank nor *Doing a Dam Better* own up to is the Bank's role in creating these governance challenges due to its own conflict of interest as self-appointed developer, financier, and de facto environmental regulator.

The fundamental flaw in the Bank's new business approach to hydro finance is that it offers protection and guarantees to private investors and commercial lenders without providing commensurate protection and guarantees to affected citizens and ratepayers. The Bank's response to unmitigated or intractable problems associated with NT2 will be more grants and loans to client governments—more public debt kept separate from NTPC's balance sheet.

A better approach to investment design and decision making would be to put affected people and electricity ratepayers at the center, instead of the periphery. Affected people expected to shoulder power project risks should be afforded the right to say "no" if they deem a project's social and environmental risks unacceptably high. Thai ratepayers are entitled to impartial regulatory oversight to protect their interests and to ensure that no private power company unfairly transfers social or environmental costs to other jurisdictions. If projects proceed despite known high risks to the public or if developers overlook certain costs in their initial assessment, ensuring full legal recourse to project owners for unmitigated damages should be standard within any contractual frame-work. Without such measures to ensure legal and financial accountability to the affected public, the unsustainable NT2 model is one of private profit amid rising public liabilities.

NOTES

The authors wish to thank Cheunchom Sangarasri Greacen, David Hubbel, and Bruce Shoemaker for their contributions to this chapter. Any errors are of course the responsibility of the authors.

1. NTPC, EGAT power purchase agreement, summary for public disclosure, March 2005, www.namtheun2.com/images/Document_for_website/Summary%20of%20 CA%20&%20PPA/041006%20-%20EGAT%20PPA%20%20Summary%20for%20 Public%20Disclosure.pdf.

2. Ital-Thai subcontracted to Vancouver-based Klohn Crippen Berger for civil, hydro-technical, geotechnical, electrical, and mechanical services for the project's civil works ("Klohn Crippen Berger Nam Theun 2 Hydro," *Canadian Consulting Engineer*, October 1, 2010, www.canadianconsultingengineer.com/features/klohn-crippen-berger-nam-theun-2-hydro).

3. For a useful schematic of NT2 developers, financiers, and financial flows before and after the dam's commissioning, see Vincent Merme, Ahlers Rodante, and Joyeeta Gupta, "Private Equity, Public Affair: Hydro Financing in the Mekong Basin," *Global Environmental Change* 24 (2014).

4. From the NTPC website: "In June 1993, the Government of the Lao PDR and the Government of the Kingdom of Thailand signed a Memorandum of Understanding [MOU] to support the development of power projects in the Lao PDR through the supply of up to 1,500 MW of electricity to Thailand. In June 1996, the agreement was superseded by a new MOU increasing the scope of supply to 3,000 MW. Since then further under-standings between the two countries have been signed agreeing on supply of 5,000 MW to Thailand up to 2015 and another 2,000+ MW after 2015" (www.namtheun2.com/index .php/about-us/project-in-brief).

5. World Bank, NT2 project appraisal document, March 31, 2005, 48, http://docu ments.worldbank.org/curated/en/250731468277466031/pdf/317640corr.pdf.

6. Teresa Serra, Mark Segal, and Ram Chopra, "The Project Is Prepared," in *Doing a Dam Better: The Lao People's Democratic Republic and the Story of Nam Theun 2*, ed. Ian C. Porter and Jayasankar Shivakumar (Washington, DC: World Bank, 2011), 72.

7. According to the North American Electric Reliability Corporation, an interna-tional regulatory authority, reserve margin is "the difference between available capacity and peak demand, normalized by peak demand shown as a percentage to maintain reliable operation while meeting unforeseen increases in demand (e.g. extreme weather) and unex-pected outages of existing capacity." For planning purposes, it assumes "a 15 percent reserve

margin for predominately thermal systems and 10 percent for predominately hydro systems." By inference, anything above 15 percent is unnecessary capacity because demand is insufficient to warrant that investment (www.nerc.com/pa/RAPA/ri/Pages/PlanningReserveMargin.aspx).

8. Serra, Segal, and Chopra, "The Project Is Prepared," 73.

9. EGAT, *2010 Annual Report*, 18 (www.egat.co.th/en/images/annual-report/annualReport-2010.pdf).

10. EGAT, *2005 Annual Report*, 6, 10 (www.egat.co.th/en/images/annual-report/annualReport-2005.pdf).

11. EGAT, *2010 Annual Report*, 18.

12. EGAT, *2015 Annual Report*, 12, 14 (www.egat.co.th/en/images/annual-report/2015/egat-annual-eng-2015.pdf).

13. EGAT website (in Thai), peak demand data, www.egat.co.th/index.php?option=com_content&view=article&id=348&Itemid=116.

14. For a history of EGAT's privatization, see Chuenchom Sangarasri Greacen and Chris Greacen, "Thailand's Electricity Reform: Privatization of Benefits and Socialization of Costs and Risks," *Pacific Affairs* 77, no. 3 (2004): 517–41.

15. Nazir Ahmad, "Working with Stakeholders," in *Doing a Dam Better*, 99.

16. The only valid economic rationale for building a hydro dam or taking on any kind of power project is to serve a particular market or set of customers in need of power at a price acceptable to both producers and consumers.

17. Norconsult, *Regional Indicative Master Plan on Interconnection in the Greater Mekong Subregion*, ADB, July 2002. See also Gráinne Ryder, "Ten Reasons Why the World Bank Should Not Finance the NT2 Power Company in Lao PDR," Probe International, Toronto, June 2004, 11-12, http://probeinternational.org/library/wp-content/uploads/2011/12/nt10reasons.pdf.

18. Tim Sharp, "The Gas-Fired Threat to SE Asian Hydro Power," *International Water Power and Dam Construction* 50, no. 8 (1998).

19. Electrowatt, *Power Sector Strategy Study*, final report, vol. 1, Asian Development Bank, 2001, 91.

20. ADB, "Vietnam: Phu My 2.2 Power Project," Project Number 35914, February 2011. Completed in 2005, the Phu My 2.2 power plant is part of Vietnam's largest power plant complex, all gas-fired combined cycle plants, providing roughly 40 percent of the country's power supply. https://www.adb.org/sites/default/files/evaluation-document/35553/files/35914-vie-validation.pdf.

21. Mark Segal, *Nam Theun 2*, interim summary report, World Bank, August 21, 2004, 11, http://documents.worldbank.org/curated/en/660941468045590805/pdf/925850WP0P076400Box385315B00PUBLIC0.pdf.

22. World Bank, Nam Theun 2 hydroelectric project, project appraisal document, 43.

23. Claudio Fernandez and Ismail Dalla, *Increasing Private Sector Participation and Improving Efficiency in State Enterprises*, vol. 2, Main Report, Industry and Energy Operations Division, Country Department I, East Asia and Pacific Regional Office, World Bank,

October 11, 1994, http://documents.worldbank.org/curated/en/857581468761095177/pdf/multiopage.pdf, 71.

24. World Bank, "REToolKit Case Study: Small Power Producers of Thailand," undated, 2, http://siteresources.worldbank.org/EXTRENENERGYTK/Resources/51382 46-1238175210723/ThailandoSmalloPoweroProduceroProgramo.pdf.

25. Serra, Segal, and Chopra, "The Project Is Prepared," 74.

26. Serra, Segal, and Chopra, "The Project Is Prepared," 72.

27. Serra, Segal, and Chopra, "The Project Is Prepared."

28. Part of this table originally appeared in Witoon Permpongsacharoen, *Technical Review of the World Bank's "Nam Theun 2 Hydro Power Project Regional Economic Least-Cost Analysis, Draft Final Report" and "Nam Theun 2 Project Economics Interim Summary Report,"* National Economic and Social Advisory Council, Bangkok, March 14, 2005, 2, www.terraper.org/web/sites/default/files/key-issues-content/1283331157_en.pdf.

29. Mark Segal, *Nam Theun 2*, interim summary report, 2004, 11.

30. World Bank, "REToolKit Case Study," 3.

31. Permpongsacharoen, *Technical Review*, 10.

32. Permpongsacharoen, *Technical Review*, 10.

33. Permpongsacharoen, *Technical Review*, 2.

34. Peter du Pont, *Nam Theun 2 Hydropower Project (NT2): Impact of Energy Conservation, DSM, and Renewable Energy Generation on EGAT's Power Development Plan*, final report, World Bank, August 28, 2004, 5.

35. *Nam Theun 2 Hydropower Project (NT2): Impact of Energy Conservation, DSM, and Renewable Energy Generation on EGAT's Power Development Plan*, 5; World Bank, Nam Theun 2 hydroelectric project, project appraisal document. The report by du Pont was not publicly released until days before the board's approval of NT2 financing.

36. Serra, Segal, and Chopra, "The Project Is Prepared," 74.

37. For an overview of EGAT's privatization politics see, Apsara Palettu, "Thailand's Power Sector Reform: Privatisation or Piratisation?" *Watershed* 9, no. 2 (2004).

38. "Nam Theun 2: No Time for Another Mistake," editorial, *Watershed* 10, no. 1 (2004); Gráinne Ryder, "Ten Reasons Why the World Bank Should Not Finance NT2," Probe International briefing, July 1, 2004, http://probeinternational.org/library/wp-content/uploads/2011/12/nt10reasons.pdf.

39. World Bank, "REToolKit Case Study," 3.

40. Norconsult, *Subregional Energy Sector Study for the Greater Mekong Subregion*, ADB, 1995, 597.

41. Norconsult, *Subregional Energy Sector Study*, 597.

42. "From Pak Mun: Ten Years Later," *Watershed* 10, no. (2004).

43. "Hike in EGAT Deal Delayed," *Nation*, September 7, 1995.

44. Ian C. Porter and Jayasankar Shivakumar, overview, *Doing a Dam Better*, 8.

45. World Bank, Nam Theun 2 hydroelectric project, project appraisal document, 25.

46. https://en.wikipedia.org/wiki/Limited_liability.

47. Norconsult, *Subregional Energy Sector Study*, 596.

48. Norconsult, *Subregional Energy Sector Study*, 593.

49. Norconsult, *Subregional Energy Sector Study*, 589.

50. Norconsult, *Subregional Energy Sector Study*, 589; World Bank, Nam Theun 2 hydroelectric project, project appraisal document, 29, 18.

51. World Bank, Nam Theun 2 hydroelectric project, project appraisal document, 22.

52. NTPC, "EGAT Power Purchase Agreement: Summary for Public Disclosure."

53. World Bank, NT2 project appraisal document, 45.

54. World Bank, NT2 project appraisal document, 45.

55. Sidharth Sinha, "Nam Theun 2 Hydroelectric Project," undated, World Bank, https://ppiaf.org/sites/ppiaf.org/files/documents/toolkits/Cross-Border-Infrastructure-Tool kit/Cross-Border%20Compilation%20over%2029%20Jan%2007/Resources/Sinha %20-%20Case%20Study%20Nam%20Theun.pdf.

56. NTPC, summary of the concession agreement between the GoL and NTPC, November 2005, 8, www.namtheun2.com/images/Document_for_website/Summary%20 of%20CA%20&%20PPA/SummaryofCA,%20for%20public%20disclosure.pdf; World Bank, Nam Theun 2 hydroelectric project, project appraisal document, 18.

57. See http://www.namtheun2.com/index.php/environment-main/environ ment-content.

58. NTPC, summary of the concession agreement between the GoL and NTPC, 28.

59. Peter Stephens, "The Communications Challenge," in *Doing a Dam Better*, 125.

60. Porter and Shivakumar, overview, 15.

61. Paul Cargill, "Decision Framework for Processing the Proposed Nam Theun 2 Project," paper presented at the World Bank-GoL Symposium "Nam Theun 2—Window to the Future," Vientiane, July 3, 2002.

62. World Bank, NT2 project appraisal document, 24; Multilateral Investment Guaran-tee Agency, *Hydropower in Asia*, June 2006, 3, www.miga.org/documents/NT206.pdf.

63. MEE Net, *Following the Money Trail of Mekong Energy Industry*, Bangkok, Septem-ber 2013, 45, www.meenet.org/wp-content/uploads/2015/08/Following-the-Money-Trail-of-Mekong-Energy-Industry-2013_English.pdf. The other NTPC owners are "limited lia-bility" subsidiaries of government-owned entities EGAT and EdF.

64. Khampha Phairath, "Italian-Thai Bank on Profit Track and NT2 Project to Go Ahead," January 30, 2002, www.reocities.com/chainat_prov/4502/THA-italthai-0201 .html.

65. Serra, Segal, and Chopra, "The Project Is Prepared," 67. The base budget for addressing downstream impacts was US$16 million; according to Patchamuthu Illangovan, the budgeted cost overrun was about US$40 million ("NT2: A Transformative Endeavor," in *Doing a Dam Better*, 164).

66. Illangovan, "NT2: A Transformative Endeavor," 159.

67. Nicholas Hildyard, *More than Bricks and Mortar: Infrastructure-As-Asset Class, Financing Development or Developing Finance?* (Dorset, UK: Corner House, 2012), 3, www .thecornerhouse.org.uk/sites/thecornerhouse.org.uk/files/Bricks%20and%20Mortar.pdf.

68. "Construction Forges ahead at Xayaburi Dam," *Bangkok Post*, July 22, 2012; for

details about the Xayaburi project ownership and investment model, see MEE Net, *Following the Money Trail of Mekong Energy Industry*, 38–39.

69. For more information on the post-NT2 investment model for EGAT and Thai companies in large hydro export projects in Lao PDR, see MEE Net, *Following the Money Trail of Mekong Energy Industry*, 26–39.

70. TRIS, September 16, 2015, www.egati.co.th/images/egati/ensite/company_credit /EGATi81-e-160915.pdf, 1.

71. World Bank, *Natural Resource Management for Sustainable Development: Hydropower and Mining*, Lao PDR development report, June 1 2010, http://siteresources.world bank.org/LAOPRDEXTN/Resources/293683-1301084874098/LDR2010_Full_Report.pdf.

13

Branding Dams

Nam Theun 2 and Its Role in Producing the Discourse of "Sustainable Hydropower"

CARL MIDDLETON

In the 1990s, the global hydropower industry—in particular the industry of Northern countries—was facing a growing crisis of legitimacy. The number of opponents to large dams had grown, and become increasingly vocal, claiming that development benefits were exaggerated. This cumulated in the publication of the World Commission on Dams (WCD) report in 2000, which affirmed many of the opponents' criticisms.[1] In this context, the World Bank, seeking a means to once again finance large hydropower, put forward the Nam Theun 2 (NT2) hydropower project as a new, best-practice approach.[2] Meanwhile, the International Hydropower Association (IHA) sought to counter the WCD with its own sustainability guidelines in 2004 and subsequently a Hydropower Sustainability Assessment Protocol (HSAP) launched in 2011. From this significant and combined effort of large dam proponents emerged the policy discourse of "sustainable hydropower," the purpose of which was to relegitimize the industry.

This chapter deconstructs how NT2 has been discursively produced as a "brand" and how it has been woven in to the discourse of sustainable hydropower. I argue that in public relations the World Bank and the hydropower industry have regularly drawn on NT2 as a model to legitimize their claim that sustainable hydropower is possible. Needless to say, this claim is fiercely disputed.[3] Indeed, behind closed doors among the project's proponents and in specialist hydropower industry conferences, more provisos and nuances are considered that bracket the public claims of success. It is not the primary purpose of this chapter to analyze the broader discourse of sustainable hydropower

271

and its global diffusion beyond NT2's already significant role. However, the chapter does touch on the implications of NT2 within these regional and global debates—for example, in relation to the IHA's HSAP. Furthermore, while I address some aspects of the counter-NT2 discourse because it has engaged with and shaped the pro-NT2 discourse, a detailed analysis is also beyond the chapter's scope.

In the next section, I introduce the key concepts of the chapter, focusing on the production of discourses. Following are two sections examining first how NT2 has been claimed as a "model" dam and then how a narrative has been produced based on it. The chapter then explores the role of NT2 in a second narrative about how dams in Laos contribute to poverty reduction and development. I go in subsequent sections to detail how Laos's hydropower narrative has been disseminated regionally and globally and how it has also legitimized the World Bank's reentry into hydropower. The last section of the chapter considers the role of the NT2 brand in producing the broader sustainable hydropower discourse as a "nirvana concept," thus reflecting NT2's positioning within global debates about development and the role of hydropower.

Discourses, Actors, Interests, and Networks

The discourse of sustainable hydropower claims that hydropower dams should be principally understood as development projects for poverty reduction rather than as literal industrial concrete artifacts for water storage and electricity generation. To explain how such a claim is produced and then reproduced, this section briefly introduces an analytical approach that considers discourses and policy narratives and the interests and networks of actors.[4]

Discourses and Policy Narratives

A discourse is "a shared set of concepts, categories, and ideas that provides its adherents with a framework for making sense of situations, embodying judgments, assumptions, capabilities, dispositions, and intentions."[5] A discourse thus brings together groups of people around a shared understanding of the world, establishes relations between them, and structures and coordinates actions. Carl Death writes, "Within discourses particular things are made visible and others invisible, truths are created and regimes of knowledge established, practices and technologies are concretized and subjects are produced."[6] The language of discourses gives meanings to material objects and practices, while practice itself also reinforces the discourse.[7] The planning, construction, and operation of the various aspects of NT2 intersect with the production of the narrative of NT2 and the wider discourse of sustainable hydropower in which it is embedded.

Relatedly, the process of discourse creation and reproduction is intimately tied to knowledge production. The World Bank and other actors' political economic power is of course important in outcomes on the ground, but words also matter. They are in fact mutually reinforcing. It is through discourses such as sustainable hydropower that the legitimacy of such a project as NT2 becomes normalized in practitioners' consciousness or becomes common sense over time.[8]

As the production and reproduction of discourses are social processes, they are in summary bound up with networks of actors and their interests, institutions and their norms and rules, and political power. Discourses need not be hegemonic; John Dryzek, for example, identifies various discourses that nucleate around a central theme of the environment, while Carl Death names four discourse variations emerging from the concept of "green economy."[9]

In producing discourses, actors generate "narratives" around policy problems, which are simple stories with beginnings defining the problem, middles elaborating the consequences, and ends outlining the solutions. They often appeal to common sense but in the process reduce and simplify the complexity of reality. The typical affirmative narrative for Laos's large hydropower dam development pathway, with NT2 at its center, goes like this: Laos has great natural wealth, including water resources and thus hydropower potential, yet it also has high levels of material poverty. Laos has struggled to attract investment into hydropower due to weak government capacity and a limited proven track record in building large dams, and thus the country remains in poverty. By supporting NT2 as a development project, it could generate government revenue, implement programs for poverty reduction, and attract further private sector investment.

To further understand the production of discourses, François Molle has proposed "nirvana concepts" and "models." Nirvana concepts are "concepts that embody an ideal image of what the world should tend to. . . . Although, just as with nirvana, the likelihood that we may reach them is admittedly low, the mere possibility of achieving them and the sense of 'progress' attached to any shift in their direction suffice to make them an attractive and useful focal point."[10] Nirvana concepts ideationally underpin discourses and their narratives or storylines and are often a photonegative of the chaotic, problematic real world. Sustainable hydropower is such a nirvana concept.

Models, meanwhile, are conceptual objects that are "based on particular instances of policy reforms or development interventions which ostensibly embody a dimension of 'success.' . . . They are apparently sanctioned by experience, approved by experts and powerful institutions."[11] NT2 is an archetypal model according to this definition and has regularly been presented as such by the World Bank and other project proponents.

Actors, Interests, and Networks

Discourses, narratives, nirvana concepts, and models are interrelated ideational objects produced by networks of actors that together stake claims to truth. John Dryzek emphasizes that in the realm of governance, discourses are produced by formal policy-making authorities, usually understood as governments, but also through deliberative processes in national and international public spheres in which "NGOs, individual activists, journalists, corporations, and members of governments and international governmental organizations acting in non-authoritative fashion" participate.[12] Thus, actors pursue their interests, make claims, and engage in decision making in multiple arenas, where they are subject to various influences including discourses and institutions.[13] Furthermore, as emphasized by Michael Goldman in his book *Imperial Nature*, even influential actors such as the World Bank cannot and do not work alone; instead they form coalitions and engage in wider networks aligned around shared goals and interests.

In producing knowledge, experts work within communities of practitioners that share conceptual frameworks, analytical approaches, and practices toward their discipline, as well as political values. These have been termed "epistemic networks."[14] Experts and their epistemic networks play a particularly significant role in the production of development discourses, coproducing science and policy by working in tandem with policy makers. Policy makers define the areas and agendas of investigation, and technical experts create and contribute knowledge within those bounds.[15] In producing knowledge that ultimately shapes discourse, this expert–policy maker nexus can often downplay situational (i.e., local) knowledge and marginalize those who do not share the same worldview. Since the early 2000s, the World Bank has reformed itself into a self-proclaimed neutral "knowledge bank," and in this role it is active in the production and circulation of knowledge that heavily influences how "development" in principle, policy, and practice is understood.[16] In the case of NT2, the World Bank, the project developers, and the government of the Lao PDR (GoL) have worked with a wide array of technical experts in the process producing a particular frame for NT2.

Thus, in this chapter I consider how NT2 as a model, the broader Laos hydropower sector as a narrative, and sustainable hydropower as a nirvana concept have interacted to produce the emergent global discourse around sustainable hydropower that partly frames contemporary global debates on the role of large hydropower in development. It is to this analysis that we now turn.

Claiming a "Model" Dam

NT2 has been named by academic Ben Boer and colleagues as the World Bank's and Laos's "showpiece hydropower project."[17] The World Bank seeks to frame NT2 not as a hydropower infrastructure project but as a poverty reduction intervention and a sustainable development project. Furthermore, in an effort to attain these framing objectives, NT2 has been heavily promoted by the World Bank as a model project. Nowhere is this more evident than in Bank staffers Ian C. Porter and Jayasankar Shivakumar's edited volume *Doing a Dam Better*, which serves to lock in NT2's model status and consolidate its legacy.

Given this chapter's focus on knowledge production, it is worth noting that *Doing a Dam Better* is a highly positioned book, despite seeking to give the impression of objectivity. The book does not assess a wide array of literature on NT2 or incorporate work from a diverse range of authors but rather explains the project—strengths and weaknesses—ultimately from the perspective of the Bank itself. It reflects a widely made observation that World Bank research in general is highly self-referential and underrepresents research that is unfavorable of its work and position.[18]

According to the book's introduction, penned by Porter and Jayasankar, the objectives of NT2 were to generate "revenues, through the environmentally and socially sustainable development of NT2's hydropower potential, that will be used to finance priority poverty reduction and environmental management programs."[19] In the the introduction, the editors also note that NT2 "demonstrates that hydropower projects can be designed and implemented to deliver sustainable outcomes through state-of-the-art environmental and social practices and strengthened public financial management systems, but this takes a long time."[20]

Overall, the book offers many "lessons learned" from NT2. A critical reading of the book shows that it doesn't demonstrate that a hydropower project can be sustainable per se but rather that unsustainable projects of the past can be improved on.

The intention of creating best practices that are replicable, which according to François Molle is a trait of producing a "model," was integral to NT2's design. *Doing a Dam Better*, in acknowledging the environmental and social risks associated with NT2 that triggered all ten of the World Bank's safeguards policies, explains that "with its large geographic footprint and multiple impacts, it [NT2] constitutes a test case for project-specific environmental and social protection policies that have the potential to be broadly replicated throughout the country."[21]

To understand the interests of the World Bank in affirming NT2's model status, it is important to recognize that the stakes were high. At the time of NT2's approval in 2005, the World Bank had not financed a major hydropower dam for a decade. In order to reenter hydropower, the World Bank essentially had to prove that it could build a sustainable project, or at least claim to have done so. In this context, according to Goldman, NT2 became a "litmus test for the Bank's ability to respond to its critics."[22] *Doing a Dam Better* acknowledges that NT2 was particularly complicated, however, because it was prepared during challenging times that included the dam debate of the 1990s, which culminated in the World Commission on Dams, the Asian financial crisis of 1997, the strengthening of environmental and social safeguard policies and practices at the World Bank and other financial institutions, and the greater scrutiny of governance arrangements for the transparent use of natural resource rents by countries.[23]

It's important to note, however, that even as the higher standards aimed for with NT2 were in response to the WCD report, the World Bank largely resisted the WCD recommendations to fully internalize the environmental and social costs of large dams and to fundamentally rework decision-making toward these high-risk projects. Hence, despite improvements in their practices, the World Bank—and the wider hydropower industry—refused to endorse the WCD report itself.[24]

This reflects a wider global context that led to the World Bank reinventing itself as a purveyor of sustainable development. This ultimately crystallized in the form of what Goldman calls "green neoliberalism." He observes how, remarkably, the World Bank was able to transform an environmentalist agenda that rallied against it in the 1980s and 1990s into a new investment opportunity.[25] According to Goldman, who was writing in 2005 at the time of NT2's approval, "That few development practices, beliefs, and truths can be expressed today outside the parameters of environmentally sustainable development, on the one hand, and neoliberalism, on the other, is a testament to the efficacy of the Bank's latest power/knowledge regime."[26] In this context, it is understandable that the World Bank has repeatedly stated that NT2 has resulted in poverty reduction, that resettled communities are better off, that it is a climate-friendly project, and that the impacts on communities downstream are being managed. As evidenced throughout this book, however, many of these claims are only partly correct, and important dimensions are increasingly in doubt.

For example, the November 2015 International Environmental and Social Panel of Experts (PoE) report raises important questions.[27] Meanwhile, Thayer Scudder, a member of the PoE, was quoted in an article in the New York Times in August 2014 as stating that "Nam Theun 2 confirmed my long-standing suspicion that the task of building a large dam is just too complex and too damaging to priceless natural resources."[28] Furthermore, the World Bank's own assessment toward the "Nam Theun 2 Social and Environment Project" rated it in 2016 as "moderately unsatisfactory" in implementation and considered it "high" risk, revised to "moderately satisfactory" in 2017.[29] Challenges are also acknowledged in the World Bank's country partnership strategy progress report, published in September 2014. What is noteworthy here is that these official assessments diverge from the more optimistic note commonly struck by the World Bank and NT2's proponents in other public communications on the project.[30]

Academics have also drawn more measured conclusions. Ben Boer and colleagues suggest that it's likely correct that the greater attention paid to NT2 left villagers with a better resettlement arrangement that they would otherwise have received, but they also argue that "relocated villagers do not appear to have fared as well as expected in the long run, in material and political terms."[31]

Communicating the Narrative of NT2 as a "Model Dam"

Both the positive and negative international public images of NT2 were projected through savvy media campaigns by the World Bank and international nongovernmental organizations (NGOs). To promote NT2 as a model, the World Bank invested heavily in communication. According to *Doing a Dam Better*, "From the beginning, NT2 was a lightning rod for criticism; the debate on dams and NT2 had a long and contentious history. The World Bank had to be on guard against reputational risk from misinformation. Over time, it came to use communications as a strategic lever to influence the debate on NT2."[32] Over several chapters, *Doing a Dam Better* details an array of strategies that the World Bank's team adopted with respect to communication within participatory processes directly related to the project and through the media for wider public consumption. For example, in his contribution titled

"Working with NGOs Opposed to the Project: Forging a Path to Constructive Engagement" Nazir Ahmad writes:

> NT2 attracted criticisms from the outset. Most vocal were activist NGOs that fundamentally dislike dam projects based on the adverse environmental and human consequences of many other projects they have witnessed. Over the years, it became increasingly necessary for the World Bank to develop a strategy to manage communications more proactively and constructively so that balanced, factual information was made available to all stakeholders and the World Bank's reputation was protected from unfair accusations. Communications would become a strategic lever to facilitate the debate and make it constructive; however, this was more easily said than done.[33]

The World Bank's focus on communications and media strategy is significant, as it acknowledges that technical knowledge production alone—in the form, for example, of project reports—was insufficient and that proactive public framing via the media was also important to maintain the World Bank's legitimacy in supporting NT2. Some news outlets spoke favorably of NT2. For example, in August 2007 *Newsweek* published a by now famous article titled "Laos Dam Raises Ethical Bar," in which the reporter observed, "There's a lot riding on NT2. Laos needs the boost to its economy and its human-rights credentials. The World Bank wants to prove that kinder, gentler megaprojects are possible."[34]

A piece penned by the World Bank one month later titled "Nam Theun 2: A Way to Better Hydro Projects" quoted the *Newsweek* article's mention of a "kinder and gentler dam," while extolling the virtues of the project, noting, for example, how "a group of social and environmental experts who advise on the project said it had the potential to become a global model."[35] Reflecting just how controversial the dam was, however, within months of the *Newsweek* article, the *Economist* also ran a story titled "Dam the Consequences: Big, Bad Dams Return to South-East Asia," and the *Associated Press* published an article titled "Critics: Lao Dam Was Bad for Villagers."[36]

In Laos, where civil and political rights are curtailed, the level of "transparency" of and "stakeholder participation" in NT2 has made it a remarkably public project. The controversy that the project courted raised the project's visibility, as did the "institutional gaze" of the external monitors of the project, in particular the PoE.[37] Needless to say, a tension existed between the closed political space to discuss hydropower in general in Laos and the project's implications for the country's "development" and thus NT2's transparency was "tethered to the individual site of the project."[38] But it can be argued that the effort to make NT2 visible to particular audiences beyond project-affected communities, such as those concerned about the project's compliance with the World Bank's safeguard standards, contributed to raising the project's profile and, ultimately, to legitimizing its claims to be a "model."

For example, in 2004, a year before project approval, the World Bank supported the GoL in its effort to organize a series of "international technical workshops" in Bangkok, Paris, Tokyo, and Washington, DC. These unprecedented workshops were held in response to civil society pressure and indicate the extent to which the project was in the public eye. There were criticisms of the workshops' process, including that reports were released too late to be useful during the workshops and that they were overly technical. However, Ahmad observes that for the GoL the workshops also unexpectedly ended up promoting Laos as a hydropower investment destination:

> Government officials had been hesitant about holding these workshops, fearing multifaceted and relatively unscripted public dialogue and potential public challenges by NGOs and Lao expatriate groups. As the workshops unfolded, however, officials appreciated the value of such engagement, both in explaining the project and in introducing Lao PDR to the outside world on the government's terms. The workshops were also successful in demonstrating the willingness of the government and the World Bank to engage with critics of the project.[39]

The Narrative of "Dams for Poverty Reduction and Development" in Laos

An important component of the NT2 narrative was its positioning as a "development project" rather than merely a hydropower dam. It was, furthermore, a development project central to the GoL's World Bank–backed country development strategy since the 1990s. Both claimed that large hydropower dams, together with mining and agricultural concessions, would enable Laos to transition from a least developed country by generating dividends, royalties, and taxes for the government and by attracting foreign direct investment. NT2 was central to the debate about Laos's future development pathway at the time.

Noting the profound economic and political scale of the project in Laos at the time of its construction, Goldman describes NT2 as "a national project that will consume most of the government's resources to finance a wide range of components, including new regimes of law, regulation, and management of both the country's natural resources (its rivers, minerals, forests, wildlife) and the people whose livelihood directly depends on these natural resources."[40] NTPC's website emphasizes NT2's status as a "development project," opening on its "About Us" page with the following:

> The Nam Theun 2 Power Company (NTPC) is an industrial and development investment owned by two private shareholders and the Lao Government, backed by commercial lenders and international financial institutions including the World Bank and the Asian Development Bank. It is described by the Lao Government as "an essential part of the country's development framework" that "is likely to provide the first real possibility for Laos to gradually reduce its dependence on Official Development Assistance."[41] Furthermore, NTPC's mission statement states three goals that frame NT2 as more than a run-of-the-mill hydropower project and that suggests its "model" status: to "generate electricity in a reliable and sustainable manner" "contribute to the development of Lao PDR," and "be a reference for the hydro industry."[42]

The website of the Ministry of Energy and Mines of Laos PDR's Department of Energy Business, meanwhile, describes NT2 as "an outstanding example of how the Government of the Lao PDR is working with the private sector and multilateral organisations to develop a model of sustainable development with strong economic, social, and environment fundamentals. The Project has long been recognized by independent experts as having great potential to achieve the country's development objectives."[43]

It is widely considered by a range of development experts together with hydropower investors that the approval of NT2 demonstrated that the GoL could handle complex projects. Furthermore, given the large number of investors in NT2, including many international ones, it gave "substantial name recognition" to Laos.[44] Thus, it was a turning point in terms of investor confidence. Indeed, in Laos, a major hydropower construction boom is under way. According to the government's website, in 2016 there were twenty-two hydropower projects in operation, twenty-five under construction, thirty for which a memorandum of understanding had been agreed on, and twenty-three for which a project development agreement had been signed.[45]

In *Doing a Dam Better*, the Lao PDR country director at the time of NT2's construction, Patchamuthu Illangovan, voices a mix of concern and optimism about this construction boom:

> Although developments are mostly positive, some disturbing elements are emerging amidst the flurry of activity. . . . Currently, private sector developers, including some that may not be reputable hydropower companies, appear to be driving the agenda. To support long-term sustainable development of the country's

hydropower resources, it will be important for the government to remain focused on its priorities and core principles.[46]

However, he goes on to claim that NT2 has had a transformative effect on Laos, noting its potential as a "model" and the implications for the hydropower industry globally:

> Achievement of financial closure on NT2 in June 2005 buoyed the hydropower industry worldwide. Many countries began redrawing their energy plans to include hydropower generation, subsequently aided by the climate change debate. There was considerable interest, from many quarters, in learning more about NT2 and its evolution. Learning about NT2 and hydropower developments will continue for many years, as the industry draws vital lessons from the project's evolving practices in engineering and construction techniques, benefit sharing, environmental and social sustainability, and transparency and accountability. Through NT2, Lao PDR has a project that is playing a role in defining the direction of the industry in East Asia.

While civil society and academic researchers have critiqued claims that large hydropower dams in Laos are a form of sustainable development, representatives of the GoL have also, on numerous occasions, made clear that they would not follow NT2 as a standard again.[47] The head of the Department of Electricity within the Ministry of Energy and Mines was quoted in 2010 as stating that "yes, they are saying that Nam Theun 2 is a very good project. But to use it as a standard, it's not possible. We can use it as a good example, a good guideline, but not as a standard. All the developers say that it is not possible to use Nam Theun 2 as a standard."[48] Ben Boer and colleagues cite a senior representative of the GoL who observes that "the concession of Nam Theun 2 is too complicated and it is very difficult even for well-trained lawyers to understand." The representative explained that pre-NT2 dams were "first-generation projects," that NT2 was a "second-generation project" that involved a significantly expanded concession agreement "to meet the requirements of international funders," and that subsequent projects are "third generation," which "we tried to simplify."[49]

Promoting the Laos Hydropower Narrative Regionally and Globally

Since NT2, the GoL has sought to build Laos's credentials as a sustainable hydropower laboratory. For example, Laos hosted the Sixth International Conference and Exhibition on Water Resources and Hydropower

Development in Asia in March 2016, organized by the industry's flagship journal, the *International Journal on Hydropower and Dams*. In addressing the question "Why meet in Asia?" the conference promotional flyer states that "there are major business opportunities for all involved in advancing sustainable hydropower and multipurpose water infrastructure in Asia." Unsurprisingly, given the location, NT2 was very visible as a presenter; there were eight individual presentations on NT2, including one full session titled "NT2: A Retrospective Look at Environmental Management."

The World Bank Group has also sought to build regional institutional arrangements to build on NT2. For example, in September 2007 it convened a high-level hydropower forum between Lao PDR and Thailand for "peer-to-peer learning opportunities," although in the end it was a one-off event.[50] More recently, and more substantively, in 2012 the World Bank Group's International Finance Corporation (IFC) created a regional hydropower advisory service to work with companies, banks, and governments toward ensuring that "hydropower development follows good international industry practices so that new projects are developed and operated in an environmentally and socially sustainable way in the Mekong region." It works and networks actively in Laos, Myanmar, Pakistan, and Nepal. To this end, in 2013 the IFC and the Lao National Chamber of Commerce launched the Laos Hydropower Developers Working Group. This served as the model for a similar working group launched by the IFC in Myanmar in 2016.

NT2's Affirmative Power: World Bank's Global Reentry into Hydropower

Since the publication of the World Bank's *Water Resources Sector Strategy* in 2003, which affirmed its "high risk-high reward" approach to water infrastructure projects including large dams, subsequent reports have further asserted with increasing confidence the World Bank's reentry into large hydropower, including *Directions in Hydropower* in 2009 and *Towards a Sustainable Energy Future for All* in 2013. A Bloomberg news article detailing its reentry into hydropower, published in July 2013, observes:

> The Bank has said its newest hydropower projects are larger and more complex than ever, part of a more recent trend toward "transformational" projects, which was outlined in its infrastructure strategy for 2012–2015. The Bank's transformational projects, such as regional power grid connections and large-scale renewable energy, are intended to address systemic development challenges. . . . One

transformational project funded by the World Bank is the $1.3 billion Nam Theun 2 hydropower project in Laos, which is often regarded as the first symbol of development banks' return to large hydropower.[51]

The World Bank's (since retired) chief technical specialist for hydropower, Jean-Michel Devernay, affirmed this strategy in an interview given to the IHA in February 2014:

> The World Bank and its clients recognize that sustainable hydropower is part of the solution for tackling the development challenges outlined in our mission, which is to eradicate poverty by 2030 and promote shared prosperity in an environment that is strongly marked by climate change. . . . We plan to enhance the support that we have been providing for the past ten years.[52]

When asked which projects he would like to highlight for their potential benefits, he offered NT2 as one example: "[There] are projects of special significance, potentially with very high transformational effects on the host countries in terms of sustainable development. One example is the Nam Theun 2 project in Laos, which the Bank supported."[53]

This interview raises another notable issue regarding experts and the circulation of expertise. Devernay joined the World Bank in July 2012 and previously worked with Électricité de France (EdF) from 2002 to 2012 as deputy managing director of the Hydro Engineering Centre, where he was also involved in developing the NT2 project.[54] He is also a former vice president of the IHA. Numerous other experts who were active at the operational level of NT2 have now proceeded to more senior and influential levels of the industry.

"Sustainable Hydropower" as a Nirvana Concept: The Role of NT2

Having established that NT2 has been promoted as a "model" as an individual project, and then deployed within the narrative of the role of hydropower in Laos's broader development, as well as legitimizing the World Bank's reentry into the hydropower sector, the chapter now turns to the broader idea of sustainable hydropower as a nirvana concept. Reframing hydropower as sustainable is an important strategy the hydropower industry has used to address its legitimacy crisis. Furthermore, being able to claim hydropower as sustainable is anticipated to be important to access climate finance in the context of climate change. The focus here, however, is on how the hydropower industry, including construction companies, dam operators, and financiers, has sought to position and promote NT2 within the wider sustainable hydropower discourse.

The 1990s marked the peak of a heated debate over the costs and benefits of hydropower. The World Bank was heavily criticized for its involvement in a number of projects, such as the Pak Mun Dam in Thailand completed in 1994. In response, in 1998, the International Union for Conservation of Nature (IUCN) and the World Bank established the multistakeholder WCD. The overall conclusion of the WCD's 2000 report was that "dams have made an important and significant contribution to human development, and the benefits derived from them have been considerable." but that "in too many cases an unacceptable and often unnecessary price has been paid to secure those benefits, especially in social and environmental terms, by people displaced, by communities downstream, by taxpayers and by the natural environment."[55]

While on the whole, civil society groups supported the report's recommendations, the hydropower industry, its financiers, and many governments with plans to build dams were less supportive.[56] Some considered the WCD's recommendations too difficult to put into practice, and others found that the report downplayed the positive impacts of dams. The hydropower industry, represented by the IHA, pursued an intensive research and communication strategy to recapture the definition of "sustainable hydropower," launching the *IHA Sustainability Guidelines* in 2004 and the website sustainablehydro power.org in 2006.

The publication of the guidelines led to the preparation of an auditing tool in 2006 and in turn the creation of the Hydropower Sustainability Assessment Forum (HSAF) to develop and refine the tool in 2009. The fourteen-member forum included the IHA, commercial and development banks, governments, and large civil society groups such as the Nature Conservancy, WWF, and Transparency International. The final Hydropower Sustainability Assessment Protocol (HSAP) was officially launched at the 2011 IHA Congress. In the process of preparing the protocol, NTPC hosted a visit of the forum to the NT2 project site in early 2010. While NTPC applied the protocol tool both at its draft and final stage, the company chose not to publicly release the results.

The HSAF process and the network of actors involved in it actively produced the discourse of sustainable hydropower. Significantly, this process has led to a deepening relationship between the hydropower industry and some civil society groups. This process mirrors the one that, as Michael Goldman observes, the World Bank used to encourage some NGOs, such as IUCN and CARE International, to participate in the NT2 project, transforming them "from critical observers into constructive participants."[57]

The protocol claims to aim to improve the quality of hydropower and to address public concerns about it. Yet whether hydropower can be sustainable has been heatedly and publicly contested.[58] In addition, the idea of sustainable development is a discourse in its own right and subject to contested definitions, ranging, for example, between weak and strong versions of sustainability.[59] While the protocol has been referenced by a range of private, state, and civil society organizations and has attracted interest by the World Bank and others in Southeast Asia, not all civil society actors who assessed it were impressed.[60] In March 2012 at the World Water Forum in Marseille, the NGO International Rivers policy coordinator responded to the IHA's presentation of the HSAP by saying that it is "a greenwash of the world's dam industry" that "allows dam builders to claim they are sustainable while they continue to violate international and national environmental and human rights law."[61]

More recently, in a January 2016 article titled "Damming the Mekong: the Myth of 'Sustainable Hydropower'" published in the *Ecologist* magazine, journalist Tom Fawthrop calls "sustainable hydropower" the "new mantra of dam builders." He writes: "This term identifies a discourse that argues a well-mitigated 'nice dam,' [sic] does not inflict too much damage on the ecosystem. It is a position that offers great comfort and solace to dam developers, investors and banks under fire from environmentalists and scientists."[62] In Southeast Asia, the concept of sustainable hydropower has been debated in various forums and has spawned programs and projects. In 2008, as hydropower construction boomed in the region, including on the Mekong River's mainstream, the Mekong River Commission launched an initiative on sustainable hydropower.[63] Numerous projects were introduced to explore sustainable hydropower, including, for example, a project sponsored by SPLASH to encourage private sector involvement in research collaboration on sustainable development in the lower Mekong region.[64] Meetings exploring sustainable hydropower were also held; for example, in September 2011, M-POWER, Challenge Program on Water and Food, and WWF China organized a roundtable on sustainable hydropower in Vientiane. At this meeting, it was concluded that "while it is generally agreed that hydropower should be developed in a sustainable manner, further research and practical experience is still needed as to how sustainable hydropower can be achieved."[65]

Within this debate, NT2 was often highlighted and debated as a case study. As part of the SPLASH project, for example, Tira Foran and colleagues produced a critical review of issues related to more sustainable development of hydropower in the lower Mekong region.[66] They document a range of well-established challenges, including developer-led screening and assessment of projects, weak state capacity to regulate hydropower, and limited transparency and accountability of both private developers and the state to the public. In the report, NT2 is drawn on as a case study regarding use of the equator principles as utilized by the private-sector international lenders of NT2 and NT2's revenue management framework. The equator principles are an initiative of mainly Northern international banks meant to ensure their project financing is consistent with the IFC's performance standards. Foran and colleagues observe that whether NT2 was compliant with the equator principles has been a matter of debate between NGOs and the World Bank.

Hydropower Industry Promotes NT2: Reproducing the Sustainable Hydropower Discourse

Within the discourse of sustainable hydropower at hydropower conferences and other forums, NT2 continues to be a topic of discussion and presentation, shaping, for example, the current debate about the role of large hydropower dams in development. At World Water Week 2014 in Stockholm, Jean Comby, EdF's managing director for hydropower in France, in a session titled "Building Effective Regulatory Frameworks for Hydropower: Lessons from Water Governance" presented a case study on why NT2 is "financially, socially and environmentally viable."[67] A similar presentation was made by EdF at the World Hydropower Congress in 2015, while the chairman of the NTPC joined a panel convened by Transparency International titled "Good Corporate Governance: CEO Roundtable."

EdF promotional material, one of the NT2's main investors, unsurprisingly also highlights NT2:

> Nam Theun 2, a genuine industrial success, was designed to integrate a comprehensive set of economic, environmental and social programs, in order to improve the living conditions on the entire project area and to mitigate the effects of the project on the local populations and the surrounding ecosystems. . . . The achievements of the [NT2] project are internationally recognized and NT2 is promoted worldwide by the World Bank as a model of [a] responsible and sustainable project.[68]

Other hydropower industry groups, including law firms and commercial banks that were important in brokering NT2, also promote it as a model. The law firm DFDL operates in Laos and is now expanding its operations in Myanmar, which in many ways is the region's new hydropower frontier. At a workshop organized by the World Bank and IHA in January 2015 in the capital Nay Pyi Daw, DFDL advised on its experience in Laos and with NT2.[69] At the same meeting, the commercial bank ANZ shared its experience with NT2 and with the implementation of the equator principles, touting NT2 as an example of project financing in partnership with IFIs.[70]

While NT2 has been significant for global hydropower in general, it is especially so for Northern developers and financiers, for whom it heralded a revival of the industry under the new guise of "sustainable hydropower." Yet for another segment of the global hydropower industry originating in China and other emerging economies, NT2 is far less significant because this new generation of hydropower developers is not subject to the same environmental and social safeguard quandaries.

Conclusions: Deconstructing the NT2 Brand

This chapter has sought to explain how NT2 can be understood as a "model," how the broader problematic of Laos's hydropower construction has been constructed as a "narrative" for poverty reduction drawing on the NT2 model, and how, in sum, the "branding" of NT2 has contributed to creating and spreading a new sustainable hydropower discourse that seeks to repackage large dams and thus relegitimize the global hydropower industry. In the process, NT2 has become a symbol of that industry's revival.[71] Though the fact that the hydropower industry is backed by a large and influential set of actors and a political economy that gives it privileges within power planning practices of government cannot be ignored, the language used within the discourse of sustainable hydropower also matters.

Putting forth NT2 as a model promotes it in places beyond its history and sociopolitical context and thus divorces it from the full details of its reality. On the ground in Laos, NT2's model status is being challenged by increasingly dominant hydropower developers from emerging economies, transforming the political economy of its hydropower industry.[72] Indeed, in Laos, NT2 now stands as an anachronism, as a new wave hydropower industry has boomed rapidly around it, backed by construction companies and financiers mainly from Thailand, China, and Vietnam that mostly adhere to weaker environmental and social standards and supply less transparency and accountability.

Despite this, the World Bank and its client governments are still keen on large dams in the name of international development.[73] NT2 played, and continues to play, a key role in this debate. NT2 was a pivotal test case in the post-WCD reentry of the World Bank into hydropower. Subsequently, as the global hydropower industry rallied in response to the WCD report with the HSAP, which required defining "sustainable hydropower" itself, the practices and experiences of NT2 have become important. Most recently, as large hydropower seeks to position itself to access climate financing, the protocol and "sustainable hydropower" have been invoked as evidence by the industry of its transformation.[74] Meanwhile, in Southeast Asia, alongside Laos, Myanmar is now the new boom market for large hydropower, and there too, hydropower construction firms and financiers are seeking to demonstrate their sustainability credentials. Here, the World Bank Group's IFC has been a key actor proposing the possibility of sustainable hydropower, based on its earlier experience in Laos.

There are, of course, aspects of NT2 that improve on prior hydropower dams in Laos, but significant problems remain. This chapter does not claim that the World Bank and the wider industry wholly ignore these challenges. Yet each framing of NT2—as a model itself, within Laos's hydropower narrative, and as a part of the nirvana concept—has contributed to the discourse of sustainable hydropower. This discourse has created a knowledge regime that has revived the large hydropower dam industry and, in discursively repackaging hydropower beyond NT2, mostly perpetuated a "business as usual," or at best "business as a bit better" approach. Yet if there is to be a more genuinely sustainable energy transition, it is important to reframe the debate beyond sustainable hydropower and to look toward comprehensive forms of energy options assessments that seriously consider the now compelling arguments for more benign renewable technologies, demand-side management, and energy efficiency.[75]

NOTES

1. WCD, *Dams and Development: A New Framework for Decision-Making* (London: Earthscan, 2000).

2. Ben Boer, Philip Hirsch, Fleur Johns, Ben Saul, and Natalia Scurrah, *The Mekong: A Socio-Legal Approach to River Basin Development* (London: Routledge, 2016), 174.

3. International Rivers, *The World Bank and Dams*, pt. 2: *Dispelling the Myths of Nam Theun 2* (Berkeley, CA: International Rivers, 2015), www.internationalrivers.org/resources /9157; Bruce Shoemaker, Ian G. Baird, and Kanokwan Manorom, "Nam Theun 2: The World Bank's Narrative of Success Falls Apart," *World Rivers Review* 29, no. 4 (2014): 10–11.

4. Knowledge, Technology, and Society Team, *Understanding Policy Processes: A Review of IDS Research on the Environment* (Brighton: Institute of Development Studies, University of Sussex, 2006).

5. John S. Dryzek, *Deliberative Global Politics: Discourse and Democracy in a Divided World* (Cambridge, UK: Polity Press, 2006), 1.

6. Carl Death, "Four Discourses of the Green Economy in the Global South," *Third World Quarterly* 36, no. 12 (2015): 2211.

7. Dryzek, *Deliberative Global Politics*, 3.

8. Michael Goldman, *Imperial Nature: The World Bank and Struggles for Social Justice in the Age of Globalization* (New Haven, CT: Yale University Press, 2005), 153.

9. John S. Dryzek, *The Politics of the Earth: Environmental Discourses*, 2nd ed. (Oxford: Oxford University Press, 2005). Some writers, such as Michel Foucault and Michael Goldman, lean toward viewing discourses as hegemonic.

10. François Molle, "Nirvana Concepts, Storylines and Policy Models: Insights from the Water Sector," *Water Alternatives* 1, no. 1 (2008): 132.

11. Molle, "Nirvana Concepts, Storylines and Policy Models," 138.

12. Dryzek, *Deliberative Global Politics*, 24; see also John Dore, "An Agenda for Deliberative Water Governance Arenas in the Mekong," *Water Policy* 16, no. S2 (2014).

13. John Dore, Louis Lebel, and François Molle, "A Framework for Analysing Transboundary Water Governance Complexes, Illustrated in the Mekong Region," *Journal of Hydrology* 466–67 (2012).

14. Peter M. Haas, "Introduction: Epistemic Communities and International Policy Coordination," in "Knowledge, Power, and International Policy Coordination," special issue, *International Organization* 46, no. 1 (1992): 1–35.

15. Knowledge, Technology, and Society Team, *Understanding Policy Processes*.

16. Molle, "Nirvana Concepts, Storylines and Policy Models," 144.

17. Boer et al., *The Mekong*, 2.

18. Molle, "Nirvana Concepts, Storylines and Policy Models," 144.

19. Porter and Shivakumar, overview, *Doing a Dam Better: The Lao People's Democratic Republic and the Story of Nam Theun 2*, edited by Ian C. Porter and Jayasankar Shivakumar (Washington, DC: World Bank, 2011), 4.

20. Porter and Shivakumar, overview, 2.

21. Porter and Shivakumar, overview, 8.

22. Goldman, *Imperial Nature*, 153.

23. Porter and Shivakumar, overview, 1.

24. Robert. Goodland, "The World Bank versus the World Commission on Dams," *Water Alternatives* 3, no. 2 (2010).

25. Goldman, *Imperial Nature*, 5.

26. Goldman, *Imperial Nature*, 6–7.

27. PoE 24.

28. Jacques Leslie, "Large Dams Just Aren't Worth the Cost," *New York Times*, August 22, 2014, www.nytimes.com/2014/08/24/opinion/sunday/large-dams-just-arent-worth-the-cost.html.

29. "Nam Theun 2 Social and Environment Project," World Bank, http://projects.worldbank.org/P049290/nam-theun-2-social-environment-project?lang=en&tab=ratings.

30. Melinda Boh, "A Dam Too Far in Laos," *Asia Times*, April 12, 2013, www.atimes.com/atimes/Southeast_Asia/SEA-01-120413.html.

31. Boer et al., *The Mekong*, 192.

32. Porter and Shivakumar, overview, 23.

33. Nazir Ahmad, "Working with Stakeholders," in *Doing a Dam Better*, 108.

34. Jonathan Kent, "Lao Dam Raises Ethical Bar," *Newsweek*, August 11, 2007, www
.newsweek.com/laos-dam-raises-ethical-bar-99271.

35. "Nam Theun 2: A Way to Better Hydro Projects," *World Bank News*, September
19, 2007, www.worldbank.org/en/news/feature/2007/09/19/nam-theun-2-a-way-to-bet
ter-hydro-projects.

36. "Dam the Consequences: Big, Bad Dams Return to South-East Asia," *Economist*,
June 13, 2007, www.economist.com/node/9325886; Michael Casey, "Critics: Lao Dam Was
Bad for Villagers," International Rivers, June 27, 2007, https://www.internationalrivers
.org/resources/critics-lao-dam-was-bad-for-villagers-2919.

37. Boer et al., *The Mekong*, 158–64.

38. Boer et al., *The Mekong*, 164.

39. Ahmad, "Working with Stakeholders," 112.

40. Goldman, *Imperial Nature*, 153.

41. NTPC, "At a Glance," www.namtheun2.com/index.php/about-us/project-in-
brief.

42. NTPC, "About Us: Strategy," www.namtheun2.com/index.php/about-us/strategy.

43. NTPC, "Nam Theun 2 Background," www.poweringprogress.org/new/17-nam-
theun-2/168-nam-theun-2-background.

44. Patchamuthu Illangovan, "NT2: A Transformative Endeavor," in *Doing a Dam
Better*, 159.

45. See Ministry of Energy and Mines, Department of Energy Business, www.power
ingprogress.org/new/power-projects/operation, www.poweringprogress.org/new/power-
projects/construction, and www.poweringprogress.org/new/power-projects/plan.

46. Illangovan, "NT2," 159.

47. International Rivers, *Power Surge: The Impact of Rapid Dam Development in Laos*
(Berkeley, CA: International Rivers, 2008); Fleur Johns, "On Failing Forward: Neoliberal
Legality in the Mekong River Basin," *Cornell International Law Journal* 48 (2015).

48. Sari Jusi, "Challenges in Developing Sustainable Hydropower in Lao PDR," *International Journal of Development Issues* 10, no. 3 (2011).

49. Boer et al., *The Mekong*, 84.

50. Illangovan, "NT2," 179.

51. Andrea Vittorio, "Development Banks Step Up Lending for Hydropower, Sustainability Remains Issue," *Bloomberg BNA*, July 3, 2013, www.bna.com/development-banks-
step-n17179874891.

52. IHA, "Interview: Jean-Michel Devernay, World Bank," February 28, 2014, www
.hydropower.org/blog/interview-jean-michel-devernay-world-bank.

53. IHA, "Interview."

54. Suzanne Pritchard and Jean-Michel Devernay, "Responsible Hydropower Is Part
of the Solution," May 1, 2014, www.waterpowermagazine.com/features/featureresponsible-
hydropower-is-part-of-the-solution-4255331; www.hydropower.org/jean-michel-devernay.

55. WCD, *Dams and Development*.

56. Cathleen Seeger, Kirsten Nyman, and Richard Twum, "The Role of the German Development Cooperation in Promoting Sustainable Hydropower," *Water Alternatives* 3, no. 2 (2010).

57. Goldman, *Imperial Nature*, 160.

58. Gabriel Chong, "Challenges to Advancing Sustainable Hydropower," *CSR Asia*, May 28, 2013, www.csr-asia.com/weekly_news_detail.php?id=12259; Vittori, "Development Banks Step Up Lending For Hydropower."

59. Dryzek, *Deliberative Global Politics*, 16–18.

60. IHA, *Hydropower Status Report 2016* (London: IHA, 2016), 12.

61. International Rivers, "Activists Protest Greenwashing of Dams at World Water Forum," March 14, 2012, www.internationalrivers.org/resources/activists-protest-green washing-of-dams-at-world-water-forum-3683.

62. Tom Fawthrop, "Damming the Mekong—The Myth of 'Sustainable Hydro-power," *Ecologist*, January 16, 2016, www.theecologist.org/News/news_analysis/2986895 /damming_the_mekong_the_myth_of_sustainable_hydropower.html.

63. Mekong River Commission, "Initiative on Sustainable Hydropower," www.mrc mekong.org/about-mrc/programmes/initiative-on-sustainable-hydropower.

64. Schools Promoting Learning Achievement through Sanitation and Hygiene (SPLASH), "Water and Energy: Sustainable Development of Hydropower Involving the Private Sector in Research Collaboration in the Lower Mekong Region," http://splash-era .net/news_events3.php.

65. M-POWER, Challenge Program on Water and Food, and WWF China, "Sustainable Hydropower in the Mekong," roundtable summary, September 27, 2011, Vientiane, Lao PDR, www.mpowernetwork.org/Knowledge_Bank/Key_Reports/Dialogue_ Reports/Sustainable_Hydropower_Development_Mekong.html.

66. Tira Foran, Timothy Wong, and Shawn Kelley, "Mekong Hydropower Development: A Review of Governance and Sustainability Challenges," M-POWER Research Network, Bangkok, 2010, www.mpowernetwork.org/Knowledge_Bank/Key_Reports/Re search_Reports/Mekong_Hydropower_Development.html.

67. Alex Trembath, "Building Effective Regulatory Frameworks for Hydropower," IHA, September 12, 2014, www.hydropower.org/blog/building-effective-regulatory-frame works-for-hydropower.

68. Électricité de France regional brochure for China, Southeast Asia, South Asia, Japan and Korea (2012).

69. DFDL (Dirksen, Flipse, Doran and Le), "Attracting Investors in Hydropower: What's Needed—Lessons from Laos," paper presented at the World Bank/IHA Sustainable Hydropower and Regional Cooperation in Myanmar Workshop, Nay Pyi Daw, 2015.

70. Nicolas Le Clerc, "The Role of Equator Principle Banks in the Myanmar Context," paper presented at the Workshop on Sustainable Hydropower and Regional Development, Nay Pyi Taw, Myanmar, January 19–20, 2015, www.ifc.org/wps/wcm/connect/5e 05b580471f3cb284beec57143498e5/2.7.Le+Clerk+N.pdf?MOD=AJPERES.

71. Johns, "On Failing Forward," 356–58.

72. Carl Middleton, Jelson Garcia, and Tira Foran, "Old and New Hydropower Players in the Mekong Region: Agendas and Strategies," in *Contested Waterscapes in the Mekong Region: Hydropower, Livelihoods and Governance*, ed. François Molle, Tira Foran, and Mira Käkönen (London: Earthscan, 2009), 23–54.

73. Sophie Harman and David Williams, "International Development in Transition," *International Affairs* 90, no. 4 (2014).

74. Jamie Skinner, "Should the Green Climate Fund Flow to Hydropower?," October 31, 2016, www.iied.org/should-green-climate-fund-flow-hydropower.

75. Cheunchom Sangarasri Greacen and Chris Greacen, *Proposed Power Development Plan (PDP) 2012 and a Framework for Improving Accountability and Performance of Power Sector Planning* (Bangkok: Palang Thai, 2012).

Conclusion

Transforming Loss

BRUCE SHOEMAKER and

WILLIAM ROBICHAUD

When I argue with reality, I lose. But only 100 percent of the time.

Byron Katie, *Loving What Is* (2002)

Nam Theun 2 (NT2) was to be a new model—a large "multipurpose" hydropower project that would pair public and private investment to deliver diverse and unprecedented social and environmental benefits. It was promoted and branded, at various times and in various ways, as a project that would play a key role in meeting Thailand's growing demand for electricity; generate revenues for nationwide poverty alleviation in Laos; produce energy for Lao domestic use; deliver effective conservation of a globally important protected area; improve the lives of local people affected by the project; benefit from the engagement of independent monitors and international development and conservation organizations; expand the engagement of civil society and thereby nudge communist Laos in a more participatory direction; and stimulate a reform of the country's investment climate—all while succeeding as a profitable commercial enterprise.

Of this ambitious list, NT2 has certainly succeeded as a profitable enterprise. Indeed, with the assurances provided in NT2's power purchase agreement, concession agreement, and political risk loan guarantees, along with the project's other subsidies, it would have been difficult for it not to be successful financially, at least for its private sector investors. It has delivered large amounts of electricity to Thailand at what has turned out to be an inexpensive price—albeit electricity so far not needed in the country.

Supplying electricity to Thailand was not, however, NT2's main attraction for the World Bank, its financial partners, and the international development community, including several reputable nongovernmental organizations (NGOs) and independent monitors. The cornerstone rationale and promise of NT2, what would set it apart from large hydropower projects of the past, is that it would yield clear net benefits for both the local people and the environment of the project area, and contribute to poverty alleviation in Laos nationwide. On balance, success has remained elusive and those promises largely unmet. Neither those resettled on the Nakai Plateau nor communities affected downstream have had their livelihoods sustainably restored. The Nakai-Nam Theun National Protected Area (NNT NPA) is anything but well protected; loss of its wildlife, timber, and other biodiversity continues. And the World Bank has been unable to document that project revenues are alleviating poverty in the country.

Ironically, an area in which NT2 has had significant impact is contributing to a revival of the international hydropower industry and the branding of dams as "sustainable hydropower," as well as serving as a new, defensible template for private investment in hydropower in Laos, through which developers and investors can largely escape liability for unanticipated social and environmental costs. This institutionalized separation of revenues from a dam's true costs and liabilities in a country where public opposition to these projects is not tolerated has created an attractive environment for private hydropower financiers and developers. The phenomenon extends beyond hydropower. Investors in other sectors with significant social and environmental impacts—from mining to industrial plantations to privatized roads and railways—are often attracted to repressive political environments where they can operate under the radar and without the burden of troublesome civil society opposition.[1] Although the result in the case of NT2 is a stream of revenue for the government of the Lao PDR (GoL), there is little evidence that much of the revenue has been directed to benefit affected communities or the Lao citizenry as a whole.

It would be natural at this juncture to provide detailed recommendations for improvements in the planning, management, and implementation of such projects. This is largely the narrative of the World Bank's book *Doing a Dam Better*—that the concept of NT2 was sound and that only some aspects of the project's preparation and implementation needed tweaking to make it even more successful.

Yet a deeper critique is called for, one that goes beyond fine-tuning how such megaprojects are planned and implemented. In the midst of a rapidly changing development finance environment in Southeast Asia and beyond, the failure of NT2 to fulfill its many promises offers profound lessons, which argue for a broader reassessment of the rationale for, and ways in which, large infrastructure projects are financed and developed. This is particularly critical at a time when multilateral development banks are strongly promoting the idea that a massive increase (to $1.7 trillion per year) in infrastructure investment is needed in Asia in order to "maintain growth momentum, eradicate poverty and respond to climate change."[2]

The first question is why, really, was NT2 built? Why did the World Bank, at a time it was smarting from the scathing critique of the World Commission on Dams (WCD), pick such a challenging and ambitious project, one already well along in its planning, as its new model project? NT2 was risky on many levels. First, large hydropower dams are, of course, much more complicated and generally have more serious social and environmental impacts than more modest projects. Yet the Bank inaugurated its new model with the largest project to be built in the Mekong basin at the time. It jumped in at the deep end. Second, as a trans-basin diversion, NT2 affected two major rivers, resulting in especially widespread impacts. Third, the adjacent protected area is of high international conservation significance. The promise to keep it well protected if the Nakai Plateau was sacrificed for the project has proved, as predicted, difficult to keep. Fourth, in all project zones, residents (including large numbers of Indigenous Peoples) are highly dependent on natural resources, including fish and forest products, and have relatively low levels of formal education. It is challenging for people in such situations to rapidly adapt to precipitous changes in their livelihoods. Lastly, because the electricity was sold to another country, the bar was set particularly high to demonstrate widespread benefits for Laos itself. Planning for NT2 started before the WCD process, and the World Bank could have used the WCD findings in 2000 to credibly justify not going ahead with the project. Instead it repackaged, or rebranded, NT2 as a new WCD-compliant model of hydropower. The Bank opted for spin and wishful thinking.

One answer to the question of why, given the risks, NT2 was built is perhaps that it was never really about poverty alleviation (or environmental protection) as much as about wealth creation—for foreign investors, the World Bank's longtime client, the Electrical Generating Authority of Thailand, and elements within the GoL. The Bank may also have seen it as an opportunity to demonstrate that it could pull off a successful public–private partnership, hasten a socialist country's transition to the type of market economy promoted by the World Bank and its main supporters, and encourage large-scale investment to generate growth in a least developed country through a demonstrably successful and profitable project.

In striving to support projects that will be profitable for its clients and itself, the World Bank has long been attracted to large development projects and their economies of scale. Internal inertia and organizational habit may have inhibited the Bank from accepting and acting on the WCD's conclusion that large hydropower and, by implication, other large infrastructure were too socially and environmentally damaging. Rather than give up on large dams, the Bank instead tried to invent for hydropower a new rationale, a new model. This suggests an institution, rather like an addict, either in denial of the need for change or incapable of making such change.

Placing a Model Project in Laos

An important consideration is whether NT2's shortcomings are related more to specifics of the implementing environment in Laos or the challenges of constructing large infrastructure in developing countries generally.

Many Lao people, both within the GoL and in other institutions, were committed to positive outcomes and sincerely believed that NT2 offered an important opportunity for their country. Many tried very hard, with commitment and in good faith, to make NT2 successful. Still, Laos was certainly a highly questionable choice for the Bank's first try for its new hydropower model. To be considered successful, this new model was required to meet WCD-era high standards of participation, consultation, and assent from affected communities, as well as demonstrate deep commitment and accountability on the part of those tasked with implementing the social and environmental aspects of the project. As detailed in chapter 1, in 2005, when the Bank approved NT2, conditions in Laos were far short of those required.

Moreover, the country had limited experience in and capacity for managing projects as large and complicated as NT2. By definition, model projects need considerable transparency and public participation and should involve partners with relatively high capacity for flexible and effective management—all of which are in short supply in Laos. These issues were expediently overlooked amid overall enthusiasm for the project. Or perhaps some stakeholders viewed the shortcomings in transparency as useful attributes for implementation of a potentially contentious project.

Despite the Bank's rhetoric touting NT2 as a transformative project, its implementation has, as chapter 10 shows, done little to address these fundamental issues. In fact, things may be worse now than when the project commenced. For example, when the World Bank approved NT2 in 2005, the country ranked in the upper half in Transparency International's Corruption Perceptions Index (a higher ranking being indicative of lower levels corruption); as of 2015, Laos's ranking had deteriorated to the bottom 18 percent, and it is now perceived as one of the most corrupt countries in the world.[3] Clearly, expecting one large project to transform an entrenched political economy was folly.

The World Bank's engagement with the GoL through NT2 was an attempt to construct an island of accountability in a sea of poor governance, where a lack of commitment to key project objectives—namely, prioritizing the welfare of local people and the conservation of nature—was evident. Despite hopes that the island would influence the larger sea, the opposite happened—the island has been eroded and inundated by the sea around it. Those who endorsed the project, including the Bank's financial partners, some NGOs, monitoring bodies such as the International Environmental and Social Panel of Experts (PoE) and the International Advisory Group, the governments of France and Australia, multiple development consultants, diplomats, and other interested parties, all put faith in both the willingness and the ability of the World Bank to shepherd positive outcomes despite the daunting obstacles faced by NT2. That faith has not been rewarded.

The reality is that such a megaproject was mismatched to Laos's current state of development, and the country's own political priorities. In such an environment neither the World Bank's periodic expressions of concern, seldom if ever backed up with sanctions, nor the PoE's criticisms, even as they grew stronger over time, were sufficient to ensure positive outcomes for affected communities, nor effective conservation of NNT NPA.

During NT2's planning, there was much discussion about the environmental, social, and Indigenous Peoples safeguard policies of the World Bank and wide recognition among Bank staff that the safeguards would play an important role in achievement of the project's ambitious social and environmental objectives. However, the findings of our book indicate that those safeguards proved impotent in the political environment in Laos. Even less realistic were the Bank's accountability mechanisms. Established procedures were unable to overcome the political constraints on civil expression and organization in Laos, with the result that project-affected local people had (and continue to have) limited options to express and resolve project-related grievances. Use of the Bank's formal independent compliance mechanism appeared out of the question, given the repercussions local people might have faced if they initiated a formal complaint. As a result, confidence in the Bank's supposedly exhaustive due diligence processes, its capacity to accurately assess the potential risks and benefits of a large project, and its willingness and ability to hold borrowers to their promises, has been tarnished.

The World Bank and its financial partners went into NT2 describing it as a high risk–high reward project. In response, they developed strong mechanisms—political risk insurance guarantees—to shield NT2's private investors from risks to their capital. In contrast, the people and places exposed to the social and environmental risks of NT2 did not receive equivalent guarantees of protection. More than any other factor, the Bank's primary orientation toward investors rather than local communities and the environment set the tone for what followed.

Perhaps the most important lesson to be learned from this can be distilled to a general principle: supporting high-risk projects—those with the potential for severe social and environmental impacts—in countries with significant governance issues is fundamentally inappropriate and likely to cause more harm than good.

NT2 and Large Hydropower Globally

Despite the international hydropower industry's NT2-inspired rhetoric of sustainable hydropower described in chapter 13, it has become extremely difficult to build new projects in countries with reasonably open civil societies. There are few, if any, examples around the world where the type of consultative and participatory process envisioned by the WCD, if implemented, would actually result in the construction of new large hydropower projects.

Beyond issues of governance, the NT2 experience points to some basic problems with the implementation of large hydropower generally—and perhaps of any large infrastructure project.

The leitmotif of *Doing a Dam Better*, echoed by many of NT2's supporters over the years, was that the project could be made successful, or more so, by tweaks to the process of planning, the project's system of controls, and, of course, the availability and security of sufficient funding. Rarely was reflection brought to the possibility that NT2's problems (to the limited extent they have even been acknowledged) stemmed from a fundamentally flawed concept.

This optimism is rooted in a narrative within the broader international development industry—that, with enough experts and enough money (and good management of communication and public relations), success can be wrested from the jaws of even deeply problematic projects. This optimism was found in many of the firms, consultants, advisors and development professionals who engaged with and, in many cases, profited handsomely from, NT2.

Unfortunately, this misplaced optimism was a poor substitute for a sober analysis of what would happen during implementation of the grand plans and the influx of financial resources, within the reality of the country's political economy.

Despite the stake that the World Bank and others may have in the ongoing narrative of NT2 as a successful new model of global importance, it has become increasingly hard to continue to deny the project's failings. NT2 *has* become a model, of another sort: a model of how difficult, or perhaps impossible, it is to restore to predisturbance levels the ecosystems, Indigenous cultures, and local livelihoods disrupted by large infrastructure projects—to make things as good or better than before—regardless of how many studies, agreements, programs, advisors, funds, and best intentions are poured into the attempt. Not all damage can be fixed and not all impacts can be mitigated. In fact, mitigation can generally treat only the margins, leaving core social and environmental issues unresolved.

By 2000 the WCD had already cast doubt on the viability of large hydropower. In response, the World Bank and other institutions tried to craft a new model of sustainable hydropower. As manifested in NT2, however, the new model has proved untenable. This leaves the international hydropower industry, along with its financial supporters, promoting a myth rather than a model with a positive track record. Supported and promoted not just by the World Bank but a broad collaboration of international financial institutions and bilateral agencies, NT2's disappointing reality is not an outlier, and it cannot be written off as just a learning experience. In fact, it joins a long list of previous hydropower projects (many described in the report of the WCD) whose substantial social and environmental costs outweigh their benefits. It is difficult to look closely at what happened in NT2 without sharing the same conclusion as Thayer Scudder, after his long career studying hydropower and twenty years of service on the NT2 PoE: "Large dams just aren't worth the cost."[4]

Lessons Learned?

Whether the World Bank and its financial partners will acknowledge, much less apply, these lessons remains unknown. But there are ample signs for concern.

In the years following the completion of NT2, the World Bank made a series of pronouncements about how it was now back in the large hydropower business. The implication was that, with NT2, the Bank had finally gotten the model right and could justify large dams based on their social and environmental benefits. As late as September 2015, with the failures of NT2's Downstream Compensation Program already well documented by the PoE and independent reports, World Bank staff, in a public forum at the Bank's annual meeting, still claimed that the Bank had learned how to mitigate downstream hydropower impacts, citing NT2 in Laos as evidence of improvement.[5]

In his 2014 book, *Foreclosing the Future: The World Bank and the Politics of Environmental Destruction*, Bruce Rich, who has followed NT2 since 1991 and covers its planning in his book, writes about the failure of the World Bank to learn from its past mistakes, noting that "failed governance at all levels is almost invariably at the root" and that the Bank has demonstrated a chronic inability to accomplish its lofty social and environmental goals. He cites a 2011 internal report that "identified troubling perversities that critics maintained had characterized much Bank lending over the past 20 years; the Bank's negligence in carrying out its own environmental policies, the inability or unwillingness of borrowing governments to adhere to these policies, and a systemic weakness of governance in many countries (which is a polite way of referring to pervasive corruption)."[6] Rich concludes his book by noting that "for the World Bank to make a greater contribution, it will have to learn from its experience rather than flee from it. The world can ill afford institutions that have built amnesia into their bureaucratic DNA."[7]

A slowly increasing recognition and, in some quarters, begrudging acknowledgment of NT2's failings appear to be leading some hydropower proponents to institute damage control by claiming they have learned from NT2's mistakes. But have they? In late 2015, staff of International Rivers and Mekong Watch visited the headquarters of the Asian Development Bank (ADB) in Manila to discuss an ADB-supported hydropower project under construction in Laos, Nam Ngiep 1, following research in twenty-three project-affected villages. Many similarities can be drawn between NT2's history and the preparations for Nam Ngiep 1, including a lack of thorough analysis of a "no project" option; comprehensive cumulative impact assessment prior to construction; free, prior, and informed consent by Indigenous Peoples living upstream, downstream, and in the immediate project area (villagers reported that because they understood the project was backed by the GoL, they could not oppose it); and the absence of a workable complaints/monitoring mechanism. In addition, the project location overlaps with a military security zone, leaving it difficult for independent monitors to access some parts of the project area.

In the meeting, ADB staff acknowledged that NT2's social and environmental mitigation programs had largely failed to achieve their stated objectives. Still, they insisted that lessons had been learned and would be applied to make other hydropower projects in Laos, like Nam Ngiep 1, a success.[8] However, recent reports by Nam Ngiep 1's Independent Advisory Panel recite a familiar litany of problems for anyone familiar with NT2—among them that the dam's construction is on schedule while the biodiversity, environmental offset, and social programs are far behind schedule; a failure to ensure biomass clearance; poor quality of land availability at resettlement sites; and hundreds of unresolved complaints and increased tensions between Indigenous villagers to be resettled and GoL authorities. The panel's February, 2017 report notes that the situation is serious enough that the Nam Ngiep 1 Power Company is in danger of violating its concession agreement.[9]

While the World Bank and ADB have been slow, or reluctant, to absorb these lessons, some other international development agencies are taking significant steps toward real reform. In December 2016, the influential Netherlands Commission for Environmental Assessment, which advises the Dutch Ministry of Foreign Affairs regarding the environmental impacts of its overseas aid, released a comprehensive review on hydropower. It recommends a much more cautious approach to large hydropower and suggests that donors put consideration for good governance and human rights at the *center* of their decision making—a different approach than that taken with NT2.

NT2 in a Changing Development Context

The lessons of NT2 come at a time of rapid transition in how large hydropower and other infrastructure projects are justified, financed, and implemented in Southeast Asia and globally. Three distinct yet related developments highlight these transitions: the continuing growth of China's influence and the World Bank's response to that influence, the expanding role of the private sector in hydropower financing, and the relationship of infrastructure to poverty reduction.

In 2015, China led the establishment of a new regional development bank, the Asian Infrastructure Investment Bank. As its name indicates, it makes no pretense of its focus on building things. It is not only about infrastructure, however, but also geopolitics. The US is not a member, and its establishment was probably in part a response to China's limited influence within the World Bank, despite the country's growing economic strength. Given the Asian Infrastructure Investment Bank's considerable size, the role the World Bank and ADB play in determining whether risky infrastructure projects will proceed in less developed Asian countries will surely shrink.[10]

The Asian Infrastructure Investment Bank's safeguard policies, while still subject to further refinement, appear in general to be less rigorous than those of the World Bank. This will be attractive to borrowers who wish to avoid high standards of accountability and the sort of external monitoring that robust safeguards require.

While official pronouncements insist that the World Bank and ADB will not really compete with the Asian Infrastructure Investment Bank, due to the seemingly unlimited demand for infrastructure in Asia, this remains to be seen. The fact is that the World Bank and ADB are no longer the only, or even the main, shows in town when it comes to financing large infrastructure in Asia. This already appears to be stimulating a dilution of the World Bank's environmental and social safeguard standards. A paper by staff of a development bank–monitoring NGO about proposed changes to World Bank safeguards policies that would put more responsibility for monitoring and enforcing safeguards on the borrowing countries, notes the potential for this to create an "acute risk that Bank-financed projects would lead to human rights violations. This is especially true for cases in which the project would be implemented in weak governance or authoritarian environments, not uncommon amongst the Bank's clients."[11]

Beyond emerging competition from the Asian Infrastructure Investment Bank, the World Bank now also faces an Asia awash in new private sources of development financing of various types, including commercial banks and state-led export credit agencies. Meanwhile, countries like China, India, Vietnam, and Thailand increasingly have their own expertise in the construction of large dams, as well as in arranging the various contractual arrangements. In this sense, the World Bank, as well as ADB, is now less important as a source of expertise and money. An example of this trend is the Xayaburi Hydroelectric Power Project in Laos, the first dam on the Mekong River below China, and a project even larger than NT2. The project is so patently controversial and problematic that the World Bank and the ADB steered clear of it. But their involvement wasn't needed. The private sector developers procured private financing for the dam's US$2.7 billion price tag through Thai commercial banks and the Thai export–import state agency (as in the case of NT2, most of the dam's electricity will be exported to Thailand).

In Laos and recently Myanmar, the World Bank now directs much of its support toward private hydropower developers through its private sector lending arm, the International Finance Corporation (IFC). The IFC claims that its involvement is intended to improve the environmental and social standards of private developers. This assertion is controversial, to say the least. Not only does the IFC face the same political-economic issues, but here it is engaging directly with the private sector—motivated solely by profit—rather than public institutions working, as in the case of NT2, with private partners. The IFC's ability to genuinely improve environmental and social private sector standards on the ground, rather than just on paper, is questionable. For example, its performance in the financial sector has been called into question in a series of recent reports by NGOs and by its own accountability mechanism, the World Bank's Office of the Compliance Advisor/Ombudsman.[12]

NT2 was premised on the idea that nationwide poverty reduction could be achieved through construction of a large infrastructure project. Locally, the same project could benefit the lives of people directly affected. Despite the lack of evidence of either in the case of NT2—which given the resources poured into it, was the best shot for a large infrastructure project to realize these hopes—claims that large dams can reduce poverty are still made by hydropower proponents, including in Laos, both by the development banks and among the new private sector players. For instance, the Pak Beng hydropower project, now proposed by a Chinese company as another mainstream Mekong dam, uses poverty reduction as a justification throughout its social planning documents. This seems ingenuous at best. No mechanisms are evident that would direct project revenues towards poverty reduction at either the local or national levels, and the budget for social mitigation and compensation is a small fraction of NT2's. The discourse of poverty alleviation is used to justify the large projects, which then result in the opposite—by displacing or removing Indigenous and other rural communities from the natural resource base, be it land, forests or rivers, on which they have depended for their livelihoods.

Some observers believe that the justification of large infrastructure as a vehicle for poverty alleviation is losing its credibility and is increasingly downplayed within the World Bank.[13] Whether or not the NT2 experience has contributed to this change is unclear, but the project certainly offers fertile ground.

Implications: Beyond Development by Destruction

The Nam Theun River probably meandered across the Nakai Plateau for more than a million years, sustaining a wealth of living things, including, for thousands of years, human residents of the plateau. It took only a few years of NT2 construction to destroy this ancient ribbon of life, and we must now ask ourselves if the costs and the benefits have been worth it. The findings of this book suggest that they have not.

This still leaves the consequences of NT2, scattered about the project area as if after a storm: resettled people who still struggle for basic, secure livelihoods; more people downstream along the Xe Bang Fai whose livelihoods remain disrupted; and ongoing loss of wildlife, timber, and other elements of biodiversity from a globally important protected area. While it is undoubtedly tempting for the World Bank and its financial partners to try to arrange a face-saving exit from the project as soon as possible, that would be ill advised. Although much of NT2's damage cannot be undone, a debt is still owed to the people and the environment of the project area. To at least approach satisfaction of this obligation, the World Bank and its partners must continue their assistance and engagement for a long time to come and in ways that are more effective than those to-date.

In the meantime, the myth of NT2's success persists. Hydropower proponents cite it and the concept of sustainable hydropower and poverty alleviation to justify new projects—not only in Laos and the Mekong region but elsewhere, in places like Myanmar, Nepal, Pakistan, and a number of African countries. Large hydropower projects supported by international financial agencies continue to be proposed, planned, and implemented in the developing world.

Still, some recent trends are starting to work against large hydropower, including the emergence of renewables and, particularly, as mentioned in chapter 11, solar power (unfortunately, far less so to date in Southeast Asia than some other regions the World Bank is active in). In places like Myanmar, where past restrictions on civil society have eased, strong movements against large dam projects have emerged. In the end, NT2 may well be seen as an aberration during a brief and misguided period of World Bank return to support for large hydropower.

The NT2 experience has shown that, if anything, World Bank safeguards are either not strong enough or are too difficult to apply, especially in a country like Laos. The question that emerges is how the World Bank, at a time when it faces increased pressure to lower these standards, will respond. Will it join a race to the bottom and further weaken its safeguards, dispensing with all but a rhetorical commitment to social and environmental benefits? What is needed now is not another model based on claims of having learned technical and procedural lessons, but rather a profound and unflinching understanding by the Bank of NT2's failings, and their broader implications, followed by sincere and sustained efforts to redress the damage the project caused. The Bank would learn best by first making amends, rather than embarking on new model projects elsewhere.

In the wake of NT2, many things are dead in the water, both literally and figuratively: trees of a forest that once lined the banks of the middle Nam Theun River and provided nesting sites for some of Laos's last white-winged ducks and fish eagles; natural mineral licks once visited by the plateau's wild elephants; traditional village sites of the plateau's residents; grasses that once fattened villagers' cattle and water buffaloes; and finally, perhaps, a misplaced confidence that human livelihoods and the environment are best supported by first destroying them, and a reductionist and puerile belief that the complex processes and relationships that define a society can be easily transformed by constructing a large thing, at one instant in time.

But like a lotus, which in largely Buddhist Laos is an important symbol of enlightenment for its ability to rise through mud and water to bloom at the water's bright surface, truth and something better can surface from Nam Theun 2's reservoir of disappointment. The project still has potential to be transformative, just not in the way its proponents envisioned. The needed transformation is within the World Bank and its financial partners. These institutions would do well to step back from financing large projects in environments that lack the conditions necessary to ensure positive, sustainable results, especially for affected people and the planet's remaining areas of high conservation value.

For the World Bank to achieve this, it will need to mature beyond its culture of wishful thinking, and change its orientation from the wants of the private sector to the needs of communities and the environment in the countries it serves. A helpful step will be to accept and acknowledge the disappointing results of NT2.

NOTES

1. The same type of poverty alleviation rhetoric is often used as justification for such projects. For example, an industry overview of the Lao mining sector notes that "the Lao government has clear strategies and policies to promote mining in Laos in order to stimulate economic development and to eradicate poverty" ("Overview of the Lao Mining Sector," SES Professionals, http://sesprofessionals.com/overview-of-laos-mining-industry).

2. ADB, *Meeting Asia's Infrastructure Needs*, February 2017, xi, https://www.adb.org /sites/default/files/publication/227496/special-report-infrastructure.pdf.

3. See www.transparency.org/research/cpi/cpi_2005/o and www.transparency.org /cpi2015#results-table.

4. This is the title of the *New York Times* piece discussed in chapter 2, in which Scudder reveals his final disillusionment with large dams.

5. Joshua Klemm, "Bad Student: Has the World Bank Learned Its Lessons?," International Rivers, October 14, 2015, https://www.internationalrivers.org/blogs/352-3.

6. Bruce Rich, *Foreclosing the Future: The World Bank and the Politics of Environmental Destruction* (Washington, DC: Island Press, 2013), 8.

7. Rich, *Foreclosing the Future*, 240.

8. Tanya Roberts-Davis, former International Rivers staff, personal communication to Bruce Shoemaker, November 2016.

9. ADB, Nam Ngiep 1 Hydropower Project, report 8, February 20, 2017.

10. As of mid-2017, Asian Infrastructure Investment Bank capital is $100 billion, making it two-thirds the size of the ADB and about half the size of the World Bank.

11. Natalie Bugalski, "The Demise of Accountability at the World Bank," *American University International Law Review* 31, no. 1 (2016), 16.

12. See Dustin Roasa, *Outsourcing Development: Lifting the Veil on the World Bank Group's Lending through Financial Intermediaries*, Inclusive Development International, Asheville, NC, October 2016, www.inclusivedevelopment.net/wp-content/uploads/2016/09/Outsourcing-Developmnet-Introduction.pdf; Sophie Edwards, "IFC Still Failing to Track Impact of Its Investments on Local Communities," DEVEX, March 17, 2017, www.devex.com/news/ifc-still-failing-to-track-impact-of-investments-on-local-communities-reports-say-89821.

13. Joshua Klemm, policy analyst for International Rivers, personal communication to Bruce Shoemaker, April 2017.

Afterword

Bookending Nam Theun 2

PHILIP HIRSCH

I have only been to the Nakai Plateau twice. The first time was in February 1991, when I spent ten days on it conducting a short research trip soon after the Snowy Mountains Engineering Corporation (SMEC) had submitted a draft report on social and environmental implications of the proposed Nam Theun 2 (NT2) Dam.[1] The second time was in November 2012, a few years after the dam had been completed. Both visits were memorable and extraordinary. Even more extraordinary is what happened to the Nakai Plateau and the people living there in the intervening years.

It took two days to travel from Vientiane to Nakai for my first visit; a *laisse passe* permit with a ministerial signature was required for our group to travel outside Vientiane. Crowded into an old *lot katien* (Russian jeep) with dreadful suspension were our driver Inpan—with a zany but slightly repetitive sense of humor, the frequent bumps in the road punctuated with "You'll never have kids now!"—a minder from the Department of Forestry, a research team of three (one Australian, one Thai, one Lao), and, from the Khammouane provincial capital of Thakhek onward, a young security staffer with a rifle. At our overnight stop at the town of Pakxan, along what was then a rutted and dusty Route 13, the main road running the length of Laos, we joined an evening *boun*, whose lighting and sound system were powered by a diesel generator in what was still a pre-mains electricity era outside Vientiane. Every second dance or so I was called on as the *siewsaan* (expert) from Australia who was helping build the friendship bridge across the Mekong. This was very much the old Laos, on the cusp of the development era.

On reaching the plateau, our first concern was whether we'd have enough fuel to visit the villages we had identified for a circular route along the road toward Lak Xao, then by boat up river from the Nam Theun bridge as far as Ban Don, and back to Thakhek, as well as for a side trip to the proposed dam site downstream of where the river flows off the plateau. We were lucky. A military fuel truck headed in the opposite direction kindly—and unofficially— sold us another tankful. We bumped our way along the dusty tracks from village to village, stopping to conduct interviews on livelihoods and people's awareness of and thoughts about the impending dam, assessing the likely impacts of what had been the object of the US$1 million study recently carried out by SMEC. We spent longer periods of time in two villages, Ban Don and Ban Sop-On, both reached by taking a small boat up the Nam Theun River while our vehicle was sent to pick us up several days later at Sop On. Once amid the isolation of the plateau, we had more or less free rein to travel wherever we wanted and talk to whomever we wished.

Our study trip came up with several main findings. One was that life was pretty hard for people living on the Nakai Plateau. Not only were they making a living off farming poor soils, with their swiddens more reliable than permanent paddy cultivation on flood-prone land with low clay content, but their crops and livestock were subject to regular predations by elephants and tigers. Another was that the mainly ethnic Makong and Thai Bo people, as they called themselves, had a close association with the plateau despite having had to move in the past, as the area had been bombed when it was used as a western route of the Ho Chi Minh trail during the Second Indochina War. And yet another—most poignant for the purposes of our research—was that very few people had heard of the proposed NT2 dam that was slated to flood their homes, and even the village leaders who were aware saw it as a distant prospect not worth spending too much time worrying about. There was great faith, in any case, that "the Party [would] lead the way" (*phak nam phaa*) and that in any case decisions depended on "superiors" (*khang theung*).

Our side visit to the proposed dam site itself showed us some of the beauty of the forested river as it left the plateau. We also encountered Japanese foresters overseeing the operations of the pine logging that was run together with the Lao military's development company, Bolisat Phattana Khet Phoudoi. They were traveling around the plateau more luxuriously than ourselves, in Land Rovers and, very sensibly, with masks to keep out the fine road dust that ultimately cost me two or three days without a voice by the end of the visit.

When I returned to Thailand from this trip I was invited to write two feature pieces for the *Nation* newspaper in Bangkok.[2] One was specifically about Nakai and NT2, while the other questioned whether all the "projects" that were mushrooming in Laos really foreshadowed development. When I returned from my sabbatical a couple of months later, a letter from the Australian ambassador was waiting for me, expressing displeasure at the fact that I had used my academic position to write for a newspaper. Concerned that I had overstepped the mark, I showed the NT2 article to two Lao colleagues, both in senior government roles (one is now a minister). Neither thought that anything I had written was particularly problematic. This was a time of innocence compared to what was to come, in a country that, on the one hand maintained secretive one-party political control, but that on the other had yet to face the cutting edge of debates over large dams and other controversial development projects. I heard later that the ambassador was relaying complaints he had received from Australian consultants rather than Lao authorities.

In September 1991, the SMEC assessment report was finalized.[3] I published a working paper in October that combined findings from our research trip with a critique of the SMEC study.[4] I sent the report to various places, including the World Bank. The response this time was much more positive, albeit bizarre. Three weeks after putting it in the post (this was of course long before the days of email), I was woken up at my Sydney home at 1 a.m. by a phone call from Jamil Sopher, the NT2 task manager. He told me that the report was one of the more informative items he had read on NT2, and he invited me to come and discuss it when I was next in Washington, with an eye to establishing a consultancy of some kind.

Fast forward a few years. In March 1995, on my next sabbatical, I spent a few days at the World Bank's headquarters in Washington, DC. Jamil Sopher was most helpful, both in giving his own views of what would and would not help make NT2 a good project and by introducing me to some of those in various departments who were also involved. These included Robert Goodland, who was instrumental in establishing the Environment Department at the World Bank and who, even at that relatively early stage, was very negative about the Bank's involvement in the dam project. Much more upbeat was a bright young South Asian sociologist who had recently been given the portfolio for resettlement and social issues. Excited to meet someone who had spent time on the plateau (she had yet to visit), she suggested a consultancy for further study and asked me to jot down a few key points of concern. I told her that one of my main surprises was that there had been no mention, either in my reading of World Bank documents or conversation with the task manager, of the Bank's operational directive on Indigenous Peoples, despite the fact that from my observation the people whose homes were to be flooded clearly matched the criteria for indigeneity under the Bank's own definitions. She immediately cautioned me that this would go nowhere: the task manager was growing impatient with the protracted delays to the project and invoking the need for an Indigenous Peoples development plan would draw things out further, so it was better not to bring this up.

Fast forward again, this time to November 2012. Arriving at a rough and ready shop in the village of Ban Phone Sa-On on a minibus with four Australian academic colleagues, I descend to ask whether—as suggested by the name's reference to the On River, combined with the Lao word meaning "raised area" (*phone*) and the term for "pleasant" (*sa-on*)—the village had moved from the original location of Ban Sop-On. The first person we encounter is a young woman selling a few convenience goods. She is too young to remember the old village but points me to her father, whose back is to us. As he turns, we both recognize each other from nearly twenty-two years previously, when I stayed with the family for a couple of nights. Following this extraordinary re-union, we spend a couple of hours listening to him and a growing group of curious neighbors describe their experience of the dam resettlement process, mainly the hardship they face in losing their cattle, in not been able to make a living from cultivating the very limited area of rocky land allocated to farming, and in seeing the initially abundant reservoir fishery start to decline. It is not clear whether the dwindling fish catches are due to the natural tail off in primary productivity that is a feature of tropical reservoirs or whether it is due to competition from outsiders who are circumventing regulations reserving the fishing to resettled communities. To be fair, the villagers also express appreciation for some of the comforts that have come with electricity and road access at the same time that they voice concerns over how much longer it will be possible to make a living on the plateau.

That one can arrive at Ban Phone Sa-On after just several hours' drive from Vientiane makes for a stark contrast to the 1991 journey. Finding the village at the edge of an enormous reservoir also makes the place quite unrecognizable. The hardship that the villagers most emphasize is that of having to pretend to all the regular visiting delegations that life is now so much better than it was pre-dam. We are told that when international visitors come as part of the frequent occasions to showcase the dam and the resettlement villages, local authorities prepare villagers ahead of the visit with thinly veiled warnings that speaking out of line will carry consequences. There are hardly opportunities for direct interaction with such visitors, as there are language barriers, and most communication happens at staged meetings in the presence of the authorities. The fact that we have showed up sans entourage, with no official minders, and are able to communicate in Lao, as well as the familiarity that comes with recognition from the much earlier visit, seems to provoke an outpouring of complaint. But it is a very brief encounter.

Earlier in the day, prior to ascending the escarpment, we had stopped at the visitor center to view the impressive displays and to be shown around the powerhouse where water from the reservoir exits the penstock tunnel that takes it through a 350-meter drop from the plateau, where it turns the huge turbines. The Australian manager of the center had been both gregarious and apologetic as he explained that we would have to make our own way around the project area unchaperoned, as the NT2 International Environmental and Social Panel of Experts (PoE) had just arrived and needed looking after. Of course, we were delighted with this transparency in a country whose official-dom has long since become very wary and controlling of information flow, impressed by the island of free rein that is the NT2 project area.

We were also conscious, of course, that the NT2 project provides a partly internationalized island of governance in which the norm of transparency is purveyed to outsiders.[5] The unimpeded access is definitely not a continuing product of the isolation that gave us relatively free rein in our conversations on the plateau two decades earlier.

An equally bizarre encounter was to occur later the same evening after we checked into the Wooden Guesthouse, a comfortable lodge operated by the Nam Theun 2 Power Company (NTPC). The members of the PoE were staying there too, and we arranged to have dinner with them. An impressive group of octogenarians with experience running international organizations and advising US presidents, they introduced themselves as having a combined age of 247 years. The three of them regaled us with stories of their travels and findings during the twenty trips they had made since the late 1990s. All this conversation took place at an upmarket French restaurant near the Wooden Guesthouse, in Ban Oudomsouk, where the road descends from the plateau, over a gourmet meal washed down with ample French wine. The contrast with the circumstances of the 1991 visit could not have been starker.

Just as stark was the way NT2 had brought global players and institutions to what had previously been one of the more remote places that I had had the opportunity to visit and study. Ten years previously, I had written an essay on the extent to which the debates and interactions on NT2 tended to be framed largely as a discourse among foreigners, engendering tensions between com-pliance by governmental as well as local actors, on the one hand, and the global norms brought to the process by institutions such as the World Bank and NGOs alike, on the other.[6] It was only with the strange encounters during my visit in 2012, however, that the internationalization of the project and the ways in which local residents and environments had become roped into these wider agendas really hit home.

Clearly something extraordinary had happened during the two decades between my visits. What had happened carries meaning not only for the Nakai Plateau and the wider impact area of NT2 but also for many other places in a world in which global institutions, expectations, and practices can transform lives, locales, and landscapes to such an extent.

This book should be read with this wider significance in mind; its message should therefore not be taken only as a critique of one particular dam, nor indeed should it be understood as restricted to lessons from the construction of large dams in general. Rather, the message can be carried to the host of other large, internationalized infrastructure projects whose proponents make big claims and whose public and private financiers and regulators continue to shift risks away from investors and onto the people and environments most affected.

NOTES

1. SMEC, *Nam Theun 2 Hydroelectric Project: Situation Report*, UNDP/World Bank, 1990.

2. Philip Hirsch, "Projects Galore; but Development?," *Nation* (Bangkok), April 27, 1991; Philip Hirsch, "Development Dilemmas Facing Laos," *Nation* (Bangkok), April 28, 1991.

3. SMEC, *Nam Theun 2 Hydroelectric Project Feasibility Study: Environmental Assessment*, UNDP/World Bank, 1991.

4. Philip Hirsch, "Environmental and Social Implications of Nam Theun Dam, Laos" (working paper no. 5, Environmental and Regional Restructuring Research Unit, Departments of Economics and Geography, University of Sydney, October 1991).

5. Ben Boer, Philip Hirsch, Fleur Johns, Ben Saul, and Natalia Scurrah, *The Mekong: A Socio-legal Approach to River Basin Development* (London: Routledge, 2016). See chapter 6.

6. Philip Hirsch, "Global Norms, Local Compliance and the Human Rights-Environment Nexus: A Case Study of the Nam Theun II Dam in Laos," in *Human Rights and the Environment: Conflicts and Norms in a Globalizing World*, ed. Lyuba Zarsky (London: Earthscan Press, 2002), 147–71.

Bibliography

Abugre, Charles. *Still Sapping the Poor: The IMF and Poverty Reduction Strategies.* World Development Movement, June 2000.

Adams, James W. Foreword to *Doing a Dam Better: The Lao People's Democratic Republic and the Story of Nam Theun 2*, edited by Ian C. Porter and Jayasankar Shivakumar, ix–x. Washington, DC: World Bank, 2011.

Adams, Patricia. "Patronage Canada." Probe International, April 2, 1997. https://journal.probeinternational.org/1997/04/02/patronage-canada.

ADB, *Meeting Asia's Infrastructure Needs.* February 2017. www.adb.org/sites/default/files/publication/227496/special-report-infrastructure.pdf.

ADB. Nam Ngiep 1 hydropower project. Report 8, February 20, 2017.

ADB. *Vietnam: Phu My 202 Power Project.* Project Number 35914, February 2011. https://www.adb.org/sites/default/files/evaluation-document/35553/files/35914-vie-validation.pdf.

ADB. *Summary Environmental and Social Impact Assessment: Nam Theun 2 Hydroelectric Project in Lao People's Democratic Republic.* November 1, 2004. http://documents.worldbank.org/curated/en/524881468266127390/pdf/383810LA0IDASECM20041079 20k01PUBLIC1.pdf.

Ahmad, Nazir. "Working with Stakeholders." In *Doing a Dam Better: The Lao People's Democratic Republic and the Story of Nam Theun 2*, edited by Ian C. Porter and Jayasankar Shivakumar, 99–116. Washington, DC: World Bank, 2011.

Alonso i Terme, Rosa, and Homi Kharas. "Lao PDR Gets Ready for NT2." In *Doing a Dam Better: The Lao People's Democratic Republic and the Story of Nam Theun 2*, ed. Ian C. Porter and Jayasankar Shivakumar, 33–50. Washington, DC: World Bank, 2011.

Alton, Charles, and Latsamay Sylavong. *Socio-Economic Technical Report.* Vientiane: IUCN, 1997.

Ansar, Atif, Bent Flyvberg, Alexander Budzier, and Daniel Lunn. "Should We Build More Large Dams? The Actual Costs of Hydropower Megaproject Development." *Energy Policy* 69 (2014): 43–56.

Arizu, Beatrice, Luiz Maurer, Jamil Saghir, and Bernard Tenenbaum. "Pass Through of Power Purchase Costs: Regulatory Challenges and International Practices." Discussion paper no. 10, Washington, DC, World Bank Energy and Mining Sector Board, February 2004.

Arthington, Angela H., and Stephen R. Balcombe. "Extreme Flow Variability and the 'Boom and Bust' Ecology of Fish in Arid-Zone Floodplain Rivers: A Case History with Implications for Environmental Flows, Conservation and Management." *Ecohydrology* 4, no. 5 (2011): 708–20.

Bakker, Karen. "The Politics of Hydropower: Development the Mekong." *Political Geography* 18, no. 2 (1999): 209–32.

Baird, Ian G. "Land, Rubber and People: Rapid Agrarian Changes and Responses in Southern Laos." *Journal of Lao Studies* 1, no. 1 (2010): 1–47.

Baird, Ian G. "Translocal Assemblages and the Circulation of the Concept of 'Indigenous Peoples' in Laos." *Political Geography* 46 (2015): 54–64.

Baird, Ian G., and Keith Barney. "The Political Ecology of Cross-Sectoral Cumulative Impacts: Modern Landscapes, Large Hydropower Dams and Industrial Tree Plantations in Laos and Cambodia." *Journal of Peasant Studies* 44, no. 4 (2017): 769–95.

Baird, Ian G., and Noah Quastel. "Rescaling and Reordering Nature-Society Relations: The Nam Theun 2 Hydropower Dam and Laos-Thailand Electricity Networks." *Annals of the Association of the American Geographer* 105, no. 6 (2015): 1221–39.

Baird, Ian G., and Bruce Shoemaker. *Aiding or Abetting? Internal Resettlement and International Aid Agencies in the Lao PDR.* Probe International, August 2005.

Baird, Ian G., and Bruce Shoemaker. "Unsettling Experiences: Internal Resettlement and International Agencies in Laos." *Development and Change* 38, no. 5 (2007).

Baird, Ian G., Bruce Shoemaker, and Kanokwan Manorom. "The People and Their River, the World Bank and Its Dam: Revisiting the Xe Bang Fai River in Laos." *Development and Change* 46, no. 5 (2015): 1080–105.

Ball, Jeff, Jim Elston, Majorie Sullivan, and Andrew Walker. *Review of Nam Theun 2 Hydroelectric Dam: Final Report to AUSAID.* Australian Agency for International Development, February 21, 2005.

Banker, Kadra, Michael J. Pathak, and Joshua M. Pearce. "A Review of Solar Photovoltaic Levelized Cost of Electricity." *Renewable and Sustainable Energy Reviews* 15, no. 9 (2011): 4470–82.

Baran, Eric, Ian G. Baird, and Gregory Cans. *Fisheries Bioecology in the Khone Falls Area (Mekong River, Southern Laos).* Penang: WorldFish Center, 2005.

Baranson, Mara T. "Reflections on Implementation." In *Doing a Dam Better: Lao People's Democratic Republic and the Story of Nam Thuen 2,* ed. Ian C. Porter and Jayasankar Shivakumar, 147–56. Washington, DC: World Bank, 2011.

Barney, Keith. "China and the Production of Forestlands in Lao PDR: A Political Ecology of Transnational Enclosure." In *Taking Southeast Asia to Market: Commodities, Nature and People in the Neoliberal Age,* ed. Joseph Nevins and Nancy Lee Peluso, 91–107. Ithaca, NY: Cornell University Press, 2008.

Baxter, Willam H., and Laurent Sagart. *Old Chinese: A New Reconstruction.* New York: Oxford University Press, 2014.

Blake, David J. H. "Independent Technical Review: NT2 Impacts on Xe Bang Fai Fisheries." IRN and Environmental Defense, January 2005. www.internationalrivers.org/sites /default/files/attached-files/nt2fishimpacts.05.02.09.pdf.

Boer, Ben, Philip Hirsch, Fleur Johns, Ben Saul, and Natalia Scurrah. *The Mekong: A Socio-Legal Approach to River Basin Development.* London: Routledge, 2016.

Boonratana, Ramesh. "DUDCP: Draft Lessons Learned, Wildlife Expert's Contribution." Unpublished report, DUDCP, 2003.

Bugalski, Natalie E. "The Demise of Accountability at the World Bank." *American University International Law Review* 31, no. 1 (2016): 1-56.

Canonico, Gabrielle C., Angela H. Arthington, Jeffrey K. McCrary, and Michele L. Thieme. "The Effects of Introduced Tilapias on Native Biodiversity." *Aquatic Conservation: Marine and Freshwater Ecosystems* 15, no. 5 (2005): 463–83.

Chamberlain, James R. "Eco-Spatial History: A Nomad Myth from the Annamites and Its Relevance for Biodiversity Conservation." In *Landscapes of Diversity: Indigenous Knowledge, Sustainable Livelihoods and Resource Governance in Montane Mainland Southeast Asia,* ed. Xu JianChǔ and Stephen Mikesell, with the assistance of Timmi Tillmann and Wan Shum, 421–36. Kunming: Yunnan Science and Technology Press, 2003.

Chamberlain, James R. "Kra-Dai and the Proto-History of Southern China and Vietnam." *Journal of the Siam Society* 104 (2016): 27–77.

Chamberlain, James R. "Mène: A Tai Dialect Originally Spoken in Nghệ An (Nghê Tinh), Viêtnam—Preliminary Linguistic Observations and Historical Implications." *Journal of the Siam Society* 79 (1991): 103–23.

Chamberlain, James R. *Nature and Culture in the Nakai-Nam Theun Conservation Area.* Vientiane: privately published, 1997.

Chamberlain, James R. "The Origin of the Sek: Implications for Tai and Vietnamese History." *Journal of the Siam Society* 86 (1998): 27–48.

Chamberlain, James R. *Participatory Poverty Assessment: Lao PDR.* Vientiane: National Statistics Center, 2001.

Chamberlain, James R. *Participatory Poverty Assessment: Lao PDR.* Vientiane: National Statistics Center, 2006.

Chamberlain, James R. "Vietic Speakers and Their Remnants in Khamkeut District (Old Khammouane)." In *Festschrift for Prof. Udom Warotamasikkhadit.* Forthcoming.

Chamberlain, James R., Charles Alton, Latsamay Silavong, and Bounlieng Philavong. *Socio-Economic and Cultural Survey: Nam Theun 2 Project Area.* Vientiane: CARE International, 1996.

Chamberlain, James R., Charles Alton, Latsamay Silavong, and Panh Phomsombath. *Cultural Diversity and Socio-Economic Development in the Context of Conservation: Environmental and Social Action Plan for Nakai-Nam Theun Catchment and Corridor Areas.* Vientiane: IUCN, 1997.

Chanudet, Vincent, Stéphane Descloux, Atle Harby, Håkon Sundt, Bjørn Henrik Hansen, Odd Brakstad, Dominique Serça, and Frédéric Guérin. "Gross CO_2 and CH_4 Emissions from the Nam Ngum and Nam Leuk Sub-Tropical Reservoirs in Lao PDR." *Science of the Total Environment* 409, no. 24 (2011): 5382–91.

Chanudet, Vincent, Pierre Guédant, Wanidaporn Rode, Arnaud Godon, Frédéric Guérin, Dominique Serça, Chandrashekhar Deshmukh, and Stéphane Descloux. "Evolution of the Physico-Chemical Water Quality in the Nam Theun 2 Reservoir and Down-stream Rivers for the First 5 Years after Impoundment." *Hydroécol* 19 (2016): 27–61.

Chape, Stuart. *Nakai-Nam Theun NBCA and Proposed NT2 Hydropower Dam: A Status Report on Key Issues and Implications for IUCN.* IUCN, May 2000.

Chirarattananon, Surapong, Pipat Chaiwiwatworakul, Vu Duc Hien, Pattana Rakkwa-musuk, and Kuskana Kubaha. "Assessment of Energy Savings from the Revised Building Energy Code of Thailand." *Energy* 35 (2010): 1741–53.

Chirarattananon, Surapong, and Juntaken Taweekun. "A Technical Review of Energy Conservation Programs for Commercial and Government Buildings in Thailand." *Energy Conversion and Management* 44, no. 5 (2003): 743–62.

Cottet, Maud, Stéphane Descloux, Pierre Guédant, Philippe Cerdan, and Régis Vigouroux. "Fish Population Dynamic in the Newly Impounded Nam Theun 2 Reservoir (Lao PDR)." *Hydroécol* 19 (2016): 321–55.

Coudrat, Camille N. Z., Chanthalaphone Nanthavong, Sengphachanh Sayavong, Arlyne H. Johnson, Jim B. Johnston, and William Robichaud. "Non-Panthera Cats in Nakai-Nam Theun National Protected Area, Lao PDR." *CATNews* 8 (2014): 45–52.

Creak, Simon. "Laos in 2013: International Controversies, Economic Concerns, and the Post-Socialist Rhetoric of Rule." *Southeast Asian Affairs* (2014): 149–71.

Cuisinier, Jeanne. *Les Mường: Géographie humaine et sociologie.* Paris: Institute d'ethnologie, 1948.

Daviau, Steeve. "Organisations à but non lucratif: Timide émergence de la société civile en République démocratique populaire lao." *Canadian Journal of Development Studies/Revue canadienne d'études du développement* 30, nos. 3–4 (2010): 403–20.

Death, Carl. "Four Discourses of the Green Economy in the Global South." *Third World Quarterly* 36, no. 12 (2015): 2207–24.

deBuys, William. *The Last Unicorn: A Search for One of the Earth's Rarest Creatures.* New York: Little, Brown, 2015.

Del Rosario, Teresita Cruz. *The State and the Advocate: Development Policy in Asia.* London: Routledge, 2014.

Demarty, Maud, and Julie Bastien. "GHG Emissions from Hydroelectric Reservoirs in Tropical and Equatorial Regions: Review of 20 Years of CH4 Emission Measurements." *Energy Policy* 39, no. 7 (2011): 4197-206.

Descloux, Stéphane, Pierre Guedant, Dousith Phommachanh, and Ruedi Luthi. "Main Features of the Nam Theun 2 Hydroelectric Project (Lao PDR) and the Associated Environmental Monitoring Programmes." *Hydroécol* 19 (2016): 5–25.

Dheeraprasart, Veerawat. "Why NT2 Will Not Save Wildlife." *Watershed* 1, no. 3 (1996): 41–43.

Diffloth, Gérard. "Vietnamese as a Mon-Khmer Language." In *Papers from the First Annual Meeting of the Southeast Asian Linguistics Society*, ed. Martha Ratliff and Eric Schiller, 125–39. Tempe: Arizona State University, Program for Southeast Asian Studies, 1992.

Dore, John. "An Agenda for Deliberative Water Governance Arenas in the Mekong." *Water Policy* 16, no. S2 (2014): 194–214.

Dore, John, Louis Lebel, and François Molle. "A Framework for Analysing Transboundary Water Governance Complexes, Illustrated in the Mekong Region." *Journal of Hydrology* 466–67 (2012): 23–36.

Dryzek, John S. *Deliberative Global Politics: Discourse and Democracy in a Divided World.* Cambridge, UK: Polity Press, 2006.

Dryzek, John S. *The Politics of the Earth: Environmental Discourses.* 2nd ed. Oxford: Oxford University Press, 2005.

Duckworth, J. William, Richard E. Salter, and Khamkhoun Khounboline, comps. *Wildlife in Lao PDR.* 1999 status report. Vientiane: IUCN /WCS/CPAWM, 1999.

Duke Center for International Development. "Some Cross-Cutting Lessons." In *Doing a Dam Better: Lao People's Democratic Republic and the Story of Nam Thuen 2,* ed. Ian C. Porter and Jayasankar Shivakumar, 127–45. Washington, DC: World Bank, 2011.

Dung, Vu Van, Pham Mong Giao, Nguyen Ngoc Chinh, Do Tuoc, Peter Arctander, and John MacKinnon. "A New Species of Living Bovid from Vietnam." *Nature* 363 (1993): 443–45.

Dunn, Bruce, Haresh Kamath, and Jean-Marie Tarascon. "Electrical Energy Storage for the Grid: A Battery of Choices." *Science* 334, no. 928 (2011): 928–35.

du Pont, Peter. *Nam Theun 2 Hydropower Project (NT2): Impact of Energy Conservation, DSM, and Renewable Energy Generation on EGAT's Power Development Plan.* Danish Energy Management, Bangkok, March 24, 2005. http://siteresources.worldbank.org /INTLAOPRD/Resources/DSMmarch2005.pdf.

du Pont, Peter. *Nam Theun 2 Hydropower Project (NT2): Impact of Energy Conservation, DSM and Renewable Energy Generation on EGAT's Power Development Plan.* Final report, World Bank, August 28, 2004.

Dyson, Megan, Ger Bergkamp, and John Scanlon, eds. *Flow: The Essentials of Environmental Flows.* Gland, Switzerland: IUCN, 2003.

EGAT. *2005 Annual Report.* Nonthaburi: EGAT, 2005. https://www.egat.co.th/en/images /annual-report/annualReport-2005.pdf.

EGAT. *2010 Annual Report.* Nonthaburi: EGAT, 2010. www.egat.co.th/en/images/annual-re port/annualReport-2010.pdf.

EGAT. *2015 Annual Report.* Nonthaburi: EGAT, 2015. https://www.egat.co.th/en/images /annual-report/2015/egat-annual-eng-2015.pdf.

Electrowatt. *Power Sector Strategy Study.* Final report, vol. 1, Asian Development Bank, 2001.

Enfield, N. J., and Gérard Diffloth. "Phonology and Sketch Grammar of Kri, a Vietic Language of Laos." *Cahiers de linguistique—Asie oriental* 38, no. 1 (2009): 3–69.

Environmental Defense. "Review of the Nakai-Nam Theun Social and Environmental Management Framework and First Operational Plan (SEMFOP-1) for the Nam Theun Hydropower Project." Environmental Defense, 2005.

Environmental Investigation Agency. *Borderlines: Vietnam's Booming Furniture Industry and Timber Smuggling in the Mekong Region.* London: Environmental Investigation Agency, 2008.

Environmental Investigation Agency. *Checkpoints: How Powerful Interest Groups Continue to Undermine Forest Governance in Laos*. London: Environmental Investigation Agency, 2012.

Environmental Investigation Agency. *Crossroads: The Illicit Timber Trade between Laos and Vietnam*. London: Environmental Investigation Agency, 2011.

Ferlus, Michel. "Langues et peuples viet-muong." *MKS* 26 (1996): 7–28.

Ferlus, Michel. "Le maleng brô et le vietnamien." *MKS* 27 (1997): 55–66.

Ferlus, Michel. "Sur l'origine des langues Việt-Mường." *MKS* 18–19 (1992): 52–59.

Fernandez, Claudio, and Ismail Dalla. *Increasing Private Sector Participation and Improving Efficiency in State Enterprises*. Vol. 2, Main Report, Industry and Energy Operations Division, Country Department I, East Asia and Pacific Regional Office World Bank, October 11, 1994. http://documents.worldbank.org/curated/en/857581468761095177/pdf/multiopage.pdf.

Foppes, Joost. *Domestication of Non-Timber Forest Products in the Nakai-Nam Theun NBCA*. DUDCP, June 2001.

Foran, Tira, Peter du Pont, Panom Parinay, and Napaporn Phumaraphand. "Securing Energy Efficiency as a High Priority: Scenarios for Common Appliance Electricity Consumption in Thailand." *Energy Efficiency* 3, no. 4 (2010): 347–64.

Foran, Tira, and Kanokwan Manorom. "Pak Mun Dam: Perpetually Contested?" In *Contested Waterscapes in the Mekong Region: Hydropower, Livelihoods and Governance*, ed. François Molle, Tira Foran, and Mira Käkönen, 55–80. London: Earthscan, 2009.

Foran, Tira, Timothy Wong, and Shawn Kelley. "Mekong Hydropower Development: A Review of Governance and Sustainability Challenges." M-POWER Research Network, Bangkok, 2010. www.mpowernetwork.org/Knowledge_Bank/Key_Reports/Research_Reports/Mekong_Hydropower_Development.html.

Fozzard, Adrian. *Technical Brief, Revenue and Expenditure Management*. Nam Theun 2 Hydroelectric Project, The World Bank, Washington DC, March 16, 2005.

Fraisse, André. "Les sauvages de Nam-Om." *BSEI* 24, no. 1 (1949): 27–36.

Franklin, Barbara A. K. *A Review of Local Public Consultations for the Nam Theun 2 Hydroelectric Project*. World Bank, September 1997.

"From Pak Mun: Ten Years Later." *Watershed* 10, no. 1 (2004): 38–44.

"Gas Turbine Power Plant Suppliers Adapting to Global Project Demand." *Gas Turbine World* 34, no. 2 (2004): 14–17.

Geller, Howard. "Fostering a Clean Energy Revolution." *Cogeneration and On-Site Power Production* 4, no. 5 (2003): 26–31.

Goldman, Michael. *Imperial Nature: The World Bank and Struggles for Social Justice in the Age of Globalization*. New Haven, CT: Yale University Press, 2005.

Goldsmith, Edward, and Nicholas Hilyard. *The Social and Environmental Effects of Large Dams*. Wadebridge, UK: Wadebridge Ecological Centre, 1984.

Goodland, Robert. "The World Bank versus the World Commission on Dams." *Water Alternatives* 3, no. 2 (2010): 384–98.

Greacen, Cheunchom Sangarasri. "Falling Demand for Electricity, Rising Demands for

Change: EGAT and Its Legacy in the Era of Privatization." *Watershed* 4, no. 1 (2004): 33–40.

Greacen, Cheunchom Sangarasri, and Chris Greacen. *Proposed Power Development Plan (PDP) 2012 and a Framework for Improving Accountability and Performance of Power Sector Planning.* Bangkok: Palang Thai, 2012.

Greacen, Cheunchom Sangarasri, and Chris Greacen. "Thailand's Electricity Reform: Privatization of Benefits and Socialization of Costs and Risks." *Pacific Affairs* 77, no. 3 (2004): 517–41.

Greacen, Chris. *Decentralizing Thai Power: Towards a Sustainable Energy System.* Bangkok: Greenpeace Southeast Asia and Palangthai, 2006.

Greacen, Chris, and Apsara Palettu. "Electricity Sector Planning and Hydropower in the Mekong Region." In *Democratizing Water Governance in the Mekong Region*, ed. Louis Lebel, John Dore, Rajesh Daniel, and Yang Saing Koma, 93–125. Chiang Mai: Mekong Press 2007.

Greacen, Chris, and Detcharut Sukkamnoed. *Did the World Bank Fudge Figures to Justify Nam Theun 2?* Bangkok: Palangthai, 2005. www.palangthai.org/docs/NT2EconMalfeas Refs.pdf.

Grossin, Pierre. *Notes sur l'histoire de la province de Cammon.* Hanoi: Imprimerie d'extrême orient, 1933.

Guttal, Shalmali, and Bruce Shoemaker. "Manipulating Consent: The World Bank and Public Consultation in the Nam Theun 2 Hydroelectric Project." *Watershed* 10, no. 1 (2004): 18–25.

Haas, Peter M. "Introduction: Epistemic Communities and International Policy Coordination." In "Knowledge, Power, and International Policy Coordination." Special issue, *International Organization* 46, no. 1 (1992): 1–35.

Haas, Peter M. *Saving the Mediterranean: The Politics of International Environmental Cooperation.* New York: Columbia University Press, 1990.

Hardin, Garrett. "The Tragedy of the Commons." *Science* 162, no. 3859 (1968): 1243–48.

Harman, Sophie, and David Williams. "International Development in Transition." *International Affairs* 90, no. 4 (2014): 925–41.

Higham, Charles. "Hunter-Gatherers in Southeast Asia: From Prehistory to the Present." *Human Biology* 85, no. 1 (2013): 21–43.

Hildyard, Nicholas. *More Than Bricks and Mortar: Infrastructure-As-Asset Class, Financing Development or Developing Finance?* Dorset, UK: Corner House, 2012. www.thecorner house.org.uk/sites/thecornerhouse.org.uk/files/Bricks%20and%20Mortar.pdf.

Hirsch, Philip. "Environmental and Social Implications of Nam Theun Dam, Laos." Working paper no. 5, Environmental and Regional Restructuring Research Unit, Departments of Economics and Geography, University of Sydney, October 1991.

Hirsch, Philip. "Global Norms, Local Compliance and the Human Rights-Environment Nexus: A Case Study of the Nam Theun II Dam in Laos." In *Human Rights and the Environment: Conflicts and Norms in a Globalizing World*, ed. Lyuba Zarsky, 147-71. London: Earthscan, 2002.

Hoanh, Chu Tai, Thierry Facon, Try Thuon, and Ram C. Bastakoti. "Irrigation in Lower Mekong Basin Countries: The Beginning of the New Era." In *Contested Waterscapes in the Mekong Region: Hydropower, Livelihoods and Governance*, ed. François Molle, Tira Foran, and Mira Käkönen, 143–72. London: Earthscan, 2009.

Hodgdon, Benjamin. "Frontier: The Political Culture of Logging and Development on the Periphery in Laos." *Kyoto Journal* 69 (2008): 58–65.

Hodgdon, Benjamin. "No Success Like Failure: Policy versus Reality in the Lao Forestry Sector." *Watershed* 12, no. 1 (2007): 37–46.

Horn, Robert. "Laos' Old Guard Masks Future Prospects." *Asia Today International* 18, no. 7 (2000): 15.

IAG. "Nam Theun 2: Handing Over." Report 10, June 2011.

IAG. *World Bank's Handling of Social and Environmental Issues in the Nam Theun 2 Hydropower Project in the Lao PDR.* Report 1, August 19, 1997. http://documents.worldbank .org/curated/en/860761468276563271/pdf/multi-page.pdf.

IHA. *Hydropower Status Report 2016.* London: IHA, 2016.

Illangovan, Patchamuthu. "NT2: A Transformative Endeavor." In *Doing a Dam Better: The Lao People's Democratic Republic and the Story of Nam Theun 2*, edited by Ian C. Porter and Jayasankar Shivakumar, 157–76. Washington, DC: World Bank, 2011.

Imhof, Aviva, and Shannon Lawrence. "An Analysis of Nam Theun 2 Compliance with WCD Strategic Priorities." IRN and Environmental Defense, February 2005. www .internationalrivers.org/sites/default/files/attached-files/nt2wcdanalysis2005.pdf.

International Rivers. *Failure to Restore: An Assessment of the Impacts of the Theun-Hinboun Dam Projects on Downstream Communities in Laos.* Berkeley, CA: International Rivers, 2014.

International Rivers. *Power Surge: The Impact of Rapid Dam Development in Laos.* Berkeley, CA: International Rivers, 2008.

International Rivers. *The World Bank and Dams.* Pt. 2: *Dispelling the Myths of Nam Theun 2.* Berkeley, CA: International Rivers, 2015. https://www.internationalrivers.org/re sources/9157.

IRN. *Agriculture and Livestock Development Plan.* Berkeley, CA: IRN, 2005.

IRN. *Power Struggle: The Impacts of Hydro-Development in Laos.* Berkeley, CA: IRN, 1999.

IRN and Friends of the Earth and Environmental Defense Fund. *Gambling with People's Lives: What the World Bank's New "High-Risk/High-Reward Strategy Means for the Poor and the Environment.* June 2003.

IUCN. *Environmental and Social Management Plan Management Plan for the Nakai Nam Theun Catchment and Corridor Areas.* May 1, 1998.

Janus, Heiner, Stephan Klingebiel, and Sebastian Paulo. "Beyond Aid: A Conceptual Perspective on the Transformation of Development Cooperation." *Journal of International Development* 27, no. 2 (2015): 155–69.

Johns, Fleur. "On Failing Forward: Neoliberal Legality in the Mekong River Basin." *Cornell International Law Journal* 48, no. 2 (2015): 347–83.

Jusi, Sari. "Challenges in Developing Sustainable Hydropower in Lao PDR." *International Journal of Development Issues* 10, no. 3 (2011): 251–67.

Karim, Lamia. *Microfinance and Its Discontents: Women in Debt in Bangladesh.* Minneapolis: University of Minnesota Press, 2011.

Karlgren, Bernhard. *Grammatica Serica Recensa. Bulletin of the Museum of Far Eastern Antiquities* 29 (1957).

Katie, Byron. *Loving What Is.* New York: Harmony Books, 2002.

Korzybski, Alfred. *Science and Sanity: An Introduction to Non-Aristotelian Systems and General Semantics.* Lancaster, PA: Science Press Printing, 1933.

Kottelat, Maurice. "Fishes of the Nam Theun and Xe Bangfai Basins, Laos: With Diagnoses of Twenty-two New Species (Teleostei: Cyprinidae, Balitoridae, Cobitidae, Coiidae, and Odontobutidae)." *Ichthyological Explorations of Freshwaters* 9, no. 1 (1998): 1–128.

Knowledge, Technology, and Society Team. *Understanding Policy Processes: A Review of IDS Research on the Environment.* Brighton: Institute of Development Studies, University of Sussex, 2006.

Kuenzer, Claudia, Ian Campbell, Marthe Roch, Patrick Leinenkugel, Vo Quoc Tuan, and Stefan Dech. "Understanding the Impacts of Hydropower Developments in the Context of Upstream–Downstream Relations in the Mekong River Basin." *Sustainability Science* 8, no. 4 (2013): 565–84.

Kujala, Saara. *Improving Power System Efficiency with Fast Flexible Power.* Wärtsilä Singapore, 2012. http://pennwell.sds06.websds.net/2012/bangkok/pga/papers/T2S3O1-paper.pdf.

Lahmeyer International and Worley International. *Nam Theun 2 Study of Alternatives.* March 1998.

Lamech, Ranjit, and Kazim Saeed. "What International Investors Look For When Investing in Developing Countries." Discussion paper no. 6, World Bank, May 2003.

Lauginie, Francis. "Organizational Review of the WMPA, Inception Report: Main Observations and Recommendations." Working document, World Bank and the GoL Department of Planning and Cooperation of the Ministry of Natural Resources and Environment, 2014.

Lawrence, Shannon. "The Nam Theun 2 Controversy and Its Lessons for Laos." In *Contested Waterscapes in the Mekong Region: Hydropower, Livelihoods and Governance,* ed. François Molle, Tira Foran, and Mira Käkönen, 81–110. London: Earthscan, 2009.

Lawrence, Shannon. "World Bank Hypes Nam Theun 2 as Project Deadline Looms." *World Rivers Review* 19, no. 5 (2004): 16.

Lawrence, Shannon. *The World Bank's International Technical Workshops on Nam Theun 2.* Civil society summary, Environmental Defense, October 1, 2004. www.international rivers.org/sites/default/files/attached-files/techwkspsum11.11.04.pdf.

Lazarus, Kate. "Driving Change in the Hydro Sector." International Water Power and Dam Construction, Hydropower Developers Working Group, April 14, 2015.

Leslie, Jacques. *Deep Water: The Epic Struggle over Dams, Displaced People, and the Environment.* New York: Picador, 2005.

Liddell Hart, B. H. *Strategy.* London: Faber and Faber, 1954.

Lohmann, Larry. "Mekong Dams in the Drama of Development." *Watershed* 3, no. 3 (1998): 50–60.

Louis Berger International. "Economic Impact Study of Nam Theun 2 Dam Project." World Bank, Washington, DC, June 12, 1997.

Lovei, Laszlo. "The Single Buyer Model: A Dangerous Path to Competitive Electricity Markets." *Public Policy for the Private Sector*, note no. 225 (December 2000): 1–4. http://siteresources.worldbank.org/EXTFINANCIALSECTOR/Resources/2828 84-1303327122200/225Lovei-1211.pdf.

Lovins, Amory. *Small Is Profitable: The Hidden Economic Benefits of Making Electrical Resources the Right Size.* Boulder, CO: Rocky Mountain Institute, 2003.

Macey, Paul. "Etude ethnographique et linguistique sur les K'Katiam-Pong-Houk, dits: Thai Pong (province du Cammon-Laos)." *Revue indochinois* 5 (1906): 1411–24.

Malaluan, Jenina Joy Chavez, and Shalmali Guttal. *Poverty Reduction Strategy Papers: A Poor Package for Poverty Reduction.* Focus on the Global South, Bangkok, January 2003.

Mayes, Warren Paul. "Unsettled Post-Revolutionaries in the Online Public Sphere." *Sojourn* 24, no. 1 (2009): 89–121.

McCully, Patrick. *Silenced Rivers: The Ecology and Politics of Large Dams.* London: Zed Books, 1996.

McCully, Patrick. "World Bank Takes U-Turn on Supporting Critical Nature Area." *World Rivers Review* 10, no. 3 (1995).

MEE Net. *Following the Money Trail of Mekong Energy Industry.* Bangkok, September, 2013. www.meenet.org/wp-content/uploads/2015/08/Following-the-Money-Trail-of-Mekong-Energy-Industry-2013_English.pdf.

MEE Net. "Know Your Power: Toward a Participatory Approach for Sustainable Power Development in the Mekong Region." Conference report, Chulalongkorn University, Bangkok, January 18–19, 2012.

Mekong Watch. Nam Theun 2 dam project site, field survey report, December 2010. http://www.mekongwatch.org/PDF/NT2FieldReportNov2010.pdf.

Merme, Vincent, Rhodante Ahlers, and Joyeeta Gupta. "Private Equity, Public Affair: Hydro Financing in the Mekong Basin." *Global Environmental Change* 24 (2014): 20–29.

Middleton, Carl, Jelson Garcia, and Tira Foran, "Old and New Hydropower Players in the Mekong Region: Agendas and Strategies." In *Contested Waterscapes in the Mekong Region: Hydropower, Livelihoods and Governance*, ed. François Molle, Tira Foran, and Mira Käkönen, 23–54. London: Earthscan, 2009.

Mirumachi, Naho, and Jacopo Torriti. "The Use of Public Participation and Economic Appraisal for Public Involvement in Large-scale Hydropower Projects: Case Study of the Nam Theun 2 Hydropower Project." *Energy Policy* 47 (2012): 125–32.

Molle, François. "Nirvana Concepts, Storylines and Policy Models: Insights from the Water Sector." *Water Alternatives* 1, no. 1 (2008): 131–56.

Molle, François, Louis Lebel, and Tira Foran. "Contested Mekong Waterscapes: Where to Next?" In *Contested Waterscapes in the Mekong Region: Hydropower, Livelihoods and*

Governance, ed. François Molle, Tira Foran, and Mira Käkönen, 383–431. London: Earthscan, 2009.

Monoram, Kanakwan, Ian G. Baird, and Bruce Shoemaker. "The World Bank, Hydropower-Based Poverty Alleviation and Indigenous Peoples: On-the-Ground Realities in the Xe Bang Fai River Basin of Laos." *Forum for Development Studies* 44, no. 2 (2017): 275–300.

Multilateral Investment Guarantee Agency. *Hydropower in Asia*. June 2006, www.miga .org/documents/NT206.pdf.

"Nam Theun II Power Deal Signed." *Watershed* 1, no. 1 (1995): 5.

"Nam Theun 2: No Time for Another Mistake." Editorial, *Watershed* 10, no. 1 (2004): 2–3.

NTPC. *Environmental Assessment and Management Plan*. Vol 2., March 1, 2005. http:// documents.worldbank.org/curated/en/221591468090579103/pdf/E3850v9orev0 EAMPoMarch005.pdf.

NTPC. *Nakai Resettlers' Reality: From the Past to the Future*. August 2014. www.namtheun2 .com/images/Document_for_website/Nakai%20Resettlers'%20Reality%20From%20 the%20Past%20to%20the%20Future/Nakai%20resettlers%20reality%20-%20Final .pdf.

NTPC. *Social Development Plan*. Final draft, 4 vols., March 2005.

NT2 WMPA. *Social and Environmental Management Framework and First Operational Plan*. April 1, 2005, to September 30, 2011. World Bank, January 2005.

Norconsult, *Regional Indicative Master Plan on Interconnection in the Greater Mekong Subregion*. ADB, July 2002.

Norconsult. *Subregional Energy Sector Study for the Greater Mekong Subregion*. ADB, 1995.

Pahlman, Charlie. "Build-Operate-Transfer (B.O.T.): Private Investment in Public Projects . . . or Just More Public Subsidies for the Private Sector?" *Watershed* 2, no. 1 (1996): 49–52.

Pahlman, Charlie. "Where Investors Fear to Tread: Risks and the Nam Theun 2 Dam." *Watershed* 3, no. 1 (1997): 53–55.

Palettu, Apsara. "Thailand's Power Sector Reform: Privatisation or Piratisation?" *Watershed* 9, no. 2 (2004): 10–18.

Permpongsacharoen, Witoon. *Technical Review of the World Bank's "Nam Theun 2 Hydro Power Project Regional Economic Least-Cost Analysis, Draft Final Report," and "Nam Theun 2 Project Economics, Interim Summary Report."* National Economic and Social Advisory Council, Bangkok, March 14, 2005. www.terraper.org/web/sites/default/files /key-issues-content/1283331157_en.pdf.

"Plan for Thailand Electricity Sector: 'Economic Nonsense.'" *Watershed* 9, no. 2 (March 2004): 7.

PoE. Nam Theun 2 hydropower project. Report 1, February 7, 1997 (PoE 1).

PoE. Nam Theun 2 hydropower project. Report 2, July 26, 1997 (PoE 2).

PoE. Nam Theun 2 hydropower project. Report 3, January 21, 1998 (PoE 3).

PoE. Nam Theun 2 hydropower project. Report 4, January 24, 1999 (PoE 4).

PoE. Nam Theun 2 hydropower project. Report 5, January 22, 2001 (PoE 5).

PoE. Nam Theun 2 hydropower project. Interim report, March 2002 (PoE 5.5).

PoE. Nam Theun 2 hydropower project. Report 6, March 21, 2003 (PoE 6).

PoE. Nam Theun 2 hydropower project. Report 7, March 2, 2004 (PoE 7).

PoE. Nam Theun 2 hydropower project. Report 8, February 7, 2005 (PoE 8).

PoE. Nam Theun 2 hydro project. Report 9, February 15, 2006 (PoE 9).

PoE. Nam Theun 2 multipurpose project. Report 10, October 30, 2006 (PoE 10).

PoE. Nam Theun 2 multipurpose project. Report 11, February 23, 2007 (PoE 11).

PoE. Nam Theun 2 multipurpose project. Report 12, September 29, 2007 (PoE 12).

PoE. Nam Theun 2 multipurpose project. Report 13, February 8, 2008 (PoE 13).

PoE. Nam Theun 2 multipurpose project. Report 14, April 4, 2008 (PoE 14).

PoE. Nam Theun 2 multipurpose project. Report 15, April 30, 2009 (PoE 15).

PoE. Nam Theun 2 multipurpose project. Report 16, February 25, 2010 (PoE 16).

PoE. Nam Theun 2 multipurpose project. Report 17, November 22, 2010 (PoE 17).

PoE. Nam Theun 2 multipurpose project. Report 18A, February 12, 2011 (PoE 18A).

PoE. Nam Theun 2 multipurpose project. Report 18B, July 15, 2011 (PoE 18B).

PoE. Nam Theun 2 multipurpose project. Report 19, March 20, 2012 (PoE 19).

PoE. Nam Theun 2 multipurpose project. Report 20, Lao PDR, February 2, 2013 (PoE 20).

PoE. Nam Theun 2 multipurpose project. Report 21A, March 12, 2013 (PoE 21A).

PoE. Nam Theun 2 multipurpose project. Report 21B, August 30, 2013 (PoE 21B).

Poe. Nam Theun 2 multipurpose project. Report 22, May 8, 2014 (PoE 22).

PoE. Nam Theun 2 multipurpose project. Report 23, December 29, 2014 (PoE 23).

PoE. Nam Theun 2 multipurpose project. Report 24, October 23, 2015 (PoE 24).

PoE. Nam Theun 2 multipurpose project. Report 25, September 2016 (PoE 25).

PoE and IAG. Joint report, August, 2005.

Porter, Ian C., and Jayasankar Shivakumar, eds. "Overview." In *Doing a Dam Better: The Lao People's Democratic Republic and the Story of Nam Theun 2*, edited by Ian C. Porter and Jayasankar Shivakumar, 1–32. Washington, DC: World Bank, 2011.

Porter, Ian C., and Jayasankar Shivakumar, eds. Preface to *Doing a Dam Better: The Lao People's Democratic Republic and the Story of Nam Theun 2*, edited by Ian C. Porter and Jayasankar Shivakumar, xi–xii. Washington, DC: World Bank, 2011.

Proschan, Frank. "Cheuang in Kmhmu Folklore, History, and Memory." In *Tamnan kiaw kap Thaaw Hung Thaaw Cheuang: Miti thaang pravatisat lae Wattanatham*, ed. Sumitr Pitiphat, 174–209. Bangkok: Thammasat University and the Thai Studies Council, 1996.

Rich, Bruce. *Foreclosing the Future: The World Bank and the Politics of Environmental Destruction*. Washington, DC: Island Press, 2013.

Richter, Brian D., Sandra Postel, Carmen Revenga, Thayer Scudder, Bernhard Lehner, Allegra Churchill, and Morgan Chow. "Lost in Development's Shadow: The Downstream Human Consequences of Dams." *Water Alternatives* 3, no. 2 (2010): 14–42.

Richter, Brian D., and Gregory A. Thomas. "Restoring Environmental Flows by Modifying Dam Operations." *Ecology and Society* 12, no. 1 (2007): art. 12. www.ecologyandsociety .org/vol12/iss1/art12.

Roasa, Dustin. *Outsourcing Development: Lifting the Veil on the World Bank Group's Lending through Financial Intermediaries*. Inclusive Development International, Asheville, NC, October 2016. www.inclusivedevelopment.net/wp-content/uploads/2016/09/Outsourcing-Developmnet-Introduction.pdf.

Robequain, Charles. *Le Thanh Hoá*. Paris: G. Van Oest, 1929.

Roberts, Christopher B. "Laos: A More Mature and Robust State?" *Southeast Asian Affairs* (2012): 153–68.

Roberts, Tyson R. "Fluvicide: An Independent Environmental Assessment of the Nam Theun 2 Hydropower Project in Laos, with Particular Reference to Aquatic Biology and Fishes." Unpublished report, Bangkok, 1996.

Robichaud, William. *Lessons-learned from the District Upland Development and Conservation Project (DUDCP), Nakai-Nam Theun National Biodiversity Conservation Area, Lao PDR: A Report to the World Bank*. DUDCP, October 2003.

Robichaud, William. *Motivation for Payment for Ecosystem Services in Laos: The Essential Alignment*. Bogor, Indonesia: International Centre for Forestry Research, 2014.

Robichaud, William. "Nakai-Nam Theun National Protected Area." In *Evidence-Based Conservation: Lessons from the Lower Mekong*, ed. Terry C. H. Sunderland, Jeffrey Sayer, and Minh-Ha Hoang, 110–24. Bogor, Indonesia: Council to Improve Foodborne Outbreak Response, 2013.

Robichaud, William. *Saola Conservation Action Plan for Lao PDR*. Vientiane: WCS, 1997.

Robichaud, William. *Saola Conservation Action Plan for Lao PDR*. Rev. ed. Vientiane: WCS and IUCN, 1999.

Robichaud, William, Clive. W. Marsh, Sangthong Southammakoth, and Sirivanh Khounthikoummane. *Review of the National Protected Area System in Lao PDR*. Vientiane: Lao-Swedish Forestry Programme, 2001.

Robichaud, William G., Anthony R. E. Sinclair, Naa Odarkor-Lanquaye, and Brian Klinkenberg. "Stable Forest Cover under Increasing Populations of Swidden Cultivators in Central Laos: The Roles of Intrinsic Culture and Extrinsic Wildlife Trade." *Ecology and Society* 14, no. 1 (2009): art. 33.

Robichaud, William, and Bryan L. Stuart. *Saola, Herpetological and Wildlife Trade Studies in Nakai-Nam Theun National Biodiversity Conservation Area and the Proposed Nam Theun Extension*. Rev. report. Vientiane: WCS and IUCN, 1999.

Ryder, Gráinne. "Behind the Mekong Power Grid: ADB Master Plan Serves Power Monopolists Not the Powerless." *Watershed* 9, no. 2 (March 2004): 25–30.

Ryder, Gráinne. "The Political Ecology of Hydropower Development in the Lao People's Democratic Republic." Master's thesis, York University, 1996.

Ryder, Gráinne. "Small Power Producers in Thailand." Probe International Power Sector Reform Series Paper no. 3, March 1, 2005.

Ryder, Gráinne. "Ten Reasons Why the World Bank Should Not Finance Nam Theun 2." Probe International briefing, July 1, 2004. http://probeinternational.org/library/wp-content/uploads/2011/12/nt10reasons.pdf.

Ryder, Gráinne. "Thailand's Flawed Electricity Privatization: The Case for Citizen-Oriented Reform." Probe International Power Sector Reform Series paper no. 4, pt. 1, February 20, 1999. https://journal.probeinternational.org/1999/02/20/thailands-flawed-electricity-privatization-2.

Salter, Richard E. *Wildlife in Lao PDR: A Status Report.* Vientiane: IUCN, 1993.

Samuelsson, Marika. "Livelihood Diversification into the Rural Nonfarm Economy: A Case of the Resettled Households of the Nam Theun 2 Hydropower Project." Department of Human Geography, Lund University, 2015. https://lup.lub.lu.se/student-papers/search/publication/5434849.

Santasombat, Yos. *The River of Life: Changing Ecosystems of the Mekong River.* Chiang Mai: Mekong Press, 2011.

Sayavongkhamdy, Thongsa, and Viengkeo Souksavatdy. "Excavations of Cave Sites at Pha Phen." In *Recherches nouvelles sur le Laos,* ed. Yves Goudineau and Michel Lorrillard, 25–35. Paris: École Français d'Extrème-Orient, 2008.

Schaller, George B., and Alan Rabinowitz, "The Saola or Spindlehorn Bovid *Pseudoryx nghetinhensis* in Laos." *Oryx* 29, no. 2 (1995): 107–14.

Schönweger Oliver, Andreas Heinimann, Michael Epprecht, Juliet Lu, and Palikone Thalongsengchanh. *Concessions and Leases in the Lao PDR: Taking Stock of Land Investments.* Bern: Centre for Development and Environment, University of Bern, 2012.

Schuessler, Axel. *ABC Etymological Dictionary of Old Chinese.* Honolulu: University of Hawaii Press, 2007.

Scudder, Thayer. "Recent Experiences with River Basin Development in the Tropics and Subtropics." *Natural Resources Forum* 18, no. 2 (1994): 101–13.

Scudder, Thayer. *The Future of Large Dams: Dealing with Social, Environmental, Institutional and Political Costs.* London: Earthscan, 2005.

Seeger, Cathleen, Kirsten Nyman, and Richard Twum. "The Role of the German Development Cooperation in Promoting Sustainable Hydropower." *Water Alternatives* 3, no. 2 (2010): 453–62.

Segal, Mark. *Nam Theun 2.* Interim summary report, World Bank, August 21, 2004, 11. http://documents.worldbank.org/curated/en/660941468045590805/pdf/925850WP0P076400Box385315B00PUBLIC0.pdf.

Serra, Teresa, Mark Segal, and Ram Chopra. "The Project is Prepared." In *Doing a Dam Better: The Lao People's Democratic Republic and the Story of Nam Theun 2,* ed. Ian C. Porter and Jayasankar Shivakumar, 51–98. Washington, DC: World Bank, 2011.

Sharp, Tim. "The Gas-Fired Threat to SE Asian Hydro Power." *International Water Power and Dam Construction* 50, no. 8 (1998): 14–15.

Shoemaker, Bruce. *Trouble on the Theun-Hinboun: A Field Report on the Socio-Economic and Environmental Effects of the Nam Theun-Hinboun Hydropower Project in Laos.* Berkeley, CA: IRN, 1998.

Shoemaker, Bruce, Ian. G. Baird, and Monsiri Baird. *The People and Their River: A Survey of River-Based Livelihoods in the Xe Bang Fai River Basin in Central Lao PDR.* Vientiane: Lao PDR/Canada Fund for Local Initiatives, 2001.

Shoemaker, Bruce, Ian G. Baird, and Kanokwan Manorom. "Nam Theun 2: The World Bank's Narrative of Success Falls Apart." *World Rivers Review* 29, no. 4 (2014): 10–11.

Singh, Sarinda. "Contesting Moralities: The Politics of Wildlife Trade in Laos." *Journal of Political Ecology* 15 (2008): 1–20.

Singh, Sarinda. "Developing Bureaucracies for Environmental Governance: State Authority and World Bank Conditionality in Laos." *Journal of Contemporary Asia* 44, no. 2 (2014): 322–41.

Singh, Sarinda. "Living within the State: A Dormitory Community in Central Laos." In *Tai Lands and Thailand: Community and State in Southeast Asia*, ed. Andrew Walker, 141–65. Singapore: Institution of Southeast Asian Studies, 2009.

Singh, Sarinda. *Natural Potency and Political Power: Forests and State Authority in Contemporary Laos*. Honolulu: University of Hawaii Press, 2012.

Singh, Sarinda. "Religious Resurgence, Authoritarianism, and 'Ritual Governance': *Baci* Rituals, Village Meetings, and the Developmental State in Rural Laos." *Journal of Asian Studies* 73, no. 4 (2014): 1059–79.

Singh, Sarinda. "World Bank-Directed Development? Negotiating Participation in the Nam Theun 2 Hydropower Project in Laos." *Development and Change* 40, no. 3 (2009): 487–507.

Sinha, Sidharth. "Nam Theun 2 Hydroelectric Project." Undated, World Bank, https://ppiaf.org/sites/ppiaf.org/files/documents/toolkits/Cross-Border-Infrastructure-Toolkit/Cross-Border%20Compilation%20over%2029%20Jan%202007/Resources/Sinha%20-%20Case%20Study%20Nam%20Theun.pdf.

SMEC. *Nam Theun 2 Hydroelectric Project Feasibility Study: Environmental Assessment*. UNDP/World Bank, 1991.

SMEC. *Nam Theun 2 Hydroelectric Project: Situation Report*. UNDP/World Bank, 1990.

Smirnov, Denis. *Assessment of Scope of Illegal Logging in Laos and Associated Trans-Boundary Timber Trade*. WWF, June 2015. https://app.box.com/s/lol9on4su2pg3zqnu3lkqpr7hjpzoiem.

"Speaking of Nam Theun 2 . . . Past, Present and Future (?)." Interview with Satoru Matsumoto. *Watershed* 10, no. 1 (2004): 9–17.

Stephens, Peter. "The Communications Challenge." In *Doing a Dam Better: The Lao People's Democratic Republic and the Story of Nam Theun 2*, edited by Ian C. Porter and Jayasankar Shivakumar, 117–25. Washington, DC: World Bank, 2011.

Stuart-Fox, Martin. "Laos." In *Countries at the Crossroads: An Analysis of Democratic Governance*, ed. Jake Dizard, Christopher Walker, and Vanessa Tucker, 325–46. New York: Freedom House, 2011.

Stuart-Fox, Martin. "Politics and Reform in the Lao People's Democratic Republic." Asia Research Center working paper 126, Murdoch University, 2005.

Tanatvanit, Somporn, Bundit Limmeechokchai, and Supachart Chungpaibulpatana. "Sustainable Development Strategies: Implications of Energy Demand Management and Renewable Energy in Thailand." *Renewable and Sustainable Energy Reviews* 7, no. 5 (2003): 367–95.

Timmins Robert J., and Tom D. Evans. *A Wildlife and Habitat Survey of Nakai-Nam Theun National Biodiversity Conservation Area, Khammouan and Bolikhamsai Provinces.* New York: WCS, 1996.

Tobias, Joe, Peter Davidson, and William Robichaud. "Nakai-Nam Theun: Can Development Save One of Asia's Last Wildernesses?" *Oriental Bird Club Bulletin* 28 (1998): 24–29. http://orientalbirdclub.org/nakainam.

Torriti, Jacopo, Mohamed J. Hassan, and Matthew Leach. "Demand Response Experience in Europe: Policies, Programmes and Implementation." *Energy* 35, no. 4 (2010): 1575–83.

Vatikiotis, Michael. "Graft Games." *New Mandala: New Perspectives on Southeast Asia*, July 4, 2016. www.newmandala.org/graft-games.

Vernstrom, Robert. *Nam Theun 2 Hydro Power Project Regional Economic Least-Cost Analysis.* Final report, World Bank, March 2005. http://siteresources.worldbank.org/INTLAO PRD/Resources/RELC-2005-final.pdf.

Vickery, Michael. "Champa Revised." Working paper no. 39, Asia Research Institute, Singapore, 2005.

Victor, David G., and Thomas Heller. *The Political Economy of Power Sector Reform.* Cambridge: Cambridge University Press 2005.

Vidal, Jules. "Noms vernaculaires de plantes (Lao, Mèo, Kha) en usage en Laos." *BEFEO* 49, no. 2 (1959): 435–608.

Walker, Andrew. *Thailand's Political Peasants: Power in the Modern Rural Economy.* Madison: University of Wisconsin Press, 2012.

WCD. *Dams and Development: A New Framework for Decision-Making.* London: Earthscan, 2000.

WCS. *A Preliminary Wildlife and Habitat Assessment of the Nam Theun 2 Hydropower Project Area.* Vientiane: WCS, 1995.

WCS. *Results of a Survey of Terrestrial Wildlife in the Area To Be Affected by the Nam Theun 2 Hydroelectric Project.* Vientiane: WCS, 1995.

Whitington, Jerome. "The Institutional Condition of Contested Hydropower: The Theun Hinboun–International Rivers Collaboration." *Forum for Development Studies* 39, no. 2 (2012): 231–56.

World Bank. *Aide Memoire to the Committee on Planning and Cooperation from the World Bank Technical Mission for the Nam Theun 2 Hydroelectric Project.* November 9, 1995.

World Bank. *Decision Framework for Processing the Proposed NT2 Project.* July 2002.

World Bank. *Directions in Hydropower.* March 1, 2009. http://siteresources.worldbank.org /INTWAT/Resources/Directions_in_Hydropower_FINAL.pdf.

World Bank. "IDA Guarantee Paves Renewed Interest in Private Hydropower—The Nam Theun 2 Project." Project and Finance Guarantees Group, June 2005.

World Bank. *Implementation Completion Report (IDA-31860) on a Credit in the Amount of SDR 1.5 Million (US$2.0 Million Equivalent) to the Lao People's Democratic Republic for a District Upland Development and Conservation Project.* March 25, 2004.

World Bank. *Lao PDR Economic Monitor.* May 2012.

World Bank. *Nam Theun 2 Hydropower Project Update: Revenue Management*. September, 2017. http://documents.worldbank.org/curated/en/343791510736969520/pdf/1213 93-WP-P049290-PUBLIC.pdf.

World Bank. *Nam Theun 2 Social and Environmental Project: Implementation Status and Results Report*, June 30, 2015.

World Bank. *Nam Theun 2 Social and Environmental Project: Implementation Status and Results Report*, July 11, 2016.

World Bank. *Natural Resource Management for Sustainable Development: Hydropower and Mining*. Lao PDR development report, June 1, 2010. http://siteresources.worldbank .org/LAOPRDEXTN/Resources/293683-1301084874098/LDR2010_Full_Report.pdf.

World Bank. *Nam Theun 2 Hydro Power Project: Regional Economic Least-Cost Analysis*. Draft final report, June 2004. http://siteresources.worldbank.org/INTLAOPRD/491761-109 4074854903/20251513/Economic.pdf.

World Bank. *Operational Guidance for World Bank Group Staff: Public and Private Sector Roles in the Supply of Electricity Services*. Energy and Mining Sector Board, February 2004.

World Bank. *Policy and Human Resources Development Fund Annual Report, Fiscal Year 1997*. Vol. 1: *Resource Mobilization and Cofinancing*. January 1998.

World Bank. "RETooLKit Case Study: Small Power Producers of Thailand." Undated. http://siteresources.worldbank.org/EXTRENENERGYTK/Resources/5138246-12 38175210723/Thailand0Small0Power0Producer0Program0.pdf.

World Bank. Transcript of interview with Jamil Sopher. World Bank Oral History Project, 2005.

World Bank. *Water Resources Sector Strategy: Strategic Directions for World Bank Engagement*. January 1, 2004.

World Bank. *The World Bank Operational Manual, Operational Policies: Natural Habitats*. OP 4.04, September 1995.

World Bank. *World Bank Statement on EDF's Withdrawal from Nam Theun 2 Hydroelectric Project*. August 12, 2003.

World Bank and ADB. *Nam Theun 2 Board Update: Project Progress during 2011*. March 23, 2012. http://documents.worldbank.org/curated/en/211891468300318225/pdf/676790 BR0P07640CR0IDA0SECM201200159.pdf.

World Bank and ADB. *Nam Theun 2 Board Update: Project Progress during 2012*. December 31, 2012. http://documents.worldbank.org/curated/en/872361468045088739/Nam-Theun-2-Board-update-project-progress-during-2012.

World Bank and MIGA. *Project Appraisal Document on a Proposed IDA Grant (Nam Theun 2 Social and Environmental Project)*, Report No: 31764-LA. March 31, 2005. http:// documents.worldbank.org/curated/en/250731468277466031/pdf/317640corr.pdf.

"World Bank Still Upbeat on NT2, but Expecting Delays . . . While Thai Economic Crisis Hits EGAT and Thai NT2 Companies." *Watershed* 3, no. 3 (1998): 4.

"World Bank Up Support for Nam Theun 2 Despite Thai Economic Meltdown." *Watershed* 3, no. 2 (1998): 4.

WWF. *WWF Position Statement: Nam Theun 2 Dam Project.* Bangkok, May 9, 2003.

Wyatt, Andrew. "Infrastructure Development and BOOT in Laos and Vietnam: A Case Study of Collective Action and Risk in Transitional Developing Economies." PhD diss., University of Sydney, April 2004.

Contributors

IAN G. BAIRD is an associate professor of geography at the University of Wisconsin–Madison. He has been studying wild capture fisheries and hydropower dams in the Mekong River basin, particularly in Laos, Cambodia, and Thailand, for twenty-five years. He is especially interested in the downstream impacts of large-scale dams on fisheries and other river-based livelihoods, including those caused by NT2 in the Xe Bang Fai River basin but also in the mainstream Mekong River, the 3S River basin, and the Mun River basin.

JAMES R. CHAMBERLAIN received his PhD in 1977 from the University of Michigan and has been engaged in the study of Laos for more than fifty years, focusing on language, literature, anthropology, history and protohistory, and social development. He was team leader of the first independent sociocultural and socioeconomic studies related to NT2 beginning in 1995. In 2004–5 he oversaw the local consultation process for the World Bank that was carried out in every village in all project areas. Currently, he resides in Vientiane.

N. J. ENFIELD is professor of linguistics and director of the Sydney Social Sciences and Humanities Advanced Research Center at the University of Sydney. He has carried out linguistic and ethnographic fieldwork in the uplands of the Nam Theun 2 project area for over fifteen years, working closely with speakers of Kri, a Vietic language of the Nam Noy Valley. His research on language, culture, and cognition is based on extended field work in mainland Southeast Asia, especially Laos.

SATOMI HIGASHI is Lao program director of Mekong Watch, an environmental NGO based in Tokyo. She was engaged with a community-based watershed management project in Oudomsay Province, northern Laos, for seven years, in cooperation with the National University of Laos. She has also been monitoring social and environmental impacts of hydropower projects in Laos, including, for many years, the Nam Theun 2 project. She completed her PhD in social sciences from Hitotsubashi University in Japan, and her research focuses on political ecology on natural resource management in Southeast Asia, especially in Laos.

PHILIP HIRSCH is an emeritus professor of human geography at the University of Sydney. He has published extensively on environment and development in the Mekong region, drawing on more than three decades of fieldwork in the region. This includes work in communities affected by dams in Laos, Thailand, and Vietnam. Hirsch first conducted research on Nam Theun 2 in early 1991, and he has written several articles on the impacts and politics of the dam. His most recent books are his edited *Handbook of the Environment in Southeast Asia* (Routledge, 2017); *The Mekong: A Socio-Legal Approach to River Basin Development* (with Ben Boer, Fleur Johns, Ben Saul, and Natalia Scurrah; Routledge/Earthscan, 2016); *Powers of Exclusion: Land Dilemmas in Southeast Asia* (with Derek Hall and Tania Murray Li; University of Hawaii Press and Singapore University Press, 2011); and *Tracks and Traces: Thailand and the Work of Andrew Turton* (edited with Nicholas Tapp; Amsterdam University Press, 2010).

DAVE HUBBEL has been researching issues relating to the environment and development in the Mekong region since 1990. As a writer and editor of the Thai environmental journal *Watershed* from the mid-1990s until 2005, he closely followed the NT2 project as well as other hydropower and natural resource conflict issues in the region. Since 2006 he has been working with Indigenous communities and NGOs in Ratanakiri Province in northeast Cambodia.

GLENN HUNT, originally from Sydney, Australia, has lived and worked in Southeast Asia since 2004 and currently works with the Centre for Development and Environment, University of Bern. He spent ten years working for NGOs on land and forest rights in southern Laos while also conducting graduate research into the impact of foreign investment on local livelihoods. From 2004 to 2008 he worked with a development organization in Khammouane Province that supported communities in Nakai District, during which time he observed the development of NT2 as the dam was constructed and communities resettled. He has continued to follow the development of NT2 since its completion, undertaking various independent assessments on livelihood restoration programs.

KANOKWAN MANOROM is an associate professor at the Faculty of Liberal Arts, Ubon Ratchathani University, Thailand. She earned her PhD in rural sociology from University of Missouri–Columbia. Since graduation in 1997, she has been working in water and land governance and impact assessment in Thailand and the Mekong Region.

CARL MIDDLETON is deputy director for Research Affairs on the MA in International Development Studies (MAIDS) Program and director of the Center for Social Development Studies (CSDS), in the Faculty of Political Science, Chulalongkorn University, Thailand. His research interests orientate around the politics and policy of the environment in Southeast Asia, with a particular focus on environmental justice and the political ecology of water and energy.

WITOON PERMPONGSACHAROEN is director of the Mekong Energy and Ecology Network (MeeNET) as well as a founding director of Thailand's Foundation for Ecological Recovery, and its sister organization, TERRA, which focuses on regional issues. He has closely followed NT2 since the early 1990s and is a prominent authority on Thai energy issues. In 1996 he was a research fellow at the Agrarian Studies Program at Yale University.

NOAH QUASTEL is a lawyer and geographer whose research interests include sustainability governance and electricity systems. He is currently a postdoctoral fellow at Simon Fraser University in Burnaby, British Columbia, Canada.

WILLIAM ROBICHAUD is a conservation biologist who has worked on wildlife and bio-diversity conservation projects in Laos since the mid-1990s. He is a former Laos country director for the Wildlife Conservation Society (WCS) and has worked on the Nam Theun 2 project in various capacities since 1995—for WCS, the International Union for the Conservation of Nature (IUCN), and the World Bank. From 2006 to 2009, during construction of the Nam Theun 2 dam, he lived near the project while serving as a conservation technical advisor to the Nam Theun 2 Watershed Management and Protection Authority. In 2015, the IUCN Species Survival Commission recognized him with its Harry Messel Award for Conservation Leadership, for his contributions to conservation in Laos and Vietnam.

GRÁINNE RYDER is a lecturer in International Development, Faculty of Environment, St. Paul's University College at the University of Waterloo in Canada. From 1990 to 1995 she worked with Bangkok-based TERRA challenging global and regional drivers of Mekong hydropower development. She subsequently led the Canadian campaign against global financing for NT2 and has written extensively on the destructive economic and environmental effects of big dams.

MARIKA SAMUELSSON holds a MSc in environmental technology at Imperial College London, with a focus on environmental resource management. In 2015 she conducted research for Lund University on NT2 regarding resettlers' livelihood restoration and diversification. She continued monitoring hydropower issues in Southeast Asia when working at the Mekong Energy and Ecology Network and has previously worked with several NGOs in Thailand, Laos, and Vietnam.

YOS SANTASOMBAT received his PhD in anthropology at the University of California, Berkeley, in 1985 and is currently a professor of anthropology and the chairperson of the PhD Program in Social Sciences at Chiang Mai University in Thailand. He is also a senior research scholar with the Thailand Research Fund. He has written numerous books in English; his most recent include *The River of Life: Changing Ecosystems of the Mekong Region* (Mekong Press, 2011), *Impact of China's Rise on the Mekong Region* (Palgrave Macmillan, 2015), and *Chinese Capitalism in Southeast Asia: Cultures and Practices* (Palgrave Macmillan, 2017).

BRUCE SHOEMAKER is an independent researcher based in northern California whose focus is natural resource conflict issues. He lived in Laos for eight years, beginning in 1990, and has continued to visit and conduct research in the country on a regular basis. He has followed Nam Theun 2 since the first 1991 presentation described in the preface and subsequently attended various informational meetings and consultations while working with NGOs in Vientiane. He was an active member of the Rivers Group (described in chapter 3) and engaged with the public participation process in 1996–97. After leaving Laos in mid-1997 he assisted a coalition of groups advocating against the project's approval, including in a series of meetings with World Bank staff and directors in Washington, DC. He returned to Laos in 1998 to do field research on hydropower. In 2001 he participated in the river-based livelihoods study of the Xe Bang Fai River described in chapter 8. In 2014 he returned to the Xe Bang Fai for a post-project study and has subsequently authored or coauthored several additional articles and reports on various aspects of the project.

SARINDA SINGH has studied environment, development, and governance in Laos and Cambodia and is currently a research fellow at the George Institute for Global Health as well as an honorary research fellow at the University of Queensland. She has published a book, *Natural Potency and Political Power: Forests and State Authority in Contemporary Laos*, with the University of Hawaii Press, and has published articles on NT2 in *Development and Change* and other journals.

Index

Page references followed by *fig* indicate an illustrated figure or photograph; followed by *t* indicate a table.

NEW PERSPECTIVES IN
SOUTHEAST ASIAN STUDIES